The Best Places to Buy a Home in *France*

A Survival Handbook

by

Joe Laredo

SURVIVAL BOOKS • LONDON • ENGLAND

First Edition 2003
Second Edition 2007

Survival Books Limited
26 York Street, London W1U 6PZ, United Kingdom
+44 (0)20-7788 7644, +44 (0)870-762 3212
info@survivalbooks.net
www.survivalbooks.net

British Library Cataloguing in Publication Data.
A CIP record for this book is available from the British Library.
ISBN-10: 1-901130-14-2
ISBN-13: 978-901130-14-0

Printed and bound in India by Ajanta Offset.

ACKNOWLEDGEMENTS

My sincere thanks to all those who contributed to the publication of this book, in particular Joanna Styles for her rigorous editing, Kerry Laredo for the new two-colour design and layout and Jim Watson for the superb cover design, illustrations and maps. I would also like to thank the people who contributed to the first edition, especially Wanda Glowinska-Rizzi, the late Michael Keyte, Beverly Laflamme and Richard Whiting, as well as John Evans (Eclipse Overseas) for information on Normandy and Brittany, Miranda Neame (Editor, The News) for help in finding knowledgeable writers, Sarah Cooper-Williams for extensive research on the south-west, Paul Owen and Stephanie Basibé (VEF) and Nicholas Smallwood (French Property Shop) for information on the property market in the south-west, Chris Rankin (Bordeaux British Community) for useful contacts, Marilyn Riley (President, Americans in Toulouse) for information about obtaining foreign products, Alison Monnier for information about Brittany, and Jean-Noël Brunet, Pamela Cooley, Françoise Labarbe, Petra Lugtig and the staff of the Conseil régional de l'Auvergne and the Conseil général du Lot for information on those areas.

What Readers & Reviewers

'If you need to find out how France works then this book is indispensable. Native French people probably have a less thorough understanding of how their country functions.'

Living France magazine

'The ultimate reference book. Every subject imaginable is exhaustively explained in simple terms. An excellent introduction to fully enjoy all that this fine country has to offer and save time and money in the process.'

American Club of Zurich

'Let's say it at once. David Hampshire's Living and Working in France is the best handbook ever produced for visitors and foreign residents in this country. It is Hampshire's meticulous detail which lifts his work way beyond the range of other books with similar titles. This book is absolutely indispensable.'

Riviera Reporter magazine

'A must for all future expats. I invested in several books but this is the only one you need. Every issue and concern is covered, every daft question you have but are frightened to ask is answered honestly without pulling any punches. Highly recommended.'

Reader

'In answer to the desert island question about the one how-to book on France, this book would be it.'

The Recorder newspaper

'It's everything you always wanted to ask but didn't for fear of the contemptuous put down. Its pages are stuffed with practical information on everyday subjects.'

Swiss News magazine

'A must for all future ex-pats. Deals with every aspect of moving to Spain. I invested in several books but this is the only one you need. Every issue and concern is covered, every daft question you have on Spain but are frightened to ask is answered honestly without pulling any punches. Highly recommended!'

Reader

'If I were to move to France, I would like David Hampshire to be with me, holding my hand every step of the way. This being impractical, I would have to settle for second best and take his books with me instead!

Living France magazine

HAVE SAID ABOUT SURVIVAL BOOKS

'The amount of information covered is not short of incredible. I thought I knew enough about my birth country. This book has proved me wrong. Don't go to France without it. Big mistake if you do. Absolutely priceless!'

READER

'A mine of information. I might have avoided some embarrassments and frights if I had read it prior to my first Swiss encounters. Deserves an honoured place on any newcomer's bookshelf.'

ENGLISH TEACHERS ASSOCIATION, SWITZERLAND

'A thoroughly interesting and useful read, it crams in almost every conceivable bit of information that a newly-arrived immigrant could need. A great book to read and have close at hand when you arrive in Canada to begin your new life. The best all-round handbook on Canada.'

READER

'A concise, thorough account of the DO's and DON'Ts for a foreigner in Switzerland. Crammed with useful information and lightened with humorous quips which make the facts more readable.'

AMERICAN CITIZENS ABROAD

'Covers every conceivable question that might be asked concerning everyday life — I know of no other book that could take the place of this one.'

FRANCE IN PRINT

'I found this a wonderful book crammed with facts and figures, with a straightforward approach to the problems and pitfalls you are likely to encounter. The whole laced with humour and a thorough understanding of what's involved. Gets my vote!'

READER

'We would like to congratulate you on this work: it is really super! We hand it out to our expatriates and they read it with great interest and pleasure.'

ICI SWITZERLAND, AG

'If you are thinking of moving to New Zealand this is the book for you. Of all the books about New Zealand I've bought, this is the only one I still refer to.'

READER

'A vital tool in the war against real estate sharks; don't even think of buying without reading this book first!'

EVERYTHING SPAIN MAGAZINE

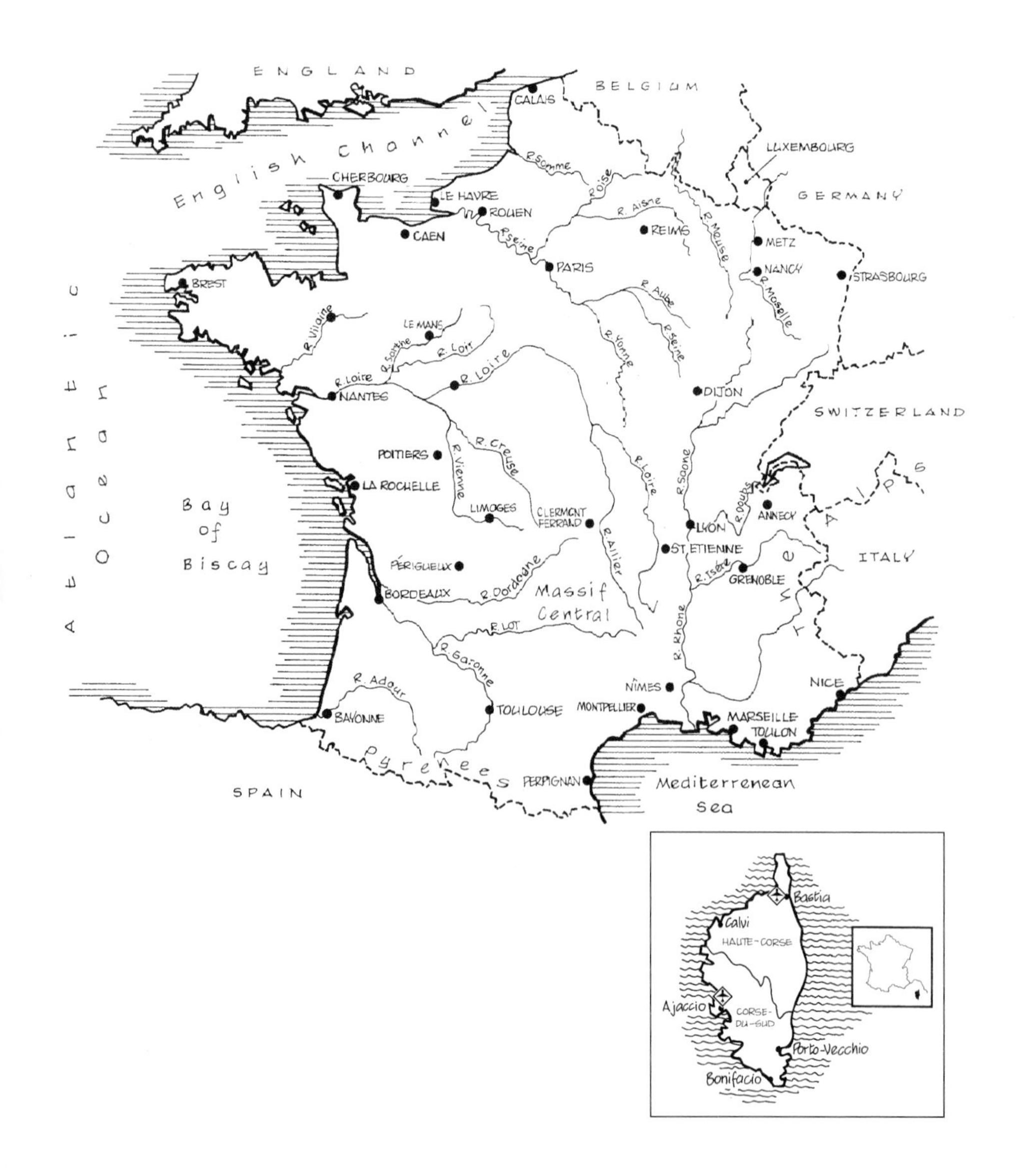
ENGLAND
BELGIUM
English Channel
CALAIS
LUXEMBOURG
R.Somme
R.Oise
GERMANY
CHERBOURG
LE HAVRE
ROUEN
R. Aisne
REIMS
R. Meuse
CAEN
R.Seine
METZ
PARIS
NANCY
STRASBOURG
BREST
R. Moselle
R. Aube
R. Vilaine
LE MANS
R. Sarthe
R. Loir
R. Seine
R. Yonne
Atlantic Ocean
R. Loire
R. Loire
NANTES
DIJON
SWITZERLAND
R. Creuse
POITIERS
R. Vienne
R. Saone
LA ROCHELLE
R. Loire
R. Doubs
Bay of Biscay
LIMOGES
CLERMONT FERRAND
LYON
ANNECY
Alps
R. Allier
ST. ETIENNE
ITALY
PÉRIGUEUX
R. Dordogne
R. Isère
GRENOBLE
BORDEAUX
Massif Central
R. Rhone
R. LOT
R. Garonne
R. Adour
NÎMES
NICE
TOULOUSE
MONTPELLIER
BAYONNE
MARSEILLE
TOULON
Pyrenees
PERPIGNAN
SPAIN
Mediterrenean Sea
Bastia
Calvi
HAUTE-CORSE
Ajaccio
CORSE-DU-SUD
Porto-Vecchio
Bonifacio

CONTENTS

FOR SALE

THE AUTHOR

Having obtained a Modern Languages degree and worked for a number of years in the marine industry, Joe Laredo became a freelance translator, proofreader and writer in 1996. Since then he has written six books for Survival Books – *The Best Places to Buy a Home in France*, *Buying a Home in Ireland*, *Culture Wise France*, *Living and Working in Ireland*, *Making a Living in France* and *Renovating & Maintaining Your French Home* – as well as regularly updating *Buying a Home in France* and *Living and Working in France* and editing and proofreading many other titles.

Joe moved from his native Surrey, England to Normandy in 2001, where he lives with his wife and daughter and numerous cats. In his spare time Joe contributes to newspapers and magazines about France and to squash and piano magazines.

AUTHOR'S NOTES

- Property prices should be taken as guides only, although they were mostly correct at the time of publication.
- His/he/him also means her/she/her (please forgive me ladies). This is done to make life easier for both the reader and (in particular) the author, and isn't intended to be sexist.
- All spelling is (or should be) British English and not American English.
- Warnings and important points are shown in **bold** type.
- The following symbols are used in this book: ☎ (telephone), 📠 (fax), 💻 (internet) and ✉ (email).
- Lists of useful information, further reading and useful websites are contained in **Appendices A**, **B** and **C** respectively.
- For those unfamiliar with the metric system of weights and measures, imperial conversion tables are included in **Appendix D**.
- Maps of France, showing the regions and departments, of the high-speed train (*TGV*) network, the road network and major airports are included in **Appendix E**, and a map showing the major cities and geographical features is on page 6. Maps of each region and sub-region showing the major towns and places of interest and the major airports and ports are included in the relevant chapters.
- **Appendix F** contains details of airline services from the UK and Ireland.
- **Appendix G** contains a rating of towns in France by *Le Nouvel Observateur* and *Le Point* magazines.

Jim Watson

INTRODUCTION

If you're planning to buy a home in France but aren't sure where you would like to live, or just wish to compare towns in your chosen area – this is **THE BOOK** for you! The purpose of *The Best Places to Buy a Home in France* is to provide you with the information necessary to help you choose the most appropriate region or town for you and your family.

France offers something for everyone, but where should you buy your home? Perhaps you wish to live on an island off Brittany or in Corsica. Or maybe you fancy a home in one of France's many coastal regions, such as the Côte d'Azur, Normandy or Vendée. Or you may hanker after the fast pace of life in a French city such as Paris, Nice or Toulouse. With so many inviting regions and towns to choose from it can be a difficult decision, particularly as the climate, lifestyle and cost of property can vary considerably from region to region, and even within a region.

Your choice will depend on a range of factors, including your preferences, your financial resources and, not least, whether you plan to work. If you intend to look for employment or start a business, you must live in an area that allows you the maximum scope. On the other hand, for a holiday home accessibility may be the key factor, and for a retirement home, the proximity of amenities and services.

For many people, choosing the location for a home in France has previously been a case of pot luck. However, with a copy of *The Best Places to Buy a Home in France* to hand you'll have a wealth of priceless information at your fingertips – information derived from a variety of sources, both official and unofficial, not least the hard-won experiences of the author and his acquaintances.

This book will reduce your risk of making an expensive mistake that you may bitterly regret later and help you to make informed decisions and calculated judgements, instead of uneducated (and possibly costly) guesses.

Buying a home in France is a wonderful way to make new friends, broaden your horizons and revitalise your life, and it may provide you with a welcome bolt-hole in which to recuperate from the stresses and strains of modern life. I trust this book will help you choose your ideal location and smooth your way to many happy years in your new home in France, secure in the knowledge that you've made the right decision.

Bon courage !

Joe Laredo
June 2007

Conques – The Dordogne

1

WHY BUY A HOME IN FRANCE?

With some 75m visitors annually, France is the world's most popular country in which to spend a holiday. It's also popular among those looking for a holiday home or to move permanently abroad. Many thousands of Europeans have settled in France, particularly Britons (over half a million of them have homes there and it's estimated that as many as 200,000 live there permanently), and in several villages foreign residents outnumber locals!

There are many excellent reasons for buying a home in France, although it's important to ask yourself **exactly** why you want to buy a home there. For example, are you primarily looking for a sound investment or do you plan to work or start a business in France? Are you seeking a holiday or retirement home? If you're seeking a second home, will it be mainly used for long weekends or for lengthier stays? Do you plan to let it to offset the mortgage and running costs? If so, how important is the property income? You need to answer these and many other questions before deciding on the best (and most appropriate) place to buy a home in France.

Often buyers have a variety of reasons for buying a home in France: for example, many people buy a holiday home with a view to living there permanently or semi-permanently when they retire. If this is the case, there are many more factors to take into account than if you're 'simply' buying a holiday home that you will occupy for just a few weeks a year (when it's usually wiser not to buy at all!). If, on the other hand, you plan to work or start a business in France, you will be faced with a completely different set of criteria. An increasing number of people live in France and work in another European country (e.g. neighbouring England, Belgium, Luxembourg, Germany, Switzerland and Italy), commuting back and forth by road, rail or air.

All this means, of course, that there's no such thing as 'the best place to buy a home in France' – or at least no single best place for everyone. Your choice will depend on your circumstances, your intentions and your preferences. Hopefully the information in this book will help you to make the right choice.

Unless you know exactly what you're looking for and where, it's best to rent a property until you're familiar with an area. As when making all major financial decisions, it's never wise to be too hasty. Many people make expensive (even catastrophic) errors when buying homes abroad, usually because they do insufficient research and are in too much of a hurry, often setting themselves ridiculous deadlines, such as buying a home during a long weekend break or a week's holiday. Not surprisingly, most people wouldn't dream of acting so rashly when buying property in their home country. It isn't uncommon for buyers to regret their decision after some time and wish they'd purchased a different property in a different region (or even in a different country!).

ADVANTAGES & DISADVANTAGES

There are both advantages and disadvantages to buying a home in France, although for most people the benefits far outweigh any drawbacks. France has many attractions: much of the country enjoys a sunny and warm climate all year round, with over 300 days of sunshine annually and high temperatures in southern areas; access to France has never been easier or cheaper, especially from the UK, thanks mainly to the proliferation of low cost flights offered by airlines such as Buzz and Ryanair, but also to an increase in the number of cross-Channel ferries, the introduction of new routes and even new operators and the widespread freezing of ferry prices; France's motorway network is second to none (although expensive to use) and is constantly being improved, and most regions can now be reached by motorway; Europe's fastest trains (*TGV*) not only serve an increasing number of major towns and cities, but also link with a Europe-wide network via the new hub at Lille, and the government has recently 'ordered' the (nationalised) railway operators to compete with the low-cost airlines, so lower train fares can be expected.

France is famous for its huge variety of cultural and leisure activities, and the French people, although not renowned for their friendliness and hospitality, are generally welcoming to foreigners who make the effort to integrate. The standard of living is generally high and the cost of living reasonable by western European standards, including good value homes (if you avoid fashionable areas). Although prices have risen rapidly in many popular areas of France in recent years, property remains far cheaper than its equivalent in the UK, for example, with the bonus that it's often accompanied by generous amounts of land. A modest €75,000 (£50,000/$90,000) will buy you a small modern house or a large property in need of renovation in Normandy or Brittany, Limousin or Poitou-Charentes, or a studio apartment in a major city (except Paris), while for €200,000 (£134,000/$241,000) you can purchase a detached, three-bedroom house in the country (except the most popular areas) or a small apartment on the Côte d'Azur or in Paris. Those with half a million euros to spend can stretch to a *maison de maître*, a *château* or even an entire hamlet (*hameau*), which in remote areas such as the Cévennes or the *départements* of Lozère and Ardèche in the south-east, can be picked up for €500,000 or less (you can even find them in Nord-Pas-de-Calais) – ideal if you **really** want to get away from the neighbours!

Among the many other advantages of buying a home in France are low interest rates (currently around 3.5 per cent), good rental possibilities (in many areas – although in many others the market is saturated), good local tradesmen (though the better ones have long waiting lists), fine food and wine (some would argue, the best in the world) at reasonable prices, a relaxed pace of life in rural areas, excellent public transport (in cities), one of the world's best healthcare systems, plenty of open space, and some of the most beautiful architecture and scenery in Europe. When buying property in France, you aren't simply buying a home but acquiring a lifestyle, and in terms of quality of life the country has few equals.

Naturally, there are also a few disadvantages, including the high purchase costs associated with buying a home in France, high taxes and social security contributions if you're working, unexpected renovation and restoration costs (if you don't do your homework), overcrowding in popular tourist areas during the peak summer season (especially on the Côte d'Azur), traffic congestion and pollution in many towns and cities, the language (unless you already speak it fluently) and the expense of getting to and from France if you own a holiday home there and don't live in a nearby country with good air connections.

CHOOSING THE REGION

France is a huge country (the largest in western Europe) with a vast array of landscapes, including low-lying areas in the north and west, mountains in the centre, east and south-east, forests, farmland and wetlands. Unlike most developed countries, France is still largely rural. Some 25 per cent of the population lives in rural areas, a percentage which has hardly changed in half a century, and average population density is among the lowest in Europe at around 100 people per km^2 (260 per mi^2). Overall, its population is growing (from 58m in 1990 to 63m in 2006), but there are currently three demographic tendencies: a general increase in migration (the French have traditionally tended to stay put); an exodus from the centre of cities and large towns into the suburbs; and a migration westwards and southwards – for example, in the period 1999-2006, the population in Champagne-Ardenne has decreased by 0.05 per cent, but the number of inhabitants in Brittany has increased by 0.85 per cent.

Many of those moving south and west are retirees: Corsica, Languedoc-Roussillon, PACA and Poitou-Charentes are among the six regions that annually attract over 100 people aged over 60 per 10,000 inhabitants, the others being Centre-Val-de-Loire and Lower Normandy, which are popular retirement destinations for Parisians.

With the exception of Paris, which has a population of almost 11m, only three cities have over 1m inhabitants – Lyon (1.6m), Marseille (1.4m) and Lille (1.1m) – and just five others (Toulouse, Bordeaux, Nantes, Strasbourg and Nice) more than half a million; on the other hand, there are over 32,600 French villages with fewer than 1,000 inhabitants.

You can choose complete isolation in Lozère in the Massif Central, authentic French village life almost anywhere, an expatriate community where you will live among your own countrymen and other foreigners (such as those in Dordogne and parts of Brittany and Provence), and an area where you can enjoy the best of both worlds. You may prefer the hustle and bustle of city life, mountain living in the Alps or the Pyrenees, nautical life in Brittany (with some of the world's best sailing on your doorstep), or mixing with the jet-set on the Côte d'Azur.

In May 2006, the magazine *l'Express* published the results of an analysis of all France's *départements* aimed at determining the best place to live. Using 42 criteria, including housing, education, health and environmental issues, the survey placed Haute-Garonne top overall, Hérault top for young people, Vendée for families and Aveyron for retirees. It's interesting to note that 19 of the top 20 *départements* include a town of more than 100,000 inhabitants, which indicates that a large town's economic and social dynamism contribute significantly to the attractiveness of the surrounding area. The survey also identified two areas with high unemployment and low economic activity: a crescent stretching from Upper Normandy through Picardy and Champagne-Ardenne to Nord-Pas-de-Calais, where economic problems, a brain drain and (by most French people's standards) inclement weather make these regions relatively unappealing; and an 'arid diagonal' running from Tarn-et-Garonne through Indre, Nièvre and Haute-Marne to Meuse, where populations are low and attractions few. Of course, one man's meat is another's poison, and not everyone will agree that, for example, Haute-Garonne offers a better quality of life than Tarn-et-Garonne; nor are all parts of a *département* similar, and so any such generalisations are inevitably oversimplifications of the variety of environments and lifestyles France has to offer. As the report concluded, 'Of course, any categorisation has its limitations, and people can be happy in Aisne (which came bottom of the league) and unhappy in Haute-Garonne (which came top).' Nevertheless, the findings mirror the general movement of the French population, away from the north and east towards the west and the south; that cannot be a coincidence.

France has four distinct climatic zones: maritime along the west and north-west coast (although its influence is felt as far inland as the *départements* of Dordogne, Lot, Tarn and Tarn-et-Garonne), continental in central and eastern areas, and Mediterranean in the south-east and in Corsica, with a mountain climate in the Alps, Pyrenees, Massif Central and Vosges. There are also numerous micro-climates making certain areas warmer, drier, wetter or colder than you might expect. The Alps and

Pyrenees experience extremes of weather, and there can be violent winds and storms in the south and north-west.

France is a world unto itself, and deciding where to live can be difficult and the choice overwhelming. For many people their choice is based on previous holidays, friends' recommendations, accessibility or simply an area's reputation. However, how do you know whether an area is a good investment and what you can expect to get for your money? Where can you find expatriate services, good hospitals or plenty of sports and leisure facilities? Which areas and resorts are busy in summer and which offer a more relaxed way of life? What are the local roads and public transport system like? Which areas are easily accessible by air and sea?

This book has been written to help answer these questions by providing comprehensive information about the most popular areas among foreign homebuyers in France and an overview of other regions. The 'best' place to live in France obviously depends on your preferences and it's impossible to specify a best location for everyone. The aim of this book is to identify the positive and possible negative aspects of each of the selected areas in order to help you to choose the part of France that suits you and your family best.

It would be impossible in a book this size to describe in detail every part of France, so we've focused on the most popular locations with foreign homebuyers and have divided these into seven chapters, starting in the north and moving around the country anti-clockwise to end with the Mediterranean coast and then considering some of France's mountainous areas and major cities. A final chapter summarises the advantages and disadvantages of the other parts of France and lists sources of further information.

- **Chapter 2** – the north-west: Normandy and Brittany;
- **Chapter 3** – the west coast : Pays-de-la-Loire and Poitou-Charentes;
- **Chapter 4** – inland south-west: Auvergne and Limousin;
- **Chapter 5** – coastal and mountainous south-west: Aquitaine and Midi-Pyrénées;
- **Chapter 6** – the Mediterranean coast: Languedoc-Roussillon, Provence-Alpes-Côte d'Azur and Corsica;
- **Chapter 7** – the Alps;
- **Chapter 8** – major cities: Paris and the surrounding region, Bordeaux, Lyon, Marseille, Montpellier, Nice and Toulouse;

- **Chapter 9** – other regions : Alsace, Burgundy, Centre-Val-de-Loire, Champagne-Ardenne, Franche-Comté, Lorraine, Nord-Pas-de-Calais, Picardy and Rhône-Alpes.

Each of the main chapters examines an area in detail with a description of the most popular towns and villages, the advantages and disadvantages of living there, the climate, regional language (if any), crime rate, local services and amenities, communications by air, sea, road and public transport, and the property market, including typical homes, the availability and cost of rental accommodation, and the average prices of different kinds of property and land. For those considering buying a property in or near a city or major town, 'attractiveness' ratings derived from nationwide surveys published by *Le Nouvel Observateur* and *Le Point* magazines are included in **Appendix G**.

FRANCE'S COAST

The Côte d'Azur isn't the only part of France's 4,000km coast to have an alluring name – nor alluring features. Here's a whistle-stop tour of the French coast from north-east to south-east, with examples of property prices in the most popular areas along the way:

- **Côte d'Opale** – The Opal Coast stretches from the Belgian border to the Somme estuary in Picardy and boasts vast stretches of sandy beach and dunes, which attract sand-yachters as well as sailors, impressive headlands and, at the Baie de Somme, a wildlife paradise. Its main resort, Le Touquet (studio apartment €100,000, three-bedroom apartment €300,000, four-bedroom villa €900,000), rivals Normandy's Deauville for exclusivity, while newer resorts such as Berck-sur-Mer (new one-bedroom apartment €75,000, five-bedroom house €250,000), Merlimont-Plage and Stella-Plage offer more affordable seaside property.
- **Côte d'Albâtre** – The Alabaster Coast is named after its impressive chalk cliffs, which stretch almost unbroken from the Somme estuary to the mouth of the Seine at Le Havre in Seine-Maritime, Upper Normandy. Beaches are mostly pebbly or stony but there are attractive resorts such as Dieppe, Fécamp (cottage €90,000), Etretat, Le Tréport (one-bedroom apartment €115,000), Varengeville (one-bedroom apartment €85,000) and Saint-Valéry-en-Caux (three-bedroom house €250,000).

- **Côte Fleurie** – The Floral Coast is the short stretch of coast between the picturesque port of Honfleur (one-bedroom apartment €70,000, three-bedroom apartment €250,000, three-bedroom old house €650,000) to the mouth of the Orne north of Caen in Calvados, Lower Normandy. It has predominantly sandy beaches and comprises some of northern France's most upmarket resorts, including Deauville (studio apartment €70,000, six-bedroom house €600,000), Trouville (studio apartment €50,000, five-bedroom house €700,000), Houlgate and Cabourg (two-bedroom apartment €175,000, three-bedroom house €350,000).
- **Côte de Nacre** – The Mother of Pearl Coast, running from the Orne estuary to Arromanches, offers vast sandy beaches (where the Allied forces landed on 6th June 1944) and tidy resorts such as Luc-sur-Mer and Courseulles-sur-Mer.
- **Côte des Iles** – The Coast of Islands (the Channel Islands are visible from the mainland) on the west side of the Cotentin peninsula (Manche, Lower Normandy) is a popular holiday area, with resorts such as Barneville-Carteret (one-bedroom apartment €50,000, three-bedroom house near the sea €500,000) and Granville (studio apartment €80,000, two-bedroom seafront apartment €350,000). The east side is less accessible and the northern tip of the peninsula is best known for its nuclear power station and reprocessing plant.
- **Côte d'Emeraude** – Brittany's Emerald Coast stretches from the attractive walled town of Saint-Malo in Ille-et-Vilaine to Saint-Brieuc Bay in Côtes d'Armor and takes in the chic resort of Dinard (two-bedroom townhouse €300,000, five-bedroom house near beach €650,000) as well as Erquy, Sables d'Or, Saint-Cast, Saint-Jacut and le Val-André. At its western end, sandy beaches give way to typical Breton fishing ports.
- **Côte de Granit Rose** – As its name indicates, this stretch of coast, from Saint-Brieuc almost to the border with Finistère, is strewn with pink granite rock formations, which give way to sand or shingle coves. There are few resorts, Perros-Guirec and Ploumanac'h being the most popular, while the most impressive rock formations are to be found at Trégastel.

  Most of the coast of Finistère has no official name, though it's sometimes called the **Côte des Légendes**, and consists of a series of bays – the Baie de Lannion and Baie de Morlaix of the north coast of Finistère (the region's wildest coast), the Baie de Douarnenez (three-bedroom house near beach €275,000) and Baie d'Audierne on the west coast (seafront studio apartment in Benodet €115,000), and the Baie de la Forêt and the Baie de Quiberon (two-bedroom apartment with sea view

€250,000, four-bedroom house €500,000), off which is the popular Belle-Ile-en-Mer, to the south. Until the last of these bays, beach resorts are few and far between – Brignognan-Plages and Licquirec being the largest – though the town of Brest has fine beaches and impressive headlands such as the Pointe de Penhir and Pointe de Raz are popular with tourists. But the Quiberon Peninsula marks the start of a gentler coastline, with long sandy beaches and dunes as Finistère gives way to Morbihan, Brittany's (and one of France's) most popular coastal area, the Golfe du Morbihan being particularly sought after.

- **Côte Sauvage** – Just across the border with Loire Atlantique in Pays-de-la-Loire, the Wild Coast is dramatic but short, covering just a few kilometres between the Pointe du Croisic (two-bedroom apartment near sea €225,000) and the Pointe de Penchâteau (two-bedroom house near sea €200,000) near the attractive resort of La Baule-Escoubiac (studio apartment €90,000, two-bedroom seaside apartment €375,000).
- **Côte de Jade** – The Jade Coast, so called on account of the colour of the sea but also known as the Côte d'Amour, marks a return to long, sandy beaches. Pornic is a pretty seaside resort (one-bedroom apartment €175,000, three-bedroom house €300,000).

  The start of Vendée's coast features the attractive islands of Noirmoutier (two-bedroom house near beach €225,000) and Yeu, while the mainland boasts the resorts of Saint-Jean-des-Monts and Saint-Gilles-Croix-de-Vie.
- **Côte de Lumière** – The Light (or Sunshine) Coast is rockier, its small resorts including Saint-Hilaire-de-Riez, Saint-Gilles (one-bedroom seaside apartment €150,000, three-bedroom house near beach €225,000) and Brétignolles.

  Les Sables d'Olonnes (one-bedroom apartment €125,000, two-bedroom house near sea €225,000) is Vendée's (and one of western France's) most popular resort, the southern part of the *département*'s coast featuring smaller, more old-fashioned resorts such as Jard-sur-Mer (one-bedroom apartment €85,000, four-bedroom villa near beach €400,000) and La Tranche.

  The attractive town of La Rochelle (one-bedroom apartment near sea €175,000) marks the start of the Charente-Maritime *département* in Poitou-Charentes, where the picturesque and upmarket islands of Ré and Oléron are attached to the mainland by bridges. Resorts include Ronce-les-Bains and, near the mouth of the Gironde, La Palmyre, Pontaillac, Saint-Palais-sur-Mer and, the least attractive but most popular, Royan (three-bedroom villa near beach €250,000).

- **Côte d'Argent** – The Silver Coast (so called because of the silvery glint of the sea) is Europe's longest straight coastline, a virtually continuous beach running some 200km from south of the Gironde estuary almost to the Spanish border, through the *départments* of Gironde, Landes and Pyrénées-Atlantiques in Aquitaine. The coast is broken by the Bassin d'Arcachon (a large inland sea – see page 177) and backed by a string of lakes. There's surprisingly little development, beaches often being inaccessible by car and devoid of facilities, and the few resorts include Biscarosse, Capbreton-Hossegor, Lacanau, Mimizan (one-bedroom apartment €80,000, three-bedroom house near beach €200,000).

- **Côte Basque** – The last stretch of France's Atlantic coast, from the famous resort of Biarritz (studio apartment €70,000, one-bedroom apartment €150,000, two-bedroom apartment €225,000) to the Spanish border, is within the Basque Country. Other resorts are Bidart, Guéthary, Hendaye (three-bedroom house near beach €275,000) and Saint-Jean-de-Luz (one-bedroom apartment €250,000, two-bedroom apartment near beach €550,000).

- **Côte Vermeille** – The only part of Languedoc-Roussillon's 200km coast to have a name, the Vermillion Coast is the short rocky section adjoining the Spanish border, with its pretty and popular fishing villages of Argelès-sur-Mer (studio apartment €75,000, three-bedroom townhouse €500,000), Cerbère (two-bedroom apartment €125,000), Banyuls-sur-Mer (two-bedroom apartment €300,000, four-bedroom villa €500,000) and trendy Collioure (two-bedroom apartment €400,000, two-bedroom villa with pool €700,000).

  Then begins an almost continuous sandy beach which, apart from a few traditional fishing villages such as Grau-du-Roi and the towns of Perpignan, Narbonne, Sète (studio apartment €60,000, three-bedroom house €200,000, two-bedroom villa with sea view and pool €500,000) and Montpellier, consists of modern resorts, purpose-built since the '60s. These include Gruissan-Plage (studio apartment €60,000, one-bedroom apartment near beach €100,000, six-bedroom house €500,000), Canet-Plage, Saint-Cyprien (one-bedroom apartment €150,000, six-bedroom house with pool €400,000), Port Bacarès, Port Leucate, La Grande Motte, Aigues-Mortes (barn for conversion €150,000, three-bedroom apartment €350,000, three-bedroom villa with pool €550,000) and Cap d'Agde (studio apartment near beach €45,000, five-bedroom villa €325,000), Europe's largest purpose-built seaside resort and its largest naturist centre. One of these resorts' advantages is relatively low property prices.

- **Côte d'Améthiste** – The Amethyst Coast is mostly taken up by the Camargue nature reserve, its only towns being the busy resort of Saintes-Maries-de-la-Mer and industrial Salin de Giraud, with its vast salt flats and works.
- **Côte des Calanques** – The Coast of Coves, between Marseille and Toulon, boasts attractive inlets between limestone cliffs, with pretty resorts such as Cassis (three-bedroom apartment with sea view €325,000, four-bedroom villa with pool €1m), En-Vau, La Ciotat (studio apartment €110,000, three-bedroom apartment with sea view €250,000, two-bedroom villa with pool €300,00), Les Lecques and Bandol.
- **Côte d'Azur** – One of the world's most famous stretches of coast, the Azure Coast, also known as the French Riviera, needs no introduction, its legendary resorts including Saint-Tropez (studio apartment €175,000, four-bedroom villa €2.8m), Cannes (one-bedroom apartment €100,000, one-bedroom beachfront apartment €275,000, three-bedroom house €475,000), Antibes (one-bedroom apartment €150,000, three-bedroom villa with sea view €800,000), Juan-les-Pins (studio apartment €100,000, one-bedroom beachfront apartment €550,000) and Nice. Hopelessly crowded in summer and with mostly narrow beaches, a high crime rate and polluted seas, it's above all a place to be seen, although there are less chic resorts, such as Cassis, Fréjus-Saint-Raphaël (two-bedroom apartment €125,000, two-bedroom villa €250,000, four-bedroom villa €1.25m), Hyères and Sainte-Maxime, smaller, family-friendly resorts such as Bandol, Bormes-les-Mimosas, Cavalaire-sur-Mer, Ciotat and Le Lavandou, and 'hideaways' such as Roquebrune, Villefranche-sur-Mer (two-bedroom apartment in old town €700,000), Eze, Beaulieu, Cagnes and Saint-Jean-Cap-Ferrat (four-bedroom apartment €1.4m).

LOCATION

The most important consideration when buying a home anywhere is usually its location – or as the old adage goes, the three most important considerations are location, location and location! A property in a reasonable condition in a popular area is likely to be a better investment than an exceptional property in a less attractive location, and there's usually no point in buying a 'dream home' in a terrible location. France offers almost everything that anyone could want, but you must choose the right property in the right place. **The wrong decision regarding location is one of the**

main causes of disappointment among foreigners who purchase property in France.

There are many points to consider regarding the location of a home, and you should take into account the present and future needs of all family members in relation to the following factors.

Climate

When consulting climate charts, don't forget to factor in the altitude of your chosen area – inland high areas tend to be cooler in winter and warmer in summer. For example, when it's 25C on the coast, it could be a mere 15C 1,000m up in the hills behind. Mountains and hills also attract cloud and rain (and sometimes thunderstorms), while river valleys can be foggy and flat land can be windy (which can be a disadvantage in winter but a boon in summer, when the breeze keeps you cool). Thunderstorms (often violent) are prevalent in the south-east but can cause power cuts and even fires in other parts of the country.

You should also bear in mind both the winter and summer climate of your chosen region, the average daily amount of sunshine, the rainfall and wind conditions. Generally, the eastern half of the country (excluding the Mediterranean coast) experiences sub-zero temperatures in winter and the southern half long periods of temperatures over 30C in the summer. The Pyrenees are an exception to both these patterns. The driest part of France is a swathe stretching from Lille to Nantes; the wettest parts are Finistère and mountainous regions, although these statistics refer to the total annual rainfall and not to the number of days' rain (rain can come in short, heavy bursts in the mountains).

The orientation or aspect of a building is vital, and if you want morning or afternoon sun (or both) you must ensure that balconies, terraces and gardens are facing the right direction (take a compass when house hunting).

An obvious point, but one that's often overlooked, is that the climate largely determines the type of plants you can grow, including grass and vegetables. If you're a keen gardener, you should make a note of what you will and won't be able to cultivate in a particular area.

Community

Do you wish to live in an area surrounded by other expatriates from your home country (as you will almost inevitably be in some parts of Provence and Dordogne) or as far away from them as possible? If you wish to integrate with the local community, you should avoid the foreign 'ghettos' and choose a French village or an area or development with mainly local inhabitants. However, unless you speak fluent French or intend to learn it, you should think twice before buying a property in a village, although residents who take the time and trouble to integrate into the local community are invariably warmly welcomed. If you're buying a permanent home, it's important to check on your prospective neighbours, particularly when buying an apartment. For example, are they noisy, sociable or absent for long periods? Do you think you will get on with them? **Good neighbours are invaluable, particularly when buying a second home in a village.**

On the other hand, if you wish to mix only with your compatriots and don't plan to learn French, living in a predominantly foreign community will be ideal. Note, however, that some towns in popular tourist areas are inhabited largely by second homeowners and are like ghost towns for most of the year. In these areas, many facilities, businesses and shops are closed outside the main tourist season, when local services such as public transport and postal collections may be severely curtailed.

Cost of Living

The cost of living varies little throughout France (with the exception of property prices – see below), although it's generally higher in cities (where the high cost of land drives up the price of just about everything) and remote areas (owing to the cost of transporting goods from their place of production). For further information about the cost of living in France, refer to *Living and Working in France* (see page 476).

Cost of Property

After an overall price rise of over 15 per cent in 2004 (the highest in Europe, according to a housing market report published by the British Royal Institute of Chartered Surveyors) and an equivalent rise during the first half of 2005, the French property market has begun to cool. According to figures released by the French estate agents' association, FNAIM, the overall rise for 2005 was only 10 per cent and the increase between July 2005 and July 2006 just 8 per cent. The table below shows overall price increases (or decreases) during this period in the 22 regions of France.

Price Change	Regions
8 to 9%	Upper Normandy, Provence-Alpes-Côte d'Azur
7 to 8%	Languedoc-Roussillon, Limousin
6 to 7%	Brittany, Champagne-Ardenne, Paris, Pays-de-la-Loire, Picardy
4 to 6%	Alsace, Aquitaine, Auvergne, Burgundy, Centre, Ile-de-France (excluding Paris), Lorraine, Lower Normandy, Nord-Pas-de-Calais, Rhône-Alpes
0 to 1%	Midi-Pyrénées
-1%	Franche-Comté
-2%	Poitou-Charentes

In October 2006, the French Housing Minister, predicted that property prices would start to fall within three years owing to the high level of new building taking place (over 400,000 new houses were started in 2005 compared with just over 300,000 the previous year, and a further increase is expected in 2006), although estate agents felt that factor this would have a negligible effect on prices.

As in most countries, property is cheapest in rural areas, where the exodus in the last 30 years has left the countryside with a surfeit of empty properties (and where employment prospects are poor or non-existent). The French tend to live close to their work and the idea of commuting long distances doesn't appeal to them. With the exception of major commuter areas such as the Seine Valley and a few popular holiday areas such as Provence, Dordogne, the Alps and most coastal areas, the price of rural property in France is relatively low. The cheapest *départements* are Allier (in Auvergne), Cher and Indre (Centre-Val-de-Loire) and Creuse (Limousin).

Prices have been driven up by foreign buyers particularly in border regions such as the Rhine *départements*, Savoy and the Lyon-Grenoble-Annecy triangle, along the coast and in some areas in the south-west, e.g. the Dordogne. However, prices are highest in areas where the French demand for holiday homes is strongest, which generally includes rural areas within 30 minutes' drive of a major city and anywhere on the coast! You usually pay a premium for a property with a sea view, although it's also easier to resell. Coastal and city properties can cost up to two or three times as much as similar inland rural properties. Property on the Côte d'Azur is among the most expensive in the world, and Paris isn't far behind.

According to specialist French property agents VEF, the average price paid by foreign buyers (mostly British) in 2005 was around €152,600, the most expensive region being Rhône-Alpes (due to the high proportion of costly ski chalets), with an average of over €400,000, and the cheapest Limousin at €123,000.

Properties in traditionally popular places, such as Provence, Dordogne and Brittany, will probably always show a steady increase in value, as it's unlikely that these regions will lose their appeal to foreign (particularly British) buyers, but there are other parts of France waiting in the wings that could soon (and suddenly) increase in popularity and where prices could therefore jump dramatically. These include the *départements* of Ariège, Aveyron, Gers and Mayenne, Auvergne, Burgundy and Limousin regions, and the Roussillon coast (see **Property Hot Spots** on page 39). Note, however, that in some remote areas (e.g. in Auvergne) the local people may be hostile to foreign buyers and integration can be difficult. Note also that, although budget airlines have recently made acessible previously remote parts of France, these services are notoriously fickle and it isn't wise to buy in a particular area purely because it's served by cheap flights; airlines create and cancel routes at the drop of a hat and you could be left stranded.

Crime Rate & Security

The crime rate in France as a whole is similar to that found in most western European countries, although lower than the UK's, with 61 reported crimes per thousand inhabitants per year compared with 72 in the UK. As elsewhere in Europe, juvenile crime is on the increase (and at an increasingly low age); it accounts for around 20 per cent of all criminal arrests and juveniles are estimated to cause around 35 per cent of street crimes and 25 per cent of crimes of assault and battery. Theft accounts for around 65 per cent of French crime, although the incidence of burglary is much lower than in the UK, for example, where there are 31 burglaries per thousand inhabitants per year compared with France's 12. However, in many resort areas (especially the Côte d'Azur) the incidence of burglary is high, which also results in more expensive home insurance.

Most violent crime takes place in certain regions of Paris and its suburbs, cities such as Strasbourg and major towns near the Mediterranean. In general, however, foreigners aren't targeted more (or less) than French people by criminals.

Check the crime rate in the local area, e.g. burglaries, stolen cars and violent crimes. Is crime increasing or decreasing? Note that professional crooks love isolated houses, particularly those full of expensive furniture and other belongings that they can strip bare at their leisure. You're much less likely to be the victim of thieves if you live in a village, where crime is virtually unknown – strangers stand out like sore thumbs in villages, where their every move is monitored by the local populace.

Developments

It's essential to find out whether any major developments are planned for the area in which you intend to buy a home. These could have a beneficial or adverse effect on your enjoyment. A new motorway, for example, might make access to your home easier or simply be a noise nuisance. Unfortunately, it's difficult to find out about proposed developments, as there's no single government or regional, departmental or local authority that coordinates all planning and you must contact innumerable offices, which will be able to inform you only about their small area of specialisation.

One of the best source of local information is town halls and inhabitants. You should also read *The News* and magazines about France (see **Appendix B**) and consult expatriate website notice boards (see **Appendix C**).

Employment

If your employer is transferring you to France, you may have accommodation found for you, but you shouldn't assume that a relocation consultant or other agent will find the best property in the best location for your particular needs and should do your own research, perhaps insisting on renting for a period until you feel more at home.

If you need to find work in France, this is obviously better done before you move definitively, although this may not be possible. The best place to find a job will depend on a number of factors, including your qualifications and experience (although the former are far more important in France than the latter), your French language skills (English may be in increasing demand, but you must also be able to communicate in French), and the type of work you're looking for (and the type of salary). For example, there's a shortage of experienced high-tech workers in many fields (notably computer-related areas) – to the extent that the government has created a special exemption in the work permit process, although the exemption doesn't automatically apply to anyone with computer experience. It helps greatly if you're a qualified engineer (*ingénieur*), as the French have great respect for technical and scientific qualifications.

You should take into account the level of unemployment in a region or *département* (see below), although this won't necessarily be relevant (e.g. if there's high unemployment in a particular sector only or, in the case of Lozère, little employment of any kind and a large proportion of retirees!).

Region	Unemployment (late 2006)
Alsace	8.0%
Aquitaine	8.5%
Auvergne	7.7%
Bourgogne	7.6%
Bretagne	7.3%
Centre-Val de Loire	7.7%
Champagne-Ardenne	9.1%
Corsica	9.3%
Franche-Comté	8.4%
Ile-de-France	8.2%
Languedoc-Roussillon	12.1%
Limousin	7.1%
Lorraine	9.0%
Midi-Pyrénées	8.9%
Nord-Pas-de-Calais	12.2%
Normandie (Basse)	8.4%
Normandie (Haute)	9.6%
Pays-de-la-Loire	7.4%
Picardie	9.9%
Poitou-Charentes	8.3%
Provence-Alpes-Côte d'Azur	10.5%
Rhône-Alpes	7.6%

The *départements* with the highest unemployment at the end of 2006 were Gard (12.8 per cent), Hérault, Pas-de-Calais, Ardennes, Nord, Aisne, Pyrénées-Orientales, Seine-Saint-Denis, Bouches-du-Rhône and Aude (11.2 per cent); those with the lowest were Lozère (4.9 per cent), Aveyron, Mayenne, Ain, Cantal, Gers, Haute-Savoie, Corrèze, Essonne, Yvelines, Deux-Sèvres, Jura, Savoie, Vendée, Ille-et-Vilaine and Côte d'Or (6.9 per cent).

Note also that unemployment is generally twice as high among immigrants (18 per cent compared with 9 per cent among native French people), the highest level applying to women between 25 and 39 (a massive 28 per cent) followed by women between 40 and 49 (18 per cent) and men between 25 and 39 (17 per cent).

Further information about finding a job, being self-employed and setting up a business in France can be found in *Living & Working in France* and *Making a Living in France* (see page 476).

Garden & Outbuildings

If you're planning to buy a country property with a large garden or plot, bear in mind the high cost and amount of work involved in its upkeep. If it's a second home, who will look after the house and garden when you're away? Do you want to spend your holidays mowing the lawn and cutting back the undergrowth? Do you want a home with a lot of outbuildings? What are you going to do with them? Can you afford to convert them into extra rooms or guest accommodation and, if so, is there a market for these?

Language

The French are generally poor at foreign languages and even in major cities few people other than professionals will speak more than basic English, so unless you choose to live in a foreign 'ghetto' (most of which use English as their *lingua franca*) you must learn French. Although there are a number of regional languages in France (e.g. Basque, Breton, Occitan and Provençal), everyone speaks French. However, there are various regional accents and local *patois* (dialects), which even the French find difficult to understand. Bear this in mind when choosing your region.

Local Council

Try to find out whether the local council is well run. Unfortunately many are profligate and simply use any extra income to hire a few more of their cronies or spend it on grandiose schemes. What are the views of other residents? If the municipality is efficiently run, you can usually rely on good local social and sports amenities and other facilities. In areas where there are many foreign residents, the town hall may have a foreign residents' department.

Natural Phenomena

Check whether an area is liable to natural disasters such as storms, floods or forest fires. If a property is located near a waterway, it may be expensive to insure against floods (or flash floods), which are a threat in some areas. Note that in areas with little rainfall there may be frequent droughts, water restrictions and high water bills.

Noise

Noise can be a problem in some parts of France, although the French are generally considerate neighbours. You should ensure that a property isn't located next to a busy road, industrial plant, commercial area, building site, restaurant, bar, discotheque or night club (where revelries may continue into the early hours). Look out for objectionable neighbouring properties and check whether nearby vacant land has been zoned for commercial activities (e.g. a nightclub!). In rural areas, make sure your neighbours don't have noisy dogs or a cockerel. In some resorts, many properties are second homes and are let short-term, which means you may have to tolerate boisterous holiday-makers as neighbours throughout the year (or at least during the summer months). In towns, traffic noise, particularly from motorcycles, can continue all night.

Parking

If you're planning to buy in a town or city, check whether there's adequate private or free on-street parking for your family and visitors. Is it safe to park in the street? In most French cities it's important to have secure off-street parking if you value your car (the French use bumpers for just that – bumping!). Parking space is at a premium in cities and most large towns, where private garages or parking spaces are unobtainable or astronomically expensive. Bear in mind also that an apartment or townhouse may be some distance from the nearest road or car park. How do you feel about carrying heavy shopping hundreds of metres to your home and possibly up several flights of stairs? If you're planning to buy an apartment above the ground floor, you may wish to ensure that the building has a lift.

Power Stations, Incinerators & Landfills

You should check where the nearest power station, incinerator and landfill site are, as well as factories that might emit smoke or unpleasant smells (check the prevailing wind direction). Most of France's electricity is generated by nuclear reactors, of which there are 19 across the country: in Cruas (*département* 07), Givet (08), Nogent-sur-Seine (10), Saint-Paul-Trois-Châteaux (26), Avoine (37), Morestel and Saint-Maurice-l'Exil (38), Laurent-Nouan (41), Ouzouer-sur-Loire (45), Les Pieux (50), Cattenom (57), Gravelines (59), Fessenheim (68), Cany-Barville and Neuville-lès-Dieppe (76), Golfech (82) and Civaux (86). Details can be found on the website of Electricité de France (💻 www.edf.fr).

Rivers & Parks

Beachfront properties are many people's dream but they're few and far between, are invariably astronomically expensive and, unless they have their own private beach, can lack privacy – not to mention be vulnerable to storm and flood damage. A river- or canalside property, on the other hand, may have none of these disadvantages (though it may have others, such as midges and mosquitoes, and constant bank erosion) and all the advantages of being 'on the waterfront'. France has 8,500km (5,300mi) of inland waterways, compared to only just over half as much coastline.

France has 44 Regional Nature Parks (*Parc Naturel Régional*), covering some 12 per cent of French territory (over 7m hectares!). Unlike the six National Parks (Cévennes, Ecrins, Mercantour, Port-Cros, Pyrénées and Vanoise), which are virtually uninhabited, the Regional Parks accommodate around 3m people, an average park consisting of 80 small towns and villages. Further information about Regional Parks can be obtained from the Ministère de l'Ecologie et du Développement Durable (💻 www.environnement.gouv.fr – choose 'Parcs naturels régionaux' from the drop-down list) or a dedicated website (💻 www.parcs-naturels-regionaux.tm.fr).

Schools

If you have school-age children or are planning to have children in France, consider how you wish them to be educated: in French state schools, in

French private schools or in foreign or international private schools. Check the choice and quality of local schools. Even if your family has no need or plans to use local schools, the value of a home may be influenced by the quality and location of schools.

Services

Check what local health and social services are provided and how far it is to the nearest hospital with an emergency department. Are there English-speaking doctors and dentists and private clinics or hospitals in the area?

Shopping

Find out what shopping facilities are provided in the neighbourhood and how far it is to the nearest large town with good shopping facilities, e.g. a super/hypermarket. Think also how you would get there if your car was out of action. Note that many rural villages are dying and have few shops or facilities, and they aren't usually a good choice for a retirement home.

Sports & Leisure Facilities

The range and quality of local leisure, sports, community and cultural facilities varies considerably from place to place. How important is it to you to be near sports facilities such as beaches, golf courses, ski resorts and waterways? Bear in mind that properties in or close to ski and coastal resorts are considerably more expensive, although they also have the best letting potential. If you're a keen skier, you may want to be close to the Alps or the Pyrenees, although there are smaller skiing areas in other regions.

Tourists

Bear in mind that if you live in a popular tourist area, i.e. almost anywhere on the Mediterranean coast, you will be inundated with tourists in the summer. They won't just jam the roads and pack the beaches and shops, but will also occupy your favourite table at your local bar or restaurant (heaven forbid!). Bear in mind that while a 'front-line' property sounds attractive and may be ideal for short holidays, it isn't always the best solution for permanent residence. Many beaches are hopelessly crowded in the peak season, streets may be smelly from restaurants and fast food outlets, parking will be impossible, services stretched to breaking point and the incessant noise may drive you crazy. You may also have to tolerate water shortages, power cuts and sewage problems. Some people prefer to move inland to higher ground, where it's less humid, you're isolated from the noise and can also enjoy excellent views. On the other hand, getting to and from hillside properties can be difficult, and the often poorly-maintained roads (usually narrow and unguarded) are for sober, confident drivers only.

Town or Country?

Do you wish to be in a town or do you prefer the country? Inland or by the sea? How about living on an island? Life on an island is more restricted and remote, e.g. you cannot jump into your car and drive to Lyon or Paris or 'pop' over the border into Andorra, Spain, Italy or Switzerland. Bear in mind that if you buy a property in the country you will have to tolerate poor (or non-existent) public transport, long travelling distances to a town of any size, solitude and remoteness, and the high cost and amount of work involved in the upkeep of a country house and garden. You may not be able to walk to the local shop for fresh bread or to the local bar for a glass of your favourite tipple, or have a choice of restaurants on your doorstep. In a town or large village, the weekly market will be just around the corner, the doctor and chemist's close at hand, and if you need help or run into any problems, your neighbours will be near by.

On the other hand, in the country you will be closer to nature, will have more freedom (e.g. to make as much noise as you wish) and possibly complete privacy, e.g. to sunbathe or swim *au naturel*. Living in a remote area in the country will suit those looking for peace and quiet who don't want to involve themselves in the 'hustle and bustle' of town life (not that there's a lot of this in French rural towns). If you're seeking peace and quiet, make sure that there isn't a busy road or railway line nearby or a local church within 'donging' distance. Note, however, that many people who buy a remote country home find that the peace of the countryside palls after a time and they yearn for the more exciting city or coastal life. If you've never lived in the country, it's wise to rent before buying. Note also that while it's cheaper to buy in a remote or unpopular location, it's usually much more difficult to find a buyer when you want to sell.

Transport

If you plan to travel extensively, you will want to be near to an airport or *TGV* station or motorway junction. Otherwise, you may be content with local public transport – if it exists (it doesn't in many rural areas). Don't believe everything you're told about the distance or travelling times to the nearest airport, railway station, motorway junction, beach or town, but check for yourself.

Type of Property

You may be dreaming of buying a tumbledown cottage and 'doing it up' in traditional style, but the availability of properties in need of renovation is diminishing while the cost of renovating them is increasing (especially if you want to do it properly, using local materials). You should therefore also consider buying a modern property – or even having one built to your own specification. New homes are usually built on the outskirts of towns and villages rather than in remote areas, so they offer quicker integration into the local community (especially as you won't be working 24 hours a day for the first two years to bring the place into a habitable condition).

PROPERTY HOT SPOTS

Brittany, Dordogne, Provence, Languedoc-Roussillon, Aquitaine, Poitou-Charentes ... recent decades have seen a succession of 'hot spots' as waves of foreign buyers, in pursuit of their French property dream, discover areas of France where the lifestyle is 'authentic' and prices are affordable. Depending on your reasons for buying, you may wish to pursue or to avoid the hot spots; either way, you will want to know what the next hot spots are likely to be.

No one can foresee the future, but the indications are that the above regions will continue to be popular (one leading estate agent predicts that Brittany and Languedoc-Roussillon will be the two main growth areas in 2007), although most of Provence has priced itself out of all but the exclusive market, while others will enjoy new-found popularity. Among these are Midi-Pyrénées, and especially the *département* of Aveyron and the area formerly known as Gascony (roughly the modern *département* of Gers), which has been described as France's 'last great wilderness'.

The recently opened A28 is making previously overlooked areas accessible, including Touraine (the area surrounding the city of Tours in Indre-et-Loire, Centre), where prices rose by 15 per cent in 2005 and 2006. Flights to Tours airport from the UK are bringing more property hunters to the area, where it's said the best French is spoken.

Elsewhere, an increasing number of foreign buyers are attracted to Burgundy – where the middle *départements* of Côte d'Or and Nièvre, being furthest from Paris and Lyon, have the lowest-priced property – and Lorraine, the cheapest of the eastern regions. But perhaps the biggest 'discovery' of this decade is the Limousin region, which is one of France's most sparsely populated (at just 42 inhabitants per square kilometre compared with England's average of 375) and cheapest in terms of property prices: a renovated village house can be bought for €100,000, a three-bedroom cottage for €150,000 and a large farm with lots of land for €250,000. The region's predominantly rural nature and the continuing exodus of local inhabitants mean that there are plenty of barns and other farm buildings available for renovation at give-away prices. Limousin has been dubbed 'the new Provence' by *Le Monde* and already there has been an influx of Britons wanting to 'cash in' on its many attractions. Most of them have settled in the *département* of Creuse and many in Haute-Vienne, where there are reckoned to be almost 2,500 British inhabitants and where Limoges airport now handles over a dozen flights per week from several UK airports (see 💻 www.aeroportdelimoges.com). So far the least attractive of Limousin's three *départements* has been Corrèze, but this is set to change. Bordering Dordogne to the east and once known as its 'poor relation', Corrèze is now being hailed as 'the new Dordogne' – it has a similar climate and landscape, equally beautiful villages and the same river, the Dordogne, running through it. Since Jacques Chirac started seeking his rural roots there, Corrèze has enjoyed a vastly improved infrastructure, with a new motorway linking its three main towns (Brive, Tulle and Ussel) and rail links with Paris and Marseille. The 'Chirac effect' is also soon to extend to the *département*'s airport at Brive (a town boasting the sobriquet 'the Paris of the South'), which is due to go international in 2007. For the time being, a three-bedroom cottage in Corrèze can be had for €150,000 and a farmhouse with land for €200,000, but these prices can only go one way.

As France continues to attract foreign property buyers, today's undiscovered areas will inevitably become tomorrow's hotspots. Thankfully for future generations, France is a big country and will always have hidden corners in which a rural idyll is indeed just around the corner. Auvergne may be the next decade's discovery as it's already being discovered by intrepid house hunters and the A89 from Bordeaux will soon reveal it to others – one leading estate agent sees the *départements* of Allier and Puy-de-Dôme (and particularly the area around Clermont-Ferrand) as impending hot spots. According to others, Béziers and Montpellier (in Hérault) are the next centres of attraction. Other areas about to be 'rediscovered' include Charente and Aquitaine's coast; Ariège and Hautes-Pyrénées in Midi-Pyrénées, where there's still a wide choice of 'renovation projects' at bargain prices; Ardèche in Rhône-Alpes, where prices are half those of neighbouring Gard (in

Languedoc-Roussillon); Indre in Centre-Val-de-Loire; and Mayenne in Pays-de-la-Loire. There's no end to the discoveries to be made in France!

RESEARCH

This book will provide you with answers to many of the above questions. However, although the information about each area is comprehensive and up to date, it isn't intended as a substitute for personal research. It's essential to spend time looking around your areas of interest. If possible, you should visit an area a number of times over a period of a few weeks, both on weekdays and at weekends, in order to get a feel for the neighbourhood (it's better to walk than to drive around). A property seen on a balmy summer's day after a delicious lunch and a few glasses of *vin de pays* may not be nearly so attractive on a subsequent visit *sans* sunshine and the warm inner glow.

If possible, you should also visit an area at different times of the year, e.g. in both the summer and winter, as somewhere that's wonderful in summer can be forbidding and inhospitable in winter (or vice versa if you don't like extreme heat). This is particularly important when choosing a holiday resort, which may be bustling and lively during the summer months but deserted in winter. If you're planning to buy a winter holiday home, you should view it in the summer, as snow can hide a multitude of sins! In any case, you should view a property a number of times before deciding to buy it. If you're unfamiliar with an area, most experts recommend that you rent for a period before buying – especially if you're planning to buy a permanent or retirement home in an unfamiliar area. Many people change their minds after a period and it isn't unusual for buyers to move once or twice before settling down permanently.

Before looking at properties, it's important to have a good idea of the type of property you want and the price you wish to pay, and to draw up a short list of the areas and towns of interest. Most importantly, make a list of what you want and don't want – if you don't do this, you're likely to be overwhelmed by the number of properties to be viewed. You should consider a property's proximity to your place of work, schools, bars and restaurants, countryside or towns, shops, public transport, beaches, swimming pools, entertainment, sports facilities, etc. If you buy a country property, the distance to local amenities and services could become a problem, particularly if you plan to retire to France. If you live in a remote rural area, you will need to be much more self-sufficient than if you live in a town. Don't forget that France is a BIG country and if you live in a remote area you will need to use the car for everything (which will increase your cost of living).

If you wish to live near a beach, particular town, airport or facilities, such as sports or other amenities, obtain a large scale map of the area and decide the maximum distance you will consider travelling. Mark the places that you've seen on the map, at the same time making a list of the plus and minus points of each property. If you use an estate agent, he will usually drive you around and you can then return later to the properties that you like best at your leisure (provided you've marked them on your map!). Note, however, that agents may be reluctant to give you the keys to visit a property on your own.

A number of companies organise 'discovery tours' of various regions of France, on which you can get a feel for an area and the type and prices of properties and maybe see a few properties that are available, although these tours aren't cheap and you may prefer to arrange your own itinerary. For example, in the UK there's Bishop & Co. (☎ 01332-747474, 💻 http://www.u2france.co.uk) and in France Moving to France (☎ 04 67 90 78 19, 💻 http://www.moving-to-france.com), which currently organises seminars and property tours in Languedoc.

The decision to purchase property, retire or relocate to France (or any other country) should only be taken after careful consideration and extensive research. There are numerous books about France (see **Appendix B**), including *Buying a Home in France* and *Living and Working in France* (Survival Books – see page 476), which are packed with important information about property purchase and daily life in France. **Note that the cost of investing in a few books or magazines (and other research) is tiny compared with the expense of making a big mistake.** Numerous websites (see **Appendix C**) also provide free information about France.

TROGLODYTE
CAVE FOR
SALE

Vitré - Brittany

2

THE NORTH-WEST

Normandy & Brittany

Normandy and Brittany have long been popular areas for foreign buyers, particularly the British on account of the regions' accessibility and similar climate and countryside, as well as their historical and cultural kinship. Like Britain, Normandy was invaded by the Vikings – 200 years before the Normans themselves invaded Britain – and it was part of England in the early Middle Ages (the Queen is still 'Duke of Normandy'!). Great Britain in French is 'big Brittany' to distinguish it from the French region, which was founded by Cornish settlers fleeing Anglo-Saxon invaders in the fifth century. They took their language with them (curiously, Breton survives but Cornish doesn't) and remain proudly Celtic. It wasn't until 1532 that Brittany officially became part of France.

There are also more recent cultural ties between the two regions and Britain, with twinnings (e.g. Rennes with Exeter, Honfleur with Sandwich in Kent, and the *département* of Calvados with Devon) and frequent cross-Channel exchanges. There's a *Normandie & South of England Magazine* (see **Appendix B**) and even the unlikely *hot dog breton*, a sausage in a pancake, and Breton whisky, distilled at Lannion!

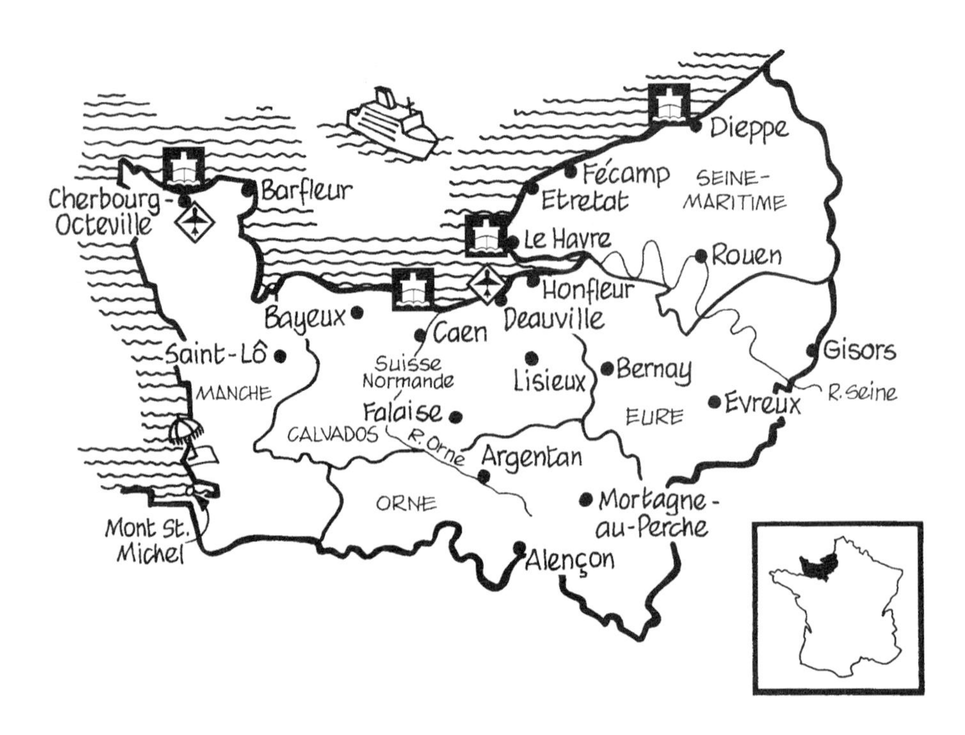

NORMANDY

Normandy (*La Normandie*) contains the *départements* of Calvados (14), Eure (27), Manche (50), Orne (61) and Seine-Maritime (76) and is officially divided into two areas: Upper Normandy (*Haute-Normandie*) to the east, comprising the *départements* of Eure and Seine-Maritime, and Lower Normandy (*Basse-Normandie*) to the west, including the other three *départements*. Upper Normandy, which covers an area of around 12,500km^2 (5,000mi^2), has a population of around 1.8m, and Lower Normandy (17,600km^2/7,000mi^2) a population of around 1.45m. This administrative division, however, has neither a historical nor a geographical basis. Historically, Upper and Lower Normandy were separated by the Seine, which now runs roughly along the dividing line between the *départements* of Eure and Seine-Maritime in Upper Normandy.

Geographically, Normandy can be said to be divided into three areas: the eastern 'plains' (roughly corresponding to Upper Normandy), interrupted by the Seine valley; the western *bocage*, a landscape of fields and hedges resulting from 19th century methods of dairy farming; and a central area divided vertically between plains to the west of the river Orne and *bocage* to the east. (Confusingly, the word *bocage* is used to describe both the area south-west of Caen and any similar landscape in Normandy or France as a whole.) Within the central area, south of Caen, is 'Swiss Normandy' (*La Suisse normande*), so called because of its supposed similarity to the Swiss landscape, with deep gorges and rocky peaks, although the highest point, Mont Pinçon, is only 365m (120ft) above sea level.

Normandy was originally divided into 'lands' (*pays*), many of which are still referred to and even marked on maps (although they often straddle *départements* and even the division between Upper and Lower Normandy), e.g. the Pays d'Argentan, Pays du Houlme and Pays du Perche in Orne, the Pays d'Auge (around Caen), the Pays de Bray (near the border with Picardy), the Pays de Caux (a largely rural and agricultural area between Rouen and Dieppe), the Pays d'Ouche (between Bernay and Verneuil-sur-Avre) and the Pays du Vexin normand in north-east Eure.

Demographically, Upper Normandy is more urbanised and Paris-influenced (the *département* of Eure is said to be in the shadow of the capital), Lower Normandy more rural and 'traditional'. The three largest towns in Normandy are Rouen (population officially 109,000 but around 400,000 including suburbs), the administrative capital of Upper Normandy, Caen (117,000), the administrative capital of Lower Normandy and Le Havre (193,000). Other major towns including Alençon, Les Andelys, Cherbourg-Octeveille, Dieppe, Evreux, Le Havre, Lisieux, Pont-Audemer, Saint-Lô, Verneuil-sur-Avre, Vernon and Yvetot (see **Major Towns & Places of Interest** on page 60).

2

PROPERTY CHECK – NORMANDY

Normandy's popularity with foreign buyers, especially the British, shows no sign of waning, though prices remain well below the national average. Traditional half-timbered (*colombage*) properties, many with thatched roofs (*en chaume*), are hard to find under €200,000 and can cost three times as much, but small village houses and properties requiring 'attention' can be had for just €100,000. There's little below this amount in Upper Normandy but in Lower Normandy restoration projects start as low as €25,000. There's more new property available in Lower Normandy than Upper Normandy, especially on the coast, where apartments in a development including tennis courts and near both the beach and a golf course start at around €130,000. Those who want a large property with a lot of land, on the other hand, should be prepared to spend at least €400,000, while chateaux range from €700,000 to €3m.

Latitudes (www.latitudes.co.uk)

Normandy is noted for its lovely countryside and wide variety of scenery, including lush meadows, orchards, rivers and brooks, quiet country lanes, and over 600km (370mi) of coastline (100km/60mi of which were the scene of the D-Day landings in June 1944). Some 30 per cent of Upper Normandy is grassland and 50 per cent of Lower Normandy (the highest percentage in France); the north-west of Calvados is known as the Bessin – land of grass, milk and marshes. A further 45 per cent of Upper Normandy and 30 per cent of Lower Normandy is arable land.

Normandy is a rich agricultural region, producing meat, milk, butter, cheese (most famously Camembert, but also numerous other cheeses, including Livarot, Neufchâtel and Pont l'Evêque), apples, cider and calvados – a spirit distilled from apple juice (Upper Normandy is sometimes referred to as 'calvaland'). It's also renowned for its cuisine, with local specialities including shellfish dishes (Calvados is a major shellfish producer) and apple tart.

Normandy is an important maritime centre, with no fewer than 50 ports along its coast, including Cherbourg-Octeville, Dieppe, Fécamp, Granville, Le Havre, Honfleur, Port-en-Bessin and Tréport, as well as the major inland ports of Rouen and Caen. France's second-longest river, the Seine, meanders through Normandy on its way from Paris to the sea, picking up the Andelle, Aube, Eure, Loing, Marne, Oise and Yonne along the way. Other

Normandy rivers include the Couesnon, Iton, Orne (which flows through Argentan and Caen), Risle, Robec, Touques and Vire.

Normandy has four *Parcs Naturels Régionaux* – Boucles de la Seine Normande (between Rouen and Le Havre), Marais du Cotentin et du Bessin (north of Saint-Lô on the Cotentin peninsula), Perche (east of Alençon, in Orne, stretching into Eure-et-Loir), Normandie-Maine (west of Alençon) – and three areas of marshland: around the mouth of the Vire in Manche (where the Parc régional du Cotentin et du Bessin is Europe's largest 'wetland'), around the mouth of the Orne in Calvados and around the mouth of the Seine in Seine-Maritime.

Normandy has long been popular with the British for holidays and second homes, particularly in and around the Channel ports and resorts. With the exception of Nord-Pas-de-Calais and Picardy, it's the most accessible region from the UK via the ports of Caen, Cherbourg-Octeville, Dieppe and Le Havre. Coastal property is relatively expensive (homes with a sea view command a steep premium) and prices increase the closer you get to Paris (Parisians weekend on the Normandy coast). Honfleur has a surfeit of British residents and Deauville is packed with chic Parisians (Deauvillians recently protested against the inauguration of Ryanair flights from London Stansted, which they believed would 'lower the tone' of the resort!); both are very expensive. On the other hand, there are still bargains to be found (particularly for British buyers) and relatively undiscovered parts, especially in the *département* of Orne.

Calvados (14)

Possibly named after the rocky ridge ('*calvadorsa*') between the Orne and Vire rivers, Calvados has given its name to the apple brandy made throughout Normandy but particularly in this *département*. The *département* is divided vertically by the Orne, which meets the sea at Ouistreham after passing through Caen. The departmental capital of Calvados and the administrative capital of Lower Normandy and the region's second-largest town, Caen, is famous for its stone (used to build the Tower of London and Canterbury Cathedral). The eastern part of the coast is known as the 'Floral Coast' (*Côte fleurie*) and the western part the 'Mother-of-Pearl Coast' (*Côte de Nacre*). Calvados attracts some 5m tourists each year, mostly to the coast and particularly to the beaches where the Allied landings took place in 1944 (four of which are in Calvados and one, 'Utah Beach', in Manche) and to see the famous tapestry in Bayeux (incidentally the first town in France to be liberated from the Nazis). The beaches are long, sandy and gently shelving but less attractive than those of western Manche (see below).

2

PROPERTY CHECK – CALVADOS

Calvados is especially popular with British buyers, who own almost 2,500 properties in the *département*, and prices, which rose sharply in 2004 and 2005, are set to surge again with the start of a Ryanair service from London Stansted to Deauville in February 2007. Nevertheless, there's still a good selection of property under €100,000, though most of it is in need of major restoration or renovation. Apartments in a modern coastal development start at around €200,000, while a traditional half-timbered home inland can be had for €250,000. Many foreign buyers aim to run bed and breakfast, self-catering or hotel accommodation, though the market is saturated in many areas and prices for suitable properties start at around €500,000.

Currie French Properties (🖳 www.curriefrenchproperties.com); Normandy Homes (🖳 www.normandy-homes.com)

The area south of Caen known as *La Suisse normande*, on account of its thickly wooded hills and few rocky outcrops by the river Orne, and the area around Falaise, with its vast, flat corn fields, are atypical of Normandy, although attractive in their different ways. On the other hand, for many, the eastern part of the *département*, known as the Pays d'Auge (bounded roughly by Pont-l'Evêque in the north, Orbec in the east, Vimoutiers in the south and Saint-Pierre-sur-Dives in the west), is the quintessential Normandy, with its lush green fields of dappled cows, apple orchards and half-timbered houses. This is where the best cider and cheeses come from: Camembert, Livarot and Pont-l'Evêque are all made here and you can follow the *Route du Cidre*, linking Cambremer, Beuvron-en-Auge, Bonnebosq and Beaufour-Druval, and the *Route du Fromage* (no longer signposted), including the cheese museums at Livarot and Saint-Pierre-sur-Dives. Another tourist route running through the *département* is the *Route des Traditions* in the *bocage*.

Eure (27)

Like many French *départements*, Eure is named after the river which flows through it, and it boasts some of the most beautiful river scenery in Normandy, along the Andelle, Iton, Risle and Seine as well as the Eure itself. Eure has no coastline (unless you count 12km/7.5mi of the Seine estuary east of Honfleur), although it's within easy reach of the beaches of Calvados and Seine-Maritime. Despite being the closest part of Normandy to Paris, it's the region's most wooded *département*, the largest forest being the Forêt de Lyons, which covers over 6,500 hectares (15,500 acres), in the north-east. The Seine valley 'corridor', served by the A13 from Paris, is noted for its light industry, especially the manufacture of pharmaceutical products. Eure's capital is the historic town of Evreux, but it's Monet's house and garden at Giverny (near Vernon) which are the *département*'s principal tourist attraction.

Manche (50)

Named after the English Channel, known to the French as 'the Sleeve' (*la Manche*) on account of its shape, Manche has more farms, cattle and horses than almost any other *département* in France. It's also the country's biggest producer of oysters as well as a major producer of mussels, meat, vegetables , cider apples, apple juice, calvados and *pommeau* (a mixture of apple juice and calvados). In contrast to Eure, the *département* is France's least forested area, although the comparative lack of trees is compensated for by the many hedgerows that characterise the *bocage*, considered by many to be the most attractive rural scenery in Normandy.

Manche has 330km (200mi) of coastline and its northern part, known as the Cotentin peninsula, has sea on three sides, where the tide is said to come in faster than a galloping horse. The west coast boasts Normandy's finest beaches – long, sandy and gently sloping – backed by a string of attractive resorts (popular with the French in summer). Less than 50km (30mi) off the west coast of Manche lie the Channel Islands (known to the French as *les Iles anglo-normandes*), as well as the French Iles Chausey, of which there are around 50, although only one is inhabited – by around 100 people. (The islands can be reached from Granville in Manche and from Saint-Malo in neighbouring Ille-et-Vilaine – see below.) In the extreme west of the *département*, on the border with Brittany, is the Mont Saint-Michel, once a place of religious pilgrimage but now Manche's principal tourist attraction (and one of the most popular in France).

Orne (61)

Another *département* named after its principal river (which has its source just north of Alençon), Orne has around 25,000 hectares (60,000 acres) of forest, including the 7,000ha (17,000 acre) Forêt des Andaines, and contains the 235,000ha (565,000 acre) Normandie-Maine 'natural park' in the south. The *département* also boasts some 2,000km (1,250mi) of horse riding trails, and the Perche area (east of Argentan) is renowned for horse breeding and racing (the *percheron* is reputed to be the world's best draught horse); Haras du Pin, the French national stud, is located here. Orne has no coastline, but is within easy reach of the beaches of Calvados and Manche. A speciality of the *département* is pear cider (*poiré*), which is made principally in the area around Passais.

Seine-Maritime (76)

As its name suggests, the Seine meets the sea in this *département*, at Le Havre, having been joined by the Andelle, Epte, Eure and Iton, among other tributaries. Seine-Maritime has an attractive coast known as the 'Alabaster Coast' (*Côte d'Albâtre*) with chalk cliffs up to 100m (330ft) high between Dieppe and Le Havre, much painted by Monet and other 'Impressionists'. Seine-Maritime's (and Upper Normandy's) capital, Rouen, the largest city in north-western France (it was once the country's second-largest city after Paris), is one of the *département*'s major tourist attractions, along with the Bénédictine factory at Fécamp and the town of Honfleur, Normandy's answer to Saint-Tropez, which attracts 3.5m visitors annually.

BRITTANY

Brittany (*La Bretagne*) is the westernmost region of France and comprises the *département*s of Côtes-d'Armor (22), Finistère (29), Ille-et-Vilaine (35) and Morbihan (56). Brittany has some 3,000km (1,875mi) of Atlantic coast – over 25 per cent of the French coastline. The west coast is characterised by dramatic cliffs and rock formations, the north by attractive coves and tiny harbours, and the south has wide estuaries and long, sandy beaches. Brittany is popular with sailors, although the sea is not without its dangers – all those who die at sea are supposed to meet in the Baie des Trépassés ('Bay of the Departed') near Douarnenez, from where they're ferried to a mythical island of the blessed! More than a third of French lighthouses are in Brittany – most of them in Finistère. The inland region, known as the *Argoat* ('land of woods'), is almost flat; only two ridges and a solitary peak rise above 250m (800ft), although the Bretons call them mountains – the Montagnes noires (Black Mountains), the Monts d'Arrée (Arée Mountains) and the Montagne de Locronan. Inland Brittany is also largely agricultural, unspoiled (some would say barren) and scenic, with delightful wooded valleys, lakes and moors.

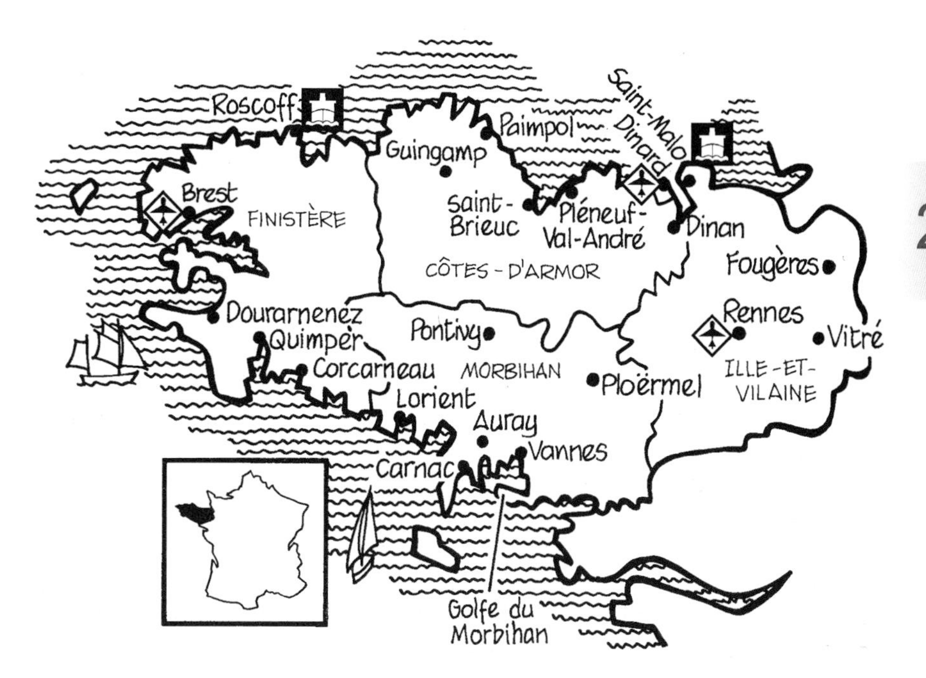

Did you know?

Breton place names can be hard to get your tongue around; it's a little easier when you know what they mean. Here's a guide to some of the most common place name components:

beg – headland

bihan – small

coat/coet/goat – wood

gui/guic/gwic – centre (of parish)

ilis/iliz – church

kastell – fortress

ker – village or hamlet

lan – consecrated land or hermitage

lann – moor or heath

menez – mountain

penn – headland

ple/pleu/plo/ploe/plou/plu/poul – parish (one of the most common place name components, which is why French people often refer to Bretons as '*ploucs*')

tre – part of a parish

ty – house

In contrast with Normandy, however, Brittany is 55 per cent arable land and only 15 per cent grassland. Vegetables and fruit are the two main agricultural products, and the *département* of Ille-et-Villaine was France's biggest cider producer until the mid-20th century (when there were over 300 varieties of cider apples; today there are fewer than 100). The average Breton is reputed to drink over 300 litres of cider per year! Brittany is also a major producer of pork, poultry, milk and fish, as well as seaweed, which is used in food additives, fertilisers and cosmetics. Cancale is reputed to be a gastronomic Mecca, and the entire region is a paradise for seafood lovers. Local culinary specialities include *crêpes* and *galettes* (different types of pancake used for sweet and savoury fillings respectively), *cotriade*, a sort of paella without the rice (the Breton equivalent of *bouillabaisse*) and *cervoise*, a beer reputed to be the favourite drink of the Gauls (or Vikings, according to which history you read).

Brittany's population is just over 3m and the regional capital, Rennes, is its largest city, having just over 200,000 inhabitants. The next largest town is Brest with around 155,000. Other main towns include Dinan, Dinard, Lorient, Quimper, Saint-Brieuc, Saint-Malo, Vannes and Vitré. Three of Brittany's towns features in the top ten 'best' in France according to a 2005 survey by *Le Point* magazine: Caen (8th), Rennes (9th) and Vannes (10th). Caen was 6th in a similar survey by *Le Nouvel Observateur* in November 2006.

The local people (Bretons) are of Celtic origin with a rich maritime tradition and a unique culture (preserved mainly in the more isolated west). Proud and independent (they claim that Brittany is a country apart), they even have their own language which has been revived in recent years (see page 70). Rennes University is a centre of Breton studies. Like Ireland, Brittany is a land of legend and folklore – the jagged coastline is said to have been carved out by the giant Gargantua, and the Forest of Broceliande is claimed to have been the hide-out of the Arthurian sorcerer Merlin. Traditional Breton costume is still worn on special occasions, one of the most colourful of which is the *Fête des Filets bleus* ('Festival of the Blue Nets') held in the fishing village of Concarneau in August.

PROPERTY CHECK – BRITTANY

After a fall in prices in the first few years of the century, Brittany's property has begun to rise in value again as demand increases. As in other parts of France, the closer you want to be to the coast, the more you must pay for a home. In a traditional Breton seaside resort, such as Damgan, studio apartments start at around €100,000, while a three-bedroom house is at least three times as much. Prices fall as you move inland, though they remain relatively high in and around the popular towns of Josselin, Malestroit, La Roche Bernard and Rocherfort-en-Terre, as in the whole of the Pays de Vilaine (on the boundary between Ille-et-Vilaine and Loire-Atlantique). Throughout Brittany there are plenty of 'neo-Breton' houses costing from around €150,000, while renovated traditional *longères* (long, straight single-storey home) start at around €200,000. Harder to find is the archetypal two-bedroom holiday cottage, though you can be lucky and snap one up for under €100,000.

VEF (🖳 www.vefuk.com)

Brittany is popular with both holidaymakers and second homebuyers, particularly the British, on account of its sea connections via the ports of Roscoff and Saint-Malo, and the nearby Normandy ports of Caen and Cherbourg-Octeville. In fact, there has been an 'invasion' of British buyers in recent years, which has pushed up property prices but also helped to regenerate many previously moribund rural areas. Property is expensive on the coast, particularly around Quimper and Bénodet (an area known as the Pays Bigouden), and very expensive on the islands (many of which are inhabited by rich Parisians and French celebrities). The triangle of land between Dinan, Dinard and Saint-Malo is also popular, which is reflected in relatively high prices. The interior is quieter and cheaper (nowhere in Brittany is more than an hour's drive from the coast), although the extreme west coast of Finistisère is also good value.

To find out more about moving to Brittany, you might consider attending the Living and Working in Brittany exhibition, held annually in September in Loudéac, near Rennes (for details contact the Comité régional du Tourisme de **Bretagne** (1 rue Raoul Poucon, 35000 Rennes, ☎ 02 99 36 15 15, 🖳 www.tourismebretagne.com).

Côtes-d'Armor (22)

The Côtes-d'Armor (Armor meaning 'land of the sea') includes the majority of the north coast of Brittany, as well as several islands – most notably the Sept-Iles, the oldest nature reserve in France (the Ile Rouzic has the country's richest 'collection' of wildlife). The *département* has some 6,000ha (15,000 acres) of forest, and the coastal area is farmed mainly for vegetables. The coastline itself is noted for fine beaches nestling between cliffs. The *département*'s principal town is Saint-Brieuc, and there are many attractive fishing ports along the coast.

Finistère (29)

Finistère, which translates as 'Land's End', includes the westernmost point in mainland Europe and more lighthouses than any other part of France. The *département*'s west coast consists mainly of high cliffs, whereas the north coast is lined with dunes. The white, sandy beaches south of Quimper are among the finest in Brittany, and La Torche offers some of the best surfing in France. There are a dozen islands (all of them bird sanctuaries) off Finistère between Le Conquet and Ouessant, and another group of islands, l'Archipel des Glenan, off the southern coast. Brest and Quimper, the departmental capital, are the two principal towns, and there are attractive resorts, such as Benodet, La Forêt-Fouesant and Pont-Aven (painted by Gaugin), as well as lots of pretty fishing villages, including Le Guilvines, Lesconil, Loctudy and Saint-Guénolé.

PROPERTY CHECK – FINISTERE

Finistère (France's 'Land's End'), formerly ignored in favour of Brittany's other *départements*, has recently begun to attract buyers thanks to its rugged coastline, attractive towns, warm weather and fascinating history. Finistère hotspots include the Crozon peninsula, the old port of Morlaix and Douarnenez bay. Throughout the *département*, village houses in need of renovation can be found for as little as €40,000. In the centre of the *département*, a two-bedroom village house needing some 'tender loving care' can be had for €70,000, a three-bedroom house with a good-size garden in a pleasant village or on the edge of a town can cost as little as €100,000, a four-bedroom farmhouse with outbuildings under €175,000 and a fully renovated traditional *longère* less than €250,000.

Ille-et-Vilaine (35)

The easternmost *département* of Brittany, Ille-et-Vilaine (named after its principal rivers) borders Manche in Normandy, and Loire-Atlantique and

Mayenne in Pays-de-la-Loire (see **Chapter 3**). Although it has the shortest coastline (70km/45mi) of any Brittany *département*, it includes the major resorts of Dinard and Saint-Malo. The so-called 'Emerald Coast' (*Côte d'Emeraude*) is dotted with cliffs, dunes and sandy beaches, Dinard boasting some of the highest tidal variations in Europe. Inland, there's a varied landscape including the Forêt de Paimpont, where King Arthur is believed (by the French) to have encountered Merlin (little of the original forest remains), and the 7,000ha (17,500 acre) Forêt de Brocéliande.

PROPERTY CHECK – ILLE-ET-VILAINE

Ille-et-Vilaine has plenty of attractions, as an increasing number of foreign buyers are discovering – agricultural activity, cultural vitality, scenic beauty, architectural and historic interest and varied sporting facilities, among others. Property prices on the popular coast, around Saint-Malo and Dinard, have risen more rapidly than in the capital, Rennes, where property starts at under €1,500 per m² and studio apartments can be had for just over €50,000. Rural restoration projects are still widely available, for as little as €45,000, while habitable four-bedroom houses start at just €150,000.

Brittany Property Web (🖳 www.brittanypropertyweb.com); French Properties Online (🖳 www.frenchpropertiesonline.com)

Morbihan (56)

The southernmost *département* of Brittany, Morbihan (meaning 'little sea' in Breton) has an almost Mediterranean micro-climate with 'exotic' flora and fauna. Its 500km (300mi) coastline includes numerous bays (most notably the Golfe du Morbihan with its 60 islands), estuaries (principally the Etel) and offshore islands (including the Ile de Groix, Ile d'Houat, Ile d'Hoëdic and Belle-Ile-en-Mer, the largest of the Breton islands). The coast is lined with dunes, the longest of which extends for 8km (5mi) at Erdeven, and Morbihan has the largest number of coastal water mills in France; a Brittany invention, these were in use until as recently as the '60s. Morbihan is famous for containing the world's greatest concentration of standing stones and also has over 250km (155mi) of navigable river and canal and some 50 *sites naturels*, including three nature reserves. Morbihan is the most visited *département* in Brittany, with over 3m visitors per year, and 25 per cent of its summer activity is tourism-related.

2

PROPERTY CHECK – MORBIHAN

A recent slowing of the market is good news for buyers and means that advertised prices are often negotiable. However, prices depend largely on distance from a main town; for example, a habitable four-bedroom house near Vannes costs almost €400,000 whereas a similar property half an hour's drive away – say, in the Locminé area – is half the price and out near Pontivy can be had for as little as €160,000. Prices are unusually high (allegedly 'thanks' to undiscerning Britsh buyers) in the areas around La Trinité-Porhoët and Guemené-sur-Scorff as well as in the Blavet valley. In most areas, old properties in need of renovation are few and far between, while modern houses are in plentiful supply. If you can find them, cottages for restoration can be had for €60,000 and larger houses with dilapidated outbuildings for little over €100,000. Restored 'character' properties start at around twice as much, while a grand *manoir* will set you back a cool €1m.

A House in Brittany (💻 www.ahouseinbrittany.com); Brittany Immobilier (💻 www.brittany-direct.com)

ADVANTAGES & DISADVANTAGES

Both Normandy and Brittany are largely unspoiled and rural with beautiful countryside, fine (mostly sandy) beaches, pretty villages and attractive properties. All of Normandy and most of Brittany are readily accessible by ferry from the UK, and parts of Normandy are within easy reach of the Paris airports. The many attractions of Paris (see **Chapter 8**) are also accessible from most parts of Normandy, there's plenty to see and do in both regions and the coast is never far away. Both regions are noted for their excellent food, particularly seafood, and everything you buy, eat and drink (except wine) is likely to be produced locally. Normandy is known as an artistic region, having inspired numerous writers, including Corneille, Flaubert, Gide, Maupassant, Maurois, Prévert and Proust, and painters, including Boudin, Braque, Dufy, Léger, Millet, Poussin and Monet, who made his home at Giverny near Vernon in Eure and captured the region's ever-changing light in his series paintings.

There are also disadvantages to buying a home in Normandy or Brittany. The weather is poor for France: it's often wet and (particularly in Brittany) windy, and summer temperatures are moderate. There are few direct international flights to airports in Normandy or Brittany, so the regions aren't readily accessible from countries other than the UK, with the exception of the *départements* of Eure and Seine-Maritime, which are within reasonably easy reach of the Paris airports. Even from the UK, Channel crossings become progressively longer – and more expensive – the further west you go (see page 95). Much of Normandy was destroyed in the Second World War and the vast majority of towns have been rebuilt in the last half-century, which means that there are few attractive old towns (though most villages remained untouched). The people of Normandy, who are descended from the Vikings (Normans means 'north men') have a reputation for being reserved, not to say secretive and suspicious, although if you make an effort you will be rewarded by true and lasting friendships. Bretons, by contrast, are reputed to be more outgoing and progressive.

Some foreign buyers have complained of a pervasive smell of chicken farms across Brittany, so drive around the area and check the prevailing wind direction before buying.

Although property generally is less expensive than on the west coast or in southern France, for example, prices have been rising steadily in recent years and bargains are few and far between, especially near the coast and within an hour's drive of Paris.

'Green' towns include Caen (14), Saint-Brieuc (22) and Saint-Malo (35), where there's over 40m² of green space for every inhabitant (in contrast with Vannes (35), which offers less than 3m² per inhabitant), and parts of Ille-et-Vilaine enjoy a lower mortality rate (from all causes) than almost any other part of France. (On the other hand, the rates of alcohol-related illnesses and suicides in Brittany are particularly high!) No fewer than 22 of the area's beaches and 28 of its marinas – the majority in Côtes-d'Armor, Manche and Morbihan – have been awarded a 'blue flag' by the Foundation for European Education and Environment (see 💻 www.pavillonbleu.com). But, almost as many beaches earned a 'black flag' from the Surfrider Foundation Europe – one each in Ille-et-Vilaine and Manche, two in Calvados, three in Morbihan, four in the Côtes-d'Armor and no fewer than seven in Finistère – which draws attention to what it considers to be unacceptable levels of pollution and has recently discontinued its black flag system in favour of positive action (see 💻 www.surfrider-europe.org). Large stretches of the Finistère coast have recently been affected by a toxic seaweed called Dinophysis, and foul-smelling weed has also affected beaches in the Côtes-d'Armor, particularly in the summer but also in spring. In addition, some of Brittany's rivers are reckoned to contain unacceptably high levels of chemical and animal waste and Brittany generally has some of the poorest quality (and most expensive) water in France.

Prospective buyers may also like to note that Normandy has three of France's 20 nuclear power stations: two on the northern coast of Seine-Maritime – at Penly between Dieppe and Tréport, and at Paluel between Dieppe and Fécamp – and one in Manche, at Flamanville on west coast of the Cotentin peninsula. Manche also has a nuclear waste reprocessing plant at La Hague on the northern tip of the Cotentin peninsula. Moreover, by 2010 there will be a 400,000 volt powerline carried by 50m-high pylons running from Flamanville through western Manche and into northern Mayenne. There are no nuclear power stations in Brittany.

MAJOR TOWNS & PLACES OF INTEREST

Calvados (14)

Calvados's capital, Caen (pop. 117,000), was largely destroyed in the Second World War but still boasts two medieval abbeys, an ancient castle and an impressive cathedral, as well as a prestigious university and several parks (even a 'prairie'!). Calvados boasts several fashionable resorts along the *Côte Fleurie*, including Cabourg (smart but unpretentious), Deauville (with its famous *Promenade* rivalling that of Nice – well, almost), Honfleur (with its picturesque harbour), Houlgate and Trouville. These are favourite locations among Parisians (and even Normans) for second homes. Less popular but equally attractive are the resorts of Arromanches and Port-en-Bessin further west.

Other main towns include Lisieux (24,000), a university town which boasts one of the world's largest churches – a place of pilgrimage – but is otherwise unprepossessing; Bayeux (pop. 15,400), one of Normandy's most attractive towns, having largely escaped destruction during the Second World War, and boasting the famous tapestry depicting the Norman conquest of England (which attracts almost half a million visitors annually); Vire (13,900), a rather unattractive industrial town which prides itself on its cultural activities; and Falaise (8,800), largely destroyed in the war but sympathetically reconstructed and boasting the castle where William the Conqueror was born; Hérouville-Saint-Clair (24,400). Also attractive are the smaller towns of Orbec, with its long main street of timbered buildings, and Saint-Pierre-sur-Dives, with an ancient abbey and a famous market. Beuvron-en-Auge is the *département*'s prettiest village and the only really 'touristy' place in the Pays d'Auge, and there are other attractive villages, including Beaumais, east of Falaise, and Clécy in the *Suisse normande*.

Côtes-d'Armor (22)

The *département*'s principal town is Saint-Brieuc (pop. 49,000), founded by the Welsh monk Brieuc in 482AD, with its imposing cathedral. Other towns of interest include Dinan (11,900), one of Brittany's finest medieval towns and a major tourist attraction; Guingamp (8,000), another town of historic and architectural as well as religious interest (it's the site of an annual pilgrimage in July); Paimpol (7,900) with its attractive harbour; Plouha (4,400), boasting Brittany's highest cliffs (104m/340ft); Pleumeur-Bodou (3,800) with its nearby leisure parks; and Pléneuf-Val-André (3,700) with its magnificent beaches and traditional fishing harbour at Dahouët. There are also many beach resorts, including Perros-Guirec, Saint-Cast and Trégastel, and fishing ports, including Binic and Saint-Quay-Portrieux. The Côtes-d'Armor boasts no fewer than six '*petites cités de caractère*', including Jugon-les-Lacs, an ancient fortress town surrounded by rivers and lakes, Portrieux with its wash houses and triangular 'squares', Quintin with its attractive *château* and other historic buildings, and Tréguier with its pretty streets and magnificent cathedral – one of the finest in Brittany.

Eure (27)

Eure's capital is the historic town of Evreux (pop. 54,000), a dynamic business centre with an attractive town centre and cathedral. Other main towns include Vernon (25,000) on the Seine with its magnificent Château de Bizy and nearby business centre of Saint-Marcel; Louviers (19,000), former textile centre on the Eure with an attractive cathedral; Bernay (11,600), with its attractive wood-beamed houses, the town recently relieved of traffic by the diversion of the N138; Gisors (11,100), with attractive streets, cathedral and castle; Les Andelys (9,300), dominated by Richard the Lionheart's Château Gaillard; and the 'new town' of Val-de-Reuil (14,000), France's newest commune created in the '70s to attract business people away from Paris but now inhabited largely by African immigrants and featuring a nearby high-security prison! The A13 motorway and main railway line from Paris run (more or less parallel) through Eure (see **Communications** on page 95), the former being something of a rat run for Parisians dashing to and from the coast for weekends and holidays. One of the *département*'s prettiest villages is Le Bec-Hellouin near Brionne. Eure also boasts France's smallest *mairie* at Saint-Germain-de-Pasquier, north-west of Louviers, measuring just 10m^2!

Finistère (29)

2

The *département*'s capital and the ancient capital of *Cornouaille* is the magnificent medieval town of Quimper (pop. 67,000) on the river Jet, the oldest city in Brittany with a splendid Gothic cathedral and a relaxed atmosphere, although Brest (156,000) is by far the largest town in Finistère, as well as easily the second-largest in Brittany after the capital Rennes. Other major towns and places of interest include Concarneau (19,400), which claims to be France's 'biggest' fishing port in terms of the number of boats (230), fishermen (1,600) and fish caught (around 30,000 tonnes per year); Morlaix (16,000) on the *Côte de Granit rose* ('Pink Granite Coast') with its impressive viaduct, jumble of lanes and unique 'lantern houses'; Douarnenez (15,800), actually four villages with three harbours; Locronan, a '*petite cité de caractère*' often used as a film set (and rated one of France's most beautiful villages, along with Le Faou and l'Ile-de-Sein); Moëlan-sur-Mer with its beautiful coastal walks; Carhaix-Plouguer (8,000), Brittany's geographical and cultural centre; Châteaulin (5,800); Plouguerneau (5,600), with its varied coastline and the tallest stone lighthouse in Europe; Pont-Aven (3,000) with its artistic heritage, and the delightful nearby port of Doelan. The coast of Finistère is dotted with fishing villages, including Le Guilvines, Lesconil, Loctudy and Saint-Guénolé.

Ille-et-Vilaine (35)

Brittany's historic capital, 2,000 year-old Rennes (pop. 212,500), which lies at the convergence of the Ille and Vilaine rivers, is one of the *département*'s four '*villes d'art*', the others being Fougères (21,800), whose castle is reckoned to be one of the finest in Europe, with a nearby 1,500ha (3,700 acre) forest, Saint-Malo (52,700) and Vitré (15,900), the 'gateway to Brittany' and one of the finest medieval towns in the region. Other towns and places of interest include Redon (10,500), at the confluence of Brittany's two largest rivers, the Oust and the Vilaine, Cancale, famous for its oysters; Dinard (10,400), considered to be one of Europe's finest seaside resorts (when the sun shines!); the small towns of Dol and Lamballe; and Paimpont (1,400), with its fine abbey. Ille-et-Vilaine has three '*petites cités de caractère*': Bécherel, with its many bookshops and *château* known as the 'Breton Versailles', Châteaugiron (5,500), with its magnificent fortress, and Combourg, whose castle is one of the finest in Brittany. The coastal towns of Saint-Malo and Dinard and the area inland as far as Dinan (22) – i.e. the area around the Rance estuary – are the most popular with homebuyers.

Manche (50)

The *département*'s largest town (and the second largest urban area in Lower Normandy after Caen) is Cherbourg-Octeville (the two towns were officially united in 1999), France's second-busiest port after Calais, with a total population of around 120,000. However, the departmental capital and also the national capital of horse-breeding and riding is Saint-Lô, whose population is only 21,500. Manche's third-largest town is Equeurdreville-Hinneville with 18,600 inhabitants, Tourlaville has 18,000, and a further 54,000 people live in the region surrounding Coutances (11,500), which boasts a magnificent cathedral and several fine churches but is otherwise lacking in charm.

Other main towns include the water-sports centre of Tourlaville (pop. 17,900), Granville (13,500), the 'Monaco of the North' with its marina and beaches, and Avranches (9,200), near Mont-Saint-Michel and the main road from Caen into Brittany, although itself also somewhat charmless. There's a number of attractive resorts on the west coast, including Portbail and Barneville-Carteret. The pretty port of Barfleur, on the east coast, is where William the Conqueror launched the Norman conquest of England, and nearby Saint-Vaast-la-Hougue, with its food shops and fish restaurants, is a favourite among 'yachties'. Inland, Bricquebec, with its medieval castle, is one of Manche's most impressive towns, but Manche's principal tourist attraction is the Mont Saint-Michel, which attracts some 3m visitors per year, despite being overcrowded and expensive (it's packed with over-priced cafés, restaurants and tourist junk shops – you can even buy Mont Saint-Michel air in cans!).

Morbihan (56)

Morbihan's capital is Vannes (pop. 55,000), an ancient town and residence of the former Dukes of Brittany. Other major towns include the modern town of Lorient (59,200), so named because of its trade with the far east; Pontivy (15,000), with its attractive medieval streets; Hennebont (13,400), a '*cité d'art*' with its medieval walls; Auray (10,900), a historic and attractive town with a pretty port; and Ploërmel (7,500). Smaller towns include Arradon, a popular sailing resort on the Golfe du Morbihan; Arzon, which faces both the Atlantic and the Golfe du Morbihan; Carnac, with beautiful beaches and the famous megalithic site nearby (see below); Erdeven, with 8km (5mi) of dunes (and naturist beach); and three '*petites cités de caractère*' – Josselin, with a splendid castle overlooking the river Oust, Lizio and Malestroit. Others are Penestin-sur-Mer, an attractive seaside resort, Port-Louis, a lively seaside resort, Rhuys, Rochefort-en-Terre, reckoned to be one of France's most beautiful villages, Suscinio with its impressive castle and La Trinité-sur-Mer, Brittany's 'yachtie' centre.

Morbihan boasts an abundance of islands, many of which can be reached by boat from the mainland, including Belle-Ile-en-Mer (20km/13mi long, 4,900 inhabitants), the largest French island in the Atlantic, with its impressive fortress at Le Palais and rocks painted by Monet; l'Ile d'Arz (3km/2mi long) with its lovely old houses and many sailing schools; l'Ile de Groix (8km/5mi long with 2,500 inhabitants) with its mild micro-climate; l'Ile d'Hoëdic (2.5km/1.5mi long with 125 inhabitants), a botanist's paradise; l'Ile d'Houat (5km/3mi long with 400 inhabitants, swollen to 1,000 in summer) with its beautiful sandy beaches and few cars; and l'Ile aux Moines (6km/4mi long), perhaps the most beautiful island in Morbihan.

Morbihan's famous standing stones, spread over some 40 separate sites, are linked by the *Route des Mégalithes*. Carnac is the world's largest megalithic site, where there are reckoned to be 2,792 stones, extending for more than 1km; a further 1,000 have been counted in a great arc between Erdeven and Plouharnel. Locmariaquer boasts the world's largest 'standing' stone (it's actually horizontal), weighing around 300 tonnes, and the nearby Musée Miln-le-Rouzic has world's largest collection of megalithic artefacts (around half a million) dating back to 450,000BC.

Orne (61)

Orne's capital is Alençon (pop. 31,000), famous for its lace and, until its recent closure, Moulinex, one of Normandy's largest employers (Alençon used to be known as 'Moulinexland'). Other main towns include Flers (17,600), 'capital' of the *bocage* and the mechanical engineering centre of Lower Normandy, Argentan (17,400), largely industrial but at the heart of horse-riding country, L'Aigle (9,300) on the river Risle, and Mortagne-au-Perche (4,900), historic 'capital' of the Perche area. One of the most attractive smaller towns is Domfront, which boasts a medieval town centre, and Saint-Céneri-le-Gérei, west of Alençon, is considered to be one of France's prettiest villages. The *département*'s main tourist attractions are the national stud, Haras du Pin, at Pin-au-Haras, east of Argentan (described as 'the Versailles of the horse'!), and Camembert, where the eponymous cheese is supposed to have been 'invented' in 1791 by one Marie Harel.

Seine-Maritime (76)

Dominated by the great river, which meanders through it between impressive chalk cliffs – on the outside of the bends – and alluvial plains on the inside, Seine-Maritime is a *département* of great contrasts: city and countryside, heavy industry and agricultural landscape, and dramatic coastline and featureless interior. The departmental and regional capital is the city of Rouen, where Joan of Arc was burnt at the stake (a modern church on the spot is dedicated to her), with its magnificent cathedral, painted by Monet. Other main towns and places of interest (most of them also featuring in Monet's paintings) include the busy port and industrial town of Le Havre (pop. 193,000), one of Europe's major ports and petrol refineries but recently declared a UNESCO World Heritage site for its unique post-war architecture (Le Havre is also one of France's most cyclist-friendly cities); Dieppe (35,700), France's oldest seaside resort with one of its longest bathing beaches; Mont-Saint-Aignan (21,800); the fishing port of Fécamp (19,900), home to the Bénédictine liqueur distillery housed in a 'Disney' fantasy of a building; Elbeuf (16,900) near Rouen by the Seine; and Etretat on the coast with its spectacular cliff arches.

POPULATION

The population of Normandy is around 3.25m (1.8m in Upper Normandy 1.45m in Lower Normandy) and that of Brittany just over 3m, divided as shown below. Each *département* covers a similar area, i.e. 5,500 to 6,000km^2 (2,200 to 2,400mi^2), which means that population figures also indicate population density, Brittany having an average of 113 people per km^2 (290 per mi^2). The populations of both Normandy and Brittany are growing at an above the average rate for France. Both Caen (14) and Rennes (35) have a very high proportion of students (around 25 per cent) among their populations, whereas the percentage of students in other towns is low, e.g. 6 per cent in Quimper (29), 5 per cent in Le Havre (76) and a mere 2 per cent in Saint-Malo (35). For populations of smaller towns, see **Major Towns & Places of Interest** above.

Normandy

Upper Normandy is one of the most densely populated areas of France with 140 people per km^2 (55 per mi^2) compared with the national average of just over 100 (40 per mi^2). Around 30 per cent of the population of Upper Normandy lives within 25km (15mi) of the centre of Rouen. It has a relatively young population (over 30 per cent are under 20) and a higher than average birth rate, although the population is growing more slowly and therefore ageing more rapidly than the national average (0.24 per cent per annum compared with 0.66 per cent) and the region suffers from net emigration; this is particularly severe in Seine-Maritime, and the region's population increase is entirely due to neighbouring Eure, which continues to attract Parisians and others. Paris is gradually 'overflowing' along the Seine valley, and Eure is growing at a rate of 0.57 per cent or around 3,000 people per annum.

Did you know?

Parisians looking for second homes are beginning to outnumber British property buyers in Lower Normandy, according to figures published by the Conseil régional des notaires de Basse-Normandie, especially in coastal areas and the eastern half of Orne, though Britons still account for almost a third of purchases in southern Manche.

Some 45 per cent of the population of Lower Normandy is concentrated around the towns of Alençon, Argentan, Caen, Cherbourg-Octeville, Flers, Lisieux and Saint-Lô, and the region's population is expected to rise by around 45,000 in the next 20 years before beginning to decline. Overall, the population has increased by almost 4,000 per year since the turn of the century, although the rate of increase is well below the national average (0.27 per cent per annum compared with 0.66 per cent) and the region tends to attract people over 60 while losing those in their 20s, most of whom migrate to Ile-de-France in search of work and excitement. Generally, the cities and large towns are losing inhabitants in favour of the surrounding, semi-rural areas (the 14 *communes* with over 10,000 inhabitants lost 12,000 people in total between 1999 and 2006). The population of Orne is already in gradual decline (30 per cent of the population is over 60), whereas that of Calvados, which is attracting people, particularly those in their early 20s, from neighbouring *départements*, is expected to continue to increase until around 2030. The population of Manche is fairly stable, although it has lost around 16,000 people between the ages of 20 and 30 and gained half as many elderly people in the last decade.

Calvados (14)

Calvados is Lower Normandy's most 'dynamic' *département*, accounting for some two-thirds of the region's population increase this century. Its total population is around 665,000, of which 4,600 are non-French EU citizens (including over 1,200 Portuguese), 1,100 Algerians, 1,000 Turks, 900 Moroccans and 3,000 of other nationalities. The capital Caen has 117,000 inhabitants but 60 per cent of the *département*'s population live in the Caen area, including nearby Hérouville-Saint-Clair – the *département*'s second-largest urban area with 24,400 inhabitants. Almost 30 per cent of Calvados's population is under 19. The next largest towns are Lisieux (24,000 inhabitants), Mont-Saint-Aignan (21,800), Bayeux (15,400) and Vire (13,900).

Eure (27)

Total population 562,500 – a similar average density to Brittany's Côtes-d'Armor – of which almost 5,000 are non-French EU citizens (including over 2,750 Portuguese), 2,500 Moroccans, 2,000 Turks, 1,700 Algerians and 4,400 of other nationalities. The capital Evreux has 54,000 inhabitants and Vernon, the *département*'s second-largest town, 25,000. The next largest towns are Louviers (19,000 and a further 40,000 in the surrounding area), Val-de-Reuil (14,000, including a high proportion of African immigrants), Bernay (11,600) and Gisors (11,100).

Manche (50)

The second-least densely populated *département* in Normandy or Brittany, with a total population of 490,000 and the lowest proportion of foreign residents, with 1,800 non-French EU citizens, 700 Moroccans, 340 Turks and 1,200 of other nationalities. The *département*'s largest town (and the second-largest urban area in Lower Normandy after Caen) is Cherbourg-Octeville with a total population of around 120,000, the departmental capital Saint-Lô having only 21,500. Manche's third-largest town is Equeurdreville-Hinneville with 18,600 inhabitants, Tourlaville has 18,000, and a further 54,000 people live in the region surrounding Coutances (11,500).

Orne (61)

The most sparsely populated *département* in Normandy or Brittany, with a total population of 290,000, of which almost 2,000 are non-French EU citizens (including over 750 Portuguese), 1,900 Turks, 1,100 Moroccans, 1,700 Algerians and 1,600 of other nationalities. Orne has few large towns; the capital Alençon has just 31,000 inhabitants. The next largest towns are Flers (17,600) and Argentan (17,400).

Seine-Maritime (76)

By far the most densely populated *département* in either region, with a total population of 1.24m, of which 8,500 are non-French EU citizens (including over 4,500 Portuguese and almost 1,000 Italians), 6,900 Algerians, 6,400 Moroccans, 1,600 Turks, 1,300 Tunisians and over 8,000 of other nationalities. Over 40 per cent of the population lives in and around the capital Rouen, although its official population is only 109,000, which has seen an influx of students since the opening of the new university science faculty in 2001. The next largest towns are Le Havre (193,900 inhabitants), Dieppe (34,300); four suburbs of Rouen, Sotteville-lès-Rouen (29,700), Saint-Etienne-du-Rouvray (28,000), Grand-Quevilly (26,200) and Petit-Quevilly (22,200), Mont-Saint-Aignan (20,500), Fécamp (19,900) and Elbeuf (16,900).

Brittany

Just over 3m people live in Brittany, whose population is growing at slightly above the national average rate (0.85 per cent per annum compared with 0.66 per cent), more so in Ille-et-Vilaine and Morbihan; in fact, Vannes in Morbihan has the fastest-growing population of any major town in France. The *département* of Ille-et-Vilaine attracts half of Brittany's immigrants. Over two-thirds of the population live in urban areas (an increase of 20 per cent in the last decade), and the capital Rennes (35) and its surrounding area, the country's third-fastest growing urban area, has over half a million inhabitants. Other expanding towns are Quimper, Saint-Brieuc and Vannes. Brest (29) is the only other town in Brittany with more than 67,000 inhabitants, though along with Lorient and Saint-Malo its population is falling. Brittany has a generally young population – the average age is 37 and 35 per cent of people are under 25 – although more people in their 20s are leaving the region than coming to it and an increasing number of older people are retiring to Brittany (it's France's third-favourite retirement destination). It's predicted that the population of Brittany will continue to increase in coming decades, although at a slower rate.

Côtes-d'Armor (22)

The least densely populated *département* in Brittany, with a total population of 565,000 – similar to that of Eure in Normandy – and the lowest proportion of foreign residents in Brittany, with over 3,000 non-French EU citizens (including almost 800 Portuguese), 500 Moroccans, 300 Turks and 1,300 of other nationalities. The capital and only large town in the *département* is Saint-Brieuc, which has 49,000 inhabitants (100,000 including suburban areas). The next largest towns are Lannion (19,350), Dinan (11,900), Guingamp (8,000) and Paimpol (7,900). The Côtes-d'Armor has a high proportion of retired people, especially in rural areas along the coast. Saint-Brieuc has the *département*'s youngest population.

Finistère (29)

Total population 875,000, of which over 4,000 are non-French EU citizens (including almost 1,600 Portuguese), 850 Moroccans, 750 Turks and 2,500 of other nationalities. The largest town is Brest with 156,000 inhabitants, followed by the departmental capital Quimper with 67,000. The next largest towns are Concarneau (19,400), Morlaix (16,000) and Douarnenez (15,800). Finistère has the most static population in Brittany: over one in three people were born in the *département*, although three-quarters of immigrants to the *département* in the last decade have come from outside Brittany. Finistère also has the region's highest proportion of one-person households (around 35 per cent). Brest and the surrounding area has the youngest population.

Ille-et-Vilaine (35)

The most densely populated *département* in Brittany, with a total population of 930,000, of which almost 4,000 are non-French EU citizens (including almost 1,200 Portuguese), 1,900 Moroccans, 1,250 Turks and 5,500 of other nationalities. The capital Rennes has 212,500 inhabitants and attracts a large mobile population, mainly because of its university. The majority of the *département*'s recent population increase has been in Rennes and along the major roads radiating from the city. The next largest towns are Saint-Malo (52,700), Fougères (21,800), Vitré (15,900), Redon (10,500) and Dinard (10,400).

Morbihan (56)

Brittany's fastest-growing *département*, whose population increased three times more between 1999 and 2006 than in the previous 25 years and its total population is now around 690,000, of which 2,600 are non-French EU citizens, 1,100 Turks and 2,000 of other nationalities. The *département*'s largest town is Lorient (59,200 inhabitants), and the capital is Vannes has 55,000. The next largest towns are Pontivy (15,000), Hennebont (13,400) and Auray (10,900). Morbihan has the most rapidly ageing population of the four Breton *départements*, as many young people leave the *département* to study or work.

LANGUAGE

French is spoken throughout the two regions, but in Brittany Breton is also spoken in some parts. Linguistically, Breton belongs to the Brittonic branch of the Insular Celtic family, the Continental branch (Gaulish, Galatian, etc.) being extinct. As a Brittonic language, Breton is close to Welsh (they became separate languages from the 16th century) and is parent to Scottish Gaelic, Irish Gaelic and Manx, although speakers of those languages won't understand much Breton (or vice versa). It was Cornish settlers who introduced their language to Brittany between the third and fifth centuries and, although Cornish has now died out, Breton survives and, like Gaelic, is currently enjoying something of a revival.

There are estimated to be around 600,000 Breton speakers, most of them in the west of Brittany, i.e. throughout Finistère and in the western part of Côtes-d'Armor and Morbihan, but also in Rennes and Nantes, which used to be the capital of Brittany, but is now in the Pays-de-la-Loire region (see **Chapter 3**). Although less than half as many use the language regularly, a recent opinion poll suggested that almost 90 per cent of Bretons would like the language to be preserved. Breton is taught in four *collèges*, one *lycée* and around 30 primary schools run by an organisation called Diwan. These bi-lingual schools were introduced in late '70s and teach only in Breton until CE1 level (age 7–8), when French is introduced (for this reason, there is opposition to them being incorporated into the state system). The number of children educated at Diwan schools is increasing by 15 to 20 per cent annually, and around 9,000 adults enrol in Breton classes every year. Around 10 per cent of the books published in Brittany are in Breton, most of them for children, and there are Breton periodicals (including the monthly *Bremañ*. Local stations of Radio France allocate a certain amount of time to Breton-language programmes, and there are Breton programmes on television in the western half of Brittany as well as plans to introduce a bilingual TV channel called *Breizh*. There are bi-lingual road signs on all major roads and in some towns (e.g. Lorient and Quimper) in the Côtes-d'Armor and Finistère regions.

It isn't necessary to learn Breton in order to integrate into the local community, although being able to get your tongue round a few words and phrases (being related to Welsh, Breton is one of the world's most complicated languages!) will undoubtedly facilitate the process.

CLIMATE

Normandy and Brittany are among the wettest areas of France, at least in terms of the number of days of rain (up to 155 days per year in the extreme west of Brittany) if not in terms of total annual rainfall (which is higher in mountainous areas). The wettest months are usually November and December, with up to 150mm (6in) of rain per month, and the driest May and June, with around 50mm (2in) per month, although January has the most rainy days (20 on average) and it's rare to have more than a week without some rain at any time of year. There can be frost from October to April but snow rarely falls. Average summer temperatures are among lowest in France, although the regions can experience very hot spells (over 30C). Annual sunshine hours vary between over 2,000 in Vannes (56) and under 1,700 in Rouen (76). Those used to a British climate will find the weather similar in many respects, although noticeably warmer even than southern England at most times of year and (slightly) less changeable.

Normandy

Although known (by the French) as 'the chamber pot of France', Normandy is less wet and windy than Brittany, which shelters it from the Atlantic. The weather is generally damp and mild and the barometer rarely strays far either side of 'variable' (Normandy's climate has been described as 'nuances of bad weather'). However, the weather is highly changeable and it's rare to have more than a few days of similar conditions; a hot, sunny spell can unexpectedly give way to cold, wet, windy weather. Generally, the further west you go, the wetter the weather. The so-called 'rotten land' (*Lande pourrie*) around Mortain in southern Manche has the highest rainfall in Normandy (over 1,200mm/47in per year), the most frequent frosts (50 to 60 days compared with only 10 in Landes-de-la-Hague on the Cotentin peninsula) and the most likelihood of snow.

Other wet areas are the Cotentin peninsula, with 155mm of rain in December (though it's among the driest in summer, with just 48mm in July) and the area to the north-east of Le Havre. Orne is also wet in winter (82mm in December, 74mm in January) and in May (66mm), while Seine-Maritime is wet in summer (60mm in July and August) and often grey – particularly around Rouen. Eure has the region's driest, most continental climate and most clearly defined seasons, and the extreme south-east of the *département* is one of driest areas in France, with less than 800mm (30in) of rain per year, spread fairly evenly between the months. Normandy is also frequently (and often densely) shrouded in fog in the mornings, although it usually clears by midday. (Curiously, most of the locals believe that England is more or less permanently fog-bound!) The table below shows the number of hours' sunshine and number of days' rainfall in selected towns in the region.

Town	Sunshine Hours	Days' Rainfall
Caen (14)	1,764	123
Le Havre (76)	1,788	125
Rouen (76)	1,687	131

Brittany

Brittany's has a generally maritime climate, being exposed to the Atlantic on three sides. It's the wettest part of France in terms of the number of days' rainfall per year (Brest is France's rainiest town). The weather can be stormy in winter, although summers are usually warm and pleasant. The north-west coast is somewhat milder, as it's influenced by the Gulf Stream, and Finistère boasts the '*Ceinture dorée*' ('Golden Belt'), whose climate allows farmers to grow over half of France's vegetables. Nevertheless, Finistère gets a lot of rain, especially in December and January (around 140mm per month), the driest month being July (48mm). Neighbouring Côtes d'Armor has less winter rain (92mm in December) but similar summer rainfall. Ille-et-Vilaine's wettest months are December (70mm), January (65mm) and May (64mm), with just 38mm in August.

The southern coast enjoys a warm micro-climate, though winters can be wet (108mm in December in Morbihan). Vannes (and indeed the whole of the coastal area from Quimper to La Baule in Loire-Atlantique) has as much sunshine as Toulouse (over 2,000 hours per year), relatively little rainfall and average maximum summer daily temperatures of around 22C (72F); parts of Morbihan are sufficiently 'Mediterranean' to support flora normally seen in the south of France. Coastal areas generally have little frost – only around a dozen days a year (no more than the Côte d'Azur). Inland areas are often misty. The table below shows the number of hours' sunshine and number of days' rainfall in selected towns in the region.

Town	Sunshine Hours	Days' Rainfall
Saint-Brieuc (22)	1,795	130
Brest (29)	1,749	155
Quimper (29)	1,749	146

Rennes (35)	1,851	115
Saint-Malo (35)	1,853	128
Vannes (35)	2,024	131

CRIME RATE & SECURITY

Crime rates in Brittany and Normandy are around average for France with 80 to 90 reported crimes per 1,000 population per year in most major towns. The 'safest' city is Saint-Brieuc (22) with 72.5 crimes, and least safe are Rennes and Saint-Malo (35) with around 94 crimes. It should also be noted that five factories in the Le Havre area are considered 'high-risk', i.e. highly polluting or in danger of explosion.

AMENITIES

Sports

There's a wealth of sporting facilities and opportunities in Normandy and Brittany, including the following:

Fishing & Hunting

There are literally hundreds of locations for fishing in both regions, on rivers, lakes and the sea. There are also hunting clubs and associations in many towns and even in some villages. Each *département* has a hunters' federation (*Fédération départemental des Chasseurs/FDC*), which can tell you how and where you can get your licence and what associations or clubs exist in the *département*.

Golf

Golf is popular in both regions, where there are over 65 courses, including the spectacular Golf de Pléneuf-Val-André (22) and Champ de Bataille at Le Neubourg (27). The table below lists the number of courses in each *département*. Information (in both French and English) on how to find courses, the cost of a round (which varies between €15 and €50), etc. is available via the internet (💻 www.backspin.com). Another useful website for golfers is 💻 www.golf.com.fr.

Département	No. of Courses
Calvados	3 x 9 holes, 5 x 18 holes, 5 x 27 holes
Côtes-d'Armor	3 x 9 holes, 5 x 18 holes
Eure	2 x 9 holes, 4 x 18 holes
Finistère	3 x 9 holes, 3 x 18 holes, 1 x 27 holes
Ille-et-Vilaine	2 x 9 holes, 4 x 18 holes, 3 x 27 holes
Manche	5 x 9 holes, 1 x 18 holes
Morbihan	1 x 9 holes, 5 x 18 holes, 1 x 27 holes
Orne	3 x 9 holes, 1 x 18 holes
Seine-Maritime	7 x 18 holes

Walking, Cycling & Horse Riding

Normandy and Brittany are ideal regions for those who enjoy these activities. Ille-et-Vilaine, for example, has 1,200km (750mi) of marked walks, 500km (300mi) of mountain bike trails and over 25 equestrian centres. Brittany as a whole has 3,000km (1,875mi) of coastline and 3,700km (2,300mi) of hiking trails. The Perche area (in eastern Orne) has over 2,000km (1,250mi) of horse riding trails, there are over 50 riding schools and equestrian centres in the Côtes-d'Armor, almost as many in Ille-et-Vilaine, a further 70 in Calvados; in Normandy's *bocage* there are some 6,000 areas dedicated to horse riding.

Watersports

Brittany is one of France's premier regions for watersports, sailing in particular. Morbihan has no fewer than 115 marinas offering moorings for 7,500 boats (Port Crouesty near Arzon and La Trinité-sur-Mer are among Brittany's largest marinas, each with over 1,000 berths) as well as two natural watersports areas in the Golfe du Morbihan and the Baie de Quiberon – the latter noted for its constant winds. There are at least 40 marinas in the Côtes-d'Armor, and many more in Finistère, including Brest (the region's largest) and Morlaix (one of the largest harbours on the English Channel). There are also numerous sailing schools, including over 50 in Morbihan, where La Trinité-sur-Mer is home to Brittany's largest sailing school, and L'Aber Wrac'h on the west coast, where thousands of Parisian children have been initiated into the joys of boating.

There's also a considerable amount of boating activity on Brittany's many rivers, lakes and canals. In the Côtes-d'Armor, for example, there are over 40 sailing schools (including ten using traditional boats), over 30 canoe/kayak clubs, 13 diving clubs, 350km (220mi) of navigable river and estuary, 3,000km (1,870mi) of fishable river bank and 26 lakes for fishing (notably the 400ha/1,000 acre Lac de Guerlédan). Another large lake for watersports and fishing is the Lac au Duc (250ha/620 acres) near Ploërmel (56). There's canoeing on the Nantes-Brest canal and fishing on the 245km (155mi) Canal d'Ille-et-Rance et la Vilaine (35), where three boat hire companies and two excursion companies operate. There's even white-water rafting on the Hyères river near Carhaix-Plouguer (29).

In Normandy, there are marinas at Cabourg, Caen, Courseulles-sur-Mer, Deauville, Dives-sur-Mer, Grandcamp-Maisy, Le Havre, Honfleur, Isigny-sur-Mer, Merville-Franceville, Ouistreham, Trouville (14), Agon-Coutainville, Barfleur, Barneville-Carteret, Carentan, Cherbourg-Octeville (France's most popular marina for visiting yachtsmen with 15,000 boats passing through it every year), Dielette, Fermanville, Flamanville, Goury, Granville, Omonville-la-Rogue, Port-Bail, Quineville, Regneville-sur-Mer, Saint-Vaast-La-Hougue, Tourlaville (50), Dieppe, Fécamp (where an annual multihull race is held and where the marina is due to be extended), Le Havre, Saint-Aubin-lès-Elbeuf, Saint-Valery-en-Caux and Le Tréport (76). There are sailing schools all along the coast.

Inland, there are numerous watersports parks in both regions, including those at Lisieux, Pont-l'Evêque, Vire and Falaise (14), Guerlédan, Jugon-les-Lacs, Port Gelin (22), La Bonneville-sur-Iton, Brionne, Grosley-sur-Risle, Léry-Poses, Toutanville (27), Chênedet near Fougères (35), Granville, which boasts the third-largest sailing school in France, Saint-Martin-d'Aubign, Tourlaville (50), Baud, Grandchamp, Ploërmel, Priziac and on the 400ha (1,000 acre) Lac de Guerlédan (56), Alençon, La Ferté-Macé, Le Mêle-sur-Sarthe, Rabodanges, Saint-Evroult Notre-Dame-du-Bois (61), Cany-Barville, Jumièges, Longroy-Gamaches, Montville, Saint-Aubin-le Cauf and Tourville-la-Rivière (76). There's also canoeing/kayaking and rowing on many rivers in both regions.

For those who like sailing without getting wet, there's sand-sailing (*char à voile*), which is particularly popular on the long, sandy beaches of Calvados, Manche and Morbihan.

Other Sports

Most towns have a municipal swimming pool, and a new pool is planned for Vire (14), as well as a new sports complex for Louviers (27). There's a 20,000 seat sports stadium in Caen (14), and a large stadium is planned for Darnétal (76). In a 19th century *château* near Verneuil-sur-Avre (27) is Center Parcs, a sporting and holiday centre (frequented mainly by over-stressed Parisians). There are many other sporting facilities in both regions, including rock climbing in Eure, Ille-et-Vilaine, Manche, Morbihan and Orne, diving in the Côtes-d'Armor, Ille-et-Vilaine and Manche, bungee jumping into the Souleuvre river in Calvados (plunge through 60m/650ft of air **and** 4m/13ft of water!), hot-air ballooning in Orne, and paragliding and hang-gliding in Calvados (organised by the discouragingly named Association Icare!).

Leisure

There's no shortage of leisure facilities in Normandy and Brittany. Brittany alone boasts over 300 listed sites and 1,000 historic monuments, including some of the world's most important megalithic remains, particularly in Morbihan (see page 57), but also in the Côtes-d'Armor and Ille-et-Vilaine, where there are some 300 megalithic monuments, Saint-Just being the most important site. Normandy is home to one of France's premier attractions, the Mont Saint-Michel (although the Bretons believe it should be theirs!). There are numerous other castles, *châteaux* and manor houses in both regions, some of which can be visited and others merely admired from the outside.

For nature lovers, there are four bird sanctuaries in the Côtes-d'Armor, as well as some 60 ports from where you can take boat trips to island bird reserves. There are also bird sanctuaries in Calvados and a spectacular nature reserve in Yeun Elez (29). Those in need of relaxation could try a little balneology (also known as thalassotherapy): Deauville, Luc-sur-Mer, Ouistreham and Trouville (14) have establishments offering seaweed baths – the *infusion de varech* (less-appealingly called 'bladderwrack' in English) is recommended by connoisseurs – and there are also centres in Dinard and Saint-Malo (35), Granville (50), Bagnoles-de-l'Orne (61) and throughout the Côtes-d'Armor and Morbihan. (For a list of all centres offering treatment, go to 💻 www.thalasso-france.com.) Or, of course, you can simply laze on the beach (only two of the nine *départements* in Normandy and Brittany have no coastline) – weather permitting!

English-language Cinema & Theatre

The best place to see films in their original language (*version originale/VO*) is Rennes (35), where three cinemas occasionally show *VO* films, including the Ciné TNB Salle Louis Jouvet, where more *VO* films are shown than anywhere else in Brittany or Normandy. The next best *département* for Anglophone cinema-goers is Finistère, where there are four cinemas showing *VO* films; the worst is the Côtes-d'Armor, which has none. In all other *départements*, there's at least one cinema regularly or occasionally showing films in *VO*, as listed below:

- Caen (14): Cinéma Lux;
- Hérouville-Saint-Clair (14): Café des Images;
- Evreux (27): Ciné Zénith;
- Le Neubourg (27): Le Viking;
- Brest (29): Le Studio;
- Douarnenez (29): Le Club;
- Quimper (29): Le Chapeau Rouge;
- Roscoff (29): Le Sainte-Barbe;
- Redon (35): Le Manivel;
- Rennes (35): L'Arvor, Ciné TNB Salle Louis Jouvet and Le Gaumont;
- Cherbourg-Octeville (50): Club 6;
- Lanester (56): Ciné Stars;
- Quistembert (56): Iris;
- Mortagne-au-Perche (61): L'Etoile.

A useful website for finding out what films are on in a given area, which also indicates whether the films are being shown in the original language, is 💻 www.cinefil.com. There's an annual British Film Festival in October in Dinard (35) (💻 www.festivaldufilm-dinard.com) and an annual American cinema festival in Deauville (14) in early September.

There's little English-language theatre in the area. The *Scène nationale* in Dieppe (76) has an annual festival (in April) of plays in English called (typically incongruously) 'Too Much' and occasionally stages productions in

English during the rest of the season, as do the Théâtre d'Evreux (27) and Le Volcan in Le Havre (76). In Brittany, there are theatres in Dinan, Guingamp, Saint-Brieuc (22), Brest, Morlaix, Quimper (29) and Redon and three in Rennes (35), but little is performed in English.

Festivals

The regions' many festivals and other cultural events include a variety of music festivals: avant-garde, blues, classical, jazz, medieval, rock, and traditional music; Brittany is especially renowned for its music festivals, which include the Festival Saint-Loup (August) in Guingamp, the festival of sea songs (August) in Paimpol, the Artrock festival (June) and *Jazz dans les feuilles* (September) in Saint-Brieuc (22), *Les Tombées de la Nuit* (July), Rock'n Solex (August) and *Les Transmusicales* (December) in Rennes (35), *Le Pont du Rock* (July) in Malestroit and an opera festival (July/August) in Belle-Ile-en-Mer (56), a jazz festival (June) in Blainville-Crevon (76). *Octobre en Normandie* is an extensive festival of music and dance in Rouen, Le Havre and other towns in Normandy throughout October. Ille-et-Vilaine claims to be the 'home' of the accordion (especially the Pays de Fougères area), and the annual *Fête de la Bouëze* (which in French has nothing to do with drinking!) in June attracts 200 to 300 players. There are also many traditional Breton festivals, particularly in Finistère, including the *Festival de Cornouaille* (July) in Quimper, in which some 4,000 people take part. One of the largest, however, is the *Festival interceltique* (August) in Lorient (56), which involves some 4,500 performers.

There are also many film, drama, dance, and literary festivals, most notable among the last being the Brittany Book Fair (August) in Carhaix-Plouguer, the maritime book fair (April) in Concarneau and the book fairs (Easter and August) in Bécherel (35). There are traditional fishermen's festivals in Honfleur, Livarot (14), Concarneau (29), Granville (50), Le Havre, Saint-Valéry-en-Caux, Veules-les-Roses and Veulettes (76), apple festivals in late September in several towns and villages, a chestnut festival (October) in Redon (35), an oyster festival (April) on the Rhuys peninsula (56), and 'horse days' throughout Calvados in the autumn. Other events include a balloon festival in Balleroy (14) in June, medieval festivals in Deauville (14) in August and in Rudepont (27) in April, the Joan of Arc Festival in Rouen (76) in May, and a spectacular procession of tall ships up the Seine as far as Rouen every four years (the next one is in 2008).

Brittany is known for its religious festivals (*pardons*), one of the biggest being the pilgrimage to Locronan in honour of Saint Ronan, known as *la*

Grande Troménie, which takes place every six years (the next is in 2008), and there are village festivals throughout the region from spring to late autumn.

Museums & Galleries

The regions' major museums and galleries include the Musée de Normandie in Caen (14) with 80,000 artefacts tracing the region's history, the Breton museum in Rennes (35), fine arts museums in Caen (14), with a major collection of paintings and engravings displayed in William the Conqueror's castle, Brest and Quimper (29), Rennes (35) and Rouen (76), where there's a particularly good collection of Impressionist paintings. Local history museums are at Saint-Brieuc (22), Caen and Evreux (27), Saint-André-de-Bohon and Saint-Lô (50), Alençon (61), Le Havre and Rouen (76). Modern art galleries include Artothèque in Caen, Cherbourg-Octeville (50) and Sotteville-lès-Rouen, the Centre culturel de Cherbourg-Octeville, Galerie Hélène Lemarque in Rouen, Centre d'Art contemporain in Hérouville-Saint-Clair (14), the Château de Vascoeil (which also houses the permanent Musée Michelet), the Palais Bénédictine at Fécamp, and SPOT at Le Havre.

In Calvados, Manche and Orne, there's a number of museums commemorating the D-Day landings and the Battle of Normandy, e.g. at Arromanches, Bayeux, Caen (where the Mémorial de Caen/Musée pour la Paix contains an illustrated history of the 20th century), Ranville (the first French village to be liberated) and Vierville-sur-Mer (14), Avranches, Cherbourg-Octeville, Quinéville and Sainte-Mère-l'Eglise (50), and L'Aigle and Montormel (61), as well as numerous military cemeteries.

There are also many specialist museums in the two regions, covering subjects as diverse as balloons, granite, posters, seaweed, bicycles, monastic life, cider, witchcraft, fire-fighting equipment and childhood. Of particular note are the museum of *haute couture* in Granville (50), in the house where Christian Dior was born, and the lace museums in Alençon and Argentan (61). There are also several museums dedicated to horses. For those who like to sample the local produce, the Bénédictine factory at Fécamp (76) is worth a detour, and of course you can visit cheese, cider and calvados-making factories to your heart's (and stomach's) content!

Parks, Zoos & Theme Parks

There's a wealth of zoos, aquariums and theme parks in Normandy and Brittany, including the following:

- Aquarium de la Pointe-du-Raz in Audierne (29): unusual sea creatures;
- Aquarium de Saint-Malo (35): mysteries of the sea;
- Aquarium intra-muros de Saint-Malo (35): freshwater fish;
- Aquarium marin de Trégastel (22): Breton sea life;
- Aquarium de Vannes (56): tropical and other fish;
- Aventure Parc in Quelneuc (56): activity park;
- Bel Air Land in Landudec (29): various children's activities;
- Canyon Park in Epretot (76): amusement park for young children;
- Le Cerza in Herminal-les-Vaux (14): wild animals in 'natural' surroundings;
- Cité de la Mer in Cherbourg-Octeville (50): museum of the sea, including an aquarium, bathyscaphe and nuclear submarine;
- Cobac Parc in Lanhélin (35): leisure park with aquatic and land-based attractions;
- Cosmopolis in Pleurmeur-Bodou (22): scientific park incorporating a planetarium and telecommunications museum;
- Domaine de Branfère between Vannes and La Roche-Bernard (56): zoological and botanical park with almost 2,000 animals, including many endangered species;
- Driver's Club in Deauville (14): vehicles of all kinds (including boats) to drive;
- Ecomusée in Hennebont (35): 19th century history brought to life;
- L'Estran in Dieppe (76): museum/aquarium depicting the history of the sea and seafaring;
- Festyland in Bretteville-sur-Odon (14): 'historical' theme park;
- La Galopette in Hanvec (29): activities for children and adults;
- Le Jardin aux Papillons in Vannes (56): butterfly park;
- La Maison de la Mer in Courseulles-sur-Mer (14): cold-water fish and shellfish;
- Natur'Aquarium in Trouville (14): 60 aquariums;
- Le Naturospace in Honfleur (14): tropical butterflies;
- Océanopolis in Brest (29): everything to do with the sea;

- Parc animalier du Quinquis in Clohars-Carnoët (29): wild animals and plants;
- Parc de Branféré in Le Guerno (56): exotic animals and plants;
- Parc de Préhistoire de Bretagne in Malansac (56): including life-size dinosaurs;
- Parc Zoologique de Champrepus in Villedieu-les-Poeles (50): wildlife park;
- Parc Zoologique de Clères (76): botanical garden with 1,200 species of bird;
- Parc Zoologique de Pont-Scorff (56): endangered species;
- Port Musée de Douarnenez (29): floating maritime museum;
- Souterroscope des Adroisières in Caumont-l'Eventé (14): caves;
- Tolysland in Tosny (27): amusement park;
- Tropical Parc in Saint-Jacut-les-Pins (56): tropical plants and landscapes;
- Zoo de Jurques (14): 500 animals;
- Zoo Loisirs in Tinteniac (35): zoo and water park.

Casinos

Somewhat surprisingly, the greatest concentration of casinos in France outside Alpes-Maritimes and Var on the Côte d'Azur is to be found in Calvados and Seine-Maritime in Normandy, where there are no fewer than 17 casinos: at Bagnoles-de-l'Orne, Cabourg, Deauville, Houlgate, Luc-sur-Mer, Ouistreham, Saint-Aubin-sur-Mer, Trouville and Villers-sur-Mer (14), and Dieppe, Etretat, Fécamp, Forges-les-Eaux, Saint-Valéry-en-Caux, Le Tréport, Veulettes-sur-Mer and Yport (76), with a new casino soon to open in Le Havre. There are also four casinos in Manche: at Agon-Coutainville, Cherbourg, Granville and Saint-Pair-sur-Mer. Brittany has almost as many: at Fréhel, Pernos-Guirec, Pléneuf-Val-André and Saint-Quay-Portrieux (22), Bénodet, Plouescat and Roscoff (29), Dinard and Saint-Malo (35), and Arzon, Carnac and Quiberon (56). Details of all casinos and what they offer are available via the internet (e.g. 💻 www.journaldescasinos.com – partly in English).

Libraries

Normandy's main libraries are to be found at Caen, Rouen, Ranville (14), Evreux (27), Saint-Lô (50), Alençon, Mont-Saint-Aignan (61) and Mont-Saint-

Aignan (76). Brittany's major libraries are in Plerin (22), Landivisiau, Quimper (29), Rennes (35), Caudon, Pontivy and Vannes (56). There are also university libraries at Caen (14), Brest (29), Rennes (35), Le Havre and Rouen (76).

Shopping Centres & Markets

There are major shopping centres in Caen (14), Paimpol (22), Evreux, Louviers and Vernon (27), Brest and Quimper (29), Rennes (35), Barentin, Bolbec, Dieppe, Le Havre, Rouen and Yvetot (76). The largest retail park in Normandy is at Tourville-la-Rivière near Rouen, where there are reputedly 59 super and hypermarkets.

As in other parts of France (and Europe), small shops are gradually giving way to supermarkets, hypermarkets and retail parks. In Lower Normandy, for example, some 35 per cent of small shops have disappeared since 1980, and there's now one grocer for every four communes with under 250 inhabitants compared with one in every small commune 20 years ago. Only the *bocage* region around Flers, Mortain and Saint-Lô has managed to retain a high proportion of small shops. In most other rural areas, you must travel an average of 7km (4mi) to find a shop selling anything other than bread and newspapers.

Nevertheless, small and large towns still have their daily or weekly markets – some consisting of just one or two stalls, others dozens – and there are traditional 'fairs' between May and November in Manche. The Tuesday market in Hennebont (56) is one of best known in the region, and the market in La Guerche-de-Bretagne (35), which has been running every Tuesday since 1121 (!), is reckoned to be one of the 'great' markets of France. The weekly markets in Bayeux, Saint-Pierre-sur-Dives (14) and Bricquebec (50) are also highly recommended. In Bécherel (35), there's a monthly book market, and Les Andelys (27) boasts France's second-largest *foire à tout* (an up-market car boot sale) in mid-September, with around 10km (6mi) of stalls. Lists of local markets are available from tourist offices, town halls, etc. (e.g. the leaflet *Mon Marché en Basse-Normandie* for Lower Normandy).

Foreign Food & Products

There are few specialist foreign product shops, although most supermarkets (and particularly Carrefour) stock a few foreign items, such as American hamburger buns, British-style bread, marmalades and sauces (e.g. HP), Australian wines, and foreign spirits (e.g. Scotch and Bourbon), Dutch and Greek cheeses and Italian pasta. In towns with a high proportion of immigrants, there's usually a number of shops selling North African products (e.g. in Val-de-Reuil in Eure). There's an English bookshop in Rouen (76), the ABC Book Shop (☎ 02 35 71 08 67), and La Bouquinerie du Centre in Rennes (35) stocks many second-hand English-language novels and children's books.

Restaurants & Bars

As in other parts of France, there's no shortage of bars and restaurants in Normandy and Brittany, and tourist towns are positively overflowing with them. However, in rural areas and even in many towns, most bars close at around 8pm and are frequented largely by men. Restaurants vary from bistrot-style, serving salads, *crêpes* and snacks, and café-style, serving a set menu for around €10, to exclusive establishments with menus costing up to €100. (Rouen boasts four Michelin-starred restaurants, including the two-star Restaurant Gill, specialising in fish, on the quai de la Bourse.)

In rural areas, an alternative to a restaurant is the *ferme auberge*, a working farm offering simple home-cooking using local produce. The Normandy Tourist Board (see **Useful Addresses** on page 99) publishes a leaflet called *Bienvenue à la Ferme en Normandie*, which lists *fermes auberges*. In the towns, there are also Chinese restaurants, pizzerias and fast-food outlets such as MacDonald's and Quick. Orne boasts one of France's few vegetarian hotels and restaurants, run by an English couple, at Ticheville, south-east of Vimoutiers (☎ 02 33 36 95 84); the hotel is open all year but the restaurant opens only during the summer.

SERVICES

Services generally have become more centralised in the last 20 years, although to a lesser extent in Manche, while in some areas where the population is ageing (e.g. in Orne), health services have become more widespread.

International & Private Schools

There are no international schools in either region (the nearest is the Ecole Internationale de Lille) and just two private schools with facilities for English-speaking pupils: in Normandy, the Ecole des Roches in Eure (BP 710, 27130 Verneuil-sur-Avre, ☎ 02 32 60 40 05, 💻 www.ecoledesroches.com) has French as a Foreign Language *département* in both its *école maternelle/*

primaire and *collège/lycée*, for pupils spending a year or two in France who wish to continue studying towards Cambridge, SAT or TOEFL exams (and obtain a *Diplôme d'Etudes de Langue Française* or *Diplôme Approfondi de Langue Française*) or those settling permanently who need to be progressively integrated into the French curriculum; in Brittany, the Lycée Privé Mixte Sainte-Geneviève in Ille-et-Vilaine (14 rue Genguené, BP546, 35006 Rennes, ☎ 02 99 65 10 08, 💻 www.ste-genevieve.org) accepts pupils from the age of 11 for periods of as little as a month.

Did you know?

The Brittany *département* of Côtes d'Armor recently launched a 'welcome programme' for English-speaking children (and their parents) to help them integrate into the French education system and learn French. The programme is currently focused on the area around Guingamp and Loudéac.

Language Schools

Language lessons are offered by a number of public and private bodies in the area, including those listed below. Language courses are also offered by local Chambres de Commerce et d'Industrie and Centres culturels.

- CEFA Normandie in Lisieux (14);
- A Breath of French Air in Montviette (14);
- Ecole des Roches in Verneuil-sur-Avre (27) – see above;
- Centre international d'Etudes des Langues (CIEL Brest) in Le Relecq-Kerhoun (29);
- Action Langues vivantes in Rennes (35);
- Langue et Communication in Rennes (35);
- Maison des Langues in Rennes (35);
- University of Rennes (35);
- Centre d'Etudes des Langues in Saint-Malo (35);
- Inlingua Normandy in Le Petit-Quevilly near Rouen (76);
- Alliance française in Rouen (76).

Details of the above schools can be found on 💻 www.europa-pages.com. The French Consulate in London (see **Appendix A**) publishes a booklet called *Cours de français Langue étrangère et Stages pédagogiques du français Langue étrangère en France*, which includes a comprehensive list of schools and organisations providing French language courses throughout France.

Hospitals & Clinics

In Normandy, there are major hospitals in Aunay-sur-Odon, Bayeux, Equemauville, Falaise, Lisieux, Pont-l'Evêque, Trouville, Vire (14), Bernay, Evreux (a new one is planned for nearby Cambolle), Gisors, Mortagne-au-Perche, Saint-Sébastien-de-Morsent, Verneuil-sur-Avre, Vernon (27), Avranches, Carentan, Cherbourg-Octeville, Coutances, Granville, Saint-Hilaire-du-Harcouët, Saint-Lô, Valgnes (50), Aigle, Alençon, Argentan, Domfront, la Ferté-Macé, Flers (61), Darnétal, Dieppe, Elbeuf, Fécamp, Le Havre, Lillebonne, Mont-Saint-Aignan and Montivilliers (76). In Brittany, there are main hospitals in Lannion and Saint-Brieuc (22), Brest, Landernau and Quimper (29), Antrain, Dinard and Rennes (35), and Pontivy, Ploermel and Vannes (56).

There are teaching hospitals (*Centre hospitalier universitaire/CHU*) in Brest, Caen, Rennes and Rouen, where all services and medical procedures are available, and the Groupe hospitalier du Havre is the largest non-teaching hospital in France, with over 2,000 beds. The *CHU* in Rouen is Upper Normandy's second-largest employer with 1,300 medical staff and comprises the Charles Nicolle, Bois-Guillaume, Satin-Julien and Oissel hospitals as well as the Boucicaut retirement home. There are also specialist clinics and hospitals in many towns, with a particularly large number in Rouen (76). A full list of hospitals and clinics, including details of specialisms, can be found at 💻 www.chu-rouen.fr/ssf/ hopfr.html.

English-language Media

There's no local radio in English, and the only local English-language periodical is *Normandie & South of England Magazine* (330 rue Valvire, BP414, 50004 Saint-Lô, ☎ 02 33 77 32 70, 💻 www.normandie-magazine.fr), a bimonthly current affairs magazine in French and English. There's also the *Central Brittany Journal*, providing information about businesses and services in this area (see 💻 www.thecbj.com). There are also two English-language monthlies published in France and distributed nationally, *The Connexion* and *The News* (see **Appendix B**).

Embassies & Consulates

Both Normandy and Brittany are covered by the British Embassy and Consulate in Paris (see page 355), although information can also be obtained (often far more easily!) from the consulates in Bordeaux, Lille, Lyon and Marseille (see **Appendix A**). There's an American Presence Post in Brittany (30, quai Duguay-Trouino, 350000 Rennes, ☎ 02 23 44 09 60). For details of the US Embassy and Consulate in Paris, see **Appendix A**.

Places of Worship

Churches in the following towns hold regular services in English (where no church is specified, it's the only one in the village):

- Bonen (35) – Rostrenen parish church ;
- Caen (14) – Chapelle de la Miséricorde;
- Dinard (35) – Saint Bartholomew;
- Guénin (56) – Interdenominational Church of Saint Andrew;
- Guerlesquin/Huelgoat (29);
- Le Havre (76) – Bethel Baptist Church;
- Ploërmel (35) – Maison Mère des Frères de la Mennais;
- Rouen (76) – All Saints.

There are also a few churches near campsites in Brittany where English services are held during the summer months only, including:

- Bénodet (29) – RC church by quayside, Port de la Plaisance;
- Carnac (56) – La Chapelle de la Congrégation;
- Névez (29) – Sainte Thumette Parish Church.

Further details of English-language church services in Brittany can be found on 💻 www.christchurchbrittany.org.uk. Those in southern Brittany may be able to attend services in Loire-Atlantique (see page 133). The Intercontinental Church Society in the UK publishes a *Directory of English-Speaking Churches Abroad* (see **Appendix A**).

There are mosques in Hérouville-Saint-Clair (14), Châteaudun, Evreux, Gaillon, Louviers (27), Brest, Quimper (29), Rennes (35), Cherbourg-Octeville (50), Lorient, Vannes (56), Candher, Elbeuf, Le Havre and Rouen (76); details can be found on 💻 http://mosquee.free.fr. There are only two synagogues in the area: in Deauville (14) and Rouen (76). Details can be found on 💻 www.pagesjaunes.fr (enter 'Synagogues' in the first box and the name of the town).

Clubs

There are no English-language clubs in either region, although those in Upper Normandy may be able to access clubs in Ile-de-France (see page 357). For French speakers, the Accueil des Villes françaises (AVF), a French organisation designed to welcome newcomers to an area, is an option (there's often at least one fluent English-speaker in each group). There are at least 25 AVF groups in Normandy – in Bayeux, Caen, Honfleur, Lisieux, Vire (14), Evreux, Louviers, Le Vaudreuil, Verneuil-sur-Avre, Vernon (27), Cherbourg-Octeville, Granville (50), Alençon, Flers (61), Bonsecours, Dieppe, Eu, Fécamp, Fontaine-la-Mallet, Le Havre, Le Mesnil-Esnard, Mont-Saint-Aignan, Montivilliers, Notre-Dame-de-Gravenchon and Rouen (76) – and 29 in Brittany: in Lannion, Loudeac, Paimpol, Saint-Brieuc (22), Bannalec, Bigouden, Brest, Concarneau, Crozon, Guipavas, Landerneau, Loperhet, Moelan-sur-Mer, Morlaix, Plougastel, Quimper, Roscoff, Saint-Pol-de-Léon (29), Cesson-Sévigné, Dinard, Fougères, Rennes, Saint-Malo, Vannes (35), Auray, Baden, Lorient, Ploemeur and Ploermel (56). The AVF website (💻 www.avf.asso.fr) includes a directory (*annuaire*) of local groups by *département* as well as an online form for contacting your local AVF before you move to the area. Listings indicate whether information and services are available in English or other languages. Other sources for clubs in the area are *The Connexion* and *The News* (see **Appendix B**) and English-speaking churches (see above).

PROPERTY

The popularity of Normandy and Brittany, particularly among British buyers, means that the demand for properties exceeds the supply. There was a spate of house building in the '80s in Upper Normandy, when the number of houses grew three times as fast as the population, mainly on account of Parisians (and others) building and buying second homes in the area, particularly in Eure (and especially the western part of the *département*). The rate of increase slowed in the '90s, to around 1 per cent per year. House building in Brittany enjoyed a boom in 1999 and 2000, when the number of houses increased by around 5 per cent per year, but the rate has since slowed to around 1 per cent. However, the demand for new properties in Brittany is still high, especially in coastal areas, where second homes represent almost 10 per cent of the property market. (In some communes, there are over 100 second homes per km^2.)

The most popular areas in Normandy are those within a short drive of the Channel ports (i.e. Caen, Cherbourg, Dieppe and Saint-Malo), particularly the southern half of the Cherbourg peninsula, and the coast of Calvados near Deauville and Honfleur. In Brittany, the area around Dinan, Dinard and Saint-Malo is especially popular. This is reflected in relatively high prices, which have caused buyers to look further west along the coast of the Côtes-d'Armor and into Finistère. If there are bargains to be found, they're in central Brittany and the extreme west of Finistère and in the *département* of Orne in Normandy, which is among the least popular parts of the area.

The demand for holiday accommodation in Brittany in particular is as great as anywhere in France, so second homebuyers usually have little difficulty in letting their properties, although competition is intense in most areas.

Typical Homes

Normandy is famous for its half-timbered *colombage* houses (often simply referred to as '*style normand*'), which are either original (with real timbers and much sought-after) or modern imitations (with wooden facings on breezeblock). *Colomage* houses often feature a protruding roof known as a *queue* or *cul de geai* ('jay's tail' or 'bottom') at one end and some are thatched (traditionally with irises growing along the apex of the roof!), which are generally much more expensive. Another typical house found in both Normandy and Brittany is the *longère* – as its name suggests, a long, straight, single storey building (although often with added bedrooms in the roof).

Among the most popular homes in Brittany are the characteristic Breton cottage, built mainly of granite with a slate roof. As with the Norman *colombage*, there are many modern imitations (known as '*néo-breton*'). Equally prevalent throughout both regions are stone and brick houses, often rather plain but sometimes in flamboyant 'gothic' style and sometimes with a distinctive glass 'porch' above the front door. Houses are often built end-on to the street and surrounded by high stone walls and solid gates to ensure privacy. Almost every house in Normandy is adorned with geraniums in window boxes, and hydrangeas, irises and hollyhocks are common in gardens throughout the area. Many modern houses are without any particular stylistic features – simply four white walls and a roof, often semi-bungalow with one or two rooms in the roof (called *chambres mansardées*). Modern homes are often raised on earth mounds with a basement (*sous-sol*) as large as the ground floor and incorporating a garage.

Cost of Property

Normandy

The table below gives the average selling price of houses in 2006. Note, however, that there may be a higher percentage of large houses or small houses in a particular area, which can distort the figures.

Town/Area	**Average House Price**			
	2-bed	**3-bed**	**4-bed**	**5+-bed**
Avranches	€110,000	€155,000	€215,000	€310,000
Caen	€145,000	€195,000	€275,000	€440,000
Deauville	€205,000	€300,000	€385,000	€580,000
Dieppe	€125,000	€205,000	€285,000	€380,000
Honfleur	€205,000	€230,000	€335,000	€450,000
Rouen	€150,000	€160,000	€265,000	€400,000
Trouville	€175,000	€235,000	€465,000	€430,000

The average price of a period property in 2006 in Lower Normandy was around €86,500 (national average €102,250, the average for a new house €109,300 (average €117,650) and for a building plot €19,500 (average €23,000). Note, however, that average property prices aren't always a reliable indication of the relative price of similar properties in different areas, as one may have a preponderance of cheaper or more expensive properties.

Brittany

The table below gives the average selling price of houses in 2006. Note, however, there may be a higher percentage of large houses or small houses in a particular area, which can distort the figures.

2

Town/Area	Average House Price			
	2-bed	3-bed	4-bed	5+-bed
Brest	€125,000	€160,000	€220,000	€280,000
Dinan/Dinard/St-Malo	€120,000	€170,000	€260,000	€300,000
Guingamp	€90,000	€135,000	€210,000	€280,000
Gulf of Morbihan	€160,000	€220,000	€300,000	€490,000
Lorient	€130,000	€200,000	€270,000	€300,000
Quimper	€115,000	€130,000	€185,000	€275,000
Rennes	€115,000	€180,000	€215,000	€260,000

The demand for homes in Normandy and Brittany has led to a steady overall increase in prices in recent decades, with sharp rises in certain parts. Brittany in particular has experienced steep price rises, especially on islands, where property has increased in value by 300 per cent in 15 years. A 100m^2 house with a sea view on the island of Bréhat off Paimpol, for example, can cost up to €450,000, and similar properties on islands such as Moines and Arz in the Golfe de Morbihan can fetch up to €600,000. (Houses in need of renovation are cheaper, but restoration costs on islands can be 30 per cent higher than on the mainland.) Elsewhere, prices are more reasonable, although the days when you could pick up a habitable farmhouse for €30,000 are long gone.

The average price of a period property in 2006 in Brittany as a whole was around €107,000 (national average €102,250, the average for a new house €131,600 (average €117,650) and for a building plot €29,000 (average €23,000). Note, however, that average property prices aren't always a reliable indication of the relative price of similar properties in different areas, as one may have a preponderance of cheaper or more expensive properties.

Properties for Restoration

Despite what estate agents might tell you, there are still plenty of properties to restore in Normandy and Brittany, although you should always check whether there are problems associated with a property (e.g. whether it's in an area liable to flooding or whether there's a complicated inheritance situation associated with it). Prices vary enormously according to the condition (as well as location and other factors) of a property, and you should have a detailed survey done in order to find out exactly how much work (and therefore cost) will be involved in realising a 'renovation project' – often a euphemism for 'ruin'!

In Brittany, for a complete renovation 'project' (read 'nightmare'), prices start at €10,000 for a tiny roofless village property; for €70,000 you could buy a habitable village house, needing 'only' central heating and interior and exterior finishing; while for under €200,000 you could own a stone *longère* needing 'some work' – e.g. a septic tank, new windows and internal renovation.

Modern Homes

Modern houses in reasonable condition start at around €120,000, and for just €200,000 you could buy a five-bedroom property with central heating, double-glazing and 5,000m^2 of landscaped gardens on the outskirts of a small town.

Land

Building land is available in all areas, although it isn't plentiful. Prices vary enormously according to location and whether main services are connected. Land in or near a small village, where there's no mains drainage, can be bought for less than €2 per m^2, whereas land with connections to all services, including electricity and telephone, and near a town can cost as much as €100 per m^2. Plots range from around 400m^2 to several hectares, the average plot being between 1,000 and 3,000m^2 and costing between €10,000 and €50,000. Most local estate agents sell building plots (*terrains à bâtir* or *terrains constructibles*).

Did you know?

Gardens range from around 400m^2 for a town house (sometimes as much as 600m^2, sometimes virtually nothing) to several hectares for a farmhouse in the country, where the average plot is around 2,000m^2 (half an acre). However, plot size has little direct bearing on the cost of a property; in fact, a large plot (e.g. over 5,000m^2) may reduce the price, as few people want the work required to maintain a large garden.

Rental Accommodation

Apartments

Apartments are available for long-term rent in all *départements*, although few have more than three bedrooms (in Rennes and Cherbourg, there are few with more than two). The majority of rental apartments are to be found in the principal towns in each *département* (except in Côtes-d'Armor, where the few available apartments are spread among several towns, and Morbihan, where the majority are in Lorient), and few are available elsewhere. Price ranges for these towns (and the *département* of Côtes-d'Armor) are shown below.

Town (*Département*)	**No. of Bedrooms**	**Monthly Rental**
Caen (14)	Studio	€250 to 400
	1	€325 to 500
	2	€375 to 600
	3	€525 to 800
Evreux (27)	Studio	€350 to 500
	1	€350 to 600
	2	€600 to 800
	3	€900 to 1,200
Brest (29)	Studio	€250 to 400
	1	€300 to 500
	2	€350 to 550
	3	€500 to 700
Rennes (35)	1	€400 to 600
	2	€525 to 800
St-Malo (35)	Studio	€250 to 400
	1	€300 to 500
	2	€400 to 550
	3	€500 to 600
Cherbourg-Octeville (50)	Studio	€150 to 250
	1	€250 to 450

	2	€400 to 500
Lorient (56)	Studio	€250 to 300
	1	€300 to 400
	2	€400 to 550
	3	€450 to 700
Alençon (61)	Studio	€225
	1	€250 to 400
	2	€350 to 500
	3	€400 to 700
Rouen (76)	Studio	€175 to 350
	1	€250 to 600
	2	€350 to 750
	3	€600 to 1,200

Houses

Rented houses are less common than apartments, and very few are to be found in or near the main towns. The table below gives an indication of the rental prices for houses in each *département*.

Département	**No. of Bedrooms**	**Monthly Rental**
	3	€600 to 1,200
Calvados	2	€425 to 650
	3	€650 to 1,000
	4	€700 to 1,100
	5	€700 to 1,250
Côtes-d'Armor	2	€350 to 550

	3	€400 to 700
	4	€500 to 800
Eure	2	€450 to 600
	3	€650 to 800
	4	€750 to 1,250
Finistère	3	€500 to 800
	4	€650+
	5	€700+
Ille-et-Vilaine	3	€550 to 1,000
	4	€600 to 1,100
	5	€750 to 1,100
Manche	2	€500 to 650
	3	€550 to 800
	4	€600+
Morbihan	3	€500 to 750
	4	€800 to 1,500
	5	€1,200+
Orne	2	€350 to 600
	3	€450 to 650
	4	€500 to 700
	5	€600 to 900
Seine-Maritime	2	€400 to 550
	3	€450 to 750
	4	€550 to 1,200
	5	€750 to 1,500

COMMUNICATIONS

Air

There are several airports in Normandy and Brittany with links to Paris and other major French cities as well as a few European cities, including London (Stansted), although international services tend to be unreliable – in the sense that they're started and terminated at short notice (for example, Buzz started a Rouen/Stansted service in March 2002 and cancelled it the following September!). Other airports accessible from Upper Normandy are Charles-de-Gaulle-Roissy and Orly in Paris (see page 369) and Beauvais (in the *département* of Oise in Picardy ☎ 03 44 11 46 66). Nantes airport (in Loire-Atlantique, ☎ 02 40 84 80 00) is well placed for southern Brittany (see page 139). Direct flights from British and Irish airports are listed in **Appendix F**. Details of all French airports and their services can be found on 💻 www.aeroport.fr.

Sea

Normandy is well provided with ports accessible from England. Furthest east (and therefore offering the shortest and usually cheapest crossing) is Dieppe (76), followed by Le Havre (76), Caen (14) and Cherbourg-Octeville (50) – France's second busiest port for cross-channel traffic after Calais, with 1.5m passengers per year. For Upper Normandy, it may be quicker/or and cheaper to cross the Channel between Dover and Dunkerque, Calais or Boulogne and drive down the coast; Calais-Rouen, for example, takes only around two hours. Brittany has only two major ports: Saint-Malo (35), connecting with Portsmouth in England, and Roscoff (29), connecting with Plymouth in England and Cork in Ireland. The details below were correct in December 2006; prices are minimum return fares for a standard car with four passengers in July/August 2007 (prices can depend on day of travel, sailing times and type of overnight accommodation as well as season).

- Newhaven-Dieppe (Transmanche Ferries, 💻 www.transmanche ferries.com): two ferries daily throughout the year, 4 hours, from £220;
- Newhaven-Le Havre (LD Lines, UK ☎ 0870-458 0401, 💻 www.ld lines.co.uk): one crossing daily throughout the year, 5 hours 30 minutes daytime (Le Havre-Newhaven) or 8 hours night time (Newhaven-Le Havre), from £180;

- Portsmouth-Le Havre (LD Lines): one crossing daily throughout the year, 5 hours 30 minutes daytime (Le Havre-Portsmouth) or 8 hours night time (Portsmouth-Le Havre), from £180;
- Portsmouth-Caen (Brittany Ferries, UK ☎ 0870-536 0360, 💻 www.brittany-ferries.co.uk): up to four crossings daily, 6 hours, from £400;
- Portsmouth-Saint-Malo (Brittany Ferries): daily crossing, 8 hours 45 minutes, from £450;
- Portsmouth-Cherbourg (Brittany Ferries): fast ferry, 3 hours 30 minutes, from £460; conventional ferry, 7 hours 15 minutes, from £480;
- Poole-Cherbourg (Brittany Ferries): up to three crossings daily by standard ferry (4 hours 15 mins), from £400;
- Poole-Saint-Malo (Condor Ferries): daily crossing by fast ferry between late May and the end of September, 4 hours 35 minutes, from £480;
- Weymouth-Saint-Malo (Condor Ferries): daily crossing by fast ferry, 5 hours 15 minutes (change of ferry required in either Guernsey or Jersey between late May and the end of September), from £360;
- Plymouth-Roscoff (Brittany Ferries): up to three crossings daily, 6 hours, from £500;
- Cork-Roscoff (Brittany Ferries): one sailing per week in each direction, 17.00 from Cork on Saturdays, 22.00 from Roscoff on Fridays (local times), 13 hours, from £700.

Public Transport

Trains

Normandy and Brittany are well connected by rail to Paris and, in the case of Brittany, to south-western France, but only Brittany is on the *TGV* network. There's a main line (not *TGV*) from Paris Saint-Lazare to Le Havre (76) via Vernon, Gaillon, Val-de-Reuil (27), Oissel, Rouen, Yvetot and Bréauté-Beuzeville (76), although services to the Vernon, Gaillon, Val-de-Reuil and Oissel are infrequent. Some trains stop at a few smaller towns along the way. (There has been talk of upgrading this line to accommodate high-speed trains, but as Le Havre is less than two hours from Paris by ordinary train, it's unlikely to happen.) There are also ordinary train services from Paris Saint-Lazare to Cherbourg-Octeville (50) via Evreux, Bernay (27), Lisieux,

Caen, Bayeux (14), Carentan and Valognes (50). Journey time to Cherbourg varies between three and three-and-a-half hours according to the number of stops en route. Again, some trains also stop at smaller towns. To get to Dieppe or Le Tréport (76), you must change at Rouen.

The *TGV* runs from Paris Montparnasse via Vitré to Rennes (35), from where there are two lines: one to Brest (29) via Lamballe, Saint-Brieuc, Guingamp, Plouaret (22) and Morlaix (29), and one to Quimper (29) via Vannes and Lorient (56). The latter line also runs south to Nantes in Loire-Atlantique. There are 20 trains a day from Paris to Rennes (just over two hours), 8 from Paris to Brest and 11 from Paris to Quimper (both journeys just under four-and-a-half hours). A new route, from Paris to Saint-Malo, opened in January 2006 with three services a day in the summer and two the rest of the year. It's also possible to travel by *TGV* from Quimper to Bordeaux without changing, although there's only one train a day and the route is rather circuitous. For details of the *TGV* network, see map in **Appendix E**. Other major towns and smaller towns in Brittany are linked by local trains.

Trams & Undergrounds

Several towns in Normandy and Brittany have tramways, including Caen and Hérouville-Saint-Clair (14), and Rouen (76). Rouen's tramway (called *métrobus*) runs partly underground from the city centre to the southern suburbs along two routes and to the western suburbs. Rennes (35) has an 'underground' railway (parts of it are elevated!) called the VAL.

Buses

All large towns have bus services, which run from the centre to the suburbs. However, these services tend to finish early in the evening. There are also some bus services between towns, particularly during rush hours and to link with train arrivals and departures. In rural areas, however, bus services (apart from school buses) can be few and far between or non-existent, and a car is often essential.

Ferries

In addition to the cross-Channel services listed above, there are ferry services to the Channel Islands (both British and French) from Granville, Barneville-Carteret and Diélette in Manche (see 💻 www.manche-iles-express.com). There are also local ferry services from Morbihan to the many offshore islands, including Belle-Ile-en-Mer (1 hour), l'Ile d'Hoëdic (1 hour 30 mins) and l'Ile d'Houat (1 hour). The islands in the Golfe de Morbihan can be reached by boat from Quiberon (daily all year) as well as from Lorient and Vannes (in summer only), from where there are also services to the l'Ile d'Arz and the Ile de Groix (45 mins from Lorient).

Roads

Major roads in Normandy and Brittany tend to run roughly from east to west, with the exception of the N137 from Saint-Malo south via Rennes (35) to Nantes (in Loire-Atlantique). Brittany has no motorways except the 45km (28mi) stretch of the A58 north-east of Rennes, but there are many dual-carriageways, most of them radiating from Rennes. These include the recently completed A84 north-eastwards to Avranches and on to Caen (14), which has greatly improved communications between the Channel ports and Brittany's capital; the N157 eastwards, which becomes the A11 to Paris at the border with Mayenne; and the N12 north-westwards to Saint-Brieuc (22). The N164, which leaves the N12 just west of Rennes, runs due west through the centre of Brittany to Châteaulin (29). There's also a major road running more or less around the coast, from the Normandy/Brittany border (near Avranches) to Brest (N176/12) and from Brest via Quimper and Vannes to Nantes (N165), all of which is dual-carriageway.

Normandy has several motorways, principally the A13 from Paris to Caen (14) via Rouen (76), with a branch (A131) leading to Le Havre (76). The Bayeux bypass has now been completed. The new A29, which links Upper and Lower Normandy, leaves the A13 south of Le Havre, passes close to Honfleur (14), crosses the A131 and continues in an arc, via Yvetot (76), to join the A28 coming out of Rouen north-east towards Abbeville in Somme; it then continues to Amiens. The A28 from Picardy comes to an abrupt halt at Rouen but it's now possible to avoid the city by taking the A29 and rejoining the new section of A28 west of Rouen to continue south-westwards towards Bordeaux. There's also a short section of motorway north from Rouen towards Dieppe (76), becoming the N27 where it crosses the A29 (around half way to Dieppe). The A13 is a particularly busy route, especially in summer, when Parisians race to the coastal resorts of Calvados for the weekends. Perhaps for this reason, it's one of the most expensive toll roads in France.

Other major roads tend to radiate from Rouen, including the N31 (east towards Beauvais in Oise), the N14 (south-east towards Pointoise in Val-d'Oise), the N15 (south to Vernon in Eure), the A154/N154 south to Evreux in Eure – only a short stretch is motorway) and the N138 (south-west to Alençon in Orne). The N13 from Paris runs parallel to the A13 until the Eure border and then west as far as Cherbourg-Octeville (50) via Evreux, Bernay (27), Lisieux, Caen and Bayeux (14). Alençon (61) is linked to Paris to the east by the N12, much of which is has recently been widened to four lanes, and Brittany to the west by the N12/176.

FURTHER INFORMATION

Useful Addresses

- Comité régional de Tourisme de **Normandie**, Le Doyenné, 14 rue Charles Corbeau, 27000 Evreux (☎ 02 32 33 79 00, 💻 www.normandy-tourism.org)
- Comité régional du Tourisme de **Bretagne** (1 rue Raoul Poucon, 35000 Rennes, ☎ 02 99 36 15 15, 💻 www.tourismebretagne.com)
- Comité départemental du Tourisme de **Calvados**, 8 rue Renoir, 14054 Caen Cedex (☎ 02 31 27 90 30, 💻 www.calvados-tourisme.com)
- Comité départemental du Tourisme des **Côtes-d'Armor**, 7 rue Saint-Benoît, BP 4620, 22046 Saint-Brieuc (☎ 02 96 62 72 01, 💻 www.cotes darmor.com)
- Comité du Tourisme de l'**Eure**, 3 rue du Commandant Letellière, 27000 Evreux (☎ 02 32 62 04 27, 💻 www.cdt-eure.fr)
- Comité départemental du Tourisme de **Finistère**, 4 rue du 19 mars 1962, 29108 Quimper Cedex (☎ 02 98 76 20 70, 💻 www.finistere tourisme.com)
- Comité du Tourisme de l'**Ille-et-Vilaine**, 4 rue Jean-Jaurès, BP 60149, 35101 Rennes (☎ 02 99 78 47 47, 💻 www.bretagne35.com)
- Comité départemental du Tourisme de la **Manche**, Maison du Département, route de Villedieu, 50008 Saint-Lô (☎ 02 33 05 98 70, 💻 www.manchetourisme.com)
- Comité départemental du Tourisme du **Morbihan**, PIBS, Allée Nicolas Leblanc, BOP 408, 56010 Vannes (☎ 08 25 13 56 56, 💻 www. morbihan.com)

- Comité départemental du Tourisme de l'**Orne**, 88 rue Saint-Blaise, BP 50, 61002 Alençon (☎ 02 33 28 88 71, 💻 www.ornetourisme.com)
- Comité départemental du Tourisme de la **Seine-Maritime**, 6 rue Couronné, BP60, 76420 Bihorel (☎ 02 35 12 10 10, 💻 www.seine-maritime-tourisme.com)
- Skol Diwan Naoned (Diwan schools), 160 rue du Corps-de-Garde, 44100 Nantes (☎ 02 51 80 50 32)

Useful Publications

- **Le Tambour de Ville** – monthly guide to what's on in Rouen available from tourist offices
- **Normandie & South of England Magazine**, 330 rue Valvire, GP414, 50004 Saint-Lô (☎ 02 33 77 32 70, 💻 www.normandie-magazine.fr) – bimonthly current affairs magazine in French and English
- **A Normandy Tapestry**, Alan Biggins (Kirkdale Books)
- **Selling French Dreams**, Alan Biggins (Kirkdale Books) – sequel to above

Useful Websites

💻 www.anarvorig.com – general information about Brittany (An Arvorig was the ancient name of Brittany)

💻 www.brittany-net.com – information on Brittany provided by the Brittany Network

💻 www.brittany-tourism.com – information on Brittany

💻 www.europe.anglican.org – details of Anglican services throughout France

💻 www.normandydev.com – information and assistance for those wishing to set up business in Normandy

💻 www.normandy-tapestry.com – Kirkdale Books' site (see above), with links to other Normandy sites

💻 www.normandy-tourism.org – information on Normandy

💻 www.normandy.worldweb.com – general information on Normandy

CHÂTEAU
FOR SALE

Château de Chenonceau
– The Loire Valley

3

THE WEST

Pays-de-la-Loire
& Poitou-Charentes

This chapter describes two administrative regions which lie on the Atlantic coast. Poitou-Charentes, covering an area of 25,809km^2 (10,066mi^2), is made up of four *départements*: Charente (16), Charente-Maritime (17), Deux-Sèvres (79) and Vienne (86). Pays-de-la-Loire (32,082km^2/12,512mi^2) comprises five *départements*: Loire-Atlantique (44), Maine-et-Loire (49), Mayenne (53), Sarthe (72) and Vendée (85). The Loire is France's longest river (1,020km/628mi), with its source in the Vivarais mountains (south of Saint-Etienne in the *département* of Loire) and its outlet at Saint-Nazaire in Loire-Atlantique. It flows through the middle of Pays-de-la-Loire, dividing the *départements* of Maine-et-Loire and Loire-Atlantique horizontally, and is fed by a number of important tributaries in the area, notably the Vienne (which flows through the *département* of the same name), the Thouet (which joins the Loire at Saumur), the Mayenne (which joins it at Angers), and the Sèvre Nantaise (which joins it at Nantes).

The two regions together occupy the Atlantic coastal area between Brittany to the north and the Bordeaux vineyards to the south. Half of the west coast area is given over to arable land, Pays-de-la-Loire consisting of 10 per cent woodland and 25 per cent grassland, while Poitou-Charentes is 15 per cent woodland and 20 per cent grassland; the remaining land in both regions is put to other uses, including urban areas. Note that the area covered by this chapter includes the western Loire valley but excludes the area in which are most of the great Loire *châteaux* (see page 399).

In the last few thousand years, the sea has been receding along the west coast leaving a flat plain. Along the border between the two regions is land which has been reclaimed from the sea, known as the *Marais Poitevin* (Poitevin Marsh). Part of the Marsh hasn't been drained, however, and consists of a pattern of tree-lined canals between small fields used for market gardening and cattle rearing – an area known as '*la Venise verte*' ('Green Venice') and one of the most unusual landscapes in France. Further south, in Charente-Maritime, the sand and mud banks which are covered at high tide are France's biggest centre for the production of oysters and other shellfish. Elsewhere, the flat shore is used for drying out sea water in shallow pans to make salt. Both regions are notable for their navigable rivers, including the Mayenne and the Charente, on which there's much boating activity.

Inland, in Vendée and Deux-Sèvres, there's gently rolling countryside with small fields, hedges, trees and woodlands called *le bocage* and similar to that found in parts of Normandy (see **Chapter 2**). Further south, in Charente and Charente-Maritime, are gently rolling chalk hills covered with cognac vines, poultry farms and grazing for dairy herds, the wooded hilltops rising to over 160m (500ft). The area is also noted for the production of white wine and cognac as well as for heavy industry, with shipyards at Saint-Nazaire, and factories near La Rochelle.

PROPERTY CHECK – COGNAC

An area tipped by many to become a property 'hotspot' in 2007 is Cognac, in the *département* of Charente. Houses here currently cost an average of €1,285 per m^2 compared with €1,600 around Carcassonne (in Aude, Languedoc-Roussillon), €2,630 near Montpellier (Hérault, also Languedoc-Roussillon) and over €3,000 near Toulon in Var (Provence-Alpes-Côte d'Azur). The town of Cognac itself has a population of less than 20,000 and plenty of green spaces as well as the famous cognac producers' factories and is surrounded by vineyards and fields of sunflowers. Just 50 minutes from the coast, Cognac enjoys a high sunshine record and is lively all year round. Property prices rose by almost 18 per cent in 2005 but have since stabilised somewhat. A two-bedroom house near the town centre costs around €120,000, a three-bedroom house in a nearby village from around €175,000. Demand is particularly strong in the €200,000 to €300,000 range, where availability is therefore limited, but you can be lucky and find a *Charentaise* (see page 135) in this bracket, while €350,000 can buy a large family house in good condition with a pool and superb views.

Cognac Property (🖳 www.cognacproperty.com)

Coastal areas benefit, of course, from tourism but, with increasing life expectancy in France, they attract more and more retired people, as well as foreigners. The *département* of Vendée in particular is attracting an increasing number of foreign homebuyers, and property prices are rising fast. In a survey of the 100 largest towns in France published in January 2005, *Le Point* magazine rated two towns in this area among the ten best to live in – Niort (79) third and Nantes (44) seventh; according to the criteria selected by *Le Nouvel Observateur* in a similar survey conducted in 2006, Angers (49) is France's third-best town and Nantes eighth (see **Appendix F**).

PAYS-DE-LA-LOIRE

The locals say that the Loire is the only river in Europe which has never been tamed by dams. In dry summers, it weaves its way through banks of shingle which cover most of its bed but are covered after winter storms. Near the

3

mouth of the river stands the great port of Nantes, which was once the capital of Brittany. This is the home of the Plantagenets, who by marrying the right heiresses became kings of an immense domain which spread from Scotland to the Pyrenees. The English Kings Henry II and Richard the Lionheart are buried at Fontevraud, near Saumur. (They weren't English, of course – neither of them could speak a word – but clever, scheming French aristocrats!)

Along the coast to the west is the industrial town of Saint-Nazaire and beyond it several attractive and fashionable seaside resorts. Inland are the vineyards which produce the famous Muscadet and Rosé d'Anjou wines, and to the north the *département* of Mayenne, named after the river that runs into the Loire – an attractive area for boating as well as for walking and cycling.

The most easterly part of the region is Sarthe, which centres on Le Mans, notable not only for its 24-hour motor races but also for its spectacular cathedral. This part of the region is less than an hour from Paris by *TGV* or under two hours' drive by car and, with its fields, hedges and beech woodlands, is popular with Parisians, many of whom have second homes in the country.

On the southern part of the coast, much of Vendée is flat and windy (its symbol is a windmill). The *département* has a dark history of mass slaughter during the religious and revolutionary wars, but now the land is smiling, with its almost endless beaches, seaside resorts and fishing villages and a soft and sunny climate which encourages mimosa.

POITOU-CHARENTES

The Poitou-Charentes region is almost completely unspoiled with virtually no industry and is one of the most tranquil in France. Its long Atlantic coastline is noted for endless, sandy beaches, marinas, golf courses and islands, which make it an ideal summer holiday destination. Two large islands, the Ile de Ré and the Ile d'Oléron, with their pine-shaded beaches and superb shellfish, were connected by road bridges to the mainland a generation ago and have seen their populations grow rapidly as a result; camp sites have also proliferated. No cars are allowed on the smaller island of Aix, where Napoleon spent his last night in France before leaving for Saint-Helena. The marshes along the estuary of the Seudre have been converted into oyster beds with lines of thick wooden posts, on which mussels are also farmed.

Inland, the landscape is flat, particularly in Charente, and the land is used for mixed farming and livestock breeding, as well as for vineyards from which the wines are used to distil cognac. The region is crossed by the medieval

routes used by pilgrims on their way to the shrine of Saint James at Compostella in Spain, a practice which is currently being revived. These routes were also used by the stone masons who built the region's many Romanesque churches, such as Saint Pierre at Aulnay (17). Other notable monuments include the 15th century church tower built by the English at Marennes (79), the fourth century baptistery in Poitiers (86)and the collection of 11th century frescos in the church at Saint-Savin (86). There are numerous places of historical interest, including the fortified town of Brouage, abandoned as a port when the sea receded, the 17th century naval port of Rochefort which replaced it, and the Vieux Port at La Rochelle (all in 17). In contrast, present-day attractions include Futuroscope near Poitiers and what is reputed to be France's best zoo at La Palmyre (see **Leisure** on page 124).

PROPERTY CHECK – POITOU-CHARENTES

Prices in Poitou-Charentes levelled out in 2005 and have fallen by 15 per cent. The new A28 motorway and increasing numbers of flights from UK airports to the region have made it easier for house hunters to visit. Prices are unlikely to increase much in the short term, **€50,000** being the average price for a barn and **€250,000** the average for a fully renovated four-bedroom farmhouse with land and outbuildings.

Papillon Properties (UK ☎ 01799 527809, 💻 www.papillon-properties.com)

Poitou-Charentes is a popular region with tourists, holiday homeowners and retirees, particularly British property buyers, many of whom favour the area around Cognac (16) and Saintes (17). There's a huge difference between the cost of property on the coast and inland, where homes are good value.

ADVANTAGES & DISADVANTAGES

The area generally enjoys a pleasant climate and a healthy lifestyle (both Pays-de-la-Loire and Poitou-Charentes enjoy lower mortality rates than most other regions of France). The Atlantic coast of Charente-Maritime in particular has an excellent micro-climate and is noted for its long hot summers and mild winters, although it can be very cold inland. The west coast boasts almost 30 resorts with 'blue flag' beaches and eight blue flag ports (see 💻 www.pavillonbleu.com), although there were also a few 'black flag' beaches – one at La Rochelle, two at Fouras and one at Aytré (17), one at Batz-sur-Mer near Le Pouliguen (44) and one on the Ile d'Yeu (85) – according to the Surfrider Foundation Europe, which draws attention to what it considers to be unacceptable levels of pollution (see 💻 www.surfrider-europe.org). La Rochelle (17) has the unusual distinction of having more cycle tracks per inhabitant than any other major town in France, as well as plenty of green space (over 53m² per inhabitant). Angoulême (16), Le Mans (72) and La Roche-sur-Yon (85) are even greener but the prize for urban open space goes to Cholet (49) with almost 100m² per inhabitant.

Homes can also be found in charming villages and countryside, although properties in coastal areas and close to the large towns can command high prices and those in Vendée are currently rising by 30 per cent per year. The road system is good, however, so it's possible to live inland and travel to the beach for the day. On the other hand, prices rise again as you approach Paris, and parts of Sarthe and northern Mayenne are very popular with Parisians for weekend and holiday homes. If you're planning to buy a rural home, learning to speak French is essential if you want to establish a satisfactory social life.

Those wishing to settle into rural houses in the area and who cannot speak French should be warned that they may well fail to establish a satisfactory social life or new friends through English-speaking associations.

Those wanting to set up a bed and breakfast or *gîte* business should note that, while there's demand among holidaymakers (increasing by around 5 per cent annually in the case of *gîtes*), it tends to be at the 'luxury' end of the market, and traditional 'rustic' *gîtes* are no longer popular. While a pool is undoubtedly a plus, it isn't essential, as an increasing number of holidaymakers visit out of season. Occupancy rates in properties owned by Gîtes de France association members average over 30 weeks in some parts.

Access by air is restricted (only two airports offer flights from the UK, for example) and there are no ferry services to the west coast, but the area is well served by the *TGV* and road access to Poitou-Charentes is good via the A10 motorway from Paris, although it doesn't run through the *département* of Charente.

There's a nuclear power station in the area, south-east of Poitiers near Lussac-les-Châteaux (86), and another nearby – on the south bank of the Loire in the Parc naturel régional Loire-Anjou-Touraine near Avoine in the western part of Indre-et-Loire (37), around 10km (6mi) north-east of Fontevraud. Also, by 2010 there will be a 400,000 volt powerline carried by 50m-high pylons running from Flamanville at the tip of the Cotentin peninsula through western Manche and into northern Mayenne.

MAJOR TOWNS & PLACES OF INTEREST

Charente (16)

The departmental capital Angoulême (pop. 43,000) is dominated by the old town within its ramparts, which you can walk right around on foot (it's also used each September as the circuit for a vintage car race). The town has a splendid (although clumsily restored) Romanesque cathedral and is home to the Centre national de la Bande dessinée et de l'Image (National Cartoon and Illustration Centre), where you can find well known cartoon characters such as Astérix, Tintin and Flash Gordon, as well as to the Musée du Papier, celebrating the area's tradition of paper-making.

PROPERTY CHECK – ANGOULEME

Just over two hours from Paris on the *TGV*, the capital of Charente is a chic but relaxed town, with beautiful period properties (many decorated with elaborate *trompe l'oeil* paintings) within its ramparts. A habitable three-bedroom townhouse with a garden and garage can be had for as little as €175,000 and a four-bedroom house, also with a garage and garden, not much over €200,000. The town offers good investment opportunities, not only in letting homes (for between €300 and €800 per month) but in renting out garages, which can be bought for less than €10,000 and let for €50 per month.

LGH France (🖳 www.lghfrance.com)

Cognac (pop. 19,500) gives its name to France's best-loved brandy and houses the distilleries of Hennesy, Martell and Rémy Martin, among others. (Many of the town's older buildings are covered by a black fungus which lives on the fumes of distillation!) The town is sited on the Charente river, which is navigable as far as the estuary beyond Rochefort (17) and offers idyllic boat trips and boating holidays.

Charente-Maritime (17)

The departmental capital La Rochelle (pop. 80,000) became an important port in the Middle Ages, especially under the Protestant Huguenots, who developed trade with Africa and North and South America. There was much commerce with Quebec, and the huge paving slabs in the old town were brought back from there as ballast in sailing ships. The old town survives virtually unchanged, alongside the Vieux Port with its many seafood restaurants and cafés, although the city has become an important industrial centre – high-speed trains are constructed here. To the west is the modern port of La Pallice.

Rochefort (pop. 25,800) is another port, built by Colbert in the 17th century and with many elements of the original docks still intact, although they've recently been abandoned by the French navy. The 375 metre-long royal rope-winding works are now a museum and international maritime centre. Behind the river front lies the town Colbert built, a little austere but with considerable charm, faithfully depicted by composer Michel Legrand in his musical film *Les Demoiselles de Rochefort*.

South of Rochefort and around 15km (9mi) into the flat marshland is Brouage, a medieval village later fortified by Vauban whose ramparts have survived in good condition. As the sea receded, its harbour became unusable and the naval port was moved to Rochefort. Brouage attracts many Canadian visitors, because it was the birthplace of Samuel de Champlain, the Protestant navigator who founded Quebec. South of Rochefort, at the mouth of the Gironde, lies Royan (17,000), almost totally destroyed by Allied bombs before its eventual liberation in April 1945 and rebuilt in the worst possible 'new-town' style. In July and August the town overflows with tourists and is best avoided.

PROPERTY CHECK – CHARENTE-MARITIME

Demand for property in this *département* has caused prices to rise considerably, though increases have been lowest in the higher price brackets (i.e. over around €500,000) and property inland is considerably cheaper than on the coast; just half an hour's drive can make a significant difference to prices. Popular areas include those around Saint-Jean-d'Angély (a busy town of around 8,000 inhabitants) and Mirambeau, while Montendre is cheaper though just as attractive.. Properties for restoration are now few and far between, though there are plenty that were renovated 20 or more years ago and are in need of 'refreshment'. You may be lucky and find an unconverted barn or dilapidated house for around €50,000. For a well renovated property, you must allow at least

€150,000, and even a modest three-bedroom property can cost €300,000. For a *Charentaise* (see page 135), you must pay at least €400,000 – up to twice as much for one in tip-top condition. Some have *pigeonniers* that can be converted into accommodation. Fishermen's cottages are popular and can be pretty but are usually small, with a maximum of three bedrooms; as they're inevitably on the coast, they can also be expensive.

La Foncière Charentaise (🖳 www.aiguillonimmobilier.com); Jacwood Estates French Properties (UK ☎ 01926-883714, 🖳 www.jacwoodestates.co.uk)

Just to the north-west of Royan are the smaller coastal resorts of Pontaillac and Saint-Palais-sur-Mer, which were undamaged in the war and have kept their character. Inland, the town of Saintes (25,600) was the region's capital in Roman times and retains a Roman arch on the east bank of the Charente and the remains of a 20,000-seat arena. The Abbaye aux Dames was consecrated in 1047 and became an important Benedictine nunnery. Pons (4,450), south of Saintes, was on the route taken by pilgrims on their way to Compostella in northern Spain. The 12th century hospice built for them has been classified by UNESCO as a 'European Historic Monument', as has the stone vault which spans the road outside, where pilgrims could sleep under cover if they arrived after the hospice had closed for the night. Pons is dominated by 30m (100ft) high ramparts, from whose roof there are fine views of the town and the surrounding picturesque countryside.

Still further south is Jonzac (4,200), a small market town well placed for exploring La Haute Saintonge, an area of rolling landscapes quite different from the *département*'s coastal plain. Les Antilles leisure centre (the French name for the Caribbean islands) has many facilities, such as shops, restaurant, health club and a fake Martinique village, all surrounding a huge covered swimming pool, which has an outdoor extension in summer adjoining the beach.

Loire-Atlantique (44)

Nantes (pop. 270,000), the departmental and regional capital, claims to be the most rapidly developing city in France, with a conurbation of over half a million people, France's largest refinery and fourth-largest port, a university, and modern industries such as electronics and aviation. Situated astride the Loire, the town was the capital of Brittany until the revolution and still has the castle that belonged to the Dukes of Brittany, although it isn't open to visitors. One of the city's most famous sons is Jules Verne, the first great science fiction writer and author of *Around the World in 80 Days* among many other novels. Around the Sainte Croix church is the medieval town, with narrow streets and timber-framed houses, and to the west, the elegant shopping arcade known as La Passage Pommeraye.

To the west, at the mouth of the Loire, Saint-Nazaire (pop. 65,000) is essentially a ship-building town, which started to develop when Scotsman John Scott started the first yard in 1862. Giant liners such as the *Normandie*, the *France* and the largest ever cruise ship, the *Queen Mary*, were built there. The town also boasts a vast factory, used to build part of the fuselages of the Airbus A380. A few miles west of Saint-Nazaire is the small resort of Saint-Marc where Jacques Tati shot his classic comedy *Les Vacances de Monsieur Hulot*.

South of Saint-Nazaire is Pornic (pop. 12,000), a fishing village that has become a popular seaside resort, once frequented by Auguste Renoir and Gustave Flaubert and now overcrowded during July and August. West of Saint-Nazaire, La Baule-Escoublac (44,500), the west coast's answer to Saint-Tropez, is a resort created in the 19th century when the railway was built (the original station has been magnificently restored); thanks to the *TGV* service, it's now less than three hours from Paris. Along the whole of the gently curved beach (reckoned by some to be the finest in Europe) and promenade, on which beach babes compete for attention, is a 'cliff' of modern apartments costing up to half a million euros each. Behind them and among the pine trees are many large 19th and early 20th century villas.

PROPERTY CHECK – LOIRE-ATLANTIQUE

With its thriving capital, Nantes, splendid beaches and pleasant climate, the Loire-Atlantique *département* has a lot going for it – as many foreign (and French) buyers have discovered. It's still possible to find a habitable property for under €100,000 and extensive renovation projects for less than €150,000, while around €250,000 can buy a four-bedroom house; a villa near La Baule costs from around €400,000. Other resorts, such as Le Croisic, Le Pouliguen and Saint-Marc, are less pricey, as are the relatively undiscovered ports on the Loire estuary, including Paimboeuf, where a substantial fisherman's house can be bought for around €150,000. Even large properties are often reasonably priced outside the most popular areas – for example an eight bedroom house for just €350,000 – where a more modest, three-bedroom property can cost as little as €175,000.

Loire-Atlantique's most popular *département* is Vendée, where prices are inevitably higher than average. Even a barn for restoration can cost €100,000, while a property with bed and breakfast potential can be in excess of €300,000.

Maine-et-Loire (49)

The departmental capital Angers (pop. 156,300), on the south bank of the river Maine near its confluence with the Loire, dates from Roman times and became the home of the Dukes of Anjou. One of them, Geoffrey V, used to wear a sprig of broom (*genêt*) in his headgear, and the family became known as the Plantagenets. The *château* became the home of Henry II of England, his wife Eleanor of Aquitaine, and sons Richard the Lionheart and King John; it was later given an immense outer wall, by Louis IX, which still stands, dominating the old town. In a specially built gallery is the rich and colourful 14th-century Apocalypse tapestry, over 100m (330ft) long and 6m (20ft) high. Nearby, in the old town, is the 12th and 13th century cathedral, with superb period stained glass.

Cholet (pop. 55,100), south-west of Angers, is a pleasant town which was almost completely destroyed during the savage civil war in 1793–94 between the royalists and the republicans, when Cholet was burnt and its inhabitants massacred. The traditional industry of weaving is celebrated in the textile museum, and the surrounding region, called the *Mauges*, is delightful countryside, with hedges and trees, lakes, *châteaux* and their parks.

Saumur (30,500), east of Angers and Cholet, boasts a *château* dominating the town from the south bank of the Loire and has changed little since it was rebuilt in the 14th century. In the 18th century, the Marquis de Sade was locked away in Saumur's prison, which now houses three museums. The famous Saumur cavalry school moved to the town before the revolution, and in June 1940 some 800 under-equipped trainee officers put up a sustained resistance to the advancing German army. The area around Saumur is well known, of course, for its wines – less so for mushrooms, around 200,000 tonnes of which are produced each year in the 800km (500mi) of galleries in the cliffs along the river valley, which were originally stone quarries.

Mayenne (53)

The most northerly *département* in this area has Laval (pop. 50,700) as its capital. The town's castle was built in the 11th century and is claimed to be unique in France for having retained all its original defences. Around the castle are ancient houses. One of them was the birthplace of the primitive painter Douanier Rousseau, and the castle itself now houses a museum of naïve art. The Port-Salut Abbey is 7km (4mi) south of the town at Entrammes, where the 13th century monastic church sells various produce but no longer the famous Port Salut cheese.

The town of Mayenne (pop. 13,600), with its traditional industry of weaving furnishing fabrics, is of limited interest, although it's surrounded by attractive countryside. The Mayenne river has once again become navigable and its restored tow path offers a perfect cycle track 85km (53mi) long. There are Roman remains and an archaeological museum at nearby Jublains.

PROPERTY CHECK – MAYENNE

Often regarded merely as a *département* for passing through on the way to somewhere else, Mayenne has a quiet charm and is ideal for those seeking an away-from-it-all rural retreat – though a new motorway from Rouen has made the area more accessible and British buyers are beginning to 'colonise' northern parts, including Domfront, Lassay-les-Châteaux and Pré-en-Pail. There's a variety of property, including attractive grey-stone cottages, and prices are on average 20 to 30 per cent lower than in neighbouring *départements*. There are also still plenty of old properties in need of restoration, costing as little as €40,000, while a fully restored cottage can be had for under €100,000 and a four-bedroom farmhouse for around €250,000.

Mayenne Properties (www.mayenne-properties.com)

Sarthe (72)

The departmental capital Le Mans (pop. 146,000) is perhaps best known for its 24-hour car race. (In fact, there are several 24-hour races: one for motorbikes in April and one for heavy vehicles in October as well as races for different types of cars in May.) The circuit is south of the town, between the N138 and the D139, and at its northern end is the Sarthe Automobile Museum. Le Mans' cathedral (where Geoffrey Plantagenet married William the Conqueror's granddaughter Mathilda) is a magnificent example of the French Gothic style, with its array of flying buttresses, and the interior is enriched with 16th century tapestries and 13th century stained glass windows. The unspoilt old town with its many historic houses boasts a wide choice of shops and restaurants.

Le Mans is situated on the river Sarthe, which gives its name to the *département* as well as to the town of Sablé-sur-Sarthe (pop. 12,500), where there are many 18th and 19th century houses. The town's *château*, built by the Colbert family, is now used by the national library as an annexe for book repair and rebinding. There are river cruises on the Sarthe and the charming countryside around the town is worth exploring.

Deux-Sèvres (79)

Niort (pop. 59,500), the departmental capital, was a Roman town which prospered under the Plantagenets, who granted the town a charter and built a castle, completed by Richard the Lionheart. The outer defence wall has been demolished, but the massive dungeon stands proudly overlooking the town and the Sèvre Niortaise river below. In the 18th century, Niort specialised in tanning skins from Canada to make top quality chamois leather for gloves (as well as breeches for Napoleon's *Grande Armée*!). The town specialises in angelica, which is sold not only candied but also as *crème* and *liqueur d'angélique*. More significantly, Niort has attracted several mutual insurance companies since 1945, which have enlivened its economy.

Bressuire (pop. 19,300) was sacked by the Protestants during the religious wars, and again by the Republicans in 1793, but is now famous for its major cattle markets and for France's only school for meat trade professionals. It's the centre of rich and picturesque countryside, known as the *bocage bressuirais*, used for cattle breeding and rearing. In many ways, the landscape is similar to that of the Dordogne (but you won't find *The Daily Telegraph* on sale here!).

Melle (4,000), south-east of Niort, is a green and florally decorated town that hides its origins as a centre for lead and silver mining (the royal silver mine and its tenth-century garden can be visited in summer) and for minting coins. The town was also once famous for mule breeding. Melle was on one of the main routes used by pilgrims heading for Compostella in Spain, who were welcomed in the church of Saint Hilaire, a superb example of the region's version of Romanesque and designated a UNESCO world heritage site.

Parthenay (10,500), north of Niort, was founded in 1020 on an outcrop of rock above the Thouet river, and the medieval town has kept its character. It also became an important staging town for pilgrims on their way to Compostella. It was for them that a local priest, Aimeri Picaud, wrote what is probably the world's oldest surviving guide book, the *Guide du Pèlerin*, indicating the best routes to take and the best places to eat, pray and find lodgings.

Vendée (85)

La Roche-sur-Yon (pop. 46,000), the departmental capital, was just a village until the Vendée *département* was created after the revolution and the village's central location prompted Napoleon to turn it into the prefecture (the event is celebrated by his equestrian statue in the Place Napoléon). Horse lovers may be interested in the local stud, one of France's largest, but otherwise there's little to interest visitors. Perhaps because of this, the town earns a top rating as a good place to live (see **Appendix F**).

Les Herbiers (pop. 14,000), north-east of La Roche, is a busy industrial town. It's an excellent centre for touring Vendée's picturesque *haut bocage*. Around 10km (6mi) north-east of the town is one of France's major theme parks, Le Puy-du-Fou (see **Leisure** on page 124).

Les Sables-d'Olonne (15,500), south-west of La Roche, was once a whaling and fishing port, but the town benefited from the fashion for sea bathing, which arrived from England at the end of the Napoleonic wars, and the later arrival of the railway from Nantes, which brought middle-class visitors. A separate port for pleasure craft, Port-Olona, providing over 1,000 berths, was built in the '60s and the town is now Vendée's chicest resort (and the finishing point of the Vendée-Globe single-handed round-the-world yacht race): its population is reckoned to increase in July and August to over 100,000 – you have been warned! Around 20km (13mi) east of Les Sables-d'Olonne is the pretty village of Jard-sur-Mer with its picturesque harbour, lovely beaches and delightful cliff-top walks through forests.

Other places of interest in Vendée include Apremont near Aizenay, a picturesque village clinging to the rocky sides of the Vie valley with the largest lake in Vendée (it even has a sandy beach); Mareuil-sur-Lay near Luçon, an attractive wine-producing town; Port-du-Bec near Beauvoir-sur-Mer on the Bay of Bourgneuf, nicknamed the 'Chinese port'; Sallertaine near Challans, a delightful village on the canals and popular with artists and craftspeople whose exhibitions are staged in the 12th-century church; Vouvant near La Châtaigneraie, one of France's most beautiful villages; and the area around the villages of Avrillé and Le Bernard, near Jard-sur-Mer, which is dotted with prehistoric stones.

Vienne (86)

Poitiers (pop. 83,500) is the departmental and regional capital and boasts France's oldest Christian building, the Saint Jean baptistery, built in the middle of the fourth century and full of archaeological relics. The town boasts some of France's finest examples of Romanesque architecture, especially Notre Dame la Grande. About 8km (5mi) north of the town is Futuroscope, France's scientific theme park (see **Leisure** on page 124). The village of Saint-Savin, around 40km (25mi) east of Poitiers, is world famous for the 11th century wall and ceiling paintings in its church, which Malraux described as "the Sistine chapel of Romanesque art".

North of Poitiers is Châtellerault (pop. 34,000), a charming town with tree-lined avenues and the imposing Henry IV bridge, built four centuries ago, which crosses the river Vienne. Across it is the Manu, a disused arms factory now a culture and leisure centre, and a museum of cars and motorbikes. To the north-west is Loudun (7,700), best known for the devils which are believed to have possessed the residents of the local nunnery. The priest found responsible for the sorcery was tortured and then burnt to death in 1634 in the main square of the town. (The story in full and repulsive detail is told by Aldous Huxley in *The Devils of Loudun*). The square tower which dominates the town was built in 1040 and offers splendid views from the top. Vienne also contains one of France's most beautiful villages, Angles-sur-l'Anglin.

Le Marais Poitevin

Known as the *marais desséché* (drained marshes), the Poitevin Marsh was recovered from the sea by Benedictine and Cistercian monks who saw it as an opportunity to create wealth, by digging drainage channels and building up dykes. In the 17th century, Dutch engineers were brought in, and by the time of the revolution the greater part of the area had been drained. The eastern part of the Marsh is subject to flooding at exceptional tides and after heavy rain. Although uniformly flat, it's picturesque, with canals running under arcades of willow, white poplar, ash and alder, market gardens on isolated and fertile plots, producing globe artichokes, onions, melons and courgettes, and fields for cereals and for grazing cattle and sheep. A 70,000ha (170,000 acre) area of the Marsh, now a regional park, has been dubbed '*La Venise verte*' ('Green Venice') and attracts many visitors, who take boat trips from points such as Arçais and Coulon on the Sèvre Niortaise river (79).

PROPERTY CHECK – MARAIS POITEVIN

The picturesque marshes are popular with both holidaymakers and property buyers. Just half an hour from the coast and near the attractive town of Niort, this haven of tranquillity is understandably sought after, and there's little to be had for under €150,000. The areas around Arçais and Coulon are particularly appealing, the former postcard-pretty and the latter at the centre of the so-called Venetian villages, though they become crowded in summer and nearby La Garette and Le Vanneau are quieter but no less picturesque. For a well renovated fisherman's cottage, expect to pay at least €175,000 and for a substantial property with land over €200,000; homes with a river or canal frontage not surprisingly attract a hefty premium.

Papillon Properties (🖳 www.papillon-properties.com)

POPULATION

Poitou-Charentes has a population of just over 1.7m (population density is just 63.5 people per km^2), whereas Pays-de-la-Loire, which is less than 30 per cent larger, has almost exactly twice as many inhabitants (3.4m – over 100 people per km^2). Pays-de-la-Loire's population is growing faster than the average for France (by 0.89 per cent annually compared with 0.66 per cent), especially in the two coastal *départements* of Loire-Atlantique (pop. 1.2m) and Vendée (587.000). Nantes (44) has the second-fastest-growing population of any major town in France (after Vannes in Brittany), and that of La Roche-sur-Yon (85) is also growing rapidly. The *départements* of Maine-et-Loire (755,000), Mayenne (298,000) and Sarthe (552,000) have around average growth.

The population of Poitou-Charentes, on the other hand, is growing at slightly below the national average rate. The *départements* of Charente (344,000) and Deux-Sèvres (352,000) have declining populations, while those of Vienne (416,000) and Charente-Maritime (593,000) are growing, the latter especially in the coastal area, where many French people choose to retire; inland, the *département* is in decline, both in population and in its economy. Poitiers (86) has a higher proportion of students among its population (32 per cent) than any town in France. Elsewhere, a dearth of young people is due largely to a lack of entry-level jobs.

The population of Pays-de-la-Loire includes 56,000 foreigners, of which 9,800 are Moroccan, 9,650 Portuguese, 6,150 Algerian and 4,380 Turkish.

There are around 1,500 foreign-owned holiday homes in Vendée and around 1,250 in Mayenne, the vast majority (some 95 per cent) owned by Britons; in Loire-Atlantique and Sarthe, on the other hand, fewer than half of non-French holiday homes are British-owned.

The population of Poitou-Charentes includes almost 40,000 foreign nationals, of which 11,600 are British, 8,300 Portuguese, 2,900 Moroccan, 1,650 Algerian and 1,150 Spanish. At least 15,000 of these have arrived in the last five years, although the percentage of immigrants in the region is still well below the national average (3.1 per cent compared with 8.1 per cent). Most of the new arrivals are Europeans and most of these British, who since the turn of the century have overtaken the Portuguese as the most numerous immigrant group and now constitute almost 10 per cent of the total number of Britons in France and the highest number after Ile-de-France (16 per cent of the total). However, 30 per cent of British residents are over 60 years old and 55 per cent over 50, which has exacerbated the 'greying' of the region. The British population is concentrated in the centre of the region, i.e. an area including south-eastern Deux-Sèvres, north-eastern Charente-Maritime, southern Vienne and northern Charente, though there are also large numbers along the border with Dordogne.

CLIMATE

The coastal *départements*, Charente-Maritime, Loire-Atlantique and Vendée enjoy a maritime climate, with mild winters. With the predominating westerly winds, clouds tend only to form some distance inland. As a result, the coastal resorts have relatively high hours of sunshine per year, almost as high as on the Côte d'Azur. The other *départements* inland have a less pronounced maritime climate, but still with mild winters and usually temperate summers. In Charente-Maritime, rainfall is lowest in July (around 35mm), rising progressively to 95mm in November. Deux-Sèvres has a similar rainfall pattern but Charente is drier in winter (88mm per month) and wetter in summer (46mm in July), while Vienne has around 70mm in December and just 40mm in August.

Vendée, in Pays-de-la-Loire, is said to have its own micro-climate, although average temperatures and rainfall are in fact similar to those throughout the region, with 110mm of rain in November and 40mm in August. Loire-Atlantique's wettest month is December (90mm), while Maine-et-Loire, Mayenne and Sarthe are drier, with just 70mm in December.

The Loire is considered to be the dividing line between the colder regions of northern France and the warmer south, although the change is gradual. An important feature of the coastal areas is the impact of winter storms, which are sometimes severe, with winds driven at up to 150km/h (90mph).

Houses and apartments with picture windows facing west, which may be delightful in summer, can be a nightmare in a winter gale, with powerful draughts letting in whistling winds and jets of rainwater.

Temperatures average around 26C (79F) in July and 10C (50F) in December and January. The table below shows the number of hours' sunshine and number of days' rainfall in selected towns in the area.

Town	Sunshine Hours	Days' Rainfall
Angoulême (16)	2,025	118
La Rochelle (17)	2,250	115
Nantes (44)	1,956	118
Angers (49)	1,944	108
Laval (53)	1,622	117
Le Mans (72)	1,825	114
Niort (79)	1,934	121
La Roche-sur-Yon (85)	1,956	113
Poitiers (86)	1,930	113

CRIME RATE & SECURITY

Both Poitou-Charentes, at 43 reported crimes per thousand population, and Pays-de-la-Loire, at 44, are well below the national average crime rate of 61 crimes per thousand. In terms of individual towns, La Rochelle has the highest crime rate of any in the area, with over 130 reported crimes per thousand inhabitants per year (the sixth highest crime rate of any major town in France). This is probably associated with an unusually high rate of drug addiction, especially among summer visitors. The crime rate in most other towns in the area is little more than half that of La Rochelle, the lowest rates being found in Cholet (49), followed by Saint-Nazaire (44), Laval (53) and Angoulême (16). (Saint-Nazaire is also one of the safest towns in France in terms of the road accident rate.) Le Mans (72), La Roche-sur-Yon (85), Nantes (44) and particularly Agen (47) have rather higher crime rates. Rates in rural areas are generally lower, but as in other areas of France, isolated houses left unoccupied for long periods can be prey to bogus removal men, who break in and take away the entire contents, sometimes even including items such as fitted cupboards and fireplaces.

AMENITIES

Sports

The regions offer a variety of sports facilities, including the Vendée Cricket Club and the following:

Boating

There are many marinas on the west coast, including those at Ars-en-Ré, Boyardville, La Rochelle, Rochefort, Royan, Saint-Georges-d'Oleron, Saint-Martin-de-Ré (17), Le Croisic, Pornichet, Pornic (44), L'Epine, Jard-sur-Mer, Les Sables-d'Olonne and Saint-Gilles-Croix-de-Vie (85). France is reported to have 150,000 more yachts and motor boats than berths, and on the Atlantic coast some marinas have long waiting lists (parents are putting down their children's names soon after birth in the hope that they can obtain a mooring by the time they're 18!), so you shouldn't expect to be able to rent one immediately.

Many resorts have sailing schools, for all ages, and the larger schools organise regular regattas. For further information, contact the Fédération française de Voile (17 rue Henri Bocquillon, 75015 Paris, ☎ 01 40 60 37 00, 💻 www.ffvoile.net), in Pays-de-la-Loire, Y. Rousse, 44 rue Romain Rolland, BP 90312, 44103 Nantes Cedex 4 (☎ 02 40 58 61 23) or in Poitou-Charentes J-L Staub, Môle central des Minimes, avenue de la Capitainerie, 17000 La Rochelle (☎ 05 46 44 58 31).

Those who prefer to sail on dry land can try their hand at sand-yachting. At low tide, the long stretches of sand on the Charente-Maritime and Vendée coasts are ideal for this sport, which uses three-wheeled, sail-powered 'karts' reaching speeds of 120kph (75mph) – three times the speed of the wind that drives them! Several clubs in the region offer classes, and details of clubs and sand-yacht builders are available from the Fédération française de Char à Voile (17 rue Henri Bocquillon, 75015 Paris, ☎ 01 45 58 75 76, 💻 www.ffcv.org). In Pays-de-la-Loire, contact the Maison des Sports, BP 167, 85000 La Roche-sur-Yon.

A more leisurely boating activity is offered in the *Marais Poitevin*, where it's possible to hire flat-bottomed boats and paddle around the maze of tiny canals.

Surfing

There's excellent surfing along the west coast, particularly in Vendée, where the best surfing beaches include those of Saint-Gilles-Croix-de-Vie, La Sauzaie, Les Dunes, Sauveterre, L'Aubraie, La Baie des Sables, Tanchet, Le Port de Bourgenay, Saint-Nicolas, Saint-Vincent-sur-Jard, Les Conches, La Terrière, La Pointe du Groin, L'Embarcadère and the unlikely sounding Bud-Bud and Le Coin à Fred.

Cycling

Much of the area is ideal for cycling, with only the gentlest of slopes to climb most of the time. There are many areas to explore, such as the *Marais Poitevin*, the Loire river banks between Angers and Nantes, and the 85km-long tow path of the Mayenne river. The tourist office in Laval (53) has a useful map of the river, which gives addresses of places to eat, sleep or camp, plus places to visit *en route*. Other guides and maps are available from departmental tourist offices (see page 141), which can also supply lists of bicycle hire companies. Further information for Pays-de-la-Loire is available from the Ligue régionale de Cyclotourisme, 6 allée des Tilleuls, 49360 Toutlemonde (☎ 05 49 68 00 62).

Horse Riding

The area offers hundreds of miles of bridle paths, across the *bocage*, through woodlands and along river banks. Along some routes, overnight accommodation is available in *gîtes*. Further information is available from the Comité national de Tourisme équestre (9 boulevard MacDonald, 75019 Paris, ☎ 01 53 26 15 50, 💻 www.tourisme-equestre.fr), which publishes an annual brochure listing riding facilities by region and by *département*. Local and departmental tourist offices also have information (see page 141).

Golf

There are around 40 golf courses in the west of France, the majority in Pays-de-la-Loire, including five near Nantes (44) and three each near Angers (49) and Sables-d'Olonne (85). The table below lists the number of courses in each *département*. Information (in both French and English) on how to find courses, the cost of a round (which varies between €15 and €50), etc. is available via the internet (💻 www.backspin.com). Another useful website for golfers is 💻 www.golf.com.fr.

Département	**No. of Courses**
Charente	1 x 9 holes, 2 x 18 holes
Charente-Maritime	2 x 9 holes, 3 x 18 holes
Loire-Atlantique	6 x 18 holes, 1 x 45 holes
Maine-et-Loire	1 x 9 holes, 4 x 18 holes
Mayenne	1 x 18 holes
Sarthe	2 x 18 holes, 1 x 27 holes
Deux-Sèvres	2 x 18 holes, 1 x 27 holes
Vendée	4 x 18 holes
Vienne	1 x 9 holes, 3 x 18 holes, 1 x 27 holes

Leisure

The following is a selection of the many leisure facilities in Poitou-Charentes and Pays-de-la-Loire.

English-language Cinema & Theatre

There are several cinemas in Pays-de-la-Loire which show films in their original language (*version originale/VO*); there are four in Nantes alone. On the other hand, Poitou-Charentes is something of a desert for English-language films, as can be seen from the list of cinemas showing *VO* films below. A useful website for finding out what films are on in a given area, which also indicates whether the films are being shown in the original language is 💻 www.cinefil.com.

- Nantes (44) – Cinématographie (occasionally), Concorde (regularly), Katorza (regularly) and UGC Apollo (regularly);
- Saint-Herblain (44) – UBC Ciné Atlantis (occasionally);
- Saint-Nazaire (44) – Cinéville (occasionally);
- Angers (49) – Les 400 Coups (regularly);
- Saumur (49) – Le Palace (occasionally);

- Laval (53) – Cinéville (occasionally);
- Le Mans (72) – Ciné Poche (regularly);
- Thouars (79) – Le Familia (occasionally).

Festivals

As in other parts of France, there are many regional, departmental and local festivals, notably the International Folk Festival in Montguyon (17) in July. Angoulême (16) calls itself the 'City of Festivals', and among the many events that take place there is an international cartoon show in January, which attracts some 100,000 people (it's fifth largest show of any kind in France). With some 3,000 students, Angoulême also boasts the liveliest nightlife in the area.

Museums & Galleries

There are numerous museums, galleries and other places of interest in both regions, including the following: in Poitou-Charentes, the Centre national de la Bande dessinée et de l'Image and the Musée du Papier in Angoulême; the cognac museum in Cognac (16), where it's also possible to visit the major distilleries (e.g. Camus, Hennessy, Martell and Rémy Martin); the natural history and automata museums in La Rochelle; the naval museum, International Maritime Centre and a unique collection of begonias (the plant was named after a local admiral named Michel Bégon) in Rochefort; historical museums in Royan (17), Niort and Poitiers; the motorbike and bicycle museum in Châtellerault; and the Maison des Marais mouillés near Coulon (86), which shows how the marshes were developed. In Pays-de-la-Loire, options include the Musée des Beaux-Arts, which houses a fine collection of French paintings, and the Jules Verne Museum in Nantes; the Ecomuseum in Saint-Nazaire (44); the Apocalypse Tapestry (see page 114), modern tapestry museum, David Museum (celebrating the native sculptor Pierre Jean David), and Pinée Museum (with a rich collection of ancient art) in Angers; the Tank Museum (which claims to house the world's largest collection of armoured vehicles) in Saumur (49); the Tessé Museum of art and the motor museum in Le Mans; and the unmissable Amusant Musée in Juigné-sur-Sarthe (72), which houses a collection of amusing, bizarre and above all useless gadgets!

Theme Parks

The area boasts a variety of attractions, including the following:

- Les Antilles in Jonzac (17): leisure centre with pool, fitness centre, shops, a fake West Indies village, and a summer outdoor pool by the beach;
- Aquarium de la Rochelle (17): sea life centre featuring sharks;
- Arche de Noé in Saint-Clément-des-Baleines (17): rare parrots;
- Atlantic Toboggan in Saint-Hilaire-de-Riez (85): water park;
- Château de Barbe-Bleue in Tiffauges (85): Bluebeard's castle – museum, *château* and theme park;
- Domaine animalier de Pescheray in Le Breil-sur-Mérize (72): wildlife park surrounding a 16th–19th century *château*;
- Domaine de la Petite Couère in Chatelais (49): reconstruction of a 1900 village;
- Labyrinthus in Gémozac near Cravans (17): mazes;
- Le Futuroscope Jaunay-Clan near Poitiers (86): everything to do with the future – France's third most popular theme park, attracting over 1.5m visitors annually;
- L'Ile aux Serpents in La Trimouille (86): snakes and other reptiles;
- Le Jardin des Oiseaux in Spay (72): 600 birds;
- Océanile in L'Epine (85): open-air water park;
- Océarium du Croisic in Le Croisic (44): Atlantic marine life;
- Papea City near Yvre-l'Evêque (72): amusement park;
- Parc d'Attractions des Naudières in Sautron (44): amusement park;
- Parc d'Attractions de Pierre Brune in Mervent (85): amusement park in the Mervent forest;
- Parc oriental in Maulevrier (49): Europe's largest Japanese garden;
- Parc zoologique in La Boissière-du-Dore (44): 500 animals;
- Planète sauvage in Port-Saint-Père (44): 'African' safari park;
- Le Puy du Fou in Les Epesses (85): spectacular displays of chariots, gladiators and marauding Vikings in a 6,000-seat Gallo-Roman amphitheatre – France's fourth most popular theme park with a million visitors per year. On Saturday evenings in summer, there's a mammoth spectacle, La Cinéscénie, which tells the story of the region, with lights,

fireworks and special effects in front of 10,000 spectators – reckoned to be the greatest sound-and-light show in Europe;

- Sealand in Noirmoutier (85): sea life, including sharks and seals;
- La Vallée des Singes in Romagne (86): ape and monkey park;
- Zoo de Doué-la-Fontaine (49): 500 animals;
- Zoo de la Flèche (72): 150 animals;
- Zoo de la Palmyre in Les Mathes (17): 1,600 animals in 'natural' environment – claims to be France's leading zoo;
- Zoo des Sables-d'Olonne (85): 200 animals;
- Zoorama européen in Villiers-en-Bois (79): 600 European animals.

Casinos

There are 11 casinos on the west coast: at Châtelaillon-Plage, Fouras, La Rochelle, Royan (17), Pornic, Saint-Brévin-les-Pins (44), La Faute-sur-Mer, Les Sables-d'Olonne-la-Plage, Les-Sables-d'Olonne-les-Pins, Saint-Gilles-Croix-de-Vie and Saint-Jean-de-Monts (85). Details of all casinos and what they offer are available via the internet (e.g. 💻 www.journaldescasinos.com – partly in English).

Walking & River Cruising

The area generally favours outdoor pursuits and is crossed by many long-distance walking routes, known as *grande randonnée* (*GR*) paths, which are numbered and signposted. (Note, however, that the approved route is not always clear, so a map is recommended.) Some departmental committees publish sets of maps and excellent ones are available for Charente-Maritime and the Anjou area. For further information, contact the Fédération française de la Randonée pédestre (64 rue Dessous des Berges, 75013 Paris Paris, ☎ 01 44 89 93 90, 💻 www.ffrandonnee.fr) or the Comités régionaux de la Randonnée pédestre: OMS, 22, place Charles de Gaulle, 86000 Poitiers (☎ 05 49 47 86 01) for Poitou-Charentes or the Maison des Sports, 44 rue Romain-Rolland, 44103 Nantes Cedex 4 (☎ 05 49 47 86 01) for Pays-de-la-Loire. The region is also noted for its outstanding parks and gardens, most of which are open to the public.

Another pleasurable way of touring the region and its countryside well away from main roads is river cruising. The area has several navigable rivers, on which you can hire and sleep aboard a cabin cruiser for a week-end or a week. Pays-de-la-Loire has the Loire, Maine, Mayenne, and Sarthe rivers, and Poitou-Charentes boasts almost 160km (100mi) of the meandering Charente and around 100km (60mi) of the Sèvre Niortaise. The main boat-hire companies are at Jarnac (16), Saintes, Savinien-sur-Charente (17), Doan and Entrammes (53).

Shopping Centres & Markets

Most sizeable towns have at least one supermarket, near which there are often various specialist shops. In large towns, there's often also a DIY superstore (which are useful for the handyman who doesn't know the French for 'Allen key' or 'Jubilee clip'). Many shopping centres in small towns are dying in the face of competition from super and hypermarkets, with only chemists', newsagents and insurance brokers remaining, as well as a few *pâtisseries*, which offer better quality cakes and pastries than the supermarkets.

In compensation, traditional street markets continue to thrive, and there are weekly and daily markets throughout the area, where local people sell their own produce, which is usually very fresh. Markets, particularly in rural areas, are also social occasions, when people from isolated farms meet their neighbours and exchange gossip. Main weekly and monthly markets in the area are listed below, as well as a few notable annual fairs (dates and times are subject to change).

Pays-de-la-Loire

Loire-Atlantique: Châteaubriant (Wednesdays); Le Loroux-Bottereau (Sundays and an annual wine fair first Sunday in March); Nantes (daily); Saint-Brevin (Thursdays & Sundays); Saint-Nazaire (daily except Mondays and an annual onion fair in mid-September); Vallet (Sundays and an annual wine fair in the third week in March).

Maine-et-Loire: Angers (daily); Beaufort-en-Vallée (Wednesdays); Chemillé (Thursdays); Cholet (Tuesdays to Saturdays); Fontevraud-L'Abbaye (Wednesdays & Saturdays); Montjean-sur-Loire (Thursdays and an annual hemp festival in mid-August); Saumur (Tuesdays, Wednesdays, Thursdays & Saturdays); Segré (Wednesdays).

Mayenne: Lassay-les-Châteaux (Wednesdays); Laval (Tuesdays & Saturdays); Mayenne (Mondays); Pré-en-Pail (Saturdays); Villaines-la-Juhel (Mondays).

Sarthe: Bonnetable (Tuesdays); La Ferté-Bernard (Mondays); La Flèche (Wednesdays & Sundays); Fresnay-sur-Sarthe (Saturdays); Le Lude

(Thursdays); Mamers (Mondays); Le Mans (daily except Mondays); Sablé-sur-Sarthe (Thursdays); La Suze-sur-Sarthe (Thursdays); Saint-Calais (Thursdays).

Vendée: Beauvoir-sur-Mer (Thursdays); Challans (Tuesdays & Fridays); Fontenay-le-Comte (Saturdays); Les Herbiers (Thursdays); Montaigu (Tuesdays, Thursdays & Saturdays); Les Sablés-d'Olonne (daily); Saint-Gilles-Croix-de-Vie (Tuesdays, Wednesdays, Thursdays & Saturdays and an annual craft and flea market every evening in July and August); Saint-Jean-de-Monts (Wednesdays & Saturdays); Saint-Michel-en-l'Herm (Thursdays); Talmont-St-Hilaire (Tuesdays & Saturdays).

Poitou-Charentes

Charente: Barbezieux (Tuesdays); Blanzac (third Saturday in month); Chalais (Mondays); Cognac (daily); Confolens (Wednesdays & Saturdays); Jarnac (daily); La Rochefoucauld (daily); Ruffac (Wednesdays & Saturdays).

Charente-Maritime: La Brée-les-Bains (daily); Château-d'Oléron (Tuesdays, Wednesdays & Thursdays); La Flotte (daily); Jonzac (Tuesdays & Fridays); Marennes (Tuesdays, Fridays & Saturdays); Mirambeau (Saturdays); Montendre (Thursdays); Pons (Wednesdays & Saturdays); Rochefort (Tuesdays, Thursdays & Saturdays); La Rochelle (daily); Saintes (daily except Sundays); Sugères (Tuesdays & Thursdays); Tonnay-Charente (Wednesdays & Saturdays); La Tremblade (Saturdays).

Deux Sèvres: Bressuire (Tuesdays); Coulonge-sur-l'Autize (Tuesdays); Lezay (Tuesdays); Mauléon (Fridays); Melle (Fridays); Niort (daily); Parthenay (Wednesdays); Saint-Maixent-l'Ecole (Wednesdays); Thouars (Tuesdays & Fridays and a lively late-night market on the last Saturday in July).

Vienne: Châtellerault (Tuesdays, Thursdays & Saturdays); Chauvigny (Saturdays); Civray (Tuesdays); Lusignan (Wednesdays); Mirebeau (Wednesdays & Saturdays and an annual donkey fair on the third Saturday in August); Poitiers (daily except Mondays); La Roche-Posay (daily); Vivonne (Tuesdays & Saturdays).

Foreign Food & Products

There are few specialist foreign product shops in the area, although most supermarkets (and particularly Carrefour) stock a few foreign items, such as American hamburger buns, British-style bread, marmalades and sauces (e.g. HP), Australian wines, and foreign spirits (e.g. Scotch and Bourbon), Dutch and Greek cheeses and Italian pasta.

Restaurants & Bars

The west coast is as well provided with restaurants and bars as any part of France and also has its share of mouth-watering regional specialities. Those in Poitou-Charentes include *mouclade* (mussels served with a white sauce flavoured with curry – the best *mouclades* are reportedly served in the old port in la Rochelle), *chaudrée* (fish soup served with garlic *croûtons*), *cagouilles* ('snails' in the local patois – usually served in their shells in bubbling melted garlic butter, but sometimes cooked in an omelette), *daube saintongeaise* (beef stew, prepared in and around Saintes, which is the region's gastronomic capital) and *gâteau charentais* (almond cake). Specialities in Pays-de-la-Loire include *rillettes du Mans* (a sort of pâté made of shredded pork), *matelote d'anguille* (pieces of eel cooked in red wine, with garlic and parsley), *fricassée de poulet à l'angevine* (chicken pieces in a creamy sauce with baby onions and mushrooms, as served in Angers since the Middle Ages) and *lièvre à la royale* (a version of jugged hare peculiar to the Vendée).

Challans in Vendée, where fowl is reared on the nearby marshes, claims to be the fowl capital of France, its *poulet noir* (the meat from black-feathered hens) being particularly renowned. Also peculiar to Vendée and found on menus throughout the *département* is *mogette*, a small, white haricot bean simmered for hours and often served with local gammon. Other specialities of the area are Pineau des Charentes, an aperitif made from unfermented grape juice blended with cognac, and Port Salut, a cheese originally made in a Cistercian monastery near the little village of Entrammes, just south of Laval (53).

Restaurants which specialise in local cuisine include La Cité in Anglouléme (16), La Ferme in Angers, Le Relais in Saumur (49), La Boîte Sel in Le Mans (72), L'Auberge de l'Ecluse in Coulon (79), La Grange au Roseaux in Lusignan and Chez Cul de Paille in Poitiers (86).

SERVICES

International & Private Schools

There are no international schools in the area; the nearest is in Bordeaux (see page 218). There are, however, a number of private schools which cater for foreign students, including the Collège privé Saint-Louis (☎ 05 46 97 00 46) in Pont-l'Abbé-d'Arnoult (17), the Lycée privé Saint Dominique (☎ 02 28 01 72 72) in Saint-Herblain (44), the Centre international pour Enfants Château de Bellevue (☎ 02 41 61 51 42) in Le Bourg-d'Ire (49), the

Lycée d'Enseignement général, Technologie et Professionnel privé Notre-Dame (☎ 02 51 69 19 33) in Fontenay-le-Compte (85) and L'Espérance (☎ 02 51 40 24 86) in Sainte-Cécile (85).

Language Schools

Language lessons are offered by a number of public and private establishments in the area, including those listed below. Language courses are also offered by local Chambres de Commerce et d'Industrie and Centres culturels.

- Séjours internationaux linguistiques et culturels (SILC) in Angoulême (16);
- Mondes nouveaux/Horizons du Monde in La Rochefoucauld (16);
- CUFLE (Université de la Rochelle) in La Rochelle (17);
- Eurocentre in La Rochelle (17);
- Université de Poitiers in La Rochelle (17);
- Centre audiovisuel de Royan pour l'Etude des Langues (CAREL) in Royan (17);
- La Ferme in Saujon (17);
- DuFoir Cours et Graductions in le Croisic (44);
- Centre d'Enseignement du français Langue étrangère (CEFLE) at the University of Nantes (44);
- Espace linguistique (CCI de Nantes et de Saint-Nazaire) in Nantes (44);
- Centre international d'Etudes françaises at the Université catholique de l'Ouest in Angers (49);
- Ecolangues in Angers (49);
- University of Angers (49);
- Château de Bellevue in Le Bourg-d'Iré (49);
- Le Poyenval in Bazoges-en-Pareds (85);
- Centre de français Langue étrangère at the University of Poitiers (86).

Details of the above schools can be found on 💻 www.europa-pages.com. The French Consulate in London (see **Appendix A**) publishes a booklet called *Cours de français Langue étrangère et Stages pédagogiques du français Langue étrangère en France*, which includes a comprehensive list of schools, organisations and institutes providing French language courses throughout France.

Hospitals & Clinics

There are teaching hospitals (*CHU*) in Angers, Poitiers and Nantes, where all services and medical procedures are available, and a main hospital in La Roche-sur-Yon (87).

Jonzac (17) boasts a thermal spa, where treatment is carried out under medical supervision, and thalassotherapy is available in Châtelaillon, the Ile d'Oléron and Ile de Ré and Royan (17), Pornic (44), Les Sables-d'Olonne and Saint-Jean-de-Monts (84).

Tradesmen

The following English-speaking tradesmen and professionals are listed with the British Consulate in Bordeaux:

- Bill Buttling (builder), chez Bonnin, 16210 Chalais (☎ 05 45 98 18 56);
- Keith Randell (builder), le Bourg, 16390 Bonnes (☎ 05 45 98 56 41);
- Susan Dixon (estate agent), ICS SARL, Les Broux 86400 Saint-Gaudent (☎ 05 49 87 45 47).

Magazines such as *French Property News* and newspapers such as *The News* (see **Appendix B**) carry advertisements by English-speaking tradesmen. French tradesmen are unlikely to speak much English but are generally reliable – and have the advantage that they often take several months to submit an invoice!

English-language Media

There's no local radio in English, but it's possible to receive BBC Radio 4 on long wave (198) in northern parts of the area and BBC Radio 1, 2, 3, and 4 can be received on your television via the Astra satellite and via the internet. The World Service is on 648MW in northern parts, as well as short wave (for frequency details, go to 💻 www.bbc.co.uk/worldservice/schedules/frequencies/eurwfreq.shtml) and via the Astra satellite in all parts of the area.

Local music stations usually broadcast 60 per cent non-French language songs, most of which are in English.

There are no local English-language publications, but there are two English-language monthlies published in France and distributed nationally, *The Connexion* and *The News* (see **Appendix B**). There's also an English-language book (and tea!) shop in Gençay, near Poitiers, in Vienne (☎ 05 49 50 61 94).

Embassies & Consulates

The Poitou-Charentes region is covered by the British Consulate General, 353 boulevard Président Wilson, 33073 Bordeaux (☎ 05 57 22 21 10) and the United States Consulate, 10, place de la Bourse, 33000 Bordeaux (☎ 05 56 48 63 80). Pays-de-la-Loire is covered by the British Consulate General, 18bis rue d'Anjou, BP 111.08, 75365 Paris Cedex 08 (☎ 01 44 51 31 02) and the US Embassy, 2 avenue Gabriel, Paris 75008 (☎ 01 43 12 22 22, 💻 www.amb-usa.fr).

Places of Worship

There are churches in the following towns which hold regular services in English (where no church is specified, it's the only one in the village):

- Chasseneuil-sur-Bonnieure (16) – Temple Protestant;
- Cognac (16) – Chapelle Ecole de la Providence;
- Le-Grand-Madieu (16);
- Saint-Léger-de-la-Martinière near Melle (79);
- La Merlatière (85);
- Puy-de-Serre (85);
- Magné near Gençay (86).

There are also a few churches near campsites in the area where English services are held during the summer months only, including:

- Royan (17) – Eglise les Mathes;
- Saumur (49) – Villebernier Church;
- Saint-Gilles-Croix-de-Vie (85) – La Chapelle.

Further details of English-language services in Poitou-Charentes can be obtained from Revd Michael Hepper, 2 place Gambetta, 86400 Civray (☎ 05 49 97 04 21). If you're in northern Pays-de-la-Loire, services in Ille-et-Vilaine or Morbihan in Brittany (see page 86) are an alternative and for those in the south of Poitou-Charentes, services in Dordogne (see page 221) or Gironde (see page 221) are a possibility. The Intercontinental Church Society in the UK publishes a *Directory of English-Speaking Churches Abroad* (see **Appendix A**).

There are mosques in Angoulême, Avignon, Soyaux (16), La Rochelle (17), Nantes, Saint-Nazaire (44), Angers, Cholet (49), Laval (53), Le Mans (72), La Roche-sur-Yon (85), Châtellerault and Poitiers (86); details can be found on 💻 http://mosquee.free.fr. There are synagogues in La Rochelle (17), Nantes (44) and Angers (49); details can be found on 💻 www.pagesjaunes.fr (enter 'Synagogues' in the first box and the name of the town).

Clubs

The area tends to attract foreigners who are keen to integrate, and there are no foreign enclaves or 'ghettos' as in some other parts of France. Nevertheless, there are a few English-speaking clubs, including the following:

- **Les Amis Solitaires** – for single English-speaking people in Deux-Sèvres (💻 www.chaslynngites.com);
- **Charente-Limousine Exchange** – covers mainly this part of the Charente *département* (💻 www.charente-limousine-exchange.netfirms.com);
- **Euromayenne** – aims to help non-French Europeans settle into Mayenne (💻 www.euromayenne.org);
- **Nous and You** – an Anglo-French association geared towards retirees (☎ 06 68 13 22 43, 💻 www.nousandyou.com);
- **Romagne International** – bilingual welcome group based in southern Vienne (☎ 05 49 87 53 93).

Anglophone contacts can also be made via English-speaking churches (see above) and through publications such as *The News* (see **Appendix B**). For French speakers, the Accueil des Villes françaises (AVF), a French organisation designed to welcome newcomers to an area, is an option (there's often at least one fluent English-speaker in each group). There are over 30 AVF groups in Pays-de-la-Loire and 11 in Poitou-Charentes. The website (💻 www.avf.asso.fr) includes a directory (*annuaire*) of local groups by *département* as well as an online form for contacting your local AVF before you move to the area. Listings indicate whether information and services are available in English or other languages.

PROPERTY

Property prices in the area rose by around 20 per cent per year in the first five years of this century but have since slowed or even fallen; prices dropped by up to 15 per cent in 2006 in Poitou-Charentes, where a renovated four-bedroom farmhouse now costs around €250,000. In Loire-Atlantique, it's still possible to find habitable properties for less than €100,000, though a modernised family home will cost at least €175,000 – more in Vendée and far more on the coast.

House-hunters are advised to visit the area between mid-October and mid-February, when agents are less busy, but you shouldn't expect a house you saw in November to still be available in March. On the other hand, it doesn't pay to be too hasty, and British buyers in particular should be wary of buying from other Britons, who often inflate the price of a property, knowing that prices in the UK are generally far higher. Note also that cheaper properties requiring renovation or modernisation with a reasonable plot on the outskirts of a small town or village (the foreign buyer's dream) are now extremely scarce in all areas.

Cholet (49), has the highest proportion of property owners (56 per cent) of any major town in France, as well as the second-highest percentage (63 per cent) of large properties (i.e. four rooms or more) and the lowest percentage (5 per cent) of vacant properties. However, the rate of new building is only average, except in Saint-Nazaire (44) with the second-highest rate of new building (2 per cent) in France, after Bastia in Corsica.

Typical Homes

The typical, traditional house in Poitou-Charentes – known as a *Charentaise* – has a central front door with one room to each side (often large enough to divide), is roomy and has up to four bedrooms. Ceilings are high and windows big, with green shutters. Roofs normally have traditional Roman tiles and outside walls are made of honey-coloured limestone, with dressed stone around windows and doors and at external corners. In wine-producing areas there's usually an extension on the north side, used for wine making and storage, called the *chais*.

Also prevalent in the area are *longères*, long, narrow single-storey buildings with low attics, originally used for storing hay. The roof structure usually has beams chest-high crossing the house from front to back, which makes conversion into bedrooms difficult – frustrating for buyers hoping to renovate.

Less attractive are many of the larger modern houses with ready-made designs intended for Provence, which look out of place on the Atlantic coast.

In Pays-de-la-Loire, most houses have slate roofs – a limited number use Roman tiles (most of them in the south of the region). Some older houses have exposed stone walls, but most are rendered and painted white. Most older rural houses are single storey, often with low roofs and attics which are impossible to convert into bedrooms. In the *Marais Poitevin*, traditional houses have thatched roofs and thick, dried-mud walls, similar to those in south-west England.

Cost of Property

Although rising rapidly, property prices in Poitou-Charentes are still competitive. They tend to be highest around Cognac and lowest in the east, although the area around Confolens is popular and therefore relatively pricey. In parts of Pays-de-la-Loire, however, the cost of property and building plots has risen beyond all expectation in recent years, probably due largely to the increase in population as people (especially retirees) rush to live by the sea. The *département* of Vendée, which has gained some 80,000 inhabitants in the last decade and is expected to reach 600,000 by 2015, has seen the steepest rises.

The area around Le Mans (72) was until recently good value but Parisian second-home buyers have pushed up prices. This isn't an area popular with visitors (except when the 24-hour race is on), who prefer to head for the coast, and therefore isn't attractive for bed and breakfast or *gîte* businesses – Angers and Saumur are better bets.

The table below gives the average selling price of houses in 2006. Note, however, that house sizes vary from area to area, which can distort average figures.

Town/Area	Average House Price			
	2-bed	3-bed	4-bed	5+-bed
Pays-de-la-Loire				
Angers/Saumur	€170,000	€190,000	€260,000	€345,000
Le Mans	€145,000	€170,000	€230,000	€375,000

Nantes	€180,000	€265,000	€320,000	€400,000
Poitou-Charentes				
Angoulême	€165,000	€200,000	€250,000	€350,000
Châtellerault	€150,000	€185,000	€210,000	€350,000
Poitiers	€160,000	€245,000	€350,000	€390,000
La Rochelle	€295,000	€375,000	€425,000	€485,000

The average price of a period property in 2006 in Pays-de-la-Loire as a whole was around €102,600 (national average of €102,250), the average for a new house €115,500 (average €117,650) and for a building plot €26,000 (average €23,000).

The average price of a period property in 2006 in Poitou-Charentes as a whole was around €86,750 (national average of €102,250), the average for a new house €108,650 (national average €117,650) and for a building plot €48,400 (average €23,000).

Note, however, that average property prices aren't always a reliable indication of the relative price of similar properties in different areas, as one may have a preponderance of cheaper or more expensive properties.

Land

There's a limited supply of sites available for building your own home. Prices vary according to whether a plot has a *certificat d'urbanisme* (*CU*), i.e. planning permission, as well as with location. Plots close to the sea or a river or which enjoy outstanding unspoilt views can be expensive. Small rural sites of around 1,000m^2 start at €10,000 euros or so, rising to €50,000 euros or more for a site near a beach.

Rental Accommodation

There's a fair amount of long-term rental accommodation available in all *départements*: most in Loire-Atlantique and Sarthe, and least in Charente-Maritime, Laval, Deux-Sèvres and Vendée. There are few houses available in coastal areas, as their owners can earn more by offering holiday lets in the summer. Where available, unfurnished houses with two or three bedrooms are offered for rents ranging from €450 to €750 per month. Apartments are more plentiful, especially in the main towns, although there are few in La Rochelle (17) and Niort (79). Approximate rental prices in selected towns are given below.

Town (*Département*)	No. of Bedrooms	Monthly Rental
Angoulême (16)	1	€250 to 350
	2	€350 to 500
	3	€425 to 600
	4	€550 to 850
	5	€700 to 1,000
La Rochelle (17)	1	€250 to 350
	2	€350 to 550
	3	€425 to 650
	4	€575 to 850
	5	€950 to 1,400
Nantes (44)	1	€350 to 500
	2	€375 to 550
	3	€525 to 775
	4	€700 to 1,000
	5	€900 to 1,350
Angers (49)	1	€250 to 375
	2	€350 to 550
	3	€525 to 775
	4	€700 to 1,000
	5	€900 to 1,350
Les Sables d'Olonne (85)	1	€400 to 600
	2	€425 to 625
	3	€450 to 700

	4	€700 to 1,500
	5	€1,200 to 2,000
Poitiers (86)	1	€325 to 500
	2	€575 to 850
	3	€825 to 1,200
	4	€1,000 to 2,250
	5	€1,500 to 2,500

COMMUNICATIONS

Air

There are three airports in the area (La Rochelle (17), Nantes (44) and Poitiers (86) – shown on the maps at the beginning of the chapter) offering direct flights from the UK as well as flights from other towns in France. If you live in the north of the area you have access to airports in Normandy or Brittany (see page 95) or the Paris airports (see page 369), while if you live in the south, Bordeaux airport (see page 230) and the airport at Périgueux (see page 169) are alternatives. Direct flights from British and Irish airports are listed in **Appendix F**. Details of all French airports and their services can be found on 💻 www.aeroport.fr.

Sea

There are no ferry services from the UK or other countries to the west coast. The nearest ferry ports are in Normandy and Brittany (see page 95).

Public Transport

The area is well served by high-speed trains (*TGV*). Angoulême (16) and Poitiers (86) are on the main *TGV* line from Paris-Montparnasse to Bordeaux, putting them an hour and a half and just over two hours from the capital respectively. (Note that trains can only run at full speed – up to 300kph/185mph – as far as Tours. New track is due to be laid as far as

Bordeaux, but not until 2016.) There's also a branch line connecting Niort (79) and La Rochelle (17). Another main *TGV* line runs from Paris to Le Croisic (44) via Le Mans (72), Angers (44) and Nantes (44). There are 15 trains a day to Le Mans and Angers (taking 55 and 90 minutes respectively) and 20 a day to Nantes (taking around two hours). Laval (53) is one-and-a-half hours from Paris on the main line to Brest and Quimper in Brittany. There are also good services from Paris to La Roche-sur-Yon (3h), Cholet (2h30), Saumur (1h30), Les Sables-d'Olonne (3h30) and Saint-Nazaire (2h35). For details of the *TGV* network, see map in **Appendix E**. There are usually special prices for return tickets from London via Paris if booked well in advance. Current examples are London-Poitiers and London-Le Mans for around €150.

There are also local trains connecting main towns, and all large towns have bus services running from the centre to the suburbs. However, these services tend to finish early in the evening. There are also some bus services between towns, particularly during rush hours and to link with train arrivals and departures. In rural areas, however, bus services (apart from school buses) can be few and far between or non-existent, and a car is often essential.

Roads

Access to the region by motorway from Paris is excellent, the A10 (known as the *Aquitaine*) running to Poitiers (86), Noirt (79) and Saintes (17). Branching off it around 50km (35mi) west of Paris is the A11 (*Océane*) to Le Mans (72), Angers (49) and Nantes (44). The A83 links the A10 near Niort to Nantes and the Le Mans-Tours stretch of the A28 is part of a uninterrupted motorway from Belgium to Spain. Yet to be completed is the A85 Tours-Angers motorway (the Tours-Saumur link is missing) but the A87 from Angers to Cholet, linking with the A83 to La Roche-sur-Yon, is virtually finished; only the Roche bypass remains (due to open in 2007). Still at the planning stage is a new Nantes-Bordeaux motorway, the A831, which, according to the English version of the Ministry of Transport's website, should 'make the road straighter'.

There's good access to the main Channel ferry ports, particularly from the north of the area. Although not classed as a motorway, the N137 north of Nantes is virtually of motorway standard for much of the way via Rennes to Saint-Malo, from where there are sailings to Portsmouth. There's also a motorway link (A84, known as the *Autoroute des Estuaires*) from Rennes north-east to Caen, from where there's a shorter ferry route to Portsmouth. Another ferry port option is Roscoff in Finistère (around 160km/100mi west of Rennes on the N12, which is dual-carriageway almost to the port).

FURTHER INFORMATION

Useful Addresses

- Centre régional du Tourisme de **Poitou-Charentes**, 62 rue Jean-Jaurès, BP 56, 86002 Poitiers (☎ 05 49 50 10 50, 🖳 www.visit-poitou-charentes.com)
- Centre régional du Tourisme des **Pays-de-la-Loire**, 44966 Nantes Cedex 9 (☎ 02 28 20 50 00, 🖳 www.paysdelaloire.fr)
- Comité départemental du Tourisme de la **Charente**, 27 place Bouillaud, 16021 Angoulême Cedex (☎ 05 45 69 79 09, 🖳 www.lacharente.com or 🖳 www.visitcharente.com – for *gîtes*: use the same address and phone number)
- Centre départemental du Tourisme de la **Charente-Maritime**, 85 boulevard de la République, 17076 La Rochelle (☎ 05 46 31 71 71, 🖳 www.charente-maritime.org – for *gîtes*: 22 rue Saint Yon, 17000 La Rochelle, ☎ 05 46 50 63 63)
- Centre départemental du Tourisme des **Deux-Sèvres**, 15 rue Thiers, BP 8150, 79025 Niort Cedex 9 (☎ 05 49 77 19 70, 🖳 www.tourisme-deux-sevres.com – for *gîtes*: 15 rue Thiers, BP 8524, 79025 Niort, ☎ 05 49 77 87 79)
- Centre départemental du Tourisme de la **Loire-Atlantique**, 11 rue du Château de l'Erauchière, 44306 Nantes Cedex 3 (☎ 02 51 72 95 30, 🖳 www.cdt44.com – for *gîtes*: 1 allée Baco, BP 93218, 44032 Nantes Cedex 1, ☎ 02 51 72 95 31/32)
- Centre départemental du Tourisme de l'Anjou [**Maine-et-Loire**], place du Président Kennedy, BP 2147, 49021 Angers Cedex 2 (☎ 02 41 23 51 51, 🖳 www.anjou-tourisme.com – for *gîtes*: same address, ☎ 02 41 23 51 53)
- Centre départemental du Tourisme de la **Mayenne**, 81 avenue Robert Buron, BP 1429, 53014 Laval Cedex 2 (☎ 02 43 53 18 18, 🖳 www tourisme-mayenne.co – for *gîtes*: same address and phone number)
- Comité départemental du Tourisme de la **Sarthe**, 19bis rue de l'Etoile, 72000 Le Mans (☎ 02 43 40 22 50 – for *gîtes*: 78 avenue du Général Leclerc, 72000 Le Mans, ☎ 03 43 23 84 61, 🖳 www.tourisme.sarthe.com)
- Centre départemental du Tourisme de la **Vendée**, 8 place Napoléon, BP 233, 85006 La Roche-sur-Yon (☎ 02 51 47 88 20, 🖳 www.vendee-

tourisme.com – for *gîtes*: 124 boulevard Aristide Briand, BP 735, 85018 La Roche-sur-Yon, ☎ 02 51 37 87 87)

- Centre départemental du Tourisme de la **Vienne**, 1bis rue Victor Hugo, BP 287, 86007 Poitiers (☎ 05 49 37 48 48, 💻 www.tourisme-vienne.com – for *gîtes*: 33 place Charles de Gaulle, BP287, 86007 Poitiers Cedex, ☎ 05 49 37 48 54)
- Gîtes de France, 59 rue Saint-Lazare, 75009 Paris (☎ 01 49 70 75 75, 💻 www.gites-de-france.fr)

Useful Publications

- *The Vendée and Surrounding Area*, Angela Bird (Malnoue Publications)

Useful Websites

💻 www.cc-facilities.com – information and assistance for those planning to visit or move to Charente-Maritime

💻 www.europe.anglican.org – details of Anglican services throughout France

💻 www.the-vendee.co.uk – information about Vendée compiled by Angela Bird, author of *The Vendée and Surrounding Area* – see above

💻 www.visaloire.com – general information about the Loire valley area

💻 www.westernloire.com – general information about the western Loire valley area

MISTRAL CORNER
FOR SALE

Rocamadour – The Lot Valley

4

CENTRAL FRANCE

Auvergne & Limousin

The area described in this chapter is one of vast contrasts, both geographically and economically. Situated south of the centre of France, it includes the following *départements*: Allier (03), Cantal (15), Haute-Loire (43) and Puy-de-Dôme (63) in the region of Auvergne; Corrèze (19), Creuse (23) and Haute-Vienne (87) in Limousin. The geography changes from west to east and from north to south. From the relatively low, rounded hills and plains in the west around Limoges (87) the terrain climbs until, in the west of the area around Clermont-Ferrand (63), the mountains reach 1,885m (6,180ft). From north to south, with a small ascent around the Plateau Millevaches (978m/3,200ft) the terrain becomes flatter and rockier as it approaches Lot in neighbouring Midi-Pyrénées. Auvergne is 25 per cent woodland, 45 per cent grassland, 20 per cent arable land and 10 per cent other uses (including urban areas). Limousin is also 25 per cent woodland, but only 30 per cent grassland and 10 per cent arable land, with 35 per cent of its land built on or unused.

Economically, the area includes some of the poorest *départements* in France; Creuse and Haute-Loire in particular are suffering from the decline of agriculture and an ageing population. On the other hand, parts of both regions are attracting increasing numbers of tourists and immigrants – especially British – and the *département* of Corrèze is being hailed as 'the new Dordogne'.

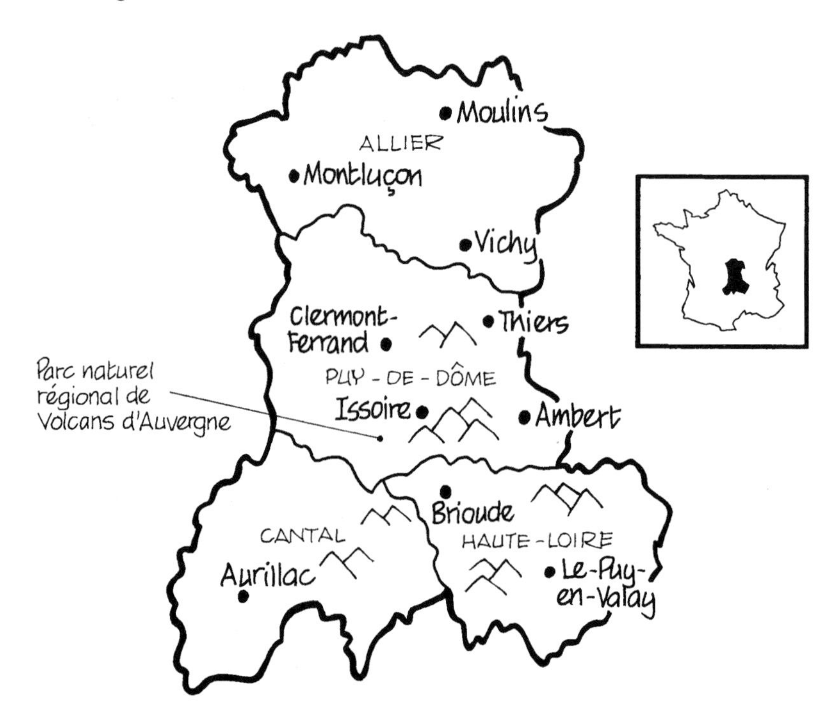

AUVERGNE

Auvergne covers an area of 26,000km^2 (16,250mi^2) at the heart of the Massif Central (the volcanic region in the centre of France) and has a population of 1.3m. The main towns are Ambert, Aurillac, Clermont-Ferrand, Le Puy-en-Velay, Moulins and Vichy. The region is unique in France, as Europe's largest group of volcanoes (now extinct) have created a landscape of mountains (Mont Dore reaches 1,885m/6,180ft), craters, lakes, rivers (the Dordogne springs from near Mont-Dore), springs (including Arvie, Mont-Dore, Saint-Yorre, Vichy and Volvic), spas and lava flows, all of which combine to create a huge geological park. The region contains two regional parks and two nature parks, and a volcano theme park with volcano-related exhibits and a guided tour around the crater of an extinct volcano (see **Leisure** on page 160).

This natural heritage is complemented by a rich cultural and historical legacy: more than 500 Romanesque churches (some of which are considered France's best), almost 50 *châteaux* and ten spa towns. Auvergne also contains ten of the 'most beautiful villages of France', four of which are in Haute-Loire. The regional capital, Clermont-Ferrand (headquarters of Michelin, the tyre manufacturer and tourist guide producer), is mainly built from dark basalt, making an impressive and unusual townscape. There are nine ski centres, 200km (125mi) of downhill runs and more than 800km (500mi) of cross-country trails.

Water plays an important part in the economy of the region. Many lakes have formed in valleys blocked by lava streams, e.g. at Aydat and Guéry, or where volcanoes have erupted in valleys, e.g. at Chambon and Montcineyre. Many anglers and watersports enthusiasts use these lakes, along with rivers such as the Allier and the Cher. The numerous hot springs in the area also owe their existence to volcanic activity. Water temperature ranges from 10C (50F) to over 80C (Chaudes-Aigues is the hottest spring in Europe at 82.3C/180F) and the springs are sought after by people who wish to 'take a cure'. Vichy, in Allier, is probably the best known spa town, having waters that are used for drinking and for balneology, and is also famous for its bottled water.

The region is predominantly agricultural with tourism slowly becoming more important. Cows are much in evidence and used for meat and milk, which is made into a number of well known cheeses: Bleu d'Auvergne, Cantal, Forme d'Ambert and Saint-Nectaire. Green lentils have been cultivated in Puy-en-Velay (43) since Gallo-Roman times and are the first vegetable to be given a quality classification as for wine. Excellent wine (both red and white) is also made from the Saint-Pourçain vineyard (one of the oldest in France) stretched along the banks of the Allier.

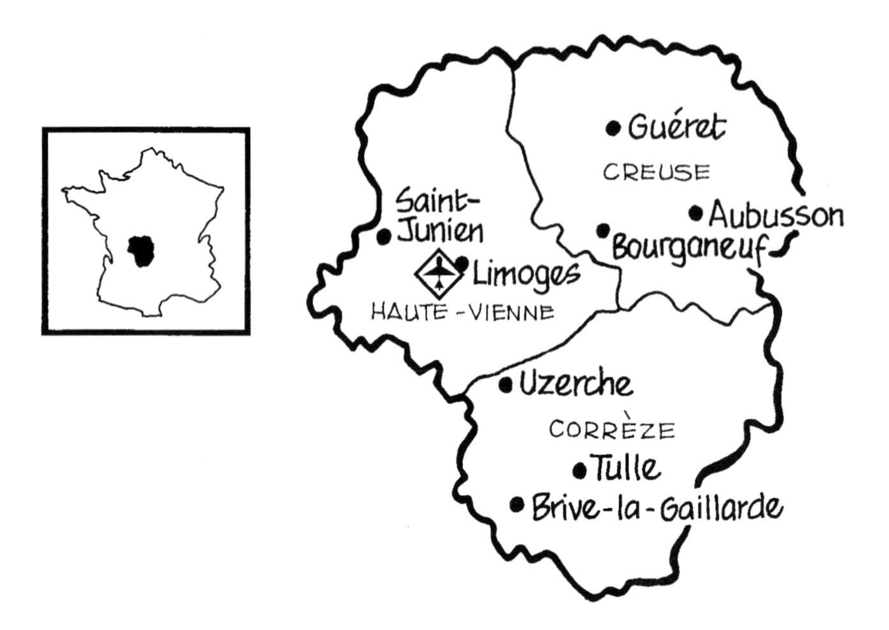

4

LIMOUSIN

Limousin is the name of the old province surrounding the town of Limoges, situated between Paris and Toulouse and west of the Massif Central. It covers an area of 16,942km^2 (10,600mi^2) and has a population of less than 725,000. It's composed of three *départements*: Corrèze (19 – the *département* of former president Jacques Chirac), Creuse (23) and Haute-Vienne (87). The main towns are Brive-la-Gaillarde (19), Guéret (23) and Limoges (87). The region is world-renowned for Limoges porcelain and enamels and the tapestries of Aubusson. The region has also given its name to a school of painting known as the Crozant school, after the place where Monet painted his first series, and is home to the Centre for Contemporary Art at Vassivière.

PROPERTY CHECK – LIMOUSIN

French Magazine recently identified a number of places in this region where property is an attractive proposition, including the following:

- **Beaulieu-sur-Dordogne** (19) – in the extreme south of the region, near Brive-la-Gaillarde, a popular spot for self-builds where scenic plots start at around €30,000;
- **Bellac** (87) – old-fashioned and off the beaten track but offering a variety of inexpensive property, including restoration projects (i.e. ruins) for under €30,000;
- **Guéret** (23) – the vibrant departmental capital has a good selection of mid-range property, and good-value homes in the higher price brackets;
- **Oradour-sur-Vayres** (87) – a pretty medieval town in the heart of the Parc naturel régional Périgord-Limousin and just 40 minutes' drive from Limoges where restoration projects start at less than €40,000 and family homes cost around €300,000;
- **La Souterraine** (23) – a lively and attractive market town, close to the A20 and numerous leisure facilities, where traditional stone farmhouses abound (from as little as €150,000);
- **Uzerches** (19) – a medieval hilltop town dubbed the pearl of Limousin and just 45 minutes' drive from Limoges, with five-bedroom properties (offering good letting potential) for under €200,000, though average prices are relatively high.

Limousin is predominantly agricultural with very little heavy industry, which makes it largely unpolluted and unspoilt by modern industrial buildings. Being in the foothills of the Massif Central, the region features rolling hills and valleys (the lowest point, around Brive-la-Gaillarde, is almost 200m/655ft above sea level and the highest is 978m/3,200ft) without the bleakness of some mountainous areas, and almost a third of the area is forested (compared with 27 per cent nationally). Its mountains and forests, coupled with the many lakes, rivers and streams that flow into either the Loire or the Garonne, make Limousin a rural holiday paradise, and it's also becoming increasingly popular with foreign homebuyers. Limousin also boasts a vast man-made lake, the Lac de Vassivière (1,100ha/2,700 acres), the largest used for water-sports in the country and featuring beaches and adjoining holiday complexes. It's also noted for its chocolate and Golden Delicious apples (reputed to be the best in the world).

ADVANTAGES & DISADVANTAGES

The main advantages of this part of France are the scenic countryside, attractive towns and villages and pleasant climate. The area is steeped in history and has many natural attractions. Being south of the Loire, the regions' weather is generally better than in the north (except for the mountainous areas) and the summers aren't as hot as in the south, although summer sun and high temperatures aren't guaranteed and it can be surprisingly cold in Limousin in all seasons except the summer. For many people, Auvergne and Limousin are unexplored territory. Those that buy houses in the region are attracted by the low prices (amongst the lowest in France) and the unspoilt countryside.

The general lack of public transport outside the main towns is a disadvantage (unless you're wedded to your car). Buses run in the largest towns but rarely venture far from the centre and in rural areas public transport stops running after 6pm. The main train lines out of Paris serve most (but not all) of the main towns and there are buses that connect the rest, but if you wish to travel east-west, there are fewer (and slower) trains and more stops. The road network follows a similar layout to the railways, although the A89 from Clermont-Ferrand to Bordeaux provides a major east-west route (see **Roads** on page 170).

Those looking to live and work in the area may be affected by the general lack of employment, and those considering buying a home in Limousin should be aware that much of the area, particularly in and around the *département* of Haute-Vienne (87), is composed of granite, which is slightly radioactive. On the other hand, the town of Limoges (87) has more green space than almost any other major town in France, with over 100m^2 per inhabitant.

Being able to speak French is almost essential in most parts of the regions, as there are few English shops, church services, newspapers, etc. Finding information outside the summer season, when the tourist offices are closed, can be difficult, although things have improved in recent years. Some newspapers publish the local diary of events in English, and local radio and television stations broadcast tourist information in English.

MAJOR TOWNS & PLACES OF INTEREST

Allier (03)

The main towns and places of interest include: Montluçon (pop. 39,800) with its attractive Saint-Pierre church and a museum of musical instruments;

Moulins (20,000), the departmental capital and 'capital' of the ancient Bourbonnais region (the pasture lands of northern Auvergne, which were once an independent state belonging to the Bourbons) with an interesting cathedral; Vichy (27,700), the quintessential spa town, with *Belle Époque* glass-roofed shopping galleries; La-Loge-des-Gardes ski resort (see page 159); and Hérisson (meaning 'hedgehog'!), one of France's most beautiful villages.

Cantal (15)

This area offers: Aurillac (pop. 30,000), the departmental capital; Salers, one of France's most beautiful villages, with typical 15th and 16th century buildings and a cheese factory; the Parc naturel régional de Volcans d'Auvergne, the biggest natural park in France (120km/75mi from north to south and covering almost 4,000km²/1,560mi²); and Le Lioran ski resort (see page 159).

PROPERTY CHECK – CANTAL

Those in search of *la France profonde* need look no further than the Auvergne *département* of Cantal. There's little development on account of its spectacular volcanic landscape (the Monts du Cantal is the largest volcanic system in Europe) making it ideal for those hankering after a rural 'paradise'. In Cantal, the mountains are high but everything else is low: the population, the crime rate and the property prices. Typical homes are built of local stone – even the roof tiles are stone (*lauze*) – with a large open fireplace. If restoration doesn't frighten you, you can pick up a traditional house for as little as **€50,000**; if it does, a fully restored 19th-century cottage can be yours for just **€100,000**..

Sélection Habitat (www.selectionhabitat.com)

Corrèze (19)

The main towns and places of interest include: Brive-la-Gaillarde (pop. 49,700), the largest town in the *département*; Tulle (16,900), the departmental capital; Uzerche (3,500) with its grey slate roofs, turrets and bell towers; medieval Turrene and the nearby 16th century collegiate church; and the villages of Collonges-la-Rouge, built from carmine sandstone, and

Saint-Robert, considered to be among the most beautiful in France and host to an annual arts festival.

PROPERTY CHECK – CORREZE

'So peaceful that road signs warn motorists to stay alert, Corrèze boasts many of the charms of neighbouring Dordogne but minus the GB *bouchons*,' stated *French Magazine* recently in a round-up of 2007 property hotspots. Here, barns still used as such can be picked up for as little as €30,000, while just over €100,000 buys a three-bedroom house in one of the three main towns (Brive-la-Gaillarde, Tulle and Ussel) or a detached house in the countryside needing only a bit of 'TLC'. However, regular Ryanair flights into Limoges have stimulated the property market in the west of the *département* and the 2007 opening of Brive-la-Gaillarde International Airport is likely to do the same for southern parts. The *French Magazine* survey identifies Beaulieu-sur-Dordogne and Brive itself as likely hotspots, along with the remote but scenic Plateau de Millevaches in the north of Corrèze, where a four-bedroom villa can be had for under €200,000.

Les Agences du Limousin (🖳 www.lesagencesdulimousin.com); Corrèze Property Consultants (🖳 *correzepropertyconsultants.com*)

Creuse (23)

This area offers: Guéret (pop. 15,800), the departmental capital; the Lac de Courtille, a large swimming and water activities lake; Aubusson (5,000), famous for tapestry making, with the Musée départemental de la Tapisserie and factory where tapestries are made and repaired; Bourganeuf (3,500) with its beautifully painted medieval church; Crozant with its ruined castle painted by Monet; Chambon-sur-Vouèze with its impressive church; and the Gorges de Verger park, where George Sand often stayed.

PROPERTY CHECK – CREUSE

Until recently, Creuse boasted France's lowest average property prices, but up to 50 per cent annual increases – largely 'caused' by an influx of British buyers – have taken the *département* off the bottom of the league table. None the less, homes are still ridiculously cheap by British standards – around a fifth of the price of those in England's Cotswolds, with which the area has been compared. Unlike the Cotswolds, however, Creuse has three times as many cows as people and isn't overrun with tourists; in fact, there are no motorways and traffic jams on local roads are rare. In villages such as Aubusson, Felletin and Guéret ruins can be bought for as little as €15,000, cottages in need of modernisation for under €100,000 and renovated farmhouses can be had for less than €150,000.

Century 21 (🖳 www.century21.com); Immobilier Guéret (☎ 05 55 41 49 49); Vert et Bleu Immobilier (☎ 05 55 64 17 68)

Haute-Loire (43)

Main towns and places of interest in this area area: Le Puy-en-Velay (pop. 19,300), the departmental capital and a medieval Holy City known for lace making and the 'Black Madonna' in its cathedral; Brioude (7,300) with its impressive Basilique St Julien church; La Chaise-Dieu with its abbey church of Saint Robert featuring carved choirs, tapestries and 'echo room'; Chapelle-Saint-Michel-d'Aiguille perched on a finger of lava rock; Arlempdes, where the remains of a medieval fortress are perched on a rock above the Loire; and Les Estables ski resort (see page 159).

Puy-de-Dôme (63)

Main towns and places of interest in this area include: Clermont-Ferrand (pop. 141,000), the regional and departmental capital, with its Basilique Notre-Dame-du-Port – one of the most important Romanesque churches in the region – and the 12th and 13th century Notre Dame de l'Assomption cathedral built from dark volcanic rock with superb stained glass windows; Issoire (15,000) with its church of Saint Austremoine – another of the region's great Romanesque churches; Thiers (15,000), a medieval town with narrow, winding streets and a knife museum; the village of Saint-Nectaire with an interesting church; Mont Dore, the highest point in central France, with its casino incorporating a children's casino(!?); six ski resorts (see page 159); and the Vulcania museum near Clermont-Ferrand (see page 161).

Haute-Vienne (87)

This area offers: Limoges (pop. 135,000), the regional and departmental capital, with its Musée national Adrien-Dubouché tracing the history of porcelain making; nearby Oradour-sur-Glane, a village burnt to the ground together its inhabitants by the Germans during World War II – its ruins are preserved as a memorial; Saint-Junien (13,000) with its 11th century collegiate church; Saint-Leonard-de-Noblat (3,650) with a Romanesque collegiate church and railway museum; Rochechouart with its *château*; Le Dorat, an attractive village; and the Lac de Vassivière (1,100ha/2,700 acres), offering many water-based activities.

PROPERTY CHECK – HAUTE-VIENNE

Haute-Vienne's sleepy surface conceals a furious property boom, with annual increases of up to 20 per cent, largely fuelled by the arrival of international flights at the departmental and regional capital, Limoges. Nevertheless, it remains one of France's cheapest *départements* to buy a home. Although restoration projects are now few and far between, they can still be found – for as little as €25,000 – and farmhouses in need of 'attention' can cost just €100,000 and small renovated houses only a little more. If you're lucky, these will feature chestnut or oak floors (both trees grow in the area) and a granite fireplace. A large renovated 'character' house with outbuildings costs from €250,000, while €400,000 will buy an extensive property with swimming pool. For investors, the town of Bellac, which is attracting people out of Limoges, offers letting potential with properties starting at just €70,000.

Agence Boineau (☎ 05 55 68 31 12); Agence Marche Limousin (🖳 www.agence-marche-limousin.com); France Limousin Properties; (🖳 www.francelimousinproperties.com)

POPULATION

The area covered by these two regions has one of the lowest population densities in France and few large towns; only Clermont-Ferrand and Limoges have over 52,000 inhabitants (for city and town populations, see **Major Towns & Places of Interest** above).

Auvergne and Limousin are the only regions in France where the death rate exceeds the birth rate, and although this decline has now been reversed, the two regions have among the slowest population growth in France: Auvergne, which has yet to return to its 1975 population level, 0.26 per cent per annum and Limousin 0.28 per cent compared with the national average of 0.66.

Auvergne has a population of 1.3m, with 51 inhabitants per km^2 (132 per mi^2). Its fastest-growing *départements* are Haute-Loire (population 217,000), which has the region's youngest population and highest birth rate, and Puy-de-Dôme (621,000, including 141,000 in Clermont-Ferrand). In fact, Clermont-Ferrand is the only major town in Auvergne that is growing. The region's population growth is concentrated in the 'corridor' linking Brioude, Issoire, Clermont-Ferrand, Riom and Vichy, the latter having the fastest-ageing population of any major town in France. Allier's population is 342,000 and Cantal's 151,000.

Limousin has 725,000 inhabitants with an average density of 42 people per km^2 (109 per mi^2) and one of the oldest populations in France (the *département* of Creuse holds the record), with a 23 per cent increase in the number of 50- to 60-year-olds between 1999 and 2004. As in many other predominantly rural regions of France, young people tend to move to the cities in search of jobs and excitement: the region has lost almost 10 per cent of its 15- to 30-year-olds in the last five years. Of its three *départements*, Haute-Vienne (pop. 364,000) is the fastest-growing – especially along the N141 linking Verneuil-sur-Vienne, Veyrac, Saint-Victurnien and the A20 between Rilhac-Rancon, Ambazac and Bonnac-la-Côte – while Corrèze (237,000) has only recently reversed its population decline (the areas that attract most newcomers are around Larche and Malemort-sur-Corrèze and near the business parks of Objat and Egletons). Nevertheless, overall the region's population increase is the fastest it has known for a century.

The British population in the area has recently increased greatly, but the Portuguese, Moroccans, Turks and Algerians still outnumber them by far. In Auvergne, of the 23,375 official non-French EU residents, 16,450 are Portuguese and the remaining 7,000 or so include all other EU nationalities as well as British (some 80 per cent of whom are retired!), whereas there are 5,460 Moroccans, 4,625 Turks and 3,750 Algerian residents. Similarly, in Limousin, a quarter of the 30,000 or so foreign residents are Portuguese; Moroccans and Turks come next at 14 per cent each, Algerians third at 10 per cent and the British fourth, though some estimates put the number of British residents as high as 3,200 and the total number of British property owners at 8,000. Haute-Vienne (87) is home to half the foreigners living in the region (including most of the British, who have congregated in the north and north-east of the *département*). More than 75 per cent of Limousin's foreign residents live in urban areas.

LANGUAGE

Southern parts of Auvergne and Limousin are within the part of France where the *Langue d'Oc* or *Occitan* is spoken (see page 262), but French is also universally spoken.

CLIMATE

The climate is basically continental but varies considerably within these two regions on account of the Massif Central mountains, where the weather is damper and colder than in the plains to the north and west. Winters are long and cold with often damaging late frosts, while summers are short and hot. Snow tends to fall later in the Massif Central than in the Alps and the Pyrenees, and the ski season doesn't usually start until January or even February. Clermont-Ferrand is one of the driest French towns north of Toulouse, with 90 days' rainfall a year.

Rainfall in Allier is higher in spring and summer (100mm in May and 62mm in August) than in winter, as it is in Puy-de-Dôme (23mm in March compared with over 80mm in May). Conversely, southern parts, around Cantal, have up to 130mm between October and December and 'only' 80mm in August. Haute-Loire has more consistent rainfall throughout the year (around 30-35mm in February and March and between 60 and 80mm the rest of the year).

Limousin's climate is oceanic and varies according to the altitude but is generally mild; summer temperatures can reach 38C, but it can be quite cold in the autumn and spring, as well as in winter. Rainfall is generally moderate, averaging 750mm (29in) per year, although Limoges is one of France's rainiest towns, with 135 days' rainfall a year. It often snows on high ground in winter.

Rainfall in Vienne is highest in winter (106mm in December) and May (90mm) and lowest in summer (68mm in July). Corrèze, on the other hand, has less rain in winter than in autumn (around 90mm per month), its driest month being March with 46mm. Summer temperatures are higher than in Vienne or Creuse, where May is the wettest month (106mm) followed by December (100mm) and August the driest (58mm).

The table below shows the number of hours' sunshine and number of days' rainfall in selected towns in the area.

Town	Sunshine Hours	Days' Rainfall
Vichy (03)	1,880	118
Brive-la-Gaillarde (19)	1,977	120
Périgueux (24)	2,025	118
Clermont-Ferrand (63)	1,907	90
Limoges (87)	1,974	135

CRIME RATE & SECURITY

This area of France is a relatively safe place to live, and car and house insurance are among the cheapest in France. Cantal, Creuse, Haute-Loire and Haute-Vienne are among the *départements* with the lowest (reported) crime rates in France. Périgueux (24) has seen the second-highest decrease in crime rates over the last two years of any major town in France and now enjoys the country's second-lowest crime rate. Allier, Corrèze and Puy-de-Dôme have only slightly higher crime rates and Montluçon (03) has the third-lowest crime rate among France's major towns. That isn't to say, of course, that crime can be ignored. In summer, in the tourist areas, there's a significant and increasing rate of theft from cars and pick-pocketing. And, as this is an area where there are many second and holiday homes which are left empty for months at a time, it's a favourite haunt of burglars. From time to time, the police remind homeowners to be on the lookout for people (generally in white vans) who 'explore' an area searching for isolated houses that are closed up; they make a number of 'passes' and, if a house is empty every time, consider it a safe target. This sort of crime is still fairly rare, but it's also on the increase.

AMENITIES

Sports

In an effort to combat unemployment and boost the local economy, all the *départements* in this area have included sport in their development strategy and, despite not having weather like the south or being close to the sea, the area offers a great diversity of sporting activities, including swimming, cycling, potholing, canoeing, hang-gliding, hiking, tennis, skiing and horse riding. From the plains around Limoges to the mountains of the Massif Central and the valleys and gorges of Lot, there's something for everyone. The information below is a selection of the facilities available; details can be obtained from regional and departmental tourist offices (see **Further Information** on page 172) and from the associations listed below.

Golf

As throughout France, golf is becoming increasingly popular in this area. The table below lists the number of courses in each *département*.

Département	**No. of Courses**
Allier	2 x 9 holes, 4 x 18 holes
Cantal	1 x 9 holes, 2 x 18 holes
Corrèze	2 x 9 holes, 1 x 18 holes, 2 x 27 holes
Creuse	1 x 18 holes
Haute-Loire	1 x 9 holes, 1 x 12 holes, 1 x 18 holes
Haute-Vienne	2 x 18 holes, 1 x 27 holes
Puy-de-Dôme	3 x 9 holes, 1 x 18 holes

Information (in both French and English) on how to find courses, the cost of a round (which varies between €15 and €50), etc. is available via the internet (💻 www.backspin.com).

Canoeing & Rafting

These sports are becoming increasingly popular among both tourists and residents on the area's many rivers, particularly through the gorges of the Dordogne and Lot rivers. Details are available from the Comité départemental de Canoë/Kayak, Bureau 218, Espace Associatif, place Bessières, 46000 Cahors (☎ 05 65 35 91 59) and the Ligue de Canoë-Kayak d'Auvergne, Plan d'Eau, rue des Laveuses, Cournon-d'Auvergne (☎ 04 73 84 30 06).

Skiing

Skiing is popular in the Massif Central (Auvergne), where there are nine ski centres offering 200km (125mi) of downhill runs and more than 800km (500mi) of cross-country trails:

- Cambon-des-Nieges (63), ☎ 04 73 88 62 62, 💻 www.grandvallee.com;
- Chastreix-Sancy (63), ☎ 04 73 21 52 00, 💻 www.sancy.com;
- Les Estables (43), ☎ 04 71 08 31 08, 💻 www.mezenc-gerbier.com;
- Le Lioran (15), ☎ 08 25 88 66 00, 💻 www.lelioran.com;
- La-Loge-des-Gardes (03), ☎ 04 70 56 44 44, 💻 www.logedesgardes.com;
- Le Mont-Dore (63), ☎ 04 73 65 20 21, 💻 www.mont-dore.com;
- Murat-le-Quaire (63), ☎ 04 73 65 53 13, 💻 www.sancy.com;
- Saint-Anthème/Prabouré (63), ☎ 04 73 95 20 64;
- SuperBesse (63), ☎ 04 73 79 52 84, 💻 www.super-besse.com.

4

Other Mountain Sports

In summer, the mountains are popular for **horse riding** (contact the Comité Régional FFME, ☎ 04 73 90 69 79), **mountain biking**, **climbing** (Montagne Auvergne, 23 place Delille, Centre Couthon, 63000 Clermont-Ferrand, ☎ 04 73 90 23 14, ✉ montagne.auvergne@orange.fr and Base de la Minoterie, 19140 Uzerche, ☎ 05 55 73 02 84, 💻 http://perso.orange.fr/vezere.passion/), **caving** (Bureau de Sports Nature, Conduché, 46330 Bouziés, ☎ 05 65 24 21 01) and **hang-gliding** (Ligue d'Auvergne de Vol Libre, 4, chemin des Garennes, 63960 Veyre-Monton, 💻 http://ligueauvergne.vollibre.neuf.fr).

Cycling

Cycling is popular, especially in Auvergne, where there are over 30 marked road circuits and hundreds of kilometres of marked off-road trails (contact the Ligue régional d'Auvergne de Cyclotourisme, rue Guérat, 03500 Saulcet, ☎ 04 70 45 56 87 and the Comité régional Cyclisme d'Auvergne, 23 place MAréchal Fayol, 63000 Clermont-Ferrand, ☎ 04 73 37 95 15) and in

Limousin, where there's a mountain bike centre with 400km (250mi) of trails and downhill slopes near Guéret (contact the Comité Limousin du Cyclisme, 3 impasse Mas Neuf, 87000 Limoges, ☎ 05 55 35 16 26 and Espace VTT-FCC des Monts de Guéret, ☎ 05 55 52 14 29). Cycling is best avoided during the peak summer season, when temperatures are high and roads are full of cars and coaches.

Other Sports

Other popular sports include **football**, **hiking** and **tennis** (contact the Ligue Régional du Limousin, 41 rue Feytiat, 87000 Limoges, ☎ 05 55 31 81 00). **Anglers** will also find plenty of opportunity for fishing, particularly for trout and carp, in the area's many rivers and lakes. Hunting is a popular 'sport', particularly in Auvergne and Limousin. There are hunting clubs and associations in many towns and even in some villages.

Leisure

The area is a paradise for nature lovers with its mountains, valleys, rivers, lakes, forests and natural parks. Those interested in architecture and history will find plenty to enjoy in the many ancient villages and *châteaux*, not to mention the caves of Lascaux and Les Eyzies, and there are also numerous vineyards (and local wines) to explore around Bergerac (24) and Cahors (46) as well as those of Saint-Pourçain in Allier. 'Taking the waters' in one of the spa towns can be combined with a (less healthy) visit to the casino, as there are no fewer than 13 casinos in the area, all in spa towns (casinos were originally permitted only in spa towns): 12 in Auvergne – in Bourbon-l'Archambault, Néris-les-Bains and Vichy (03), Chaudes-Aigues and Vic-sur-Cère (15), Allègre (43), La Bourboule, Chatel-Guyon, Le Mont-Dore, Royat and Saint-Nectaire (63) – and one in Limousin: in Evaux-les-Bains (23). These are open all year and offer shows and restaurants, as well as gambling. Details of all casinos and what they offer are available via the internet (e.g. 💻 www.journaldescasinos.com – partly in English).

There are numerous fairs and festivals in the region, including the Corrèze Festival of music and drama in Limousin in August and, in the same month, a Scottish Fête in Saint-Orse (24).

Other types of leisure facility are limited, particularly in winter, unless you live in or near a large town. There are, however, a number of zoos, animal parks, activity centres, aquariums and bird sanctuaries in the area offering (mainly in the summer months) many attractions, especially for children. The major venues are listed below.

▲ © Youssof Cader (www.123fr.com)

▲ *Gordes, Provence*
© Ciscardi Gabriel (www.123rf.com)

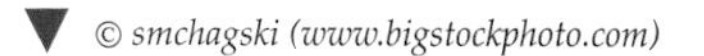

▼ © smchagski (www.bigstockphoto.com)

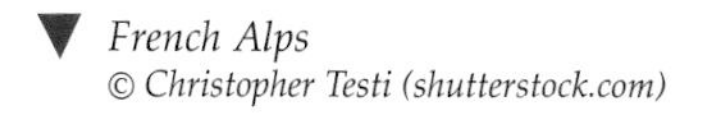

▼ *French Alps*
© Christopher Testi (shutterstock.com)

▼ *Lavender* © David Hughes (www.shutterstock.com)

▲ *St Emilion, Gironde © Lagui (www.shutterstock.com)*

◀ *© Elena Aliaga (www.bigstockphoto.com)*

▲ *Tourettes-sur-Loup, Alpes-Maritimes*
© Cyrille Lips (www.bigstockphoto.com)

◀ *Vines in autumn © Sebastion G (www.shutterstock.com)*

▲ *Painting seller, Paris*
© Dana Ward (www.istockphoto.com)

▲ *La Conciergerie, Paris* © *ErikN (www,shutterstock.com)*

© *Christopher Lofty (www.shutterstock.com)* ▶

▲ *Menton, Alpes-Maritimes*
© *John Saxenian (www.123rf.com)*

Nice, Alpes-Maritimes © *Cyrille Lips (www.bigstockphoto.com)* ▶

▲ © *Val Gascoyne*

▲ *La-Roque-Gageac, Dordogne*
© Ian Frazer (www.bigstockphoto.com)

◀ *Bordeaux Cathedral*
© Wizdata (www.bigstockphoto.com)

▲ *Colmar, Alsace* © christinaZ (www.bigstockphoto.com)

▲ © bparren (www.istockphoto.com)

▼ *Dieppe, Normandy*
© Pozzo di Borge Thomas (www.shutterstock.com)

- Hippodrome de Vichy (03): racecourse with horse racing and carriage racing;
- Aquarium du Limousin in Limoges (87): 300 species and 2,500 fish;
- Bowling Club Limousin at Feytiat, near Limoges (87);
- La Cité des Insectes in Nedde (87): the name says it all;
- Corrèze Montgolfière (19): hot-air ballooning;
- Les Loups de Chabrières near Guéret (23): wolves in their natural habitat and an astronomical observatory;
- Mirabel near Riom (63): theme and animal park;
- Le Pal near Moulins (03): animal park with 500 animals from the five continents;
- Le Parc de la Droséra near Thiers (63): 50 models of local monuments in a 10ha (25 acre) park;
- Parc Zoologique du Bouy (63): zoo with 500 animals;
- Port miniature in Ambert (63): as the name suggests, a miniature port for children;
- Vulcania near Clermont-Ferrand (63): museum dedicated to volcanoes and earth sciences.

English-language Cinema & Theatre

Some cinemas show all foreign films in the original language (*en version originale/VO*), notably Cinéma le Club in Brive-la-Gaillarde (19). A useful website for finding out which films are on in a given area, which also indicates whether the films are being shown in the original language is 💻 www.cinefil.com.

There are no theatres in the area that show plays in English, although you may find performances of English-language plays in French!

Shopping Centres & Markets

Most large towns have a shopping complex or a super or hypermarket with a car park and several smaller shops attached. The two main shopping centres in Auvergne are the Centre de Vie Saint-Jacques in Montluçon (03) and the Centre Jaude in Clermont-Ferrand (63). In Limousin, there's a multi-storey commercial centre in Limoges (87) and two large commercial areas on the outskirts of the town (Centre Beaubreuil to the north and Centre Bosseuil to the south) as well as one on the outskirts of Brive-la-Gaillarde (19) incorporating a Carrefour hypermarket.

Daily and weekly markets can be found in the largest (and some of the smallest) towns across the whole of the area. Details can be provided by local town halls and tourist offices (see **Further Information** on page 172). Some of the major regular and annual markets and fairs are listed below:

Auvergne		
June	Regional products fair	Saint-Nectaire (63)
July	Cheese and wine fair	Besse-et-Saint-Anastaise (63)
August	Cheese and cow fair	Salers (15)
	Farm market	Le Breuil (63)
	Wine fair	Saint-Pourçain-sur-Sioule (03)
	Organic fair	Charbonnières-les-Varennes (63)
October	Wine harvest and apple fair	Le Vernet (03)
	Beer fair	Vichy (03)
November	Gastronomy, apple and traditional fruit fair	Massiac (43)
Limousin		
June	Red fruit fair	Châteauneuf-la-Forêt (87)
June to Sept	Regional products market	Objat (19)
August	Regional products fair	Aubusson (23)
	Organic fair	Beaulieu-sur-Dordogne (19)
September	Bread, wine and cheese fair	Evaux-les-Bains (23)
October	Mushroom festival	Brive-la-Gaillarde (19)
November	Oyster fair	Sardent (23)

Foreign Food & Products

Most large supermarkets and the food departments in Monoprix and Galeries Lafayette have some foreign food and products. Usually, the bigger the shop, the better the selection. In some areas, there are *épiceries fines* (delicatessens) that stock foreign food.

Restaurants & Bars

As in most of France, there's a multitude of restaurants and bars in this area, especially in the tourist towns. Sadly, the typical French café is slowly disappearing. However, it's still possible to find bars in smaller towns and villages serving a set menu with wine at lunchtime for around €10. If you want something other than regional food and French cuisine (and pizza), e.g. Chinese or Indian restaurants, you must look in the larger towns, several of which also have a McDonald's (if you're that desperate).

Almost every village has a bar, which opens early in the morning and usually sells local papers and cigarettes as well as drinks. Some provide simple meals or sandwiches at lunchtime, but most are closed by 8pm. 'The Pheasant Pluckers' in Château-de-Lacomte near Carlucet (46) is a British-run bar and restaurant, and the Moulin de la Geneste campsite in Condat-sur-Ganaveix (19) has an 'English' pub, while Le Chêne Vert in Rollin near Saint-Pourçain (03) boasts the 'Irish Corner Pub'. Local specialities include lentils (in Auvergne) and locally caught fish.

SERVICES

International & Private Schools

There are no international schools in this area and the nearest are in Toulouse and Bordeaux (see page 218). However, the University of Clermont-Ferrand (63) accepts foreign students on an exchange programme. As across the whole of France, there are private schools from kindergarten to university level, and there are two in the area which cater for English-speaking students: the Lycée privé mixte Saint Joseph (☎ 05 53 31 33 00, 💻 www.saint-joseph-sarlat.org) in Sarlat-la-Canéda (24) and the Lycée privé Cénevol international (☎ 04 71 59 72 52) in Le Chambon-sur-Lignon (43).

Language Schools

Language lessons are offered by a number of public and private bodies in the area, including those listed below. Language courses are also offered by local Chambres de Commerce et d'Industrie and Centres culturels, and the YES clubs (see **Clubs** on page 166) provide English-French conversation classes.

- CAVILAM in Vichy (03);
- CEL in Montluçon, Moulins and Vichy (03), Brive-la-Gaillarde (19), Guéret (23) and Clermont-Ferrand (63);
- Centre de Langues et d'Etudes françaises in Clermont-Ferrand (63);
- CNED (Long Distance Learning) in Futuroscope (86);
- Greta in Guéret (23), Cahors (46), Clermont-Ferrand (63) and Limoges (87);
- Université Blaise in Clermont-Ferrand (63).

Details of the above schools can be found on 💻 www.europa-pages.com. The French Consulate in London (see **Appendix A**) publishes a booklet called *Cours de français Langue étrangère et Stages pédagogiques du français Langue étrangère en France*, which includes a comprehensive list of schools and organisations providing French language courses throughout France.

Hospitals & Clinics

Most large towns have both hospitals and clinics, either in the town centre or on the outskirts. There are teaching hospitals (*CHU*) at Clermont-Ferrand and Limoges, where all services and medical procedures can be found. There are also main hospitals at Montluçon and Vichy (03), Aurillac (15), Brive-la-Gaillarde and Tulle (19), Guéret (23), Périgueux (24), Le Puy-en-Velay (43), Cahors (46), Cébazat (63) and Saint-Junien (87). No hospitals or clinics in the area have English-language services, although many doctors and consultants have some knowledge of English.

Tradesmen

It's fairly easy to find English-speaking tradesmen in most areas, although they don't advertise as such in local papers. The Chambre de Métiers (Chamber of Trades) can provide a list of all builders, stonemasons and other artisans, registered in the *Répertoire des Métiers* (trades register). Beware of unregistered builders. You should therefore always ask to see a tradesman's professional card and examples of his work. Magazines such as *French Property News* and newspapers such as *The News* (see **Appendix B**) carry advertisements by English-speaking tradesmen. French tradesmen are unlikely to speak much English but are generally reliable.

English-language Media

Despite the number of Britons in the area, there's no dedicated English-language radio station (a business opportunity, perhaps?). BBC Radio 1, 2, 3, and 4 can be received on your television via the Astra satellite, and you can listen to recordings of radio programmes on Radio 1, 2, 3, 4, 5, 6 and 1Extra on your computer via the internet (go to 💻 www.bbc.co.uk/radio/aod/index.shtml). The World Service is available on short wave (for frequency details, go to 💻 www.bbc.co.uk/ worldservice/schedules/frequencies/eurwfreq.shtml) and via the Astra satellite. Local music stations usually broadcast 60 per cent non-French language songs, most of which are in English.

In larger towns it's possible to find major international newspapers such as *The International Herald Tribune* and the *Guardian* on the day of publication (although not normally before breakfast). There are two English-language monthlies published in France and distributed nationally: *The Connexion* and *The News* (see **Appendix B**).

Embassies & Consulates

The British consulate covering Limousin is in Bordeaux (353 boulevard du Président Wilson, BP91, 33073 Bordeaux, ☎ 05 57 22 21 10, ✉ postmaster.bordeaux@fco.gov.uk). Auvergne is covered by the British consulate in Lyon (24 rue Childebert, 69288 Lyon Cedex 1, ☎ 04 72 77 81 70, ✉ britishconsulate.mail@ordilyon.fr). There are also American Presence Posts in Bordeaux (BP 77, 33025 Bordeaux, ☎ 05 56 48 63 80) and Lyon (16 rue de la République, 69002 Lyon, ☎ 04 78 33 36 88), where there are consulates for most other major countries.

Places of Worship

Every town and almost every village has a Catholic church, although services in villages are usually only once a month. Mass schedules for the month are posted on church doors.

In Limousin, there's an English vicar, Michael Hepper (19 avenue René Baillargeon, 86400 Civray, ☎ 05 49 97 04 21), who offers services in English at several locations. There's a Protestant church in Clermont-Ferrand (63). There are Jehovah's Witnesses groups in Cusset (03) and La Souterraine (19), and Latter Day Saints in Brive-la-Gaillarde (19), Clermont-Ferrand (63) and Limoges (87). There are mosques in Montluçon, Moulin, Vichy (03), Le Puy-en-Velay (43), Clermont-Ferrand, Thiers (63) and Limoges (87); details can be found on 💻 http://mosquee.free.fr. There are two synagogues, in Vichy (03) and Clermont-Ferrand (63), details of which can be found on 💻 www.pagesjaunes.fr (enter 'Synagogues' in the first box and the name of the town) and 💻 www.feujcity.com (where there's also information about Kosher food shops and restaurants, Jewish associations and schools, etc.).

Clubs

Limousin has a bilingual organisation, Welcome-en-Limousin, aimed at helping English-speakers to integrate. For French speakers, the Accueil des Villes françaises (AVF), a French organisation designed to welcome newcomers to an area, is an option (there's often at least one fluent English-speaker in each group). There are around 25 AVF groups in Auvergne and Limousin – in Moulins, Monluçon and Vichy (03), Aurillac (15), Brioude, Langeac, Le Puy-en-Velay and Yssingeaux (43), Aubière, Cébazat, Chamalières, Clermont-Ferrand, Cournon, Issoire, Pont-du-Château, Riom and Thiers (63). The website (💻 www.avf.asso.fr) includes a directory (*annuaire*) of local groups by *département* as well as an online form for contacting your local AVF before you move to the area. Listings indicate whether information and services are available in English or other languages. Other sources for clubs in the area are *The News* (see **Appendix B**) and English-speaking churches (see above).

PROPERTY

There are few housing developments outside large towns and most people moving to this area are looking for houses or farms to renovate with at least 1,000m^2 (a quarter of an acre) of land. However, it's becoming difficult to find a typical stone house with a large plot. Often, when a farm or *fermette* (small farm) is sold, a local farmer will buy the land and perhaps a barn, leaving the house with a small garden or virtually no land. It's worth bearing in mind that in rural areas of Auvergne and Limousin, 10 to 15 per cent of homes have no septic tank or sanitation, and when a property is described as 'for renovation' this usually means 'requiring drainage, electricity and other basic amenities'.

New houses are generally bought (or built) by French people and tend to be either in or near a town, although there are some new housing developments that may appeal to foreigners, especially those looking to let a property to holidaymakers. For example, Souilllac Country Club (46) offers swimming pools, tennis courts, a bar, a restaurant and a golf course (Souillac Country Club, ☎ 05 65 27 56 00, 💻 www.souillaccountryclub.com). A number of two-, three- and four-bedroom chalets are available from €350,000.

Typical Properties

Houses in this area are typically built of stone, but the stone used varies from place to place – from almost black lava stone in the Massif Central to the creamy white of the Quercy plateaux. In northern parts, houses are constructed with thick walls and small windows to keep out the heat in summer and the cold in winter; in the southern parts, windows tend to be larger. In Auvergne roofs are predominantly slabs of volcanic stone and in Limousin slate. Some houses and many of the churches in Limousin are roofed with chestnut slats called *bardeaux.* The region is one of the last in France to produce *bardeaux*, and many famous buildings in other parts of the country (on the Mont Saint-Michel, for example) are roofed with Limousin *bardeaux*. However, owing to the cost of such roofing materials, modern houses throughout the area tend to be roofed with standard red tiles.

4

Cost of Property

Generally, prices within a 30km radius of Limoges are around 15 per cent higher than elsewhere.

The table below gives the average selling price of houses in 2006. Note, however, that house sizes vary from area to area, which can distort average figures.

Town/Area	Average House Price			
	2-bed	3-bed	4-bed	5+-bed
Auvergne				
Clermont-Ferrand	€145,000	€200,000	€255,000	€305,000
Countryside	€110,000	€150,000	€180,000	€225,000
Vichy	€145,000	€210,000	€270,000	€455,000

Limousin				
Limoges	€125,000	€180,000	€205,000	€260,000
Tulle	€110,000	€155,000	€190,000	€290,000

The average price of a period property in 2006 in Auvergne as a whole was around €75,000 (national average of €102,250), the average for a new house €100,000 (national average €117,650) and for a building plot €22,000 (average €23,000). The equivalent figures for Limousin were €67,800, €121,300 and €20,000. Note, however, that average property prices aren't always a reliable indication of the relative price of similar properties in different areas, as one may have a preponderance of cheaper or more expensive properties.

Land

Building land is available in all areas, although it isn't plentiful. Rather surprisingly, the largest number of plots on the market are in Dordogne, followed by Corrèze, Puy-de-Dôme and Vienne, with few in the other *départements*. Prices vary enormously according to location and whether main services are connected. Land in or near a small village, where there's no mains drainage, can be bought for as little as €5 per m², even in Lot, whereas land with connections to all services, including electricity and telephone, near a town costs at least €100 per m², although the maximum price in Auvergne and Limousin is usually around €75 per m². Plots range from around 400m² to several hectares, the average plot being between 1,000 and 3,000m² and costing between €10,000 and €50,000. Most local estate agents sell building plots (*terrains à bâtir* or *terrains constructibles*).

Rental Accommodation

Rental accommodation is easiest to find in the main towns. For example, in Clermont-Ferrand (63) and Limoges (87), there are apartments from studios to five-bedrooms, although smaller apartments are in demand from students, as both towns have universities. Outside the main towns, rental accommodation tends to be limited to *gîtes*, which can be expensive for a long period, though it's possible to find rural houses for rent. Few agencies deal solely in rentals, but most estate agents handle properties for rent. Approximate rental rates in selected towns in the area are given below.

Town (*Département*)	No. of Bedrooms	Monthly Rental
Vichy (03)	1	€200 to 300
	2	€250 to 375
	3	€400 to 600
	4	€550 to 850
	5	€700 to 1,000
Tulle (19)	1	€200 to 300
	2	€225 to 350
	3	€350 to 525
	4	€450 to 750
	5	€600 to 900
Clermont-Ferrand (63)	1	€250 to 350
	2	€350 to 500
	3	€425 to 600
	4	€550 to 850
	5	€700 to 1,000
Limoges (87)	1	€250 to 375
	2	€350 to 525
	3	€400 to 600
	4	€550 to 800
	5	€700 to 1,000

COMMUNICATIONS

Air

There are several airports in the area (shown on the maps at the beginning of the chapter), although there are few direct services from other countries and in most cases it's necessary to fly via Paris. Direct flights from the UK and Ireland are listed in **Appendix F**. Brive-la-Gaillarde's new airport (to be known as Brive-Souillac), just south of the town at Cressensac, is due to open in 2008, when it will offer flights to London, Paris and Lyon. Those in the north of the area may have access to Poitiers airport (in Vienne, around 125km/80mi north-west of Limoges – see page 139). Details of all French airports and their services can be found on 💻 www.aeroport.fr.

Public Transport

The *TGV* from Paris runs as far as Bordeaux via Poitiers (in Vienne to the north-west of Haute-Vienne) and Angoulême (in Charente to the west of Dordogne and Haute-Vienne) but doesn't serve this area, although there's talk of a Poitiers-Limoges link (backed by former president Jacques Chirac, no less). For details of the *TGV* network, see map in **Appendix E**. It's possible to catch local trains from Poitiers and Angoulême to Périgueux (24), Souillac (46), Clermont-Ferrand (63) and Limoges (87), but services are slow and infrequent. Limoges, for example, is four-and-a-half hours from Paris, Clermont-Ferrand five hours and Souillac six. Car rental is available at most of the major stations.

A cheaper but slower alternative to the train is coach travel. For example, Eurolines (💻 www.eurolines.com) offer services during the summer months from London to Limoges (direct) costing around €150 return and taking up to 12 hours and to Bellac (87) and Souillac (both with a change at Tours).

All large towns have bus services, which run from the centre to the suburbs and, in the case of Bergerac, Clermont-Ferrand and Limoges, from the station to the airport. However, these services tend to finish early in the evening. There are also some bus services between towns, particularly during rush hours and to link with train arrivals and departures. In rural areas, however, bus services can be few and far between or non-existent, and a car is often essential.

Roads

Road access to the area is easier since the completion of the A20, which runs from Paris (it starts as the A10 and A71) to Toulouse via Limoges (87), Brive-la-Gaillarde (19) and Cahors (46) and is toll-free from Vierzon (around half way from Paris to Limoges) to Brive; the A75 from Paris right down to the Mediterranean coast, crossing the spectacular new Millau viaduct between Clermont-Ferrand and Béziers; and the A77 from Paris to Nevers and Moulins. The A20 Cahors bypass is now completed and has done much to relieve traffic congestion. The A71 continues to Clermont-Ferrand, and the recently completed A89 links Clermont with Tulle (19), Brive and Périgueux and continues as far as Bordeaux. The following are approximate travelling times by motorway:

- Brive-la-Gaillarde: 5 hours from Paris and 3 hours from Toulouse;
- Cahors: 6.5 hours from Paris and 1.5 hours from Toulouse;
- Clermont-Ferrand: 4 hours from Paris and 2 hours from Lyon;
- Limoges: 4 hours from Paris and Toulouse;
- Souillac: 6 hours from Paris and 2 hours from Toulouse.

Traffic jams are almost unheard of except in the large towns and even there are usually fairly innocuous (at least by Parisian standards). Limoges and Clermont-Ferrand can become congested during rush hours, and tourist towns can be jammed in July and August. The D703, known as the *Voie de la Vallée*, along the river Dordogne from Saint-Cyprien (24) to Souillac (46) is often impassable because of the sheer volume of cars and coaches (most of them foreign). There are plans to create a diversion, but the exact route is (still) under discussion. The route along the river Lot between Cahors and Figeac is magnificent but also heavily used in summer and, with its many bends, can be extremely slow.

There are a number of major roads under development (and therefore slowed by road works), including the N145 from Montluçon (03) to Angoulême (16), which is dual-carriageway either side of Guéret (23) but otherwise only two lanes. It's a very dangerous road (it has the greatest concentration of lorry traffic of any road in France) – especially the section between Montluçon and Guéret, where there are black silhouettes of people beside the road to show how many deaths there have been! However, the recently completed A89 motorway should attract many of the lorries away from the N145 and out of Brive-la-Gaillarde and Clermont-Ferrand. (Note that Brive currently has the third-worst accident record of any major French town.) The N141/D941 from Limoges to Clermont-Ferrand is another busy road, and there have been demands for passing lanes to reduce the accident rate, although as yet nothing has been done and it looks set to remain a two-lane road for some time.

FURTHER INFORMATION

In this section, you'll find addresses for tourist information offices and estate agents in Auvergene and Limousin. In addition there's a selection of useful websites (see below).

Useful Addresses

Tourist Offices

4

- Comité régional du Tourisme d'**Auvergne**, Parc technologique Clermont-Ferrand La Paediue, 7 allée Pierre de Fernat, 63178 Aubière Cedex (☎ 08 10 82 78 28, 💻 www.auvergne-tourisme.info)
- Comité régional du Tourisme du **Limousin**, 27 boulevard de la Corderie, 87031 Limoges (☎ 05 55 45 18 80, 💻 www.tourismelimousin.com)
- Comité départemental du Tourisme de l'**Allier**, Pavillon des Marroniers, Parc de Bellevue, BP 65, 03402 Yzeure (☎ 04 70 46 81 50, 💻 www.destination-allier.com)
- Comité départemental du Tourisme du **Cantal**, 11 rue Paul Doumer, BP 8, 15000 Aurillac (☎ 04 71 46 22 00, 💻 www.cdt-cantal.fr)
- Comité départemental du Tourisme de la **Corrèze**, Quai Baluze, 19000 Tulle (☎ 05 55 29 98 78, 💻 www.cg19.fr or 💻 www.correze.net)
- Comité départemental du Tourisme de la **Creuse**, 43 place Bonnyaud, BP 243, 23005 Guéret (☎ 05 55 51 93 23, 💻 www.cg23.fr)
- Comité départemental du Tourisme de la **Haute-Loire**, Hotel du Département, 1 place Monseigneur de Galard, 43011 Le Puy-en-Velay (☎ 04 71 07 41 54, 💻 www.cg43.fr)
- Comité départemental du Tourisme du **Puy-de-Dôme**, Place de la Bourse, 63038 Clermont-Ferrand Cedex 1 (☎ 04 73 42 22 50, 💻 www.planetepuydedome.com)

Estate Agents

- Agence Couloumy, La Maze, 19140 Uzerche (☎ 05 55 73 28 92, ✉ limousin.immoblier@orange.fr). FNAIM registered, English-speaking

- Cendrillon Immoblière, 23 rue Zizim, 23400 Bourganeuf (☎ 05 55 54 95 85, ✉ j-p.pelege@orange.fr). FNAIM registered, English-speaking
- J-N Brunet, 27 avenue de la République, 23000 Guéret (☎ 05 55 51 90 90, 💻 www.fnaim.fr/brunet). FNAIM registered

Useful Websites

- 💻 www.correze.net (information on Corrèze, including a website address book – in French)
- 💻 www.cr-limousin.fr (Conseil régional du Limousin. Information on the economy and population, statistics of the region and useful links – in French and English)
- 💻 www.europe.anglican.org – details of Anglican services throughout France
- 💻 www.franceguide.com/uk/hiddenfrance – general information about Limousin
- 💻 http://limoges.cci.fr – information on services in and around Limoges (in English)
- 💻 www.meltingpot-darnac.com – English-speaking integration group in Darnac
- 💻 www.region-limousin.fr – search engine for the Limousin region (in French only)
- 💻 www.settlinginlimousin.com – information for people thinking of moving to Limousin

Lagrasse – Pyrénées

5

THE SOUTH-WEST

Aquitaine & Midi-Pyrénées

The area of France described in this chapter includes most of the Aquitaine and Midi-Pyrénées. Aquitaine is made up of the following *départements*: Dordogne (24), Gironde (33), Landes (40), Lot-et-Garonne (47) and Pyrénées-Atlantiques (64); Midi-Pyrénées comprises Ariège (09), Aveyron (12), Haute-Garonne (31), Gers (32), Lot (46), Hautes-Pyrénées (65), Tarn (81) and Tarn-et-Garonne (82). Aquitaine is perhaps most famous for its wines, beaches, surfing and of course, Eleanor of Aquitaine, mother of Richard the Lionheart. Midi-Pyrénées is renowned for skiing, spas and the pilgrimage town of Lourdes.

The most popular *départements* among foreign buyers are Dordogne (in Aquitaine) and neighbouring Lot (in Midi-Pyrénées), to which separate sections are devoted below. Until relatively recently, the regions' other *départements* haven't been especially popular with foreign property buyers, but with access becoming easier by air, rail and road, coupled with relatively low increases in property prices, a pleasant climate and wonderful wines and food, the south-west has seen an increase in the purchase of second and retirement homes – especially by the British and other Europeans.

Unlike Peter Mayle's book *A Year in Provence*, which caused Britons to flood into PACA, Ruth Silvestre's book *A House in the Sunflowers* (set in Aquitaine) and Rosemary Bailey's *Life in a Postcard* (the story of buying and renovating a 13th century monastery in the Pyrenees) haven't provoked an influx of foreigners to these regions. These two books are, however, well worth reading – especially if you're think of embarking on a renovation project (see **Useful Publications** on page 234).

Did you know?

Four of the *départements* in this area – from west to east, Pyrénées-Atlantiques, Hautes-Pyrénées, Haute-Garonne and Ariège – border Spain, which is accessible via a number of trans-Pyrenean routes as well as the Atlantic coast road. Living near the border can give you the best of two worlds, with the option to savour Spanish culture, cuisine and architecture whenever the fancy takes you without even having to change currency (and take advantage of lower prices on certain goods, including toiletries, DIY materials, cigarettes and wine). However, although in many ways the countries 'overlap': in the west, the Basque Country straddles the border with its unfathomable language and ardently separatist culture, and in the east it's Catalonia that blurs the frontier, its language almost comprehensible to a French or Spanish speaker and its culture proudly independent of either 'mother' country (residents on the French side are campaigning to have Catalan taught in local schools). This creates a fascinating mix of experiences for those who choose to live 'on the edge'.

5

AQUITAINE

Aquitaine owes its name to the Romans, who logically named the area Aquitania, as it had many rivers running through it (to which canals were later added). It has had a somewhat chequered history and, like Normandy, was once ruled by the kings of England (or vice versa), although it has been under French rule since 1650. The region, which covers an area of 41,310km^2 (16,135mi^2) and has a population of 2.7m, is largely agricultural, unspoiled and sparsely populated, and it's noted for its temperate climate. Crops include corn and peppers (the hot variety), which are hung from the window ledges and beams of houses to dry. Aquitaine is one of the most varied regions of France; although predominantly flat (the majority of the region lies less than 250m/825ft above sea level), the land rises in the south at the foothills of the Pyrenees. It has over 270km (170mi) of spectacular beaches along the Atlantic coastline, known as the *Côte d'Argent* ('Silver Coast'), 30km (20mi) of which are considered to offer the best surfing in Europe (see **Sports** on page 207).

In the north of the region is the Bassin d'Arcachon, a natural inland sea with the largest beach in Europe (where incidentally 90 per cent of French oysters are grown), while the south of Aquitaine includes the so-called

Landes de Gascogne. 'The Landes' is a flat, sandy plain (*lande* means 'moor'), roughly triangular, bounded by the sea and dunes to the west and stretching from Bordeaux (33) in the north to Dax (40) and the Golfe de Gascogne in the south and east as far as Nérac (47) and therefore covering roughly the whole of the *département* of Landes, as well as a good deal of Gironde and parts of Lot-et-Garonne. It was transformed during the 19th century by the planting of pine trees, which now cover virtually the entire area, to prevent invasion by the coastal sand dunes, creating purportedly the largest forest in Europe (some 10,000km^2); the trees are now used for making paper. Part of the forest, corresponding roughly to the basin of the river Eyre, was designated a regional park (the Parc régional des Landes de Gascogne) in 1970. The Landes is known as '*le pays de la bonne bouffe*' ('the land of good grub'), where traditional dishes include *cruchade* (a dessert), *garbure* (soup), *millas* (corn-cake) and *saupiquet* (fried ham). Gironde to the north is also generally flat (its highest point is just 165m/535ft) and much of the land is given over to vineyards.

PROPERTY CHECK – LES LANDES

The landscape of the ancient province of *Les Landes* (roughly equivalent to the modern *département* of Landes) is unique in France: flat and covered in pine forest with little industry, apart from forestry and tourism, and a small, largely rural population. *Maisons landaises* are typically chalet-like, with a wood frame and large, gently sloping roof (usually canal tiled) almost reaching the ground at the back (usually facing the prevailing westerly wind) and making an overhang at the front (*auvent*) to provide shelter. Inside, a large central living room gives onto bedrooms, a bathroom, kitchen, etc. Old *maisons landaises* in good condition are highly sought after and therefore, of course, hard to find and expensive: at least €200,000 for a small one.

Estiou Property Search (💻 www.estiou.com); Latitudes (💻 www.latitudes.co.uk)

Pyrénées-Atlantiques is part of the Basque Country (*Pays basque*), which extends from around 160km (100mi) south of Bordeaux, where the Landes give way to the foothills of the Pyrenees, across the mountains into Spain and east along the river Nive as far as Saint-Jean-Pied-de-Port. The Basque Country has its own language (see page 203), style of architecture (see

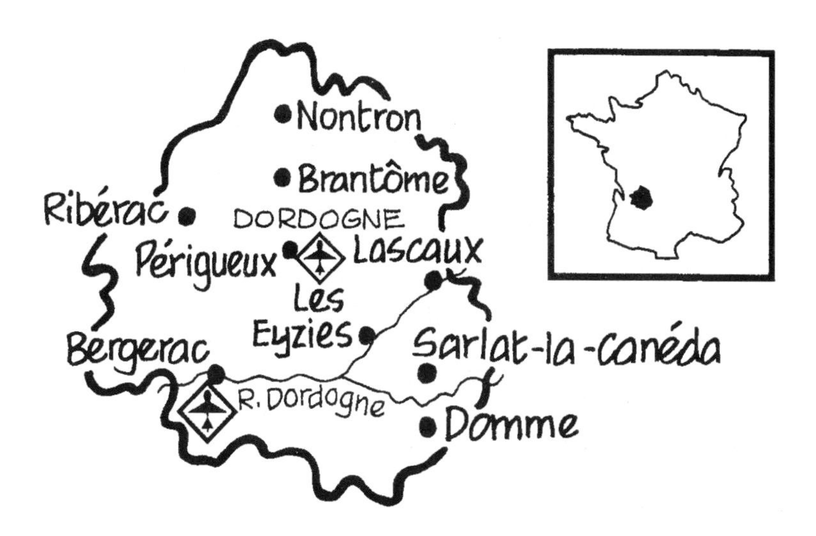

page 224), sport (*pelote* – see page 210) and traditions and is itself divided into ancient 'regions', such as Labourd, Soule and Basse-Navarre. Apart from the conurbation of Bayonne, Anglet and Biarritz (known locally as the 'BAB'), where property is fairly expensive, Pyrénées-Atlantiques is sparsely populated. To the east of the Basque Country is Béarn (famous for its *sauce béarnaise*), another ancient 'region' (its capital is Orthez) surrounding the valleys of the Aspe, Barétous and Ossau in the east of Pyrénées-Atlantiques. The inland *département* of Lot-et-Garonne is undulating and largely rural and agricultural. It's one of the largest fruit-growing areas in France, producing apples, apricots, melons, nectarines, peaches, plums (including the mouth-watering *prunes d'agenais*) and strawberries, as well as tobacco, among other crops. (There's a famous fruit fair at Prayssas, between Agen and Villeneuve-sur-Lot.) Much of Aquitaine is covered by trees, including virtually the whole of the *département* of Landes, which contains Europe's largest forest, by 30 per cent grassland, 20 per cent arable land and 25 per cent other uses, including urban areas.

Dordogne

The ancient province of Périgord, Dordogne is south-west of the centre of France and is surrounded by Charente (16) and Haute-Vienne (87) to the north, Charente-Maritime (17) and Gironde (33) to the west, Corrèze (19) to the east and Lot-et-Garonne (47) and Lot (46) to the south. It's France's third-largest *département*, covering an area of 9,060km^2 (3,533mi^2), and has a population of just under 400,000. Like many French *départements*, Dordogne is named after the main river flowing through it. It's split into four territories. In the north is 'Green Périgord', so called because of its green valleys irrigated by a multitude of streams. This territory contains the Périgord-Limousin Regional Natural Park and its main towns include Brantôme, Nontron and Riberac. In the centre is 'White Périgord', which takes its name from the limestone plateaux and contains the departmental capital, Périgueux. In the south-west corner of Dordogne is the newly identified territory of 'Purple Périgord', which includes the Bergerac area, famous for its wine grapes (hence 'purple'), and French and English fortified towns, castles and *châteaux* built during the Hundred Years War (Dordogne boasts some 10 per cent of France's 40,000 *châteaux*). In the south-east is 'Black Périgord', so called on account of the ancient oak trees covering large parts of the area and home to the valleys of the rivers Dordogne and Vézère. Perhaps the territory best known to foreigners, Black Périgord has been inhabited since prehistory and contains the famous caves at Lascaux and Les Eyzies (among others) and the picturesque towns of Saint-Cyprien and Sarlat-la-Canéda.

PROPERTY CHECK – DORDOGNE

Those put off Dordogne by its 'little Britain' image should note that this is largely confined to a few areas, Dordogne also being extremely popular with the Dutch, Germans and French, and that the 'retired stockbroker' type of British expatriate has recently given way to young families aiming to run businesses from home. With six or seven flights a day into Bergerac and others into nearby Bordeaux and Toulouse, access from the UK has never been easier – and an additional air route into Brive is planned for 2009. There has also been an increase in the number of 'help' services geared to foreigners, e.g. Lafayette After Sales Service.

There has been a steadying in house prices in the Dordogne in recent years but the market remains active. Surprisingly, average prices are on a par with the national average of around €2,000 per m^2 and significantly lower than on the Mediterranean coast. Older properties, of stone and wood beam construction, are still sought after but the increase in building means that new properties are becoming popular. On the other hand, a tightening of planning regulations means that good plots are increasingly hard to come by. Would-be buyers should also note that houses without gardens are almost impossible to sell, unless they're in a town where there's a café and public gardens nearby. Generally, look for properties that have been on the market a while, which, unless there's something obviously wrong with them, can represent 'bargains', as vendors are often prepared to drop the asking price significantly.

Under €100,000 there's nothing that doesn't require a good deal of work (e.g. reroofing!) – and the majority of old properties under €200,000 are in need of more than a lick of paint. Newer properties, on the other hand, can be found for as little as €150,000. For a character three-bedroom house, prices start at around €250,000 and can be as much as twice that.

A recent article in *French Magazine* identified the following property hotspots in Dordogne:

- **Bergerac** (in Purple Périgord/Périgord Pourpre) – Now boasting budget flights from the UK, this attractive town offers renovated townhouses from €200,000 and detached properties near the outlying vineyards for less than €400,000.
- **Brantôme** (in Green Périgord/Périgord Vert) – On the banks of the Dronne, the 'Venice of the Dordogne' is nevertheless affordable, with two-bedroom semi-detached nearby village houses for as little as €110,000.
- **Périgueux** (in White Périgord/Périgord Blanc) – This beautiful old town straddling the river Isle offers restored townhouses from around €175,000 and although detached houses in the nearby villages of Rouffignac, Saint-Astier, Thenon and Tocane are pricey (starting at €300,000), a 20-minute drive from the city brings a significant drop in prices.
- **Riberac** (in Périgord Blanc) – An attractive market town in the centre of Dordogne, Riberac has a large British population but retains its authentic charm and reasonable property prices, with restored three-bedroom houses for under €200,000. It also has a strong rental market, such a property being lettable for over €1,000 per week in high season.

Agence Immobilière Herman (💻 www.immobilier-dordogne.com); Agence Immobilière Périgord (💻 www.agenceimmobiliereperigord.com); Agence Wilson (💻 www.agence-wilson.com); Bergerac & Beyond (💻 www.bergerac-and-beyond.com); Francophiles (UK ☎ 01622-88165, 💻 www.francophiles.co.uk); IDI Périgord (💻 www.idi-perigord.com); Valora (💻 www.valora.fr)

5

Dordogne has for a long time been a holiday and migration destination for Britons (the French call the area around Ribérac 'little England') and more recently Dutch and Germans. During the late '80s, the demand was so great for ruined farms and houses that a mini-boom was created. Prices are more reasonable now and bargains can still be found, especially in the Nontronnais area in the north, but it's still the most expensive *département* in this area for the simple reason that it's one of the most scenic *départements* in France and contains some of the country's prettiest and most dramatic towns and villages, including Brantôme, Domme, La Roque-Gageac, Sarlat-la-Canéda and Trémolat. Domme and Sarlat are the jewels of Dordogne and are so popular that they're in danger of being ruined by tourism (it's almost impossible to find a grocer's amongst the tourist shops and artist's galleries along the main road in Domme).

Most of what makes Dordogne memorable is to be found in a 15km (10mi) stretch of the river between Bergerac and Souillac (in Lot), but every village has history in its buildings, whether churches, *châteaux* or ordinary houses inhabited by the same family for generations. Dordogne is also a treasure trove of caves filled with prehistoric paintings up to 30,000 years old. Lascaux and Les Eyzies are the two major sites and perhaps the best known. The river itself provides other distractions for inhabitants and holidaymakers (see **Amenities** on page 207), although the latter can be a nuisance to the former in high season. Local cuisine includes truffles and *pâté de foie gras* (the best French *foie gras* is considered to come from Sarlat) and is noted for its duck and goose dishes.

MIDI-PYRÉNÉES

France's largest region (bigger than Switzerland!) borders Spain in the south, Languedoc-Roussillon to the east and Aquitaine to the west, and encompasses the French Pyrenees with Toulouse, its capital, at the centre. Midi-Pyrénées boasts a wide variety of stunning, unspoilt scenery ranging from the majestic snow-capped peaks of the Pyrenees in the south to the pastoral tranquillity of the Aveyron, Lot and Garonne valleys in the north. The region as a whole is 25 per cent woodland, 25 per cent grassland, 35 per cent arable land and 15 per cent other uses, including urban areas.

The *département* of Gers is widely regarded as the heart of the ancient province of Gascony (sometimes called 'Guyenne' by the French), which is often described as France's 'Tuscany' on account of its rolling green countryside and numerous pretty villages. Neighbouring Haute-Garonne is dominated by Toulouse but reaches right down to the Pyrenees, while

Hautes-Pyrénées is a largely mountainous *département* boasting many ski resorts (see page 207).

PROPERTY CHECK – GASCONY

The ancient province of Gascony (*Gascogne*), which more or less corresponds to the modern *département* of Gers but spills over into Landes to the west and parts of other neighbouring *départements*, is considered by many to be the 'real' France, with its golden stone farmhouses dotted among vast fields and gently rolling hills, its down-to-earth wines, traditional cuisine and largely unspoiled architecture. Property prices aren't low, however: while a small village house can be picked up for less than €100,000, a renovated three-bedroom forest chalet costs around €300,000 and farmhouses in good condition start at around €400,000.

Au Charme Gascon (💻 www.fnaim.fr/gascon); Vialex Gers (💻 www.vialexgers.com)

In the north-east of the region, Aveyron offers a variety of landscapes, including the wild, rocky area known as Les Causses, south of Millau, the town being regarded as the gateway to the Tarn Gorges – spectacular cuts through the lower Massif Central and a Mecca for hikers, canoeists, climbers and campers (the viewpoint at the top is appropriately called the Point Sublime!). The *départements* of Tarn and Tarn-et-Garonne in the east of the region have recently become extremely popular with foreign homebuyers, particularly the British (in many parts, you're almost certain to have British neighbours), and prices have risen accordingly.

In the south-east corner of Midi-Pyrénées, the *département* of Ariège has stunning scenery and is popular with a number of British and European notables, including Tony Blair, who has spent part of his summer holidays here for the past several years. (Perhaps he has been trying to strike it lucky: around 50kg (110lb) of gold is panned every year from the *département*'s rivers.) The decline of agriculture means that there are plenty of inexpensive properties to be found, and the *département* has the dual advantages of being near the Pyrenees and close to Toulouse. On the Spanish border is the principality of Andorra, which offers its own ski resorts as well as tax-free shopping (if you don't mind sitting in a traffic jam waiting to cross back into France afterwards!).

The Pyrenees are popular for year-round outdoor activities, including cycling, hiking and, of course, skiing. There are more than 30 ski resorts in the area (see page 207), which are generally much less expensive than the Alpine resorts, although less challenging for advanced skiers. There are also numerous spa towns in Midi-Pyrénées, owing to the region's many thermal springs. Lourdes, in Hautes-Pyrénées, is probably the most visited place in the region, millions of people flocking to the Roman Catholic holy shrine each year, many in search of miracle cures.

The people of Midi-Pyrénées have long regarded themselves as a breed apart – brave and free-spirited, typified by the statue of D'Artagnan (famous as one of the 'Three Musketeers' in the novel of that name by Alexandre Dumas) in the shadow of the cathedral at Auch (32). In fact, D'Artagnan is reputed to have been modelled on Charles de Batz, Captain of the King's Musketeers and a native of Auch. Examples of the earliest forms of human art, 30,000-year old cave paintings depicting deer, bison and other animals, can be found in the grottoes of the Ariège *département*, and the region also retains influences of the Celts (who settled here in pre-Christian times), Romans and Moors (Arabs), who occupied the area for some 800 years. The local culture and especially the cuisine have therefore developed from both Roman and Arab roots and are celebrated in the region's many festivals

Several classic French dishes originate in this region, including *cassoulet*, made from Toulouse sausage, *magret de canard* (duck cutlet) and that most politically incorrect (but most typically French) of foods, *pâté de fois gras* (goose-liver pâté). Roquefort cheese is made here (in the town of Roquefort-sur-Soulzon in Aveyron) and another famous Gascon product is armagnac, a grape brandy similar to (but subtly different from) cognac, which is made in neighbouring Poitou-Charentes. (Many connoisseurs rate armagnac above cognac, claiming that is has a richer flavour thanks to its single distillation and oak casking.) Many armagnac producers also make a fine aperitif called Floc de Gascoigne, which is a blend of armagnac and wine, along with a number of armagnac-based liqueurs.

Lot

Also named after its principal river, Lot (the 't' is pronounced) is part of Midi-Pyrénées region, which stretches from Auvergne and Limousin in the north to the Spanish border in the south. Lot has borders with six other *départements*: Aveyron (12), Cantal (15), Corrèze (19), Dordogne (24), Haute-Garonne (31), Lot-et-Garonne (47) and Tarn-et-Garonne (82). It has an area of 5,200km^2 (3,250mi^2) and a population of just over 160,000. Lot is geographically diverse, which contributes to its climatic variations (see page

204). The altitude rises from west to east as you approach the Massif Central, and the highest point in the *département* is 780m (2,550ft) above sea level.

Two major rivers cross the *département*: the Dordogne in the north and the Lot, with its many tributaries, in the south. The Dordogne basin is lush with small valleys, bubbling streams and tall cliffs (on which are perched many dramatic *châteaux*). In the southern half of the *département* are the *causses*, rocky plateaux and hills full of caves, and *Quercy blanc* ('White Quercy') – so called because of the white limestone used in the area's distinctive buildings. These plateaux are mainly hot and dry with little cultivation. In the extreme south, hemmed in by cliffs, are the plains of the Lot valley, covered with the vines of Cahors.

PROPERTY CHECK – LOT

The two rivers that run through the *département* of Lot, the Dordogne and the Lot itself, have created separate areas with distinct characteristics. The north-east, being closest to the Massif Central, is the coolest part, while the north-west is greener, with more trees and softer contours. The south-east, near the river Lot, is wilder, with valleys and cliffs and the Lot valley to the west boasts the vineyards of Cahors. The southern part of the *département* is more provençal in both landscape and building style.

After a steep but unrealistic rise in 2002, property prices in this popular *département* are back to more reasonable levels, as sellers are being forced to lower their sights in a market that has changed in recent years. People are now moving to Lot from Provence and other more highly developed regions in search of tranquillity, and younger foreigners (including Britons) are joining the retirees who used to flock here. The heart of the *département* is Quercy Blanc – so called on account of its pretty white stone houses but elsewhere the architecture (as well as the landscape) is varied: from the wooded hillsides of the north and their houses with steep, stone- or clay-tiled roofs to the sunflower fields of the south, where houses are made of pale stone. Particular features of Lot properties are the *pigeonnier* (dovecot), which adds a premium to the price, and the *souillard* – a spacious kitchen alcove found in old farmhouses, which are often accessed via an external stone staircase leading to a covered terrace, the main living area

5

being on the first floor above the *cave* (wine cellar). Prices are generally lower in the north than in the south, the Lot river being the rough dividing line. Small village houses for restoration can be had for **€75,000**, larger properties, including barns, for around **€125,000**, while a restored two-bedroom stone house is in excess of **€200,000** and for a three- to four-bedroom property in good condition you should expect to pay at least **€300,000** in the north and at least **€350,000** in the south.

Agence l'Union (🖳 www.agencelunion.com); CAPI France (🖳 www.capifrance.co.uk); Le Tuc Immobilier (🖳 www.jjvimmo.com); Vialex International (🖳 www.vialex.com)

The *département* is rich in history and boasts many ancient and picturesque towns, including Rocamadour, a town built into the cliffs and France's second-most visited place outside Paris (after the Mont Saint-Michel in Brittany) and Souillac, 'where culture and history meet' (according to the tourist guides). On the other hand, parts of Lot are relatively poor in economic terms, although in the area around Cahors, with its wine industry, the economy is booming.

Tourism has contributed greatly to the economy of the *département*, as it has a lot to offer to both visitors and the many people who have second homes here (one in five properties is a second home).

ADVANTAGES & DISADVANTAGES

The south-west has a range of climates to suit almost everyone. Few European countries, let alone regions, can match the south-west's ability to offer top-class skiing conditions so close to the balmy, temperate coastal plain (Provence-Alpes-Côtes d'Azur is another – see **Chapter 6**). Many regard the climate on the Atlantic coast as better than that of the Mediterranean, equally warm and sunny but with the benefit of Atlantic breezes to clear the air. Aficionados of summer outdoor pursuits should, however, always be prepared for sudden weather changes, particularly in the eastern Pyrenean mountains and in the southern reaches of the Massif Central in Tarn and Aveyron. These areas are subject to infrequent but invariably spectacular summer storms and flash floods. For that reason care should also be taken and enquiries made if you're contemplating the purchase of a riverside property. Those who favour a temperate, northern

European climate will probably find the Pyrenean foothills of Haute-Garonne and Gers to their liking.

Midi-Pyrénées is acknowledged, even by French people from other regions, to have the country's finest and healthiest cuisine. As this is one of France's prime food producing areas, local produce is abundant, varied and reasonably priced, and the red wines of Bordeaux (and the sweet white Sauternes) are regarded by many as the best in the world. The body beautiful is also catered for in many ways – health spas and thermal springs, outdoor pursuits such as walking, cycling and skiing and, on the coast, sailing, surfing and swimming, not to mention popular local sports such as golf, rugby and *pelote* (see **Sports** on page 207). For residents in search of some Mediterranean heat, Perpignan and the western Mediterranean coast is a mere couple of hours' drive from the south-easterly *départements* of Ariège and Haute-Garonne. And, of course, Spain is within easy reach of the southern *départements*.

PROPERTY CHECK – ARIEGE & HAUTE-GARONNE

In recent years the Ariège and Haute-Garonne *départements* (in Midi-Pyrénées) have been 'discovered' by English-speaking property buyers looking for an area that offers a wealth of activities and opportunities, properties at a reasonable price and an attractive way of life. It has always been a popular destination for northern French people, Dutch and other nationalities so it's cosmopolitan and welcoming. Prices increased by around 40 per cent in 2005-06 and continue to rise due to the area's new-found popularity but it's still possible to find good properties at a reasonable price including those with *chambres d'hôte* and *gîte* potential. With budget airlines flying to Toulouse, Carcassonne and Perpignan from the UK, access is cheap and easy, and the forthcoming *TGV* line into Toulouse will increase the options. With skiing on the doorstep in the mountains, Andorra only an hour away, Barcelona three hours and Milan six, a two-hour drive to the Mediterranean and three hours to the Atlantic, the area offers everything you could want.

A farmhouse with 1ha of land needing refurbishment costs from **€180,000**, a property suitable for *chambres d'hote* from **€300,000** and a barn to renovate from **€70,000**.

Midi Pyrénées Properties (💻 www.midi-pyrenees-properties.com)

5

One of the major advantages of the region (currently) is the relatively low cost of living. With the exception of the major cities, such as Toulouse and Bordeaux, and popular holiday destinations, such as Biarritz and the ski resorts, property prices are among the lowest in France. This is probably because the region isn't as accessible to the British and other northern Europeans as the Dordogne and other more northerly regions; nor are its winter sports offerings as comprehensive as those available in the Alps. The proliferation of low-cost airline services into the region may, however, cause property prices to rise in the next few years. It's also becoming increasingly popular as a holiday destination, both summer and winter, although unless you take up residence in one of the major ski resorts or seaside resorts you're unlikely to be unduly troubled by holiday crowds.

The south-west coast has 14 resorts with 'blue flag' beaches and two blue flag ports (see 💻 www.pavillonbleu.com) but also a large number of 'black flag' beaches – one in Gironde, three in Landes and no fewer than 12 in Pyrénées-Atlantiques, including two in Biarritz and two in Saint-Jean-de-Luz – according to the Surfrider Foundation Europe, which draws attention to what it considers to be unacceptable levels of pollution (see 💻 www.surfrider-europe.org). Pau (64) is the 'greenest' major town in the south-west, with over 75m^2 of green space per inhabitant compared with just 17m^2 in Bordeaux (33) and 15m^2 in Tarbes (85), where there's also a lack of cycle track (Bayonne and Bordeaux are the towns for cyclists). In a survey of the 100 largest towns in France published in January 2005, *Le Point* magazine rated Toulouse the country's fourth-best town to live in and Bordeaux sixth; in a similar survey published in November 2006, *Le Nouvel Observateur* also rated Toulouse fourth and Bordeaux in the top ten (see **Appendix F**).

Although the appearance of the low cost airlines has improved matters, the south-west is not as accessible from outside France as is, say, the Mediterranean coast. Although several regional airports are classed as 'international', they mainly handle scheduled flights from other French and European cities. Visitors from North America, for example, would need to travel via one of the major European hubs such as Paris or London. Internal travel from elsewhere in France has, however, greatly improved in recent years thanks to the expansion of the motorway network and the introduction of high-speed train (*TGV*) services from Paris. British visitors can now travel from the Channel ports to the south-west by car or train fairly comfortably in a day.

The locals in the region have a long history of acceptance of other peoples, and are naturally friendly and outgoing. They're passionate about their food and drink and equally enthusiastic about their rugby. Display an informed interest in any of these and you're likely to be welcomed into the community.

Both Dordogne and Lot are quite 'Anglicised' with pubs, cricket clubs and English newspapers, so if you want to remain in touch with British culture they're an ideal choice. Although it's possible to avoid the Brits in Dordogne and Lot, those looking to embrace French life may do better to investigate Auvergne and Limousin.

Note that there are two nuclear power stations in the south-west: one at Braud-et-Saint-Louis (33), half way between Bordeaux and Royan, the other in Golfech (82) 20km/12mi from Agen and 80km/50mi from Toulouse. Bordeaux is also susceptible to flooding.

MAJOR TOWNS & PLACES OF INTEREST

Ariège (09)

Foix (pop. 9,100), the departmental capital (one of the smallest in France) and principal town, is steeped in history and has a medieval castle perched on a hill overlooking the town and the river. There's a number of *bastides* (medieval towns laid out on a grid) in the *département*, including Mazères, Le Mas-d'Azil, as well as fortified villages at Camon and Seintein. Other places of interest include the castle of Montségur, where 200 Cathars were burned at the stake for heresy by the Catholics in the Middle Ages, and the displays of prehistoric cave art and the Cathar fortress of Roquefixade. During the second world war, the Germans built a concentration camp near the village of Le Vernet, where there's now a museum dedicated to the camp's history.

PROPERTY CHECK – PAYS D'OLMES, CHALABRAIS & RAZES

This little-known area straddles the border between Ariège and Aude (in Languedoc-Roussillon – see page 238), and consists of contrasting landscapes – from the tree-clad Pyrenean peaks of the Pays d'Olmes, whose main town is Lavelanet, through the gentler slopes of Chalabrais to the undulating fields and vineyards of Razès to the heights of Monts d'Olmes, Ax-Bonsacre and Camurac, where skiing is possible. Forestry and textile manufacture are the traditional economic activities of the area, and textile workers' houses are sometimes for sale in Laroque d'Olmes. Property prices rose by around 9 per cent per year for the first few years of this century but have since stabilised and are low compared with those in neighbouring areas. In the Pays d'Olmes, a two-bedroom villa can be bought for just €125,000, while three- and four-bedroom properties cost less than €250,000. In Razès, to the north, you can buy a 'ruin' for a mere €25,000 or a habitable five-bedroom country house for less than €150,000, while €400,000 will buy a seven-bedroom mansion with swimming pool. In Chalabrais, to the south, prices are a little higher but still highly competitive.

Couleurs de France (🖳 www.couleurs-de-france.com)

Aveyron (12)

The departmental capital, Rodez (pop. 23,500), is an unpretentious town with a relatively unimposing cathedral and little to attract the tourist. The main attractions of the *département* lie in the spectacular countryside – the Tarn Gorge carving its way through the plateau de Larzac in the south and the rolling hills and valleys to the west. The plateau is where the Knights Templar settled in the middle of the 12th century; after the Pope suppressed the order in 1312, their possessions were transferred to the Knights Hospitallers of Saint John, who were responsible for the fortification of many of the hilltop villages – La Couvertoirade is an exceptionally well preserved example. The village of Conques, north of Rodez, with its fine half-timbered houses, is one of the nine villages in Aveyron rated among the most beautiful in France; its 11th century Abbatiale Sainte-Foy houses an exhibition of medieval gold, reckoned to be the finest in Europe. In the far south of the *département* near the town of Millau lies the quiet village of Roquefort-sur-Soulzon, famous for the production of the 'king of cheeses', made from ewes' milk.

PROPERTY CHECK – AVEYRON

Spectacular rocky outcrops, rolling pastures and fortified villages characterise the easternmost *département* in this area, the south-east end of which is within striking distance of the Mediterranean. Described by estate agents as 'green and serene', Aveyron is the Midi-Pyrénées' most unspoilt *département* and, although it boasts the largest concentration of classified 'beautiful villages', remains relatively undiscovered. As a result, property prices are still among the lowest in France – but not for long. Huge improvements in accessibility have been made in the last few years – most notably the construction of the Millau Viaduct but also with the arrival of Ryanair in Rodez airport. Low cost flights from the UK also serve Montpellier and Toulouse, both of which are only one and a half hours' drive away. Nevertheless, rural property prices are on average 30 per cent lower than in neighbouring Tarn and Tarn-et-Garonne.

Aveyron's property reflects its agricultural heritage, and there's a vast number of traditional stone farmhouses with outbuildings for sale. Barns and village houses for restoration start at around €40,000, traditional red stone cottages with stone tiled roofs can be had for just €75,000, while a four-bedroom house could cost anything between €275,000 and €500,000 depending on quality and location (especially near Rodez). 'Hotspots' include the towns of Conques, Millau, Najac, Rodez and Villefranche-de-Rouergue, the picture postcard village of Becastel and, for the adventurous, the Aubrac mountains. In the family-friendly ski resort of Laguiole a chalet can be had for just €200,000 – a fraction of the price of an Alpine chalet.

CAPI France (💻 www.capifrance.co.uk); French Property Shop (💻 www.french-property-shop.co.uk); Sélection Habitat (💻 www.selectionhabitat.com)

5

Dordogne (24)

Highlights here include: the departmental capital, Périgueux (pop. 32,000), whose Saint-Front cathedral is the largest in south-west France, with the Musée du Périgord, one of the country's most complete prehistory museums; Bergerac (28,000), famous for its wines and the Musée du Tabac; Sarlat-La-Canéda (10,500) with a concentration of medieval, renaissance and 17th century buildings and an impressive Saturday market specialising in *foie gras*, truffles and walnuts; several of France's most beautiful villages, including Beynac, Monpazier, La Roque-Gageac and Domme, a fortress town with medieval gateways perched over the Dordogne and offering spectacular views; the painted prehistoric caves at Les Eyzies and Lascaux II (an exact replica of the real thing, which is closed to the public in order to preserve the paintings).

Haute-Garonne (31)

Toulouse (pop. 900,000) is the fourth-largest city in France after Paris, Lyon and Lille and the country's second-largest university town, its population including some 100,000 students and academics in the Mirail suburb. The city has a Spanish feel and is often referred to as '*la cité rose*' because of the soft pink hue reflected from its red brick buildings. The medieval Les Jacobins quarter, with its narrow streets, is one of the city's main attractions, and the Place du Capitole is one of the great squares of France. With seven museums, over 50 historical monuments and a host of wonderfully decorated churches, including the Basilica Saint-Sernin, Europe's largest Romanesque church, Toulouse justifiably claims to be the cultural capital of the south-west. The southern spur of the *département* reaches the Pyrenees and the Spanish border and includes the spa towns of Bagnères-de-Luchon, Salies-du-Salat and Barbazan, as well as ski resorts (all above 1,400m/4,550ft) such as Superbagnères and Peyragudes (see page 207). The village of Saint-Bertrand-de-Comminges is among the most beautiful in France, and there are *bastides* at Cologne and Revel.

Gers (32)

The Gers *département* is widely regarded as the heart of ancient Gascony, with rolling green countryside. There are several fine examples of *bastides*, notably Fourcès, Plaisance and Mirande – the last now home to an annual international summer jazz festival.

PROPERTY CHECK – GERS

Described by writer Albert Camus as 'the Tuscany of France', this *département*, which more or less constitues the ancient province of Gascony, is sparsely populated and largely unspoiled. Its capital, Auch, with its splendid cathedral, has just 25,000 inhabitants and there are a few market towns, such as Lombez and Samatan (which boasts one of France's largest outdoor markets); the rest is rural. Property in the east of the *département* is becoming relatively expensive as people working in Toulouse look to live out in the country – particularly west of the city, where the airport and the Airbus factory are located.

Property to renovate starts at around €100,000 and habitable houses at around €200,000, though for a farmhouse in good condition with plenty of land expect to pay upwards of €350,000.

Auch (pop. 25,000) has been the regional capital since Roman times, when it rivalled Bordeaux in importance. It boasts a lovely cathedral (with unique choir stalls). Although the Gers region produces Madiran wine, its most famous tipple is armagnac.

PROPERTY CHECK – MADIRAN

Known for its powerful red wine, which is its economic lifeblood, this area straddles three *départements*: Pyrénées-Atlantiques, Gers and Jautes-Pyrénées. It's a patchwork of villages, such as Castetpugnon, Conchez-de-Béarn, Lascazères and Lembeye, nestling between the major towns of Pau and Tarbes. Madiran's only (small) town, known as the gateway to the ancient 'region' of Béarn, is Garlin, where there's a significant British presence. Property ranges from charming village houses (from around €150,000) to small and large farmhouses (from €200,000) and *manoirs* (from €400,000) in the vineyard-filled countryside.

PBI Conseil (www.pbiconseil.com)

5

Gironde (33)

Bordeaux (pop. 735,000), France's fifth-largest city after Toulouse in Haute-Garonne, is the capital of Aquitaine and lies on the river Garonne. It attracts tourists from all round the world as the starting point for the region's famous wine trails. Saint-Emilion (2,500) is a picturesque medieval village (one of the most beautiful in France) perched above the Dordogne river 40km (25mi) east of Bordeaux. Arcachon (11,400), south-west of Bordeaux on the southern shore of the Bassin d'Arcachon, has long, sandy beaches and safe swimming which have turned it into a major seaside resort; in summer, the population swells to around 50,000. On the north side of the Bassin lies Aquitaine's answer to Saint-Tropez – Cap Ferret. The village of Blaye on the Garonne estuary north of Bordeaux is one of the most attractive in France.

PROPERTY CHECK – GIRONDE

The world's most famous wine-growing area isn't just about vines: there are also pines (in the south) and sand and sea (in the west). France's largest *département*, Gironde is nevertheless dominated by the city of Bordeaux and the eponymous vineyards, which fan out in a semi-circle around the city. The well known names of Pauillac, Saint-Emilion and Blaye are in fact important towns. The area known as Entre-deux-Mers (actually between two rivers, the Dordogne and the Garonne) is the most attractive wine-growing area, with undulating hills dotted with medieval villages, while the coast is spectacular but forbidding other than in the Bassin d'Arcachon. The traditional Girondine house is classically proportioned, with light, airy rooms, and built of limestone, usually with attractive features such as fireplaces.

The property market is largely influenced by 'local' demand, Gironde being one of the least popular *départements* in the south-west among foreign buyers; as a result, prices are fairly stable, except around Bordeaux, which has become an 'in' place to live (see page 375) and where prices average around €2,250 per m^2. The thriving resort of Arcachon is also sought after; average prices here are more than twice as high. On the other hand, the recent downturn in the French wine industry has left a number of vineyard properties on the market at attractive prices. Three-bedroom properties requiring 'some work' can be found for less than €150,000, while villas with a pool start at around €175,000 and restored traditional stone houses at €200,000, though you will need nearer €300,000 for a really attractive one.

Currie French Properties (🖳 www.curriefrenchproperties.com); A Place in France (🖳 www.aplaceinfrance.co.uk); Waterside Properties International (🖳 www.watersideproperties-int.co.uk)

5

Landes (40)

Mont-de-Marsan (pop. 32,000) is the capital of Landes, although the town isn't particularly inspiring – except for aficionados of sculpture, as the town is littered with nude bronze sculptures by Charles Despiau and Charles Wlerick, two local artists; the museum in the town is named after them. Mont-de-Marsan also hosts two spectacular festivals, the Fête de Flamenco and the Fête de la Madeleine during July. Dax (20,900), despite having a smaller population than the capital, is a far more vibrant place; popular with the Romans, it was the first thermal spa town in France and is also the largest. Over 100,000 visitors swell the town's population each year, half of whom come to 'take the waters'. Every March, the town plays host to the national *foie gras* fair. Bullfighting is also a tradition in Dax, as is rugby (see **Sports** on page 207). The village of Saint-Sever is regarded as one of the most attractive in France.

Lot (46)

The main places of interest in Lot include: Cahors (pop. 19,750), the departmental capital, with its 12th-century cathedral and Pont Valentré, a fortified bridge with seven pointed arches (supposedly the most photographed monument in France); Figeac (10,000), a medieval centre with 13th, 14th and 15th century buildings; Rocamadour, a spectacular medieval village built into the cliffs of the river Alzou gorge; Autoire and Saint-Cirq-Lapopie, among France's most beautiful villages; the Chapel de Notre Dame, a pilgrim destination and reportedly a place of miracles; the Gouffre de Padirac, a huge crater with a succession of 'galleries', including the Salle de Grand Dôme, bigger than the world's largest cathedral.

Lot-et-Garonne (47)

Agen (pop. 32,000), despite being the departmental capital and steeped in history, isn't a particularly interesting town, although it's a busy commercial centre and renowned for its prunes. Just outside the town is the Walibi Parc d'Attractions, a vast amusement park with water rides and other attractions (see **Leisure** on page 210). Nérac, (7,450) is a small tourist town on the river Balse with plenty of historical interest, including the 16th-century Château de Henri IV. There's a number of *bastides* in the *département*, including Montflanquin, Puymirol and Sauveterre-de-Guyenne.

Pyrénées-Atlantiques (64)

Pau (pop. 90,000) is the capital of this *département* with spectacular views of the Pyrenees. It has something of an Anglophone heritage, having been a favourite winter watering hole of rich and famous Britons and Americans in the 19th century, mainly because of its mild climate (see page 204). It has much

English-style Victorian architecture, although the old town has retained a number of the medieval buildings. Pau has developed since the '60s, both as a tourist resort and as a centre of industry, but retains a genteel atmosphere. Bayonne (42,000) lies on the rivers Ardour and Nive. The town's history dates back to Roman times and it's famous throughout France for its salt-cured ham (*jambon de Bayonne*), which can only be made from pigs reared on a pure cereal diet (there's even a museum dedicated to the local art of ham-making), as well as for chocolate-making. It's a vibrant town with plenty to see and do, and the Basque language (see page 203) and customs are much in evidence (Bayonne is the capital of the Basque province of Labourd). The picturesque spa town of Salles-de-Béarn nearby is the principal producer of salt for making *jambon de Bayonne* (it naturally has a salt museum!).

PROPERTY CHECK – HAUTES-PYRENEES

This *département* has the best of two worlds: the Atlantic coast with its long, sandy beaches and cooling breezes, and the spectacular Pyrenean mountains. Hautes-Pyrénées includes the major part of the Pyrenees National Park, which attracts tourists summer and winter to its dramatic peaks, lush valleys and crystalline lakes and rivers. There are 16 skiing areas, at least one of which is within half an hour's drive of most parts of the *département*, and most of the southern villages derive much of their income from tourism – as do those around the pilgrimage centre of Lourdes. International access is easy, thanks to airports at Pau and Toulouse. Property-wise the area offers a choice between village houses ideal for 'lock-up-and-leave' holiday homes and rambling Gascony farmhouses, often suitable for bed and breakfast or *gîte* conversion, for permanent settlers. Less than €100,000 can still buy an attractive renovated holiday home, such as a one-bedroom house in a small town, while Gascony farmhouses for renovation start at under €150,000. Expect to pay at least twice as much, however, for one in pristine condition. The magnificent Aure valley in Hautes-Pyrénées stretches south from the town of Lannemzan towards Spain and boasts the attractive villages of Arreau and Saint-Lary. Its name comes from the Latin word *aura* meaning breeze, and in spring and autumn a cooling breeze sweeps along the valley. The valley has year-round activities, including, at Saint-Lary, the Pyrenees' largest ski resort, which accommodates almost 25,000 visitors annually and is therefore a good place for letting. A renovated four-bedroom house can be had for under €300,000, while modern villas sell for under €200,000 and building plots from around €50,000.

Abafim (💻 www.abafim.com/en); Couleurs de France (💻 www.couleurs-de-france.com); Gascony Estate Agents (💻 www.gasconyestateagents.com)

Biarritz (29,000) is situated on the Bay of Biscay and used to be the playground of the rich, although it has since become accessible to 'ordinary' people. Visitors come for the beaches, surfing and balneology (see **Amenities** on page 207) – and simply to relax (Biarritz is said to be France's retirement capital). The town is lively all year and particularly busy in summer. Saint-Jean-de-Luz (13,000) is a popular coastal spa town (Louis XIV was married there and authorised the local fishermen to plunder foreign ships – which they're still allowed to do!). The *département* also boasts a number of attractive villages, including Aïnhoa (reckoned to be one of the most beautiful in France), Espelette, Labastide-Clairence, Lescar, Lescun and Mauléon-Licharre.

PROPERTY CHECK – BIARRITZ & ST-JEAN-DE-LUZ

Property is distinctively Basque, with timber-framed, whitewashed houses painted red or green; even new property must be in the appropriate style. Most seafront properties in these popular resorts are large and divided into apartments. A two-bedroom apartment a minute from Biarritz beach costs a whopping €450,000, though it can be let for over €600 per week in August. Out of town prices are lower; a new studio apartment costs around €100,000, a one-bedroom apartment in Biarritz's Les Halles *quartier* even less, a similar property in chic Saint-Charles from €200,000, a three-bedroom villa in the coastal village of Bidart, just five minutes from Biarritz, under €500,000, a four-bedroom apartment in Cibourne, near Saint-Jean, €750,000. Leaseback properties are available at Ondres, around half an hour from Biarritz, with prices starting at around €200,000.

Beyond Biarritz (💻 www.beyonebiarritz.com); Couleurs de France (💻 www.couleurs-de-france.com)

Hautes-Pyrénées (65)

The departmental capital, Tarbes (pop. 46,000), is a quiet place famous (at least in France) as the birthplace of Maréchal Foch and for the *haricot tarbais*, which has been described as the 'Rolls Royce of beans'! The best-known town in the *département* (and one of the most famous in France) is Lourdes (15,700), a Roman Catholic pilgrimage centre. Over 5m pilgrims and tourists visit the town each year (only Paris has more hotel accommodation), half a million of them arriving in the spring in search of a miraculous cure.

PROPERTY CHECK – LOURDES

Many of the traditional shepherd's huts that dot the mountainside near Lourdes have been converted to holiday homes in recent years, though legislation now restricts conversions to permanent dwellings. Gascony farmhouses, often with adjoining open-fronted barns (suitable for conversion to *chambres d'hôtes* or a *gîtes*) in an L shape, typically have a central doorway leading to a large hall and an impressive staircase with rooms leading off either side. A standard farmhouse in need of renovation costs around €150,000 – and there are still plenty of needy farmhouses – while for a fully renovated property you must add at least €100,000 (though this could be far less than the cost of doing it yourself). A renovated small village house, on the other hand, can be had for just €100,000. Add 10 per cent to all prices for panoramic views.

Sife (www.sifex.co.uk); VEF (www.vef.com)

The *département* of Hautes-Pyrénées has many attractions other than Lourdes, however. These include a range of ski resorts and spas (the resort of Cauterets doubles as a spa town and a ski resort), wildlife and stunning scenery for hiking. The Parc national des Pyrénées offers panoramic views across the mountains and incorporates the spectacular Cascade du Pont d'Espagne – a 440m (1,430ft) high waterfall which freezes in winter – in the Cirque de Gavarnie, a natural amphitheatre amid the mountains.

PROPERTY CHECK – HAUTES-PYRENEES

As its name suggests, the Hautes-Pyrénées *département* includes some of the highest peaks in the Pyrenees (as well as the highest ski resort in the French Pyrenees – Tourmalet-Barèges-La Mongie). Geographically the department divides into two distinct areas more or less delineated by the A64 motorway. To the north the terrain and architecture are similar to Gers and Haute-Garonne: a mixture of plains and rolling hills with small towns and villages and old farms with their shallow clay-tiled roofs. To the south, where the Pyrenees rise to over 3,000m (10,000ft), interspersed with valleys, lakes and rivers, the architecture is quite different – almost Alpine: stone walls, slate roofs, balconies with flowers and mountain barns.

Access to the *département* has improved greatly in recent years with the advent of low-cost air services to the nearby towns of Pau and Toulouse. This, in turn, has had an effect on property prices, which went through a catching-up exercise in recent years and have now stabilised to grow steadily with inflation as elsewhere in France.

The Hautes-Pyrénées lacks heavy industry and is becoming increasingly focused on leisure and tourist activities, for which there's year-round appeal: in the summer every outdoor activity is catered for including, of course, the famous Tour de France which always includes the Cols of Tourmelet and Aspin on its route. In the winter, skiing is increasingly popular with numerous ski resorts including Cauterets, Saint-Lary-Soulan, Tourmalet and Hautacam. At other times of year the 'curists' come to spa towns such as Bagnères-de-Bigorre for treatment paid for by the French health service and over 5m pilgrims visit the town of Lourdes each year.

The most popular properties with foreign buyers are inevitably those with mountain views and in the traditional local style known as Bigordan after the ancient Bigorre region, which more or less covers the south of the *département*. Such properties are available but command a premium and may take some patience to find. Typical properties and prices include:

- a mountain barn for total renovation with 1.5ha (4 acres) of land – €117,000;

5

- a village house with three bedrooms and views of the Pyrenees – €132,000;
- a four-bedroom bigordan style cottage with 1,200 m^2 of land, ready to move into – €222,000;
- a four-bedroom renovated mountain barn in the Campan valley ten minutes from ski resort – €265,000;
- a farmhouse with four bedrooms plus outbuildings and 6ha (15 acres) of land – €353,000.

BCI-Immo (www.bci-immo.com)

Tarn (81)

Albi (pop. 64,500), the departmental capital, is situated on the river Tarn, where the light reflects off the rose-red bricks of the city. In medieval times, a blue dye was made from a plant called the *pastel* (whence our expression 'pastel blue'), a process which has been revived in the last decade. (Perhaps it was the bright blues and reds of the region that drove one of Albi's famous sons, Henri de Toulouse-Lautrec to rebel against the dull, northern greys and browns of his Parisian teachers and paint in such vivid colours.) Castres (45,500) is a historic town and the gateway to the Parc national régional du Haut-Languedoc. The nearby forest of Sidobre contains many unusual rock formations and is the world's largest granite quarrying site, where over 200 companies extract 150,000 tons of the rock each year (many of the buildings on the Champs-Elysées in Paris are made from Sidobre granite). The Sidobre region is also noted for its numerous *bastides*, such as Castelnau-de-Montmiral, Cordes-sur-Ciel, Penne-du-Tarn and Puycelci; Cordes, a fortified medieval hilltop town in the north of the *département*, is reckoned to be France's best preserved Gothic site.

PROPERTY CHECK – TARN

Small wonder this *département* is popular with British (and other foreign) buyers, with a landscape reminiscent of Tuscany – a combination of oak forests, lush river valleys, sunflower fields, vineyards, cypresses and pines – a mixture of Mediterranean,

Atlantic and mountain climates, a unique fusion of Languedocian and Pyrenean cultures and people renowned for their *joie de vivre*. Albi (the red city), Gaillac and the attractive *bastides* of Lisle-sur-Tarn and Puycelsi are among Tarn's many architectural riches and its property is varied, with many stone farmhouses, *mas*, *maisons bourgeoises* and *maisons de maître*. The downside is the property prices, which have historically been high (Tarn is a wealthy region) and have soared even higher in recent years. Nevertheless, a small *bastide* house can be had for less than €150,000 and a medium-size village property or a stone farm with outbuildings for around €250,000, although larger renovated country homes start at around €350,000. Property in the so-called 'golden triangle' – between Albi, Cordes and Gaillac – is the most sought after and consequently the most expensive, the average price of property being around €300,000. Nearby Lavaur and old-world Castres are cheaper, while in the market town of Mazamet at the foot of the Montagnes Noires bordering Languedoc prices are around 15 per cent lower than in the north.

Tarn Immobilier (💻 www.tarn-immobilier.com); Imogroup Tarn Sud (💻 www.imogroup-tarnsud.com)

Tarn-et-Garonne (82)

The departmental capital Montauban (pop. 53,800) is somewhat neglected in many French guidebooks, although it has much to offer, with its pink brick buildings (it's known locally as '*la ville rose*') and its reputation as the premier *bastide* in south-west France. Moissac (12,700) is renowned for fruit growing (apples, cherries, figs, kiwis, peaches, pears and plums, as well as hazelnuts and melons – a quarter of France's melons are grown here) and has an impressive abbey church and cloister, a masterpiece of Romanesque art. The *bastide* of Beaumont-de-Lomagne in the south-east of the *département* boasts an interesting 13th century church and holds a major garlic market in season (the Tarn valley is renowned for the production of garlic). The villages of Bruniquel and Penne are considered two of the most beautiful in France.

PROPERTY CHECK – TARN-ET-GARONNE

One of the sunniest *départements* in France, often with early winters and long summers, and mostly sheltered from the Mistral and other pernicious winds, Tarn-et-Garonne is understandably popular – not only with foreign buyers but with the French – and property prices have risen dramatically in recent years. They start at around €150,000 for a basic, habitable property but a restored typical three-bedroom farmhouse costs at least twice as much.

Cabinet International (☎ 05 63 94 09 24)

POPULATION

The population of the south-west of France comprises just over 3m in Aquitaine and 2.8m in Midi-Pyrénées, broken down among the 13 *départements* as follows: Ariège (146,000), Aveyron (271,000), Dordogne (401,000), Gers (180,000), Gironde (1.38m), Haute-Garonne (1.16m), Hautes-Pyrénées (230,000), Landes (357,000), Lot (168,000), Lot-et-Garonne (318,000), Pyrénées-Atlantiques (628,000), Tarn (363,000) and Tarn-et-Garonne (221,000).

The population of both regions is among the fastest-growing in France: Aquitaine's increasing by 0.92 per cent per annum and Midi-Pyrénées' by 1.11 per cent compared with the national average of 0.66 per cent. Haute-Garonne is the fastest-growing *département* (1.7 per cent per annum) and its capital, Toulouse, among the country's fastest-growing towns, having grown by over 10 per cent in the last six years. Tarn-et-Garonne (1.2 per cent) and Ariège (1.1) aren't far behind, followed by Tarn (0.9), Lot (0.8), Gers (0.7) and Aveyron and Hautes-Pyrénées (0.5). The region is France's second-most attractive (in population terms) after Languedoc-Roussillon (11 per cent of the population has moved there this century) and the majority are young and highly qualified.

There are around 107,000 foreign residents (including 42,500 North Africans) in Aquitaine and 100,500 (including over 33,000 North Africans) in Midi-Pyrénées. The highest concentration of North Africans is in Gironde – primarily in and around Bordeaux. Gironde also has the highest concentration of Spanish and Portuguese with around 18,000 out of a total of 40,000 in Aquitaine. Not surprisingly, a large number (14,200) also live in Pyrénées-Atlantiques. Even in Dordogne, there are over 2,300 Portuguese and almost 1,300 Moroccans. Lot has 1,250 Portuguese, 475 Moroccans, 380 Spanish and 150 Italians out of a total of 4,875 foreigners.

Other non-French EU nationals living in Aquitaine are mainly British, Dutch, German and Belgian, although they account only 0.5 per cent of the population. There are reckoned to be some 13,000 resident Britons in Dordogne alone, where there are enclaves such as the town of Eymet that are more British (in fact, English) than French. Gironde has the next largest number of British residents. Of the British population in Aquitaine, around two-thirds are retired or otherwise non-working, the proportion varying between less than 50 per cent in Gironde to around 80 per cent in Dordogne.

In Midi-Pyrénées, around 13,500 Spanish and Portuguese and 8,370 other non-French EU nationals (including around 1,700 Britons) live in Haute-Garonne, mainly in and around Toulouse. The second-largest contingent of British people is to be found in Gers (over 1,000) followed by Tarn-et-Garonne (around 600). In Hautes-Pyrénées, there are almost 13,500 Spanish and Portuguese, but fewer than 800 English, Dutch, Germans and Belgians.

Dordogne

Dordogne has a population of almost 388,400, whereas Lot has only just over 160,000, which makes it one of the most sparsely populated *départements* in France, with a density of just 31 people per km^2 (80 per mi^2) compared with the national average of around 100 people per km^2 (260 per mi^2). The population of both *départements* is growing at a slightly above average rate for France

Lot

Like many predominantly rural *départements* in France, Lot has been experiencing a decline in agriculture and a resulting decrease (and ageing) of the population. The latter trend, however, has recently been reversed and the 1999 census indicated that Lot's population had returned to its pre-1939, while more recent figures show an annual increase of 0.8 per cent – above the national average. This can in part be accounted for by the migration of both French and foreigners (mainly British) to the area.

LANGUAGE

Practically the whole of the area covered in this chapter is within the part of France where the *Langue d'Oc* or *Occitan* is spoken (see page 262), so don't be disturbed if you hear locals conversing in a 'foreign' language; they also speak and understand French, although their accent has a pronounced 'twang' (not at all like the pronunciation you learned at school), which it may take a while to get used to.

Peculiar to the extreme south-west of France is the Basque language (called *euskara*, *euskera* or *eskuara*), which is spoken in the western part of Pyrénées-Atlantiques in the historical provinces of Basse-Navarre, Labourd and Soule. The language's origin is a mystery, as it shows no resemblance to any other known language, although it has borrowed from Latin, French and Spanish (and our word 'bizarre' comes from Basque). Basque was passed on orally for centuries (it wasn't written until the 16th century and the first Basque book was published in 1545), and this tradition is kept alive, mainly in rural areas, by *bertsolaris*, who improvise Basque poems in various metres. There were originally eight dialects of Basque, but in the '60s an attempt was made to unify the language and the so-called *Euskara Batua* (Unified Basque) is now the most widely used.

During the Franco regime in Spain, it was forbidden to speak Basque, but since then it has enjoyed a revival: a school network has been set up in both Spain and France for those who want their children to learn the language (there are estimated to be 50,000 school children learning Basque at any time), and over 1,000 adults enrol in Basque classes every year. *Kilometroak* is the name of a popular movement for the preservation of Basque. Basque has no official status and isn't used in local administration, although local authorities have recently begun to erect bilingual road signs and there are a few in Basque only. It's estimated that over 600,000 people speak Basque, around 530,000 of them in Spain and only 70,000 or so in France (out of a population of around 260,000 in the Basque region of France, which is called *Iparralde* in Basque); a further 25,000 people are said to understand the language. French national television broadcasts only a few minutes of Basque each day and Radio France around an hour. However, there are three local radio stations broadcasting solely in Basque, and a weekly Basque newspaper was started in 1994.

Needless to say, it isn't necessary to learn Basque (or *Occitan*) in order to be accepted by the local community in *Iparralde*, but if you can master a few words and phrases it will probably improve your chances.

CLIMATE

Because of the varied geography of the area, the south-west of France experiences a variety of weather conditions, although in general it enjoys a pleasant, temperate climate due to the influence of both the Atlantic and the Massif Central. (Gers, for example, has a more maritime climate than

Aveyron.) Summer daytime temperatures can reach 38C (100F) during July and August with spectacular thunderstorms interrupting the sunshine, although the heat is usually alleviated by cool sea breezes. Bordeaux is the sunniest town in the area with over 2,080 hours of sunshine per year. Rainfall in the two regions is generally below the average for the country, although it varies greatly – e.g. 675mm (26in) on 101 days in Toulouse compared with Bordeaux's 850mm (33in) on 125 days. Bordeaux's wettest months are between October and January, whereas April to June are the wettest months in Toulouse. In Dordogne, winters are usually wet and cold (but not too cold and not too long) and summers are hot and humid; the most pleasant seasons are spring and autumn. Périgueux enjoys as much sunshine as Toulouse, with over 2,000 hours per year. Lot-et-Garonne is generally slightly hotter and drier than neighbouring Dordogne, while the coastal *départements* of Gironde and Landes have a pleasant, maritime climate. Inland, the climate changes as you approach the Pyrenees, and the Causses area of Aveyron can be windy and cold in winter but hot in summer. Lot has both an Atlantic and a continental climate, which means that in places the weather is predominantly mild, while in others it's hot and dry.

5

Atlantic coastal areas have the highest rainfall – up to 1,000mm (39in) per year – Bayonne is one of France's wettest towns with rainfall on 143 days per year – and the area can experience severe flooding, as in November 1999, when 22 people died after almost a year's rain fell in just 24 hours, and in September 2002, when 28 deaths were reported as a result of heavy rain in the neighbouring region of Languedoc. The wettest month in Pyrénées-Atlantiques is April (with around 115mm of rain), followed by May and November, while July and August are the driest months – but still have over 60mm of rain on average. The pattern is similar in Gironde and Landes, though overall rainfall is slightly lower. Inland *départements* are generally drier, monthly rainfall in Lot-et-Garonne varying between around 50mm (in March) and 80mm (May), while Dordogne has 52mm in July and 84mm in December, May and October also being relatively wet.

Mid-Pyrénées' wettest *département* is Hautes-Pyrénées, with up to 120mm of rain in April and May and over 60mm in the driest month, July. Ariège has a similar pattern, while Haute-Garonne, Tarn and Tarn-et-Garonne are significantly drier (from 45mm in July to 75mm in May). Aveyron, Gers and Lot are in-between, with between 45mm and 60mm in July and 80mm to 90mm in May and October.

In the mountains, the weather is often stormy. As in the rest of Europe and indeed the world, climatic changes have produced some strange and adverse weather conditions in recent years, and the south-west of France has experienced its share of strong winds and higher than average temperatures during the summer as well as the above-mentioned flooding.

In northern parts of the area, average temperatures are around 10C during December and January. In the mountains, however, temperatures are much lower and the Pyrenees are popular with skiers, the season lasting from December until March or April. The weather in the foothills of the Pyrenees is relatively mild all year. The table below shows the number of hours' sunshine and days' rainfall in selected towns in the area.

Town	Sunshine Hours	Days' Rainfall
Toulouse (31)	2,047	101
Bordeaux (33)	2,084	125
Agen (47)	1,984	111
Bayonne (64)	1,935	143
Pau (64)	1,849	130
Tarbes (65)	1,913	126
Castres (81)	2,077	106
Montauban (82)	2,029	105

CRIME RATE & SECURITY

The south-west rates fairly low in the French crime-rate stakes, probably because the majority of the area is rural. Dordogne is among the *départements* with the lowest (reported) crime rates in France. As in other regions, crime rates are higher in the major cities. Toulouse (31) has the area's highest (reported) crime rate (although not particularly high by national standards) with over 100 reported crimes per 1,000 inhabitants per year. Next come Bordeaux (33) and Montauban (82) with around 95 crimes. 'Safest' cities are Tarbes (65) and Albi (81) with under 70 crimes per 1,000 inhabitants. However, car thefts and thefts from cars are on the increase, especially from foreign registered and rented cars.

During the summer months, forest fires are a danger, both to people and to property. Where properties are in a high-risk area for forest fires, it's often a legal requirement to ensure that firebreaks surround them. During this period the local authorities ban bonfires and sometimes barbeques. Fines for ignoring theses bans are heavy.

Those considering living in the Basque region will no doubt be aware of the nationalist group known as *ETA*. While much publicity has been afforded to terrorist attacks carried out in Spain, France has been little affected.

AMENITIES

Sports

Because of its varied environment and climate, the south-west of France offers a host of sporting opportunities. Most towns have a public swimming pool and tennis courts as well as a municipal gymnasium (*salles des sports*), where there are usually facilities for a variety of sports, including basketball and volleyball. With some of the most beautiful scenery in Europe, the area offers walkers and cyclists an abundance of spectacular cycle routes and hiking trails. Bicycles can be hired in many towns for around €15 per day. For further information on cycle routes in France contact the Cyclist Touring Club (UK ☎ 0870-873 0060, 🖳 www.ctc.org.uk). Walkers should note that in some areas, especially in the mountainous, walks can be formidable and require appropriate clothing – particularly in winter. For further information contact the Fédération française de la Randonnée Pédestre (☎ 01 44 89 93 90/93, 🖳 www.ffrandonnnee.fr). Cycling is best avoided during the peak summer season, when temperatures are high and roads, particularly in Dordogne, are full of cars and coaches. Many of the roads near the river Dordogne, for example, are extremely narrow and leave little place for two cars to pass, and cyclists risk being flattened.

Hunting is a popular 'sport' throughout France, and there are hunting clubs and associations in many towns and even in some villages. Other popular sports in the area include:

Skiing

There are around 30 ski resorts in the French Pyrenees, most of them in Hautes-Pyrénées. Although not as famous or challenging as the Alps, the Pyrenees offer a good selection of downhill runs as well as plenty of cross-country skiing. Resorts include Ax, Guzet (09), Luchon/Superbagnères (31), Gourette, (64), Artouste-Fabrèges, Barèges, Cauterets, Gavarnie, La Mongie, La Pierre-Saint-Martin, Luz-Ardiden, Peyragudes-Balestas and Piau-Engaly (65), as well as four resorts in Pyrénées-Occidentales (see page 268) and five in Andorra (Arinsa/Pal, Arcalis/Ordino, La Rabassa, Pas-de-la-Casa/Grau Roig and Soldeu/El Tarter), which borders Ariège. Further information is available from La Maison des Pyrénées, 6 rue Vital Carles, 33000 Bordeaux (☎ 05 56 44 05 65) and from 💻 www.pyrenees.net and 💻 www.skiandorra.ad. Details of resorts and snow conditions can be found on 💻 www.goski.com.

Surfing & Swimming

With over 14 championship surfing beaches and a further 38 surfing beaches of varying quality between Soulac in the north and Saint-Jean-de-Luz in the south, surfing is a popular sport for those living within reach of the coast. Surfing competitions are normally held in July, August and September (the Biarritz Surf Festival in July is one of the major events), although surfing is a year-round sport. There's a number of surf schools which, for around €30 to €40 per hour, will provide individual tuition. Board hire costs around €15 per day. Further information can be obtained from the Fédération française du Surf (☎ 05 58 43 55 88, 💻 www.surfinfrance.com). The sea is less suited to swimming (this is the Atlantic, not the Mediterranean), and it can be dangerous to bathe outside the prescribed beaches, although there's a number of inland seawater lakes, such as the 3,600ha (8,900 acre) Hossegor lake and the Etang de Biscarosse, where swimming is safer.

Watersports

There are other watersports facilities along the coast, principally at La Teste-de-Buch (33), Hossegor and Léon (40). Inland, the area is crossed by a number of rivers, including the Adour, Ariège, Aveyron, Baïse, Garonne, Gave d'Oloron and Gave de Pau, Gers and Tarn, as well as the Canal du Midi, which joins the Garonne at Toulouse. There's also a number of lakes, including those at Montbels (09), Blasimon, Hostens, Hourtin-Carcans, Lacanau (33), Parentis, Sanguinet, Soustons (40), Casteljaloux, Duras, Preyssas (47), Lembeye, Oloron, Thèze (64) and Gaube (65). These offer a variety of watersports – from swimming and rowing to canoeing and rafting. The river Gave d'Oloron south of Pau (64) is renowned for white-water rafting, which can be enjoyed at Navarrenx and Oloron and in the Vallée d'Ossau; the rivers Gave de Pau, Adour and Neste d'Aure are also well suited to white-water sports. Details can be obtained from the Fédération française de Canoë Kayak (☎ 01 45 11 08 50, 💻 www.ffck.org) and local tourist information offices.

Fishing

The area's lakes and rivers are also used for fishing, and Midi-Pyrénées in particular, with some 2,500km (1,500mi) of waterways and over 2,000 lakes, is reckoned to be an angler's paradise, where fish include carp, perch, pike, shad and trout.

Horse Riding

There are many equestrian centres in the area, where mounts can be hired by the hour, half-day or day. Further information can be obtained from the Fédération française d'Equitation (☎ 01 53 26 15 50, 💻 www.ffe.com) and the Bureau des Guides équestres transpyrénéens (☎ 05 61 69 01 99, 💻 www.equipyrene.com, which has information in English).

Rugby

The French are as passionate about rugby as the Welsh or New Zealanders, and in the south-west rugby has a bigger following than soccer, all the major towns having a team. Toulouse have been national champions on more than one occasion, as have Biarritz. For further information contact the Fédération française de Rugby (💻 www.ffr.fr), which can provide a list of rugby clubs in the region.

Golf

There are over 60 golf courses in the south-west (Pau boasts France's oldest golf club, founded in 1856 – by the English, of course), many of which are considered to be the best in the country. There are more courses in Midi-Pyrénées than Aquitaine, towns with the most courses being Bordeaux (33) and Biarritz (64) with six each and Toulouse (31) with seven. The table below lists the number of courses in each *département*. Information (in both French and English) on how to find courses, the cost of a round (which varies between €15 and €50), etc. is available via the internet (💻 www. backspin.com). Another useful website for golfers is 💻 www.golf. com.fr. Fees vary, and Golf Pass packages are available in some areas during low season. The website 💻 www.touradour.com/golf includes a list of all the golf courses participating in the scheme in Aquitaine.

Département	**No. of Courses**
Ariège	1 x 18 holes
Aveyron	2 x 9 holes, 1 x 18 holes
Cantal	1 x 9 holes
Dordogne	3 x 9 holes, 3 x 18 holes
Haute-Garonne	4 x 9 holes, 4 x 18 holes, 1 x 36 holes
Gers	3 x 9 holes, 2 x 18 holes
Gironde	2 x 9 holes, 6 x 18 holes, 2 x 27 holes, 2 x 36 holes
Landes	1 x 9 holes, 3 x 18 holes, 1 x 27 holes
Lot-et-Garonne	3 x 9 holes, 3 x 18 holes
Pyrénées-Atlantiques	2 x 9 holes, 1 x 12 holes, 6 x 18 holes
Hautes-Pyrénées	1 x 9 holes, 4 x 18 holes
Tarn	1 x 9 holes, 4 x 18 holes
Tarn-et-Garonne	1 x 9 holes

Pelote

Known as *pilota* in Basque and *pelota* in Spanish, this game is unique to the Basque region and is quite dangerous, as it's incredibly fast. It's played on an outdoor court, and pairs of teams fling a leather ball against the court walls using their hands, a wooden paddle or a scooped wicker racquet.

Leisure

The south-west boasts numerous leisure activities and attractions, many of which are available all year. There are abundant varieties of flora and fauna in the area to interest both the amateur and professional naturalist; for example, the arid plateaux of the Aveyron boast over 2,000 species, including the great tawny vulture. There are many museums to visit, notably the Musée de l'Armagnac at Condom (32), which shows the traditional method of making armagnac and gives visitors the opportunity to taste the result, and the Musée Toulouse-Lautrec at Albi (81), which holds the largest collection of the artist's work. In addition to the many attractions listed under **Major Towns & Places of Interest** on page 189, there are numerous *châteaux*, including the 12th-century Château de Villandraut south of Bordeaux, which is a particularly fine example. (Note, however, that many places advertising themselves as *châteaux* are in fact vineyards, often not open to the public except by appointment.)

There's a good selection of plays, concerts and other musical events in major towns and cities, and even the smallest village holds events and festivals during the summer months. Bordeaux, Toulouse, and Pau all have excellent theatres, which attract quality productions and performances. Bordeaux has its own symphony orchestra, as does Toulouse, and Biarritz boasts a ballet company. There are no fewer than seven major jazz festivals, as well as numerous smaller ones, in the area. In the Basque region, traditional music can be heard in town squares, and both music and dance are performed in the streets of Bayonne (64). Details of festivals and events in the Basque region can be found on 💻 www.guide-basque.com.

Once considered a somewhat dowdy town, Bordeaux has recently revitalised itself, particularly in the eyes of the student population, with around 40 nightclubs on the quai de Paludate, as well as jazz clubs and tapas bars. Friday night is 'roller night', when over 500 young people rollerskate around the city! Bordeaux also boasts over 60 historical monuments, an opera house, a concert hall and a new casino. Toulouse is also a lively city, with a large student population and plenty of cheap places to eat and drink. Most bars stay open until the early hours of the morning. There's also plenty to see, including a modern art gallery, the relics of Saint Thomas Aquinas (in the Les Jacobins monastery), seven museums and over 50 historical monuments.

English-language Cinema & Theatre

Some cinemas show all foreign films in the original language (*en version originale/VO*), e.g. Cinéma le Club in Brive-la-Gaillarde (19), while others do so only on certain days of the month or on demand. The cinema in Sarlat-la-Canéda (24) shows English-language films at least once a month, and English-language films can also be seen at the Cinéma Lux in Le Buisson (24). Bordeaux (33) has three cinemas that show films in their original language, Toulouse (31) has two, and Biarritz and Pau (64) have one each. English-language films are also shown at Ciné 4 in Castillonnès (47). A useful website for finding out what films are on in a given area, which also indicates whether the films are being shown in the original language is 💻 www.cinefil.com.

There are two annual regional film festivals, one in Sarlat (24) during November, which shows a good selection of foreign and French films, and the other in Arcachon (33) in September. Although neither compares with the Cannes film festival, both attract a good selection of foreign and French films.

Parks, Zoos & Theme Parks

The area boasts an abundance of *parcs naturels*, principally the Parc régional des Landes de Gascogne (see page 178). There are also plenty of man-made attractions (many of a historical nature), including:

- Abbaye des Automates in Clairac (47): automatons;
- African Safari in Plaisance-du-Touch (31): African and other animals in a 'natural' environment;
- Aqualand de Gujan-Mestras (33): water park in the Forêt des Landes;
- Aquarium de la Garonne et des Pyrénées in Muret (31): tropical and freshwater fish;
- Aquaval in Lautrec (81): water park;
- Aquarium du Périgord Noir in Le Bugue-sur-Vézère (24): 10,000 freshwater fish;
- L'Archipel in Cahors (46): water park;
- L'Archipel in Castres (81): water park;
- Château du Colmbier in Mondalazac (12): medieval *château* and animal park;
- Le Chaudron magique in Brugnac (47): farm animals;
- Cité de L'Espace in Toulouse (31): one of the world's best space park, museum and planetarium complexes, attracting over 300,000 visitors annually;
- La Coccinelle in Gujan-Mestras (33): a combination of traditional amusement park and zoo;
- La Colline aux Marmottes in Argeles-Gazost (65): local wild animals;
- Le Donjon des Aigles in Beaucens (65): eagles and other birds of prey;

- Ecomusée de la Grande Lande in Sabres (40): relive the traditional way of life;
- La Falaise Aux Vautours (Cliff of the Vultures) in Aste-Béon near Laruns (64): all about vultures;
- La Féerie du Rail in Rocamadour (46): 'kingdom of enchanted railways';
- Ferme équestre la Haute Yerle in Alles-sur-Dordogne (24): horse-riding centre;
- La Forêt des Singes in Rocamadour (46): monkey park;
- La Ferme exotique (33): 'safari' park with over 1,000 animals;
- Les Grottes de Betharram in Saint-Pé-de-Bigorre (62): 3km (2mi) of caves;
- Le Jardin des Bêtes in Gages-le-Bas (12): animal park;
- Jardin d'Eyrignac in Salignac-Eyvigues (24): one of the finest gardens in France;
- Le Jardin des Papillons (33): tropical garden with butterflies;
- Labyrinthus du Lot in Martel (46): mazes;
- Larressingle (32): medieval life;
- La Maison des Loups in Orlu (09): wolves;
- Micropolis (12): all about insects;
- Musée Aquarium d'Arcachon (33): local and other fish;
- Parc animalier de Gramat (46): 150 rare species of animal;
- Parc animalier de Pradinas (12): 250 animals;
- Parc aux Kangourous/Zoo d'Asson (64): 400 exotic animals and birds, including kangaroos and wallabies;
- Parc de Nahuques Mont de Marsan has an open-air wildlife park;
- Parc ornithologique du Teich (33): over 250 species of bird;
- Parc Préhistologia in Lacave (46): caves and prehistory park;
- Parc du Thot Espace Cro-Magnon in Thonac (24): prehistory park;
- Préhistoparc in Tursac (24): prehistory park;

- Quercyland in Souillac (46): water park;
- La Récréation in Castelnau-Montratier (46): children's activity park;
- Repriland in Martel-en-Quercy (46): 250 reptiles, including crocodiles;
- La Réserve de Bisons d'Europe in Sainte-Eulalie (48): bison roaming 'free';
- Village Medieval d'Artisans d'Art in Gujan-Mestras (33): reconstruction of medieval village;
- Le Village du Bournat in Le Bugue-sur-Vézère (24): reconstruction of a 19th century village;
- Walibi Aquitaine in Roquefort near Agen (47): amusement park with 16 attractions, including an 18th century *château*;
- Zoo de Pessac (33): 400 animals and over 100 species.

Spas

For those who want (or need) pampering there are around a dozen spas offering a variety of water cure treatments. There are three in Ariège, three in Pyrénées-Atlantiques (at Anglet, Biarritz and Cambo-les-Bains) and several in the area around Dax (40). Costs vary according to the type and number of treatments you have, but a full day's pampering will set you back between €150 and €200. Most treatments must be booked in advance. Aquitaine is also noted for its many naturist centres, of which there are at least ten.

Casinos

For those who like to have a flutter, there are over 25 casinos in the area, most also offering meals and entertainment: one in Ariège, three in Haute-Garonne, one in Gers, five in Gironde, six in Landes, six in Pyrénées-Atlantiques, four in Hautes-Pyrénées and one in Tarn. The main casinos are in Arcachon (33), where the casino is housed in the beautiful Château Deganne, Dax (40), and Saint-Jean-de-Luz (64). Details of all casinos and what they offer are available via the internet (e.g. 💻 www.journaldes casinos.com – partly in English).

Bullfighting

In the southern *départements* of the area, bullfighting (*la corrida*) is considered a noble sport and supporters ardently celebrate both the tradition and spectacle, despite the fact that bulls suffer a slow and painful death. Matadors are treated as heroes and can earn vast amounts of money. Recently, there has been a number of protests against bullfighting, both by locals and animal rights supporters. Should you have a taste for blood, the main towns that hold festivals are Vic-Fézensac (32), Dax, Mont-de-Marsan (40) and Bayonne (64).

Shopping Centres & Markets

The Saint-Christoly shopping centre in Bordeaux has around 40 shops and the Galerie des Grands Hommes around 20. Toulouse has no fewer than five shopping centres, including the vast Portet-sur-Garonne incorporating a hypermarket (claimed to be the largest in France), a mall and a surrounding complex of home improvement centres, sporting and electronic goods outlets. Large IKEA and Habitat stores can also be found in Toulouse. The *centre commercial* Bosquet at Pau (64) incorporates a Champion supermarket.

There are few multi-storey shopping centres in Dordogne and Lot, where there tend to be 'commercial zones' – i.e. a large car park surrounded by a supermarket and several other shops. There's a Nouvelles Galeries department store in the centre of Périgueux (24) and a new shopping centre called La Feuilleraie with 50 shops on the outskirts of the town (off the RN21). There's also a covered market in Domme (24). Lot has two Leclerc hypermarkets: in Pradines (with 11 shops) and Capdenac (seven shops).

Regional markets for local produce such as *foie gras* (goose liver pâté) are held weekly; the Monday market in Samatan south-east of Auch (32) attracting buyers from all over the south-west. Most towns also have weekly or daily markets, and Toulouse (31) boasts several: food on the Boulevard de Strasbourg, flowers and 'antiques' in the Place du Capitole (on Wednesdays and Sundays), proper antiques near the Saint-Sernin basilica (Thursdays to Sundays) and a huge indoor produce market specialising in fish at Place Victor Hugo. Other major weekly markets in the area are listed below:

- Bergerac (24) – Tuesdays (organic market)
- Biron (24) – June to September (farm market)

- Couze-Saint-Front (24) – July (evening fair)
- Eyvirat (24) – August (farm market)
- Sarlat-la-Canéda (24) – Saturdays all year (general market)
- Bazas (33) – Saturdays
- Dax (40) – Saturdays
- Mont-de-Marsan (40) – Saturdays
- Peyrehorade (40) – Wednesdays
- Cahors & Gourdon (46) – June to September (evening market)
- Cahors & St Martel (46) – all year (traditional market)
- Limogne & Lalbenque (46) – December to March (truffle market)
- Agen (47) – Saturdays
- Marmande (47) – Tuesdays to Saturdays
- Villeneuve-sur-Lot (47) – Tuesdays and Saturdays
- Mauléon-Licharre (64) – Tuesdays and Saturdays
- Nay (64) – Tuesdays
- Saint-Jean-Pied-de-Port (64) – Mondays
- Saint-Palais (64) – Fridays
- Tardets (64) – every Monday in July and August; every other Monday the rest of the year

Foreign Food & Products

Most large supermarkets and the food departments in Monoprix and Galeries Lafayette have some foreign food and products. Usually, the bigger the shop, the better the selection. In some areas, there are *épiceries fines* (delicatessens) that stock foreign food. There's a stall at the Tuesday market in Le Bugue (24) selling English products, and there's a butcher in Saint-Cyprien (24) who apparently makes English sausages from spices supplied to him by Britons living in the area! The English Panier, Le Caprice, 24310 Saint-Crépin-de-Richemont (☎ 05 53 03 21 97) and The Corner Shop, 50 rue Thiers, 24700 Montpon-Menesterol (☎ 05 53 81 88 43) sell 'English' produce, and the Librarie Millescamps, 7 rue Saint-Front, 24000 Périgueux (☎ 05 53 09 53 25, ✉ millescamps@orange.fr) sells second-hand English and Australian books.

With its large expatriate community, Toulouse (31) is particuarly well provided with shops selling foreign products – probably better than anywhere outside Paris. Supermarkets and hypermarkets, especially Carrefour and Leclerc, stock a variety of foreign food, including such British staples as Marmite and peanut butter, and may even have aisles dedicated to non-French produce. Almost every grocery shop in the city also stocks Asian food and there are a number of Asian-run stores. Close to the Spanish border, many British products are available in smaller supermarkets (including products from Sainsbury, Tesco and Waitrose!), and in Andorra (near Ariège) the shops stock all kinds of foreign goods. There's a number of English-language bookshops in the area, including those in Bordeaux, Toulouse, and Pau, and most large towns and tourist regions have bookshops that sell books in Dutch, German and Spanish (especially near the Spanish border).

Restaurants & Bars

As in any part of France, wherever you go in the south-west you will find an abundance of bars and restaurants ranging from pavement cafés to gourmet establishments. Many offer regional specialities, such as *cassoulet* from Toulouse, *foie gras* from Périgord or Gascony, oysters from Arcachon and ham from Bayonne, and a fish stew called *ttoro*, the Basque Country's answer to *bouillabaisse*. There's also a variety of international restaurants in larger towns and cities offering Italian, Spanish, Arabic, Indian and Chinese cuisine, as well as Basque restaurants, which serve some of the spiciest dishes in France! Bordeaux boasts five Michelin-starred restaurants. Some restaurants (especially on the coast) are open only during the summer. Not surprisingly, prices on the coast and in cities and tourist areas tend to be a little higher that in other areas.

There are American-style fast food outlets in large towns, including Buffalo Grill, Quick and the ubiquitous McDonald's as well as self-service cafeterias such as Flunch and Casino, usually located within or near shopping complexes. Cafés and bars in villages and small towns play an important part in the local community, often serving multiple functions such as *tabac*, betting shop and *bistro*. Most open around 8 or 9pm, sometimes even earlier, especially on market days. Closing times often seem to depend on the volume of business and the mood of the *patron*!

As in most parts of France, vegetarian food is hard to find, but it's offered at Le Café de la Rivière in Le Bourg near Beynac (24) as well as English, French and Italian dishes.

SERVICES

International & Private Schools

There are two international schools in the south-west: The Bordeaux International School (252 rue Judaïque, 33000 Bordeaux, ☎ 05 57 87 02 11, 💻 www.bordeaux-school.com), which takes pupils from the age of 3 to 19 and offers facilities for day students and boarders, and The International School of Toulouse (Route de Pibrac, 31770, Colomiers, ☎ 05 62 74 26 74, 💻 www.intst.eu), which is a day school only with pupils aged between 4 and 18. Fees for these schools are several thousand euros per year. There's also a number of private schools which cater for foreign students, including the Lycée privé Institution Notre-Dame (☎ 05 34 01 36 40, 💻 www.notre-dame-pamiers.com) in Pamiers (09), the Collège privé Sainte Marie (☎ 05 59 26 20 35) in Saint-Jean-de-Luz (64) and, for primary school pupils, the Ecole privée du Sacré-Coeur (☎ 05 59 25 46 50) in Bayonne (64). The Lycée Magendie (☎ 05 57 81 61 50) in Bordeaux is an 'ordinary' state school which teaches English literature, history and geography in English.

As across the whole of France, there are private schools from kindergarten to university level, and there's one in the area which cater for English-speaking students: the Lycée privé mixte Saint Joseph (☎ 05 53 31 33 09, 💻 www.stjoseph-sarlat.fr.st) in Sarlat-la-Canéda (24)

5

Language Schools

Language lessons are offered by a number of public and private bodies in the area. The Alliance française has branches in Toulouse (31) and Bordeaux (33). Other public and private schools include those listed below. For private lessons expect to pay between €20 and €35 per hour. Language courses are also offered by local Chambres de Commerce et d'Industrie and Centres culturels.

- Langue Onze Sud-Ouest in Toulouse (31);
- Université de Toulouse Le Mirail in Toulouse (31);

- Cetradel in Bègles (33);
- BLS in Bordeaux (33);
- Centre d'Etude des Langues in Bordeaux (33);
- Greta in Guéret (23), Cahors (46), Clermont-Ferrand (63) and Limoges (87).
- AFPA in Cahors (46) and Limoges (87);
- MCB Langues in Bordeaux (33);
- Centre international d'Etudes in Saint-Aubin-de-Médoc (33);
- Département d'Etudes de français in Pessac (33);
- Centre d'Etudes des Langues in Bayonne (64);
- Institut d'Etudes françaises pour Etrangers (IEFE) in Pau (64);
- Ateliers linguistiques du Tarn (ALT) in Brens (81);
- ALS Langues in Tarn (81).

Details of the above schools can be found on 💻 www.europa-pages.com. The French Consulate in London (see **Appendix A**) publishes a booklet called *Cours de français Langue étrangère et Stages pédagogiques du français Langue étrangère en France*, which includes a comprehensive list of schools and organisations providing French language courses throughout France.

Hospitals & Clinics

There are no 'international' hospitals in the south-west, although many hospitals cater for foreign patients and there are three hospitals in Bordeaux where English is known to be spoken: the Centre Hospitalier Charles Perrens, the Fondation Jean Bergonié and the Hôpital du Groupe Pellegrin-Tripode. There are also main hospitals at Montluçon and Vichy (03), Aurillac (15), Brive-la-Gaillarde and Tulle (19), Guéret (23), Périgueux (24), Le Puy-en-Velay (43), Cahors (46), Cébazat (63) and Saint-Junien (87). Hospitals in main towns, and especially teaching hospitals (*CHU*), have English-speaking staff.

Private hospitals include the Clinique Pasteur in Toulouse, which is world-renowned for its highly specialised expertise in medical and surgical cardiology and provides translators if required.

Tradesmen

It's fairly easy to find English-speaking tradesmen, especially in Dordogne and Lot, although they don't advertise in local papers and the consulate in Bordeaux (see below) only supplies lists of tradesmen in that area. Magazines such as *French Property News* and newspapers such as *The News* (see **Appendix B**) carry advertisements by English-speaking tradesmen. French tradesmen are unlikely to speak much English but are generally reliable.

English-language Media

Sud Radio on 96.1FM broadcasts a programme in English at 12.15 each weekday which can be received in most parts of the area. In Lot and neighbouring parts of Dordogne there are broadcasts in English (called 'Britdoc') every Thursday and Sunday evening on Antenne d'Oc; frequencies vary (contact ☎ 05 65 31 92 76 for information). BBC Radio 1, 2, 3, and 4 can be received on your television via the Astra satellite, and you can listen to recordings of radio programmes on Radio 1, 2, 3, 4, 5, 6 and 1Extra on your computer via the internet (go to 💻 www.bbc.co.uk/radio/aod/index. shtml). The World Service is available on short wave (for frequency details, go to 💻 www.bbc.co.uk/worldservice/schedules/frequencies/eurwfreq.shtml) and via the Astra satellite. Local music stations usually broadcast 60 per cent non-French language songs, most of which are in English.

Only cities and large towns, towns and villages with a substantial foreign population and shops near Bordeaux and Toulouse airports tend to have English newspapers and magazines. Those that can be obtained tend to be a truncated European edition and, unless bought close to an airport, are usually the previous day's edition. There are also two English-language monthlies published in France and distributed nationally, *The Connexion* and *The News* (see **Appendix B**). There's no local English-language press, although in Toulouse a free publication listing events of interest to English speakers is available from Books and Mermaids bookshop, and the Bordeaux British Community and Bordeaux Women's Club (see **Clubs** below) publish English-language newsletters.

Embassies & Consulates

There are over 40 consulates in Bordeaux covering countries from Algeria to Togo, including the UK and the US. The British Consulate (353 boulevard du Président Wilson, 33073 Bordeaux, ☎ 05 57 22 21 10, ✉ postmaster.

bordeaux@fco.gov.uk), which covers the whole of Aquitaine and Midi-Pyrénées, is open Mondays to Fridays from 9am to noon and from 2 to 5pm and has telephone numbers for information on French administrative services in Dordogne (☎ 05 56 11 56 56) and Lot (☎ 05 62 15 15 15). The American Presence Post is at 10 place de la Bourse, BP 77, 33025 Bordeaux (☎ 05 56 48 63 80, ✉ bordeauxcons@fr.psinet.com). There's also an American presence post, but no longer a British consulate, in Toulouse – The American Presence Post, 25 allée Jean-Jaurès, 31000 Toulouse (☎ 05 34 41 36 50).

Places of Worship

The south-west has a relatively high population of Protestants (compared with the overall 2 per cent for France), and there are a number of Anglican churches in the area with regular services in English, including:

- Chancelade near Périgueux (24) – Chapelle Saint-Jean de l'Abbaye;
- Chapdeuil, Limeuil (24) – Eglise Sainte Cathérine;
- Ribérac (24) – Eglise Notre-Dame de la Paix;
- Sarlat-la-Canéda (24) – Parish Church of Sainte Nathalène (summer only);
- Toulouse (31) – Eglise Sainte Marguerite;
- Bordeaux (33) – Chapelle de l'Assomption;
- Monteton (47) – Eglise de Monteton;
- Biarritz (64) – Eglise de Saint Joseph;
- Pau (64) – Saint Andrew's.

There are also English-language services at a number of venues in Cahors (46), for which the contact is Laurie Mort (☎ 05 61 85 17 67). *The News* (see **Appendix B**) publishes the schedule of English-language services in Dordogne performed by the Anglican Church of Aquitaine (contact Rvd Michael Selman, 1 Lotissement de la Caussade, 33270 Floirac, ☎ 05 56 86 36 20, 💻 http://chapaq.free.fr). For further details of English-language services, contact Laurie Mort (☎ 05 61 85 17 67) for Toulouse, Michael Selman (☎ 05 56 40 05 12) for Bordeaux and Monteton, and John Livingstone (☎ 05 59 24 71 18) for Biarritz.

Every town and almost every village has a Catholic church, although many villages hold services only once a month. Mass schedules for the month are posted on church doors.

There's a Jehovah's Witnesses groups in Saint-Aster (24), Latter Day Saints in Périgueux (24), and Seventh Day Adventists in Notre-Dame-de-Sanilhac (24), and there's a Buddhist association (Association Dhagpo Kagyu Ling) in Dordogne.

There are mosques in Bordeaux (33), Mont-de-Marsan (40), Agen, Fumel (47), Bayonne and Pau (64); details can be found on 💻 http://mosquee.free.fr. There are several synagogues in Toulouse (31) and Bordeaux (33) as well as one each in Agen (47), Bayonne and Pau (64). Details can be found on 💻 www.pagesjaunes.fr (enter 'Synagogues' in the first box and the name of the town) and 💻 www.feujcity.com (where there's also information about Kosher food shops and restaurants, Jewish associations and schools, etc.).

Clubs

There are numerous clubs and associations for the English-speaking community, which have a wealth of local knowledge and are useful points of contact for new arrivals. The British and American Consulates (see **Consulates** above) in Bordeaux can provide a list of clubs and associations in the Aquitaine region. Clubs and associations include:

- Anglophones in Aquitaine (☎ 05 59 83 78 74, 💻 http://pau.anglophones.com) in Pau (64);
- Association France/Grande Bretagne (☎ 05 65 31 61 13) in Cahors (46);
- Bordeaux Accueil (☎ 05 56 44 62 83);
- Bordeaux British Community (💻 www.bordeaux british.com) publishes a newsletter and organises monthly meetings;
- Bordeaux Women's Club (☎ 05 57 43 69 04) publishes a monthly newsletter and organises a monthly lunch and other activities.
- Dordogne Ladies' Club (☎ 05 53 83 82 35);
- Dordogne Organisation of Gentlemen (☎ 05 53 94 73 14);
- English Kids' Club in Beynac (24) (☎ 05 53 28 35 49);
- English-speaking Ladies' Group of Toulouse (ESLG, ☎ 05 61 85 65 65);
- YES Association (24) (☎ 05 53 46 77 47).

For French speakers, the Accueil des Villes françaises (AVF), a French organisation designed to welcome newcomers to an area, is an option (there's often at least one fluent English-speaker in each group). There are around 30 AVF groups in Aquitaine and Midi-Pyrénées – in Millau, Rodez (12), Muret, Ramonville, Revel, Saint-Jean, Saint-Orens, Toulouse (31), Auch (32), Arcachon, La Teste-de-Buch, Pessac (33), Vieux-Boucau (40), Cahors (46), Agen, Marmande, Nérac, Villeneuve-sur-Lot (47), Biarritz, Billière, Pau, Saint-Jean-de-Luz (64), Argeles-Gazost, Lannemezan, Tarbes, Vic-en-Bigorre (65), Albi, Aussillon, Castres, Gaillac (81) and Montauban (82). Curiously there's no AVF in Dordogne. The website (💻 www.avf.asso.fr) includes a directory (*annuaire*) of local groups by *département* as well as an online form for contacting your local AVF before you move to the area. Listings indicate whether information and services are available in English or other languages. Other sources for clubs in the area are *The News* (see **Appendix B**) and English-speaking churches (see above).

PROPERTY

The south-west has been steadily increasing in popularity over the past 15 years or so. On the coast, Gironde is particularly popular, especially among the British, although (relative) bargains can still be found on the Garonne estuary north of Bordeaux (beyond commuting distance), including large properties with vineyards. However, in Dordogne and Lot it's difficult to find houses to renovate for the simple reason that there are very few properties left in need of renovation. It's easier to find properties that have been renovated but, of course, the price is much higher.

There are fewer properties available in Landes, and these tend to be snapped up by the French. Typical *landais* houses (see below) near the coast can fetch high prices. The extreme south-west is perhaps France's best-kept secret, although prices are beginning to shoot up here too and a lot of new properties are being built in and around Pau (64).

Inland, the *département* of Tarn and, more recently, Tarn-et-Garonne and Lot-et-Garonne becoming particularly sought-after (and consequently expensive). Those unable to find a suitable property in Dordogne and Lot look mainly to Lot-et-Garonne, and the area between Albi, Cordes-sur-Ciel and Gaillac in Tarn has become known among estate agents as the 'Golden Triangle'. Lot-et-Garonne is now so popular with tourists that there's a shortage of almost 1,000 beds each year to accommodate them, and grants of up to 50 per cent are available to those wanting to renovate properties in order to provide tourist accommodation. Therefore, there's considerable demand for such properties and generally for habitable stone houses with plenty of land which are secluded but not isolated. As a result, there's a shortage of this type of property around Agen, Villeneuve and other main towns in the *département*. Properties are easier to come by in more rural areas, mainly to the north-west of Agen and north of Villeneuve.

Elsewhere, cheaper properties can be found around Rodez in Aveyron and generally on higher ground. In fact, prices tend to drop the higher you go, as areas below around 500m (1,600ft) enjoy better weather. Above this height, tiles give way to slate roofs to keep out the rain and snow (see below). There are also fewer properties generally on higher ground, where they tend to be dotted around and many are isolated.

Typical Homes

There's a number of different styles that are typical of various parts of the south-west. Typical of the major seaside resorts are elaborate brick, stone and plaster villas, the finest examples of which are to be found at Arcachon (33). Homes in the mountains of Ariège are made of granite, slate and shale, often with a facing of chalk or sand, which makes them pale or almost white. Many have a round bread oven attached to one side and opening into the kitchen. Square pigeon houses with tiled roofs sloping on all four sides, unlike the round ones found elsewhere in France, are a feature of Gers, where almost every farm has one – either free-standing or adjoining other buildings. Single-storey houses in brick or stone attached to farm buildings, often around a courtyard, are typical of Gascony, while the area around Toulouse (as far as Bram and Villefranche to the east and Montauban to the west) is characterised by yellow and red brick and Roman or provençal roof tiles (*tuiles canal*), small stones sometimes being added to the brickwork in more southern parts between Toulouse and Saint-Félix.

Dordogne houses are characterised by warm, yellow bricks and many have small square towers. Lot houses largely follow the same style but using whiter stone. In northern parts, houses are constructed with thick walls and small windows to keep out the heat in summer and the cold in winter; in the southern parts, windows tend to be larger. In Dordogne and Lot, older houses will typically be roofed with the Roman (or provencal) tiles favoured in the south of France.

In Landes, houses tend to be half-timbered, sometimes with a first floor balcony at the front of the house, under the eaves. The typical Basque Country house, found in western Pyrénées-Atlantiques, is made of white-painted stone with red timbers and shutters (or occasionally green or dark blue – the Basque flag is red and green, the sea and the sky are deep blue!).

It also often has a first-floor balcony above a carved lintel, and a shallow-sloping roof of Roman tiles (the village of Aïnhoa in Pyrénées-Atlantiques is the quintessential Basque village). As you move east into Basse-Navarre, the houses become more austere, with narrow windows and chalk-coated walls decorated with grey stones. Usually single-storey, they have a more sloping roof than the Basque houses, covered partly with tiles and partly with slate and often with the name of the owner, the date of construction and sometimes a religious inscription on the lintel. Further east still, near the border between Pyrénées-Atlantiques and Hautes-Pyrénées, in the Béarn 'region', the houses are even plainer, although with doors and windows framed by Pyrenean marble. More often two-storey, their pointed, slate-covered roofs slope on all four sides.

Cost of Property

Prices in the south-west have been rising above the level of inflation for the last 20 years and particularly sharply in the last ten years or so; it's predicted that they will continue to outstrip inflation in the coming years. Coastal properties in Gironde and inland houses in Dordogne, Lot, Lot-et-Garonne, Tarn and Tarn-et-Garonne are particularly expensive. Cheaper areas include Ariège, Aveyron, Hautes-Pyrénées and parts of Pyrénées-Atlantiques, where prices generally drop the higher you go.

In Dordogne and Lot, many people want a house within 15km (11mi), north or south, of the river Dordogne, or within the triangle Souillac/Sarlat/Gourdon, where prices are around 25 per cent higher than elsewhere, but it's possible to find reasonably priced property in other parts of the *départements*. The average price of a restored four-bedroom house in Dordogne is around €500,000, while a similar-size new property can be had for around €350,000. Among major towns, Montluçon (03) boasts some of the lowest average prices for older properties, not only in the area, but in the whole of France, while the area's highest average prices are to be found in Périgueux (24) and the Périgord Noir area.

The table below gives the average selling price of houses in 2006. However, house sizes vary from area to area, which can distort average figures.

Town/Area	Average House Price			
	2-bed	3-bed	4-bed	5+-bed
Aquitaine				
Agen	€140,000	€260,000	€320,000	€360,000

5

Arcachon/Cap Ferret	€250,000	€385,000	€395,000	€585,000
Bayonne/Biarritz	€285,000	€345,000	€505,000	€650,000
Bordeaux	€250,000	€310,000	€355,000	€485,000
Midi-Pyrénées				
Auch	€185,000	€205,000	€270,000	€500,000
Bagnères	€175,000	€210,000	€265,000	€425,000
Cahors/Rocamadour	€140,000	€180,000	€230,000	€425,000
Toulouse	€200,000	€255,000	€380,000	€530,000

The average price of a period property in 2006 in Aquitaine as a whole was around €121,500 (national average of €102,250), the average for a new house €128,000 (national average €117,650) and for a building plot €37,000 (average €23,000). The equivalent figures for Midi-Pyrénées were €110,000, €121,000 and €29,000.

Land

Building land is available in all areas. It's most plentiful in Dordogne, Gironde, Landes and Pyrénées-Atlantiques and least plentiful in Ariège, Aveyron and Tarn. Prices vary enormously according to location and whether main services are connected. Land in or near a small village, where there's no mains drainage, can be bought for as little as €5 per m^2, even in Lot, whereas land with connections to all services, including electricity and telephone, near a town can cost €100 per m^2 or more. Plots range from around $400m^2$ to several hectares, the average plot being between 1,000 and $3,000m^2$ and costing between €10,000 and €50,000. Most local estate agents sell building plots (*terrains à bâtir* or *terrains constructibles*).

Rental Accommodation

Apartments

There are a fair number of apartments available for long-term rent in Gironde, Haute-Garonne and Pyrénées-Atlantiques but few or none in

Ariège, Gers and Hautes-Pyrénées. Most apartments are in the main towns in each *département* (i.e. Agen in Lot-et-Garonne, Toulouse in Haute-Garonne, Bayonne and Pau in Pyrénées-Atlantiques, Dax and Mont-de-Marsan in Landes, Castres in Tarn, and Montauban in Tarn-et-Garonne), and few are available elsewhere. Price ranges for each *département* (except Hautes-Pyrénées) are shown below.

Département	**No. of Bedrooms**	**Monthly Rental**
Ariège	Studio	€250
	1	€350 to 600
	2	€600
Aveyron	Studio	€200 to 400
	1	€500
	2	€500 to 650
	3	€600 to 800
Dordogne	Studio	€200 to 350
	1	€250 to 400
	2	€400 to 600
	3	€500 to 750
Haute-Garonne	Studio	€350
	1	€375 to 700
	2	€450 to 800
	3	€650 to 1,000
Gers	Studio	€225 to 300
	1	€250 to 375
	2	€450 to 650
	3	€600 to 900
Gironde	Studio	€250 to 450
	1	€400 to 575

	2	€500 to 900
	3	€600 to 1,250
Landes	Studio	€250 to 350
	1	€450 to 650
	2	€500 to 800
	3	€600 to 1,000
Lot	Studio	€200 to 400
	1	€375 to 550
	2	€400 to 650
	3	€600 to 850
Lot-et-Garonne	Studio	€375
	1	€400 to 500
	2	€650 to 850
	3	€750 to 950
Pyrénées-Atlantiques	Studio	€250 to 400
	1	€300 to 500
	2	€400 to 650
	3	€500 to 750
Tarn	Studio	€200 to 350
	1	€350 to 500
	2	€400 to 700
Tarn-et-Garonne	Studio	€250 to 400
	1	€350 to 550
	2	€525 to 900
	3	€600 to 1,025

Houses

Rented houses are less common than apartments, and very few are found in most *départements*; Gironde and Haute-Garonne have the largest number of houses for rent. The table below gives an indication of the rental prices for houses in each *département*.

Département	No. of Bedrooms	Monthly Rental
Ariège	4	€850
Aveyron	2	€600 to 750
	3	€750
	4	€750
Dordogne	2	€400 to 550
	3	€500 to 750
	4	€650 to 1,000
	5	€850 to 1,250
Haute-Garonne	3	€600 to 1,000
	4	€750 to 1,600
Gers	2	€450 to 650
	3	€600 to 900
	4	€725 to 1,000
	5	€800 to 1,250
Gironde	2	€400 to 900
	3	€525 to 1,000
	4	€700 to 2,000
	5	€1,500+
Landes	2	€475 to 850
	3	€500 to 900

	4	€700 to 1,200
	5	€800+
Lot	2	€400 to 575
	3	€550 to 850
	4	€750 to 1,200
	5	€800+
Lot-et-Garonne	2	€500
	3	€650 to 850
	4	€500 to 900
	5	€750+
Pyrénées-Atlantiques	2	€400 to 600
	3	€600 to 850
Tarn	2	€500 to 650
	3	€525 to 750
	4	€750 to 1,200
Tarn-et-Garonne	2	€550
	3	€550 to 650
	4	€750 to 900
	5	€1,000

COMMUNICATIONS

Air

There are several airports in the area (shown on the maps at the beginning of the chapter), although there are few direct services from other countries. Although some other airports in the south-west purport to be 'international', most handle only flights from within the EU and from North Africa. Travellers from other parts of the world must change at Paris, London, Amsterdam or

Brussels. Air France is the leading carrier to regional airports and has connections to all regional airports from both Paris airports: Roissy-Charles de Gaulle and Orly. Direct flights from British and Irish airports are listed in **Appendix F**.

Those in the north of the area have access to Poitiers airport (in Vienne, around 125km/80mi north-west of Limoges – see page 139), while those with property in eastern parts of Midi-Pyrénées may be able to take advantage of flights to Carcassonne in Aude (see page 251). Details of all French airports and their services can be found on 💻 www.aeroport.fr.

Sea

British people buying a home in the south-western part of the area may wish to take advantage of ferry services between the UK and northern Spain. P&O Portsmouth Ferries (UK ☎ 0870-242 4999, 💻 www.poferries.com) operates a twice-weekly service between Portsmouth and Bilbao. The outward ferry departs Portsmouth at 8pm on Tuesdays and Saturdays and takes 36 hours, with two nights on board; the return ferry leaves Bilbao at 12.30pm on Thursdays and Mondays, taking 28 hours. The typical off-peak (February) cost of a return trip for two adults with a medium-sized car and sharing a two-berth cabin is around £600, rising to over £700 if two children and a four-berth cabin are included. As always, there's a variety of special deals, and costs can compare favourably with a Channel crossing and a return drive from north to south, incurring toll charges and possibly with overnight stays in hotels *en route*. Note that travellers must book a cabin and that pets aren't allowed. The drive from Bilbao to Biarritz is less than 160km (100mi).

Alternatively, Brittany Ferries (UK ☎ 0870-907 6103 or France ☎ 02 98 29 28 00 or 08 25 82 88 28, 💻 www.brittanyferries.com) operates from mid-March to mid-November, sailing on average twice weekly between Plymouth and Santander – Mondays/Wednesdays from Plymouth and Tuesdays/Thursdays from Santander. Prices are broadly comparable with those of P&O Ferries to Bilbao, although the euro-conscious traveller can save money by opting for a couchette rather than a cabin (not an option with P&O). However, Santander is approximately 100km (60mi) further than Bilbao from the French border.

Public Transport

The *TGV* from Paris runs as far as Bordeaux via Poitiers (in Vienne to the north-west of Haute-Vienne) and Angoulême (in Charente to the west of Dordogne and Haute-Vienne). For details of the *TGV* network, see map in

Appendix E. It's possible to catch local trains from any of these towns to Périgueux (24) and Souillac (46), but services are slow and infrequent. Souillac, for example, is six hours from Paris. Car rental is available at most of the major stations.

Rail

The *TGV* runs from Paris (Montparnasse) to Bordeaux, although it must slow to a mere 200kph (120mph) from Tours (see map in **Appendix E**). South-west France has a comprehensive internal rail network, Midi-Pyrénées region alone boasting over 100 stations, and from Bordeaux there are ordinary rail links to Toulouse and beyond via Agen (47) and to Lourdes and Tarbes (65) via Dax (40) and Pau (64). There are also spurs leading to Arcachon (33) and (from Dax) to Bayonne and Hendaye (64). (There's also a spectacular train journey from Foix (09) across the Pyrenees into Spain.)

Motorail (car sleeper) services are available at all times of year from Boulogne, Calais, Dieppe and Paris to all parts of south-west France, although the cost is quite high and there are height restrictions (most 4x4s and 'people carriers' cannot be accommodated). Note that you're unable to access your vehicle during the journey, and there have been UK newspaper and TV reports of vehicles being damaged in transit.

Bus, Coach, Métro & Tram

Eurolines and National Express offer coach services from London (Victoria) to Bordeaux. Within the area, urban public transport is excellent in all areas, with comprehensive bus services in all major towns and cities. In addition, Toulouse has an underground (*métro*) system linking Basso-Cambo in the west with Joliment in the east, and Bordeaux now has started a three-line tramway. As in other parts of France, services between towns and in rural areas are infrequent or non-existent.

Roads

The south-west is generally well served by both motorways and trunk roads. Most motorways are toll roads and are very well maintained. The main motorways from the north to the south-west are the A10 Paris to Bordeaux and the A20, which branches off the A10 at Orléans and runs as far as Toulouse. The A62 links Bordeaux and Toulouse, and the A64 runs from Toulouse to Pau and beyond, linking with a short stretch of the A63 from near

Dax to Spain. Another short stretch of the A63 runs south from Bordeaux to Arcachon and towards Dax; the intervening distance is covered by the N10, which is due to be upgraded to motorway.

Bordeaux can be reached in around seven to eight hours from the Channel ports or three to four hours from the Spanish ports (see above), and Toulouse in eight to nine hours from the Channel ports or four to five hours from the Spanish ports.

Driving standards in the south-west are generally below average for France (i.e. terrible), and Gers has the highest road death rate of any *département* in the country, with over 270 deaths per million inhabitants.

FURTHER INFORMATION

Useful Addresses

- Comité régional de Tourisme d'**Aquitaine**, Cité mondiale, 23 Parvis des Chartrons, 33074 Bordeaux (☎ 05 56 01 70 00, 💻 www.tourisme-aquitaine.fr)
- Comité régional du Tourisme de **Midi-Pyrénées**, 54 boulevard de l'Embouchure, BP 2166, 31022 Toulouse Cedex 2 (☎ 05 61 13 55 55, 💻 www.tourisme-midi-pyrenees.com or 💻 www.tourism.midi-pyrenees.org)
- Comité départemental du Tourisme de l'**Ariège-Pyrénées**, 31bis avenue du Général de Gaulle, BP 143, 09004 Foix (☎ 05 61 02 30 70, 💻 http://ariegepyrenees.com)
- Comité départemental du Tourisme de l'**Aveyron**, 17 rue Aristide Briand, BP 831, 12008 Rodez (☎ 05 65 75 55 70, 💻 www.tourisme-aveyron.com);
- Comité départemental du Tourisme de la **Dordogne**, 25 rue Wilson, BP 2063, 24002 Périgueux (☎ 05 53 35 50 24, 💻 www.dordogne-perigord-tourisme.fr)
- Comité départemental du Tourisme de la **Haute-Garonne**, 14 rue Bayard, BP 845, 31015 Toulouse Cedex 6 (☎ 05 65 75 55 75, 💻 www.tourisme-haute-garonne.com)
- Comité départemental du Tourisme du **Gers** en Gascogne, 3 boulevard Roquelaure, BP 106, 32002 Auch (☎ 05 62 05 95 95, 💻 www.tourisme-gers.com)
- Comité départemental du Tourisme de la **Gironde**, 21 cours de l'Intendance, 33000 Bordeaux (☎ 05 56 52 61 40, 💻 www.tourisme-gironde.cg33.fr)

- Comité départemental du Tourisme des **Landes**, 4 avenue Aristide-Briand, BP 407, 40012 Mont-de-Marsan (☎ 05 58 06 89 89, 💻 www.tourisme-aquitaine.fr)
- Comité départemental du Tourisme du **Lot**, 107 quai Eugéne Cavaignac, 46000 Cahors (☎ 05 65 35 07 09, 💻 www.tourisme-lot.com)
- Comité départemental du Tourisme de **Lot-et-Garonne**, Maison du Tourisme, 271 rue Péchabout, 47000 Agen (☎ 05 53 66 14 14, 💻 www.cg47.fr)
- Mission touristique des **Pyrénées-Atlantiques**, 22ter rue Jean-Jacques de Monaix, 64000 Pau (☎ 05 59 30 44 01 or ☎ 05 59 40 22 30, 💻 www.tourisme64.com)
- Agence du Tourisme du **Pays Basque**, 4 allée des Platanes, BP 811, 64108 Bayonne (☎ 08 20 05 40 64, 💻 http://infobasque.free.fr)
- Agence du Tourisme du **Béarn**, 22ter rue Jean-Jacques de Monaix, 64000 Pau (☎ 05 59 30 01 30,💻 www.tourisme-bearn-gaves.com)
- **Hautes-Pyrénées** Tourisme Environnement, 11 rue Gaston Manent, 65000 Tarbes (☎ 05 62 56 70 65, 💻 tourisme-hautes-pyrenees.com)
- Comité départemental du Tourisme du **Tarn**, 41 rue Porta, BP 225, 81006 Albi (☎ 05 63 77 32 10, 💻 www.tourisme-tarn.com)
- Comité départemental du Tourisme de **Tarn-et-Garonne**, 2 boulevard Midi-Pyrénées, BP 534, 82005 Montauban (☎ 05 63 63 31 40, 💻 www.tourisme-tarn-et-garonne.com)

Useful Publications

- *A Harvest of Sunflowers*, Ruth Silvestre (Allison & Busby) – sequel to *A House in the Sunflowers* (see below)
- *A House in the Sunflowers*, Ruth Silvestre (Allison & Busby)
- *Life in a Postcard: Escape to the French Pyrenees*, Rosemary Bailey (Bantam Books)

Useful Websites

💻 www.123voyage.com – includes a guide to south-west France

💻 www.guide-basque.com – details of festivals and events in the Basque region

- www.bordeauxbritish.com – Bordeaux British Community
- www.cg46.fr – site of the Conseil régional de Lot for information on the economy and population, statistics of the region and useful links
- www.europe.anglican.org – details of Anglican services throughout France
- www.french-liaison.com – an English-speaking help centre based in Eymet, Dordogne
- www.perigord-developpement.com – Dordogne's Franco-British chamber of commerce (CCIFB), based in Périgueux
- www.quercy.net – information about the Quercy region of Dordogne and Lot (in French only)

Menton – The Mediterranean Coast
Jim Watson

6

THE SOUTH-EAST

Languedoc-Roussillon, Provence-Alpes-Côte d'Azur & Corsica

The area described in this chapter comprises the regions of Languedoc-Roussillon, Provence-Alpes-Côte d'Azur and Corsica, which together cover the whole of France's Mediterranean coast. These regions include the *départements* of Corse-du-Sud (2A), Haute-Corse (2B), Alpes-de-Haute-Provence (04), Hautes-Alpes (05), Alpes-Maritimes (06), Aude (11), Bouches-du-Rhône (13), Gard (30), Hérault (34), Lozère (48), Pyrénées-Orientales (66), Var (83) and Vaucluse (84).

Provence-Alpes-Côte d'Azur is the most popular region in France for holiday and retirement homes and has a large foreign community, the British, Germans and Italians being among the largest buyers of second homes. *The Riviera Times* recently wrote with reference to the Côte d'Azur: 'Sun, blue skies, warm sea, delicious food and tasty wines, idyllic villages and an allure of luxury. Surely that's the life we are all looking for?' There are an estimated 10,000 British residents in the region (Peter Mayle's televised book, *A Year in Provence*, caused countless Brits to pack up and head south). Popularity, of course, has its price, notably in respect of property costs, which have risen beyond the reach of many, who may look instead towards Languedoc-Roussillon, which currently has only half as many British residents as Provence-Alpes-Côte d'Azur – although the region is attracting migrants (from within France as well as abroad) at a faster rate than any other and property prices are escalating accordingly.

LANGUEDOC-ROUSILLON

Languedoc-Roussillon, often referred to simply as 'the Languedoc' (after one of the two ancient languages of France, the *langue d'Oc*, the Roussillon part corresponding approximately to the Pyrénées-Orientales *département*) or by the French, confusingly, as *le Midi*, has an area of 27,376km^2 (17,010mi^2) and a population of 2.3m. It contains the coastal *départements* (from east to west) of Gard, Hérault, Aude and Pyrénees-Orientales, as well as Lozère, which is inland. The region resembles a hammock stretched between Mount Lozère 1,700m (5,580ft) in the north and Mount Canigou 2,784m (9,135ft) in the south. Lozère has the highest average altitude in France of 1,000m (3,280ft). Bordered by the Pyrenees, Andorra and Spain in the south, Languedoc-Roussillon extends north as far as the Massif Central (where Lozère is France's most sparsely populated *département*). It has a long Mediterranean coastline of virtually uninterrupted sandy beaches, stretching some 180km (110mi) from the Petite Camargue nature reserve in Gard, through Hérault, Aude and Pyrénées-Orientales, with its beautiful beaches and cliff inlets (*calanques*) of pink rock, to the Spanish border. Overall, the

region is 30 per cent woodland, 15 per cent grassland, 10 per cent arable land and 45 per cent other uses (including urban areas – the second-highest proportion in France).

Few French regions are more steeped in history than Languedoc (home of the heretical Cathars), which encompasses the largest wine production area in Europe (Béziers claims to be France's wine capital) and offers an abundance of excellent (but under-rated) wines such as Corbières, Minervois and Côtes du Roussillon. The region has a vast range of scenery and landscape, including the beautiful Cévennes national park and Tarn valley areas (famously written about by Robert Louis Stevenson in his *Travels with a Donkey*), the tranquil Canal du Midi, the gently rolling foothills of the Pyrenees, home to a handful of protected bears living in the wild, and the dramatic beauty (not always appreciated by the Tour de France cyclists) of the high Pyrenean peaks.

Languedoc is noted for its relaxed pace of life and is a popular hideaway for those seeking peace and tranquillity. It has its own ancient language (*Occitan*) and many towns close to the Spanish border have a Catalan feel (Catalan is also spoken here). See **Language** on page 262.

A number of purpose-built resorts have been created on the *Côte vermeille* (Vermillion Coast) in the last few decades, including Argelès-sur-

Mer, Gruissan, St Cyprien, Port Bacarès, Port Leucate and Cap d'Agde, where you will find the apartment blocks mostly unattractive if you're looking for a home with character. Collioure, on the other hand, known as the 'jewel of the Vermillion Coast', is a most attractive (and expensive) port. Overall, Languedoc-Roussillon is popular with second homeowners, property being much cheaper here than in the Provence-Alpes-Côte d'Azur region, its adjacent 'competitor' on the Mediterranean coast.

PROVENCE-ALPES-COTE D'AZUR

Provence-Alpes-Côte d'Azur, abbreviated to PACA by officials and residents, contains the coastal *départements*, running west to east to the Italian border, of the Bouches-du-Rhône, Var and Alpes-Maritimes, and the inland *départements* of Alpes-de-Haute-Provence and Vaucluse. The inland *département* of Hautes-Alpes (in the Rhône-Alpes region) is also included in this section, as it 'belongs' more to the Mediterranean coast than to the Alps, which are considered in **Chapter 7**. Slightly larger than its Mediterranean neighbour, Languedoc-Roussillon, the PACA region occupies an area of 31,400km² (19,510mi²) and has a population approaching 4.6m. Economically, it's the second most important region in France after Ile-de-France. Overall, the region is 40 per cent woodland (the second-highest proportion in France), 15 per cent grassland, 10 per cent arable land and 35 per cent other uses (including urban areas).

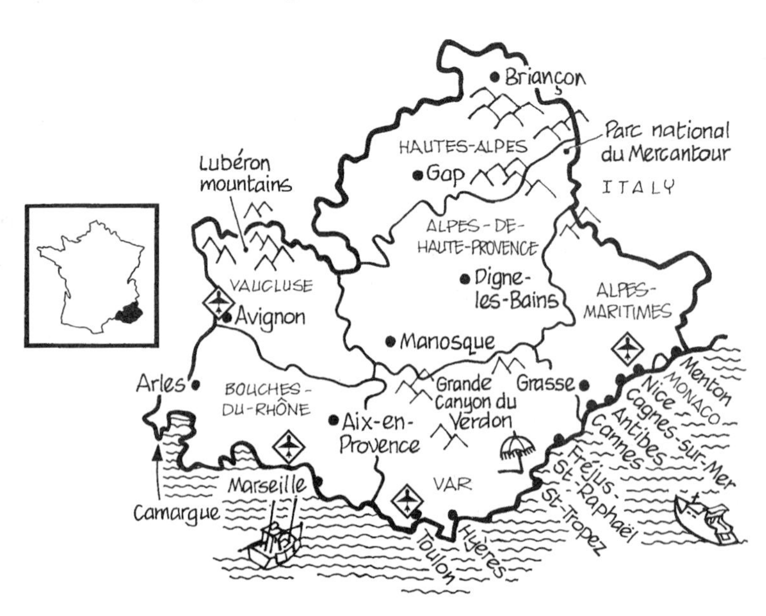

The Provence area comprises the Alpes-de-Haute-Provence, Bouches-du-Rhône and Vaucluse *départements* and part of the Var, although opinions differ as to exactly where Provence ends and the Côte d'Azur (Azure Coast) begins. The Côte d'Azur was 'discovered' by the British, who dubbed it the 'French Riviera' and helped to create the world's first coastal playground for the rich and famous. At the end of the 19th century, Queen Victoria was influential in developing the area's popularity through her visits to Hyères (just east of Toulon), which was then considered the western extremity of the Côte d'Azur. Today, many people regard Saint-Tropez, 45km (28mi) further east along the coast, as the limit of Provence and the start of the Côte d'Azur (known locally as *la Côte*). Another school of thought (whose members understandably include many local estate agents) believes that the Côte d'Azur lies between Hyères and the conurbation of Fréjus-Saint-Raphaël (east of Saint-Tropez). There are also those who consider the French Riviera as the stretch of coastline from Menton, close to the Italian border, to just beyond Cannes, the Côte d'Azur encompassing the French Riviera and extending to Saint-Tropez. (Note that Monaco, although geographically part of the Riviera/Côte d'Azur, is a separate principality and not part of France.)

PROPERTY CHECK – COTE D'AZUR

For those who hanker after the glamorous life but don't have a glamorous budget, it's still possible to find affordable properties on or near the Côte d'Azur – even in sophisticated places such as Cannes, Grasse, Juan-les-Pins and Nice, where studio apartments are available at under €100,000, and one-bedroom apartments and one-bedroom village houses at under €200,000, while luxury one-bedroom apartments with a sea view in a development with a communal pool can be found for €250,000 and two-beds for €300,000. Such developments are springing up on the outskirts of many towns on and near the coast; it's just a matter of being in the right place at the right time.

While the most expensive part of the Riviera is between Villefranche and Monaco, where one-bedroom apartments start at €300,000 and villas at a shade under €1m, the cheapest part is between Grasse and Seillans, just back from the coast, in villages such as Cabris, Callian, Fayence and Peymeinade, where villas can be had for almost half the price.

Latitudes (🖳 www.latitudes.co.uk)

6

Provence is a fascinating land of romance, history (it has its own ancient language, Provençal, now spoken only in Italy) and great beauty and is celebrated for its excellent climate, attractive scenery, fine beaches, superb cuisine and fashionable resorts. It's one of the most exclusive areas of France, and few places in Europe can compete with its ambience and allure, glamorous resorts and beautiful people. However, it's also a region of stark contrasts, with a huge variety of landscape and scenery encompassing extensive woodlands, rugged mountains, rolling hills, spectacular gorges (the Grand Canyon du Verdon is the deepest cleft in the surface of Europe), dramatic rock formations, lush and fertile valleys carpeted with lavender, extensive vineyards (which stretch to the foot of the rugged Alpilles mountains in Vaucluse), and a ravishing coastline dotted with quaint fishing villages and fine beaches.

A journey through Provence is an indulgence of the senses, and its diverse vegetation includes cypresses, gnarled olive trees, almond groves, umbrella pines, lavender, wild rosemary and thyme, all of which add to its unique and seductive sights and smells. Provence produces a number of excellent wines and includes the prestigious vineyards of Châteauneuf-du-Pape, Gigondas (mostly red) and Lilac (red, white and *rosé*) plus popular wines such as Côtes du Luberon and Côtes de Provence.

The region contains many beautiful areas, notably the Luberon National Park (Parc naturel régional du Luberon), the heart of the provençal countryside and still a fashionable area for holiday homes and visitors, in spite of (or perhaps because of) Peter Mayle. The Camargue, between Arles and the sea (from which it was reclaimed), is one of the most spectacular nature reserves in France and famous for its wild horses. Provence also contains a wealth of beautiful historic Roman towns and dramatically sited medieval villages (see **Major Towns & Places of Interest** on page 248), and both Marseille and Nice provide sea links (see **Communications** on page 287) to Corsica and North Africa, where the holiday resorts of Morocco and Tunisia are popular with the French (being former protectorates where French is still widely spoken).

Although the Alpes-Maritimes and Bouches-du-Rhône *départements* have very little coastline which isn't built-up, Var has perhaps the most attractive, unspoilt coastal stretch in the PACA region, between Hyères and Fréjus-Saint-Raphaël.

Did you know?

Three of PACA's six *départements* – Alpes-Maritimes, Alpes-de-Haute-Provence et Hautes-Alpes – border Italy, which is accessible via a number of trans-Alpine routes (including the Mont Blanc tunnel) as well as the coast road. Living near the border can give you the best of two worlds, with the option to savour Italian culture, cuisine and architecture whenever the fancy takes you without even having to change currency. In fact, the fontier is often 'blurred' by an overlap of culture, cuisine and architecture, creating a fascinating mix of experiences. When house-hunting, however, you will have to compete with Italians, who pour over the border to snap up French property (especially new developments) as well as to fill up on 'cheap' petrol.

At the other end of the area under consideration here, Pyrénées-Orientales, in Languedoc-Roussillon, shares a border with Spain, which is accessible via a number of trans-Pyrenean routes (including the A7 motorway) as well as the Mediterranean coast road (see page 176). It also borders the tiny principality of Andorra, with its attractive ski resorts and border traffic jams as visitors queue to export their tax-free purchases.

CORSICA

Containing the *départements* of Corse-du-Sud (2A) and Haute-Corse (2B), the island of Corsica (*la Corse* in French) covers an area of 8,721km² (3,367mi²) with a coastline of around 1,000km (620mi). It's situated 160km

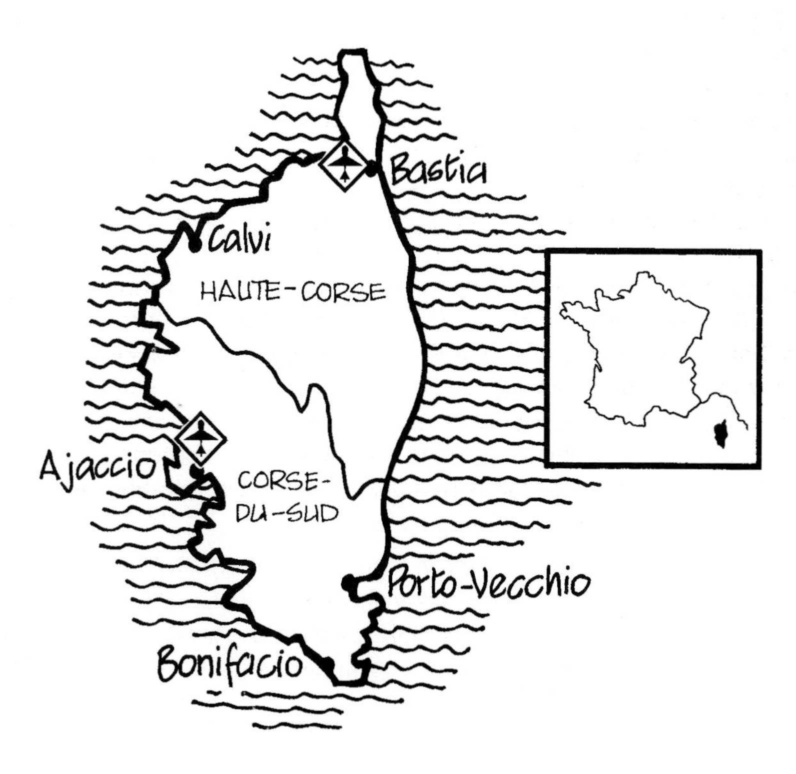

(99mi) from France and 80km (50mi) from Italy, with which it has strong historical ties, having been an Italian possession until 1768, when France purchased it from the Genoese. Corsica is quite different from mainland France, not only in its geography but in its people, culture and customs. (Corsican men are reputed to be among the most chauvinistic in France – which is saying something!) The island even has its own language, Corsican, spoken regularly by around 60 per cent of the people, although it has no official status and French is also universally spoken and understood. There's a strong local identity (and independence movement) and Corsica enjoys a greater degree of autonomy than the mainland regions.

Corsica is sparsely populated with huge areas devoid of human life and has a stark, primitive beauty with superb beaches and picturesque hillside villages; it's considered by some to be the most beautiful Mediterranean island (it's known as the *Ile de Beauté*) and is a popular holiday destination (particularly the western coast). Mountains cover most of its surface, including some 200 peaks over 2,000m (6,500ft), the highest reaching over 2,700m (9,000ft) so that skiing is possible in the winter. Around half the island is covered in vegetation, including beech, chestnut and pine forests and the ubiquitous *maquis*, a dense growth of aromatic shrubs (heather and myrtle) and dark holm oak. Corsica also boasts some of Europe's most beautiful Romanesque art.

PROPERTY CHECK – CORSICA

Corsica, which has been described as 'Scotland with sunshine' and 'the French Riviera without the concrete', isn't for those who want an easy bolt hole or a 'Little England' lifestyle. The island's attractions are many – especially its diversity, with spectacular mountains just 20 minutes from sandy beaches and a fusion of French and Italian culture – but there are few direct international flights, and these are mostly limited to the summer months, and most of the islanders don't speak English. There are also few estate agents (most property is sold by word of mouth), and some are reluctant to deal with foreigners, who even risk having their properties destroyed by bombs if they don't make sufficient effort to fit in to the local community. Most old properties, often built of granite, are in villages – only a few shepherds' houses (*pailliers*) are available in the countryside and these are small, with strict limitations on extending them – but most Corsicans now live on or near the coast, where properties are mostly modern (and not made of granite). Prices are high compared with most of mainland France, a two-bedroom house near the beach costing from €250,000 and a four-bedroom villa up to €700,000.

Agila Immobilier (www.agila-immobilier.com)

Tourism is the island's main industry (many French mainlanders holiday here), although it remains almost completely unspoiled and a haven for outdoor lovers (hikers and bikers) and those seeking peace and serenity. Not surprisingly, Corsica has a slow pace of life, which is epitomised by its ancient and spectacular mountain railway. The main towns include Ajaccio (the regional capital and birthplace of Napoleon), Bastia, Bonifacio, Calvi and Porto-Vecchio, all situated on the coast. It's popular with holiday homeowners, particularly Italians, and prices have risen in recent years following increased interest. It has, however, avoided the devastation wrought in many other Mediterranean islands by high-rise developments; buildings are restricted to two storeys and construction is forbidden close to beaches. Sardinia is only a short boat ride away.

ADVANTAGES & DISADVANTAGES

For many people the climate on the Mediterranean coast is one of its principal attractions, although you may find bright sun most of the year round boring and the stifling summers unbearable. Northern Europeans may miss the lack of marked changes of season on the coast, although the *Tramontane* mountain wind, affecting the coastal area from Perpignan to Narbonne, can be extremely nippy and parts of Languedoc-Roussillon suffer heavy rain at times. The *département* of Alpes-Maritimes is officially an earthquake risk area, although the likelihood of a serious earthquake is minimal.

Partly because of the climate, the Mediterranean coast is considered to be one of the healthiest areas to live in France, and the mortality rate (from all causes) is lower here than almost anywhere else in the country (despite worse than average driving standards!). There's no shortage of general practitioners and specialists in the Languedoc-Roussillon and PACA areas, particularly on the coast; in fact, you're almost spoilt for choice. Although the Aquitaine and Midi-Pyrénées regions in the south-west (see **Chapter 5**) are recognised by several official organisations as offering the healthiest foods in France, the Languedoc-Roussillon region is considered by many gourmets to be a second 'south-west', offering an extremely varied cuisine, with Italian and Arab influences and also a Spanish influence from the Spanish colony in Toulouse.

Another advantage of buying a property on the Mediterranean coast is that most parts of the area are easily accessible from most parts of the world, and the increase in budget flights within France and from other European countries (notably the UK) as well as recent improvements in the French high-speed train network – see **Communications** on page 287) enable you not only to travel to your property frequently and cheaply but also to escape the summer heat if you wish. Spain and Italy are quickly reached from the western and eastern ends of the coast respectively (Barcelona, for example, is just a few hours from Perpignan by road, while Florence, Venice and the Italian lakes are within striking distance of Alpes-Maritimes and parts of Alpes-de-Haute-Provence). Residents can also take advantage of the continued expansion of the Mediterranean cruise business (see page 288), which offers a leisurely way to enjoy the European and North African Mediterranean coasts and the Mediterranean islands.

On the debit side are the high rates of crime (see page 266) and unemployment, but perhaps the major disadvantage of the area is the cost of living there. The PACA region is the second most expensive in France (after Paris), although Languedoc-Roussillon has an appreciably lower cost of living. Property prices follow this pattern (see page 283) and you can pay two or three times as much for a property on the Mediterranean coast as for a similar home in a less popular area of France.

The popularity of the area causes another of its major disadvantages. Around 25m tourists visit the PACA region every year, and Languedoc-Roussillon region is in the top five French tourist areas. The entire coastline in both regions (with the exception of Marseille and, to a lesser extent, Toulon) is a tourist area in high season (June to September), when visitors from inland areas as well as other parts of France and the world triple or quadruple the population. The coast is dotted with campsites as well as hotels and self-catering accommodation, all of which are filled to overflowing. So, if you buy a property near a main resort and close to the beach, apart from paying a premium and probably having a small amount of land, you should expect traffic congestion and general noise and bustle in the high season. You can still, however, enjoy the beach and Mediterranean swims just before or after the high season (especially if you're used to English Channel temperatures) on a coast that regains its charm. The high season is of course good news if you've bought a seaside property with letting for part of the year in mind, when the Côte d'Azur is a better investment than Languedoc-Roussillon even allowing for the higher property prices.

Major inland towns and tourist attractions (see below) have similar high season inconveniences. These may also extend to certain festival periods, not necessarily in the summer. There are, however, numerous inland locations, particularly in the Languedoc area, where peace and quiet, relaxation and seclusion can be found all year round. Extreme seclusion, if you're seeking a hermit's lifestyle, can be found in the Lozère *département*, which has de-populated by some 50 per cent over the last 150 years.

Of all France's major towns, Nice (06) is the worst affected by flooding (it has been flooded 19 times in the last 30 years), closely followed by Marseille (13) and Antibes (06) with 17 and 16 floods respectively since 1982. Nice also suffers a lack of green space (a mere 1m^2 per inhabitant) and a shortage of cycle track, as do Aix-en-Provence, Béziers, Cannes, Marseille and Toulon. Carcassonne (11) has more green space than almost any other town in France (over 136m^2 per inhabitant), and keen cyclists should favour Avignon, where there's more cycle track per inhabitant than anywhere else in the area. Marseille has also been the scene of occasional attacks by Corsican terrorists. Entressen (13), 70km (45mi) from Marseille, is the site of Europe's largest open refuse tip.

On the plus side, the Mediterranean coast boasts the largest number of 'blue flag' beaches and ports of any of the areas considered in this book (34 resorts with 'blue flag' beaches and 37 blue flag ports) – the majority in Pyrénées-Orientales, Hérault and Var (see 💻 www.pavillonbleu.com), although there's also a number of 'black flag' beaches – one in Antibes (06), three in Cassis and one each in Marseille and Martigues (13), and two in Palavas-les-Flots (34) – according to the Surfrider Foundation Europe, which draws attention to what it considers to be unacceptable levels of pollution (see 💻 www.surfrider-europe.org). Even if you aren't up to surfing, the generally stable weather allows you to step out of the door and go for a long walk or cycle at a moment's notice. Golf, on the other hand, requires a not inconsiderable annual budget even if you play (or want to play) once a month on a public course. Membership of a private club costs at least €2,000 per year. Sea swimming is possible for five or six months a year (depending on your tolerance of the cold), and there are plenty of public swimming pools which, however, have a tendency to overheat the water.

As far as integration is concerned, the PACA region in particular has become such a mixture of non-Mediterranean French people, French colonials (*pieds-noirs*) from Algeria, other Mediterranean nationalities and Northern Europeans that newcomers to the area will almost certainly detect a certain apprehension, reserve and perhaps mistrust on the part of the original locals, natives of the region. Probably accounting for less than half the population, France's 'Mediterranean Man' may be difficult to really fathom and get to know, especially if you don't make the effort to show that you have a long-term contribution to make towards community or village life; persist and you should be rewarded.

Corsica

Corsica's main advantages are its great natural beauty, particularly inland, and superb climate. It's ideal for those seeking seclusion, but property is expensive, especially small apartments near the sea, and the island is relatively inaccessible (you may need to book your ferry passage well in advance). Coastal areas are crowded in summer and there are few employment opportunities. You may find it difficult to be accepted by Corsicans, who are renowned for their insularity, and the political future of Corsica is uncertain. A number of bombings are carried out each year by various Corsican terrorist groups; most of these are aimed at French government buildings, but non-Corsican property owners are also occasionally targeted, although there are rarely fatalities.

MAJOR TOWNS & PLACES OF INTEREST

Cities, towns and villages of interest to foreign homebuyers are listed below by *département* (in alphabetical order), with approximate population figures for each town or city, as well as the major tourist attractions in each *département*.

Corsica (2A/2B)

Highlights on the island include Ajaccio (2A, pop. 53,000), the capital of Corse-du-Sud, a cathedral town with an elegant crescent-shaped, palm-tree lined seafront, a tourist centre and Napoleon's birthplace (almost every other bar is called *Le Bonaparte*!); Bastia (2B, pop. 38,000) the capital of Haute-Corse, less exotic and more business-like than Ajaccio; Bonifacio (2A, pop. 2,500), a fishing port set on spectacular chalk cliffs at the southernmost tip of Corsica, facing Sardinia; Portovecchio (2A, pop. 10,000), a rare inlet on the comparatively straight eastern coastline; and Propriano (2A, pop. 3,000), one of several attractive fishing ports on the jagged west coast of Corsica, which has some beautiful creeks and inlets. Note that population figures swell enormously in peak tourist season.

Alpes-de-Haute-Provence (04)

Main towns and places of interest in this *département* are Digne-les-Bains (pop. 16,000), the unpretentious departmental capital, with its healthy mountain air at 600m (1,900ft) altitude and curative baths, and the town surrounded by some of the most beautiful countryside in France; Manosque (19,000) with a motorway link to cosmopolitan Aix-en-Provence enabling a rapid transition from the relaxed lifestyle in the southern French Alps to the animated Bouches-du-Rhône; Entrevaux, one of France's most beautiful villages; a number of good ski resorts, offering a range of altitudes and difficulties, e.g. Barcelonnette 1,135m (3,725ft), Val d'Allos 1,800 to 2,600m (5,900 to 8,530ft) and, for more experienced skiers, La Foux d'Allos, also around 1,800 to 2,600m (out of season, they're sturdy tests for walkers); and the Parc National du Mercantour, the largest conservation area in the two Mediterranean regions, some 75km (45mi) from west to east, visited by over half a million people each year – there are chamois on the upper slopes, eagles and a variety of Alpine plants. No dogs are allowed and there are no residential properties.

Hautes-Alpes (05)

Gap (pop. 38,200), at 735m (2,411ft), is the highest departmental capital in France, but Briançon (pop. 10,700), in the centre of the *département*, is more interesting historically, with its fortified medieval upper town area. At an altitude of 1,310m (4,300ft) it rivals Davros (Switzerland) as the highest town in Europe. The village of Sain-Véran is reputedly the highest in Europe.

As its name suggests, the *département* is high in the Alps and offers walking, climbing and paragliding in summer, and skiing in winter (see page 304). Its many rivers include the Buëch, Clarée, Drac, Durance, Luye and Séveraise, the Durance having been dammed to form Europe's largest man-made lake, the Lac de Serre-Ponçon, where watersports are popular. Hautes-Alpes contains the Parc National des Ecrins and a Regional Park, Queyras, covering 1,600km^2 (615mi^2) of the eastern *département*.

Alpes-Maritimes (06)

Highlights here include Nice (pop. 348,000), the departmental capital and unofficial capital of the Côte d'Azur, the quintessential Riviera town with its strong Italian architectural style; nearby Sophia Antipolis, France's 'Silicon Valley' with its concentration of high-tech businesses; Cannes (70,200), created by the English, with its famous Film Festival, the ultimate in sophistication (and prices!) and the wealthiest French town outside Ile-de-France; Grasse, 30km (19mi) inland, France's perfume capital (48,200); Cagnes-sur-Mer (47,200), between Cannes and Nice, famous for its horse racing (the only course in the *département*); Antibes (72,500), a yachting centre, particularly for the rich and famous; Menton (67,000, including suburbs up to Monaco), sedate, laid-back and aristocratic with a colourful annual lemon festival; Isola 2000, a purpose-built ski resort (the sunniest in France) two hours' drive from Nice; and two of France's most beautiful villages, Eze-Village and Peillon.

PROPERTY CHECK – ANTIBES & GRASSE

Legendary hang-out of the flaunting classes, Antibes is a cosy, lively little town with a botanical garden, a Picasso Museum, an English bookshop, an annual tall ships race, and an annual jazz festival in nearby Juan-les-Pins. The Cap d'Antibes boasts five harbours and as many narrow, sandy beaches. Property prices are understandably high, but a two-bedroom apartment in the old town or a new apartment in a nearby development can be had for under €250,000.

Famous for its perfume factories, the little town of Grasse, tucked up in the hills above Antibes, offers slightly less expensive property, with two-bedroom apartments from €150,000 and three-bedroom villas for under €500,000.

Lavender Homes (💻 www.lavenderhomes.co.uk); A Place in France (💻 www.antibes-juanlespins.com or 💻 www.grasseriviera.com)

6

If your budget enables you to purchase a superb villa with landscaped gardens and deluxe swimming pool with all the trimmings and a clear panoramic view of the nearby sea, try to avoid Saint-Tropez, the entrance to Antibes and the Corniche coastal roads near Monte Carlo, because the high season road traffic is horrendous. (A helicopter would be a good investment if you absolutely have to be in one of these localities!) In the low season, however, they're glorious.

PROPERTY CHECK – ALPES-MARITIMES

PACA's most easterly *département*, bordering Italy, Alpes-Maritimes offers lesser-known resorts, such as Cagnes-sur-Mer, Saint-Laurent-du-Var and Tourrettes-sur-Loup west of Nice as well as the exclusive Saint-Jean-Cap-Ferrat, Villefranche-sur-Mer and, of course, Cannes. Prices on the coast are unsurprisingly lofty – a large villa with pool costs in excess of €600,000 – but inland, in pretty hillside villages such as Biot, Mougins and Villeneuve-Loubet, those with a more modest budget can find two-bedroom apartments in developments with communal pools and tennis courts for around €350,000.

Escape in Provence (💻 www.escapeinprovence.com)

Aude (11)

Aude's main towns and places of interest are Carcassonne (pop. 45,800), the regional capital (known as 'Cork-assonne' by the Irish and British now flocking to the area), one of France's major tourist attractions (reckoned to be the second-most visited town after Paris) with the largest and best preserved medieval walled fortress in Europe; Narbonne (47,000), just off the coast, the ancient regional Roman capital.

PROPERTY CHECK – NARBONNE

Once the most important Roman settlement in southern France (and the first Roman colony outside Italy), and the most populous town in Aude, Narbonne maintains relics of its rich history alongside the conveniences of modern living – and it's just 15km from the Mediterranean. The nearest seaside resort is modern Narbonne-Plage, others including the village of Gruissan, the fishing ports of Bages, Peyriac-de-Mer and Saint-Pierre-sur-Mer, and the busy modern port (the third largest on France's Mediterranean coast) of Port-la-Nouvelle. Inland is the lively market town of Lézignan, 'capital' of the Corbières area. One-bedroom apartments in Narbonne centre cost less than

€100,000, two-beds under €150,000 and nearby villas with pools from €250,000, while on the coast, where most property is modern, one-bedroom apartments start at around €75,000, two-bedroom *pavillons* around €150,000, three-bedroom villas €225,000. Prices inland are even lower, building plots starting at around €70,000, three-bedroom village houses at under €100,000, four-bedroom detached houses at under €200,000.

Logic-Immo (🖳 www.logic-immo.com)

Limoux (10,200), known for its white wine (Blanquette de Limoux) and a lively town with a well known winter carnival and the only piano museum (Le Musée du Piano) in France; Lagrasses, one of France's most beautiful villages; and the Canal du Midi, a man-made canal 240km (148mi) long, running from Toulouse (Midi-Pyrénées) and crossing the Aude and Hérault *départements* to the Mediterranean near Cap d'Agde – the Midi's 'equivalent' of the UK's Norfolk Broads.

PROPERTY CHECK – AUDE

In the heart of Languedoc-Roussillon's wine country, the *département* of Aude offers a unique combination of bustling coastal resorts and peaceful retreats along the Canal du Midi or among the endless vineyards – as well as the unique medieval fortified town of Carcassonne. Canalside properties start at a reasonable €150,000, and for less than €200,000 you can buy a three- or four-bedroom house. In the west of Aude, near Narbonne, villas with pools cost around €300,000 and a large *maison de maître*, suitable for a bed and breakfast or *gîte* business, can be had for under €500,000, while one-bedroom apartments start at just €60,000. In the Corbières and Fitou areas to the south, 200-year-old cottages in picturesque villages such as Paziols can be found for less than €150,000 and barns for conversion for a third of the price, and in the coastal town of Port Leucate townhouses start at a derisory €60,000.

Languedoc Property and Leisure Services (☎ 04 68 41 77 15)

Bouches-du-Rhône (13)

Marseille (pop. city centre 820,000), capital of Bouches-du-Rhône and the PACA region and France's oldest city (over 2,500 years), has a poor reputation and a rather faded grandeur, but much restoration work is in progress and the old docks have been transformed into an up-market area with luxury waterfront apartments and classy restaurants; it isn't a tourist city (the local people are true Mediterraneans) but has plenty to offer historically and sociologically, particularly in the old port and Canebière main street areas, and since the 1998 World Cup (when several matches were played in the city) has become a fashionable place for foreigners to live and is particularly popular with the Dutch.

Other major towns and places of interest are Aix-en-Provence (pop. including suburbs 140,000), the pre-French Revolution capital of Provence, 15 minutes north of Marseille and in sharp contrast, with sophisticated boutiques and people; Arles (50,000) with its well preserved Roman arena (*les Arènes*) where bullfights are 'staged' and international exhibition centre; the Camargue conservation area, which spills over into the Gard *département*, inhabited by semi-wild bulls and horses, an unrivalled variety of birds including pink flamingos, small and larger mammals, such as red foxes, coypus and wild boar; Les-Saintes-Maries-de-la-Mer, on the south-west tip of the Camargue, the gypsies' Mecca around 25th May every year, when they celebrate their patron saint Sarah; Martigues (45,400), a modern 'Venetian' development with houses built along canals; and Les Baux-de-Provence, one of France's most beautiful villages.

PROPERTY CHECK – BOUCHES-DU-RHONE

Dominated by Marseille, this is the least popular of PACA's six *départements* with foreign property buyers, but it boasts two of France's most cultural towns, Aix-en-Provence and Arles (with its impressive Roman amphitheatre), as well as the scenic wilderness of the Camargue, known for its wild horses and bulls, less so for its rice fields. Bouches-du-Rhône's 300km coast harbours many attractive fishing ports, such as Cassis, between its fine beaches, while inland the countryside is dotted with ancient villages among the vineyards and olive groves as well as attractive towns such as Saint-Rémy-de-Provence, a magnet for artists and film makers.

Aix is one of France's wealthiest towns – a fact reflected in its property prices – but homes in nearby villages needn't cost the earth. Given the area's easy access from Paris and London, the holiday home market is particularly active, though prices are often set unrealistically high and open to negotiation. The towns are also good locations for investment properties thanks to the large number of students. Seaside villas start at around €350,000, while a four-bedroom farmhouse in good condition can cost €500,000.

Immobilier et Financement (💻 www.immobilier-financement.com); Investments Provence (💻 www.propertiesprovence.co.uk)

Gard (30)

Nîmes (pop. 143,000), the departmental capital, renowned as the best example of a Roman town outside Italy but with a curious admixture of avant-garde buildings and to be avoided at Whitsun and at grape-harvesting time (September), unless you're a bull-fighting/running aficionado and enjoy huge *ferias*; Alès (40,000), at the foot of the Cévennes slopes, once an important industrial and mining town but now turning increasingly to tourism; the Pont du Gard, a two thousand-year-old Roman bridge, one of the most visited historical sites in France; and La Roque-sur-Cèze, one of the most beautiful villages in France.

PROPERTY CHECK – GARD

Languedoc-Roussillon's most easterly *département*, rubbing shoulders with the PACA region, Gard is an area of sensational natural beauty. In the north, the Cévennes mountains rise to spectacular heights, the central plains ripple with wild thyme and rosemary, and the windswept southern tip reaches to the Mediterranean. The Roman amphitheatre in the capital, Nîmes, and Pont du Gard are among the *département*'s many architectural highlights. A new dual-carriageway linking Nîmes and Alès (currently half and hour's drive apart) is slow in coming but will facilitate access to the Cévennes.

Property prices soared in the early years of the century (including an almost 30 per cent rise in 2003), thanks largely to the 'Ryanair effect', but have since stabilised – in particular for villas with pools and stone farmhouses outside commuting distance of the cities, these two property types being the most popular among foreign buyers – and remain significantly lower than those in neighbouring Provence. Near the coast, a basic two-bedroom apartment costs around €250,000 and a four-bedroom villa at least €400,000. Inland, while villas with low-maintenance gardens and swimming pools can be found from €250,000, well appointed but characterful stone properties in a tranquil spot near a village can be difficult to find under €350,000. A pleasant substitute is a village house with terraces or patios, which can cost as little as €100,000. City centre one-bedroom apartments (e.g. in Nîmes) start at a similar price, as do brand new leaseback properties, and Nîmes is an attractive location for investment properties.

In the north, in villages such as Montclus and Saint-Laurent-de-Carnols, detached houses can be found for as little as €100,000. In the hilltop village of Barjac, studio apartments are selling for under €100,000 and three-bedroom farmhouses for less than €200,000. Near Uzès, a three-bedroom villa with pool can be had for just €250,000, in the former Roman spa town of Bagnols-sur-Cèze, a four-bedroom townhouse costs around €300,000, and in Alès, the *département*'s second-largest town, a four-bedroom villa costs around €400,000. Leasebacks are available in Uzès from around €125,000.

James Properties (💻 www.jamespropertiesfrance.com); Languedoc Property Finders (💻 www.languedocpropertyfinders.com); Lavender Homes (💻 www.lavenderhomes.co.uk); Midi Property (💻 www.midiproperty.com)

6

Hérault (34)

Highlights here include Montpellier (pop. 244,000), one of the world's oldest university seats, the capital of Hérault and the Languedoc-Roussillon region and its economic driving force with high-tech industrial zones such as

Agropolis and Euromédecine – one of the most cosmopolitan, dynamic and progressive towns in France (and recently rated among the ten best French towns to live in – see **Appendix F**).

PROPERTY CHECK – HERAULT

One of France's fastest-growing *départements*, Hérault attracts some 10,000 people every month in search of a new life or a holiday home, and its capital, Montpellier, with its large student population and major international company sites (including Dell and IBM), is one of the country's most dynamic cities – Béziers isn't far behind. Apartments here and in other cities are now expensive by national standards: for example, a new studio apartment in the centre of Béziers costs over €95,000. Such is the population boom that the local government is offering owners of old properties up to 60 per cent grants for renovation. But Hérault isn't just about business; its extensive coast with lively resorts such as Grande Motte and Cap d'Agde offers residents and visitors a vast playground.

The Millau viaduct, which opened at the end of 2004, and the completion of the motorway to Béziers has accelerated home building along the Hérault valley, which in turn has halted property price increases and led to a greater willingness among vendors to negotiate. Further transport improvements are in the pipeline: Béziers airport's runway is to be extended in 2007 (a move likely to attract budget airlines), the Montpellier-Lodève motorway is due to be completed by the end of the same year and a new *TGV* link between Perpignan and Spain is to open in 2009.

Unrestored village houses can be had for under €100,000, two-bedroom houses for less than €200,000, and new seaside apartments for €225,000. Villas with swimming pools in the countryside cost upwards of €300,000 and spacious restored stone properties with gardens over €400,000 – if you can find them.

Garrigae Investments (💻 www.garrigae.com); James Properties France (💻 www.jamespropertiesfrance.com); Lamalou Immobilier (💻 www.lamalouimmobilier.fr)

6

Béziers (72,400), with its ancient bridge (le Pont Vieux), an easy-going town and the unofficial capital of the largest wine-producing region in France; Sète (43,200), the most important fishing port on the French Mediterranean coast – in contrast to Montpellier, insular and 'authentic' and, like Marseille, inhabited largely by native French Mediterraneans; the Cap d'Agde, the largest purpose-built bathing resort in Europe with sleeping accommodation for 100,000 and incorporating a huge naturist centre; and Saint-Guilhem-le-Désert, one of France's most beautiful villages.

PROPERTY CHECK – AGDE

Founded by the Greeks some 2,600 years ago, Agde is one of the oldest towns in France. Five minutes from the modern seaside resort of Cap d'Agde, the town of Agde offers old-world charm and history, with its narrow lanes and traditional fishing port. Its almost black buildings, made from local volcanic rock, have given Agde its nickname of *la perle noire*. A recent development near the town centre, comprising over 20 apartments, saw prices starting as low as €130,000 for a one-bedroom apartment.

Couleurs de France (www.couleurs-de-france.com)

Lozère (48)

Mende (pop. 11,800), the capital, situated in the very centre of the *département*; Châteauneuf-de-Randon, a completely unspoilt (no souvenir shops), authentic village with a commanding view of the Margeride plateau in the north of the *département*; and the Cévennes, scene of Robert Louis Stevenson's *Travels with a Donkey* (his journey actually started in the adjacent Haute-Loire *département* and ended, 220km/136mi later, in Gard).

Pyrénées-Orientales (66)

Perpignan (pop. 115,000) is the departmental capital, with its strong Catalan influence (it's only 30km/19mi from the Spanish border). Inland towns and villages include Amélie-les-Bains (a popular spa town), Arles-sur-Tech (with its mysterious cathedral tomb), Le Boulou (an attractive town often clogged with traffic), Céret (boasting an important modern art museum), Le Perthus on the Spanish border (a bargain-hunter's paradise), Prades (famous for its summer music festival founded by legendary cellist Pablo Casals), Prats-de-Mollo (with an imposing fort) and Villefranche-de-Conflent (one of the country's most beautiful villages). The northern coast, from Canet to Collioure, consists of sandy beaches and salt-water inland lakes, while the remainder is rocky. From north to south, Saint-Cyprien is an upmarket resort boasting one of the largest marinas on the Med (with some 2,000 berths), Argelès-sur-Mer is popular for its superb beaches, Collioure (Languedoc-Roussillon's answer to Saint-Tropez) is a small, pretty port crammed with tourists in summer, Port-Vendres is a working port and Cerbère is a former staging post between France and Spain, Cerbère is now a relatively insignficant town.

PROPERTY CHECK – PYRENEES-ORIENTALES

Roughly equivalent to the ancient province of Roussillon, France's most southerly *département* is more gently sloping than its 'partner', Languedoc – apart from the Corbières hills just north of Perpignan and *les Albères* (the Pyrenean foothills) at its southern extreme – the Roussillon Plain interrupted only by Mont Canigou (2,784m/9,135ft) in the centre. Sometimes described as 'the poor man's Riviera', Pyrénées-Orientales is no longer as cheap as it was even in the early years of the 21st century, though prices still compare favourably with the Côte d'Azur. Beachside studio apartments can still be found for under €100,000, small inland village houses for €125,000 and detached houses with a pool for €200,000, while even in touristy Collioure a two-bedroom apartment costs under €250,000 and a nearby villa with pool less than €500,000.

Agence Paradise (💻 www.argeles-sur-mer.com)

6

Var (83)

Highlights in this K encompass Toulon (pop. 167,000), with the largest harbour in continental Europe (France's Mediterranean naval base), offering prestigious properties in the hills above the town with panoramic sea views; Hyères (53,200) with its palm trees and medieval old town, combining the attractions of Provence and the Côte d'Azur; Saint-Tropez (known as 'Saint-

Trop' – *trop* meaning 'too much'!), crowded, colourful, glamorous, outrageous, and architecturally quite pretty (pop. 6,000 in the low season; overrun in the summer); the adjoining seaside resorts of Fréjus-Saint-Raphaël (61,200), with their beautiful, sandy beaches and Roman arena; Port-Grimaud, a modern 'Venetian' development with houses built along canals; Bargème, one of France's most beautiful villages; Mont Saint-Victoire, painted by Cézanne; the Grand Canyon du Verdon (also called the Gorges du Verdon, but the locals prefer to compare it with the American Grand Canyon), Europe's deepest canyon.

PROPERTY CHECK – VAR

One of France's greenest *départements*, three-quarters of its area being wooded, Var also has olive groves, vineyards, lakes and, of course, sandy beaches. It's less built up than its neighbour Alpes-Maritimes but is far from a sleepy hollow, with a growing population and a dynamic economy centred on tourism. Claiming to be France's sunniest *département*, Var understandably attracts both foreigners and the French in search of blue skies and blue sea. To meet the continued demand for property in the heart of Provence, developers are building complexes both on the coast and inland, featuring security gates, a *concierge* service and rental management as well as the obligatory swimming pools and tennis courts; some also include a golf course. Two-bedroom detached homes in such a development start at around €400,000. Otherwise, prices start at around €100,000, for example for a one-bedroom semi-detached home in Vidauban. Villas start at around €300,000. Coastal property tends to be modern, whereas inland there are 'character' houses to be found.

EJC French Property (www.ejcfrenchproperty.com); Lavender homes (www.lavenderhomes.co.uk); Savills (www.savills.co.uk)

6

Vaucluse (84)

This area offers Avignon (pop. 90,800), City of the Popes with the Popes' Palace and, of course, the nursery-rhyme bridge (only half remains) – home to important metallurgy and textile industries and a major drama festival in July; Carpentras (26,800), which boasts France's oldest synagogue, and nearby Mont Ventoux – at 1,912m (6,270ft) the highest mountain in Provence; three of France's most beautiful villages, Bonnieux, Gordes and Roussillon; Fontaine-de-Vaucluse, a village in a natural beauty spot where a mysterious 'fountain' springs from 308m (1,010ft) below ground (Vaucluse, meaning 'enclosed valley', gave its name to the village before the *département*); and the Luberon, a mountainous conservation area extending some 50km (30mi) from the southern French Alps almost to the Mediterranean.

PROPERTY CHECK – VAUCLUSE

Those in search of the 'real' Provence – Peter Mayle country – will want to be well away from the glitzy, overdeveloped coast and up in the *arrière-pays* instead. Landlocked Vaucluse is just such a place, encompassing the Parc Naturel Régional du Luberon with its picturesque villages dotted among craggy countryside and lively towns of Avignon and Orange. An added attraction is that property costs some 30 per cent less than on the coast. Detached period homes start at under €400,000.

Escape in Provence (www.escapeinprovence.com)

POPULATION

The population of Languedoc-Roussillon is around 2.5m and that of Provence-Alpes-Côte d'Azur almost 4.8m, although the former's population has doubled in the last 50 years. Languedoc-Roussillon has the fastest-growing population of any region in France (an annual increase of 1.36 per cent compared with the national average of 0.66 per cent), Corsica is the country's third-fastest growing region (0.99 per cent per annum) and PACA the seventh-fastest (0.86 per cent), the *département* of Var and the town of Montpellier (34) being among the fastest-growing in France, though in Var's case the increase is largely in the 50-60 age group as retirees flock to the Mediterranean coast for their 'golden' years. Other fast-growing *départements* are Alpes-de-Haute-Provence and Hérault (1.6 per cent per annum), Aude, Gard and Hautes-Alpes (1.4 per cent), Var (1.3) and Pyrénées-Orientales (1.2). The only *département* to have a rate of increase below the national average is Bouches-du-Rhône (0.6 per cent).

However, these increases have been largely due to migration rather than a high birth rate, the largest number of migrants (between 2,500 and

3,000 per year into PACA alone) coming from Nord-Pas-de-Calais to escape the cold and damp. An amazing 13 per cent of the inhabitants of Languedoc-Roussillon and 10 per cent of PACA's residents lived elsewhere five years ago. Most of the new arrivals are young – two-thirds being under 40 – and highly qualified, and fewer people retire to the regions than in the previous decade, although there are still popular retirement spots, such as Cannes. The student population of the major towns in the area varies considerably: from over 30 per cent in Aix-en-Provence (13) – the second-highest proportion of any town in France – and to 5 per cent in Marseille (13), 3 per cent in Toulon (83), 2 per cent in Carcassonne (11) and Béziers (34), and a mere 1 per cent in Antibes, Cannes (06), Arles (13) and Sète (34).

In contrast with the '90s, the cities and major towns in the area have grown since the turn of the century: Marseille by some 23,000 inhabitants, Aix-en-Provence, Avignon, Nice and Toulon by between 5,000 and 6,000 each, and Arles, Cannes and Hyères by between 2,000 and 3,000 each. Among the smaller towns, only Marignane and Vitrolles (both in 13) have declining populations.

Corsica's population is just under 280,000 and fast growing (around 1 per cent per annum) thanks to migration rather than a high birth rate, attracting both young people and retirees (the over-60s accounting for a third of arrivals), particularly from mainland France: some 4,400 people move to the island every year, almost a quarter of them from Ile-de-France.

6

The approximate populations, including official foreign resident numbers, of each *département* are given below; for the populations of major towns, see **Major Towns & Places of Interest** on page 248.

- **Corse-du-Sud (2A)** – population 128,000, of which 5,900 Moroccans, 1,900 Portuguese, 1,800 Italians, 1,500 Tunisians and 65 Britons.
- **Haute-Corse (2B)** – population 149,000, of which 7,100 Moroccans, 1,200 Italians, 1,100 Portuguese, 800 Tunisians and 60 Britons.
- **Alpes-de-Haute-Provence (04)** – population 153,000, of which 1,000 are Algerians, 1,000 Moroccans, 850 Italians, 650 Portuguese and 130 Britons.
- **Hautes-Alpes (05)** – population 132,000, of which 800 are Italians, 700 Algerians, 350 Moroccans and just over 100 Britons.
- **Alpes-Maritimes (06)** – population 1.06m, of which 19,000 are Tunisians, 17,000 Italians, 9,500 Algerians, 8,500 Moroccans, 6,000 Portuguese and 4,300 Britons.

- **Aude (11)** – population 337,000, of which 3,600 are Moroccans, 2,900 Spaniards, 1,200 Algerians, 1,100 Portuguese, 700 Armenian Turks, 700 Britons and 600 Italians.
- **Bouches-du-Rhône (13)** – population 1.9m, of which 47,000 are Algerians, 14,500 Moroccans, 13,000 Tunisians, 7,600 Italians, 6,000 Spaniards and 1,400 Britons.
- **Gard (30)** – population 678,000, of which 15,500 are Moroccans, 5,000 Algerians, 3,900 Spaniards, 2,400 Portuguese, 1,600 Italians, 900 Tunisians, 650 Britons and 500 Armenian Turks.
- **Hérault (34)** – population 982,000, of which 21,000 are Moroccans, 8,200 Spaniards, 4,900 Algerians, 2,100 Portuguese, 1,800 Britons, 1,700 Italians, 1,100 Armenian Turks and 800 Tunisians.
- **Lozère (48)** – population 77,000, of which 1,250 are Portuguese, 500 Moroccans, 250 Armenian Turks and a sprinkling of Britons, Italians and Spaniards.
- **Pyrénées-Orientales (66)** – population 422,000, of which 9,000 are Spaniards, 2,500 Portuguese, 4,000 Moroccans, 3,500 Algerians, 700 Britons, 500 Armenian Turks, 500 Italians and 250 Tunisians.
- **Var (83)** – population 967,000, of which 10,000 are Moroccans, 9,000 Tunisians, 7,600 Algerians, 5,000 Italians and 1,500 Britons.
- **Vaucluse (84)** – population 529,000, of which 16,000 are Moroccans, 4,500 Spaniards, 4,000 Algerians, 2,100 Italians, 1,800 Tunisians and 600 Britons.

LANGUAGE

Languedoc-Roussillon is the homeland of France's second language, the *langue d'Oc* (also known as *Occitan*), which was once spoken throughout southern France, while those in the north spoke the *langue d'Oïl* (*oc* and *oïl* being the two medieval words for 'yes' in the respective areas). The language is sometimes called Provençal, but in fact this was just one of the dialects of *Occitan* and is now spoken only in Italy. Although the *langue d'Oïl* has become the national *lingua franca*, *Occitan* was the everyday language of most of the rural population of the south until well into the 20th century and still survives in most of southern France (in as many as 31 *départements*, according to some surveys), where it's estimated that there are around 3m speakers of *Occitan* (around a third of whom use the language daily) and a further 1.5m who can read or understand it. (It's also spoken in parts of Spain and Italy.)

Although most speakers are older people, there has recently been an attempt to revive the language, for example through *Occitan*-language pre-schools (*calandretas*), where there are around 1,500 pupils at any time, and it's taught as an optional subject in some state schools. The language has no official status, although around 40 minutes of *Occitan* programmes are broadcast every week by France 3 and there's a number of local radio programmes in the language, as well as articles in local newspapers and a number of *Occitan* magazines.

Related to *Occitan* (and to French) is Catalan, which is spoken by around 6m people, mostly in Spain but also in Andorra (where it's the official language) and parts of Pyrénées-Orientales in France (as well as in a single village in Sardinia!) – a region known as Catalonia.

Although it isn't necessary to learn *Occitan* or Catalan in order to be accepted by the local community, if you can master a few words and phrases it will probably improve your chances. Note also, however, that French is spoken with a pronounced 'twang' in southern France (not at all like the pronunciation you learned at school), which it may take a while to get used to.

CLIMATE

The Mediterranean coast proves that you cannot generalise about French weather. The climate is, of course, Mediterranean (hot, dry and sunny except for the habitual heavy rain in early spring) as opposed to continental (inland) or maritime (oceanic) climates, but the high mountains not too far from the coast mean weather conditions change suddenly. Mountainous areas inland may also have heavy rain after the middle of August. Beneficial micro-climates exist in certain localities, e.g. Hyères (83), which has a number of rest homes (so Queen Victoria obviously knew a thing or two when she elected to visit there).

The Cévennes area in Languedoc is the wettest in France with some 2,000mm (80in) of rain annually, as cold and hot air streams collide over the mountains (known as the *effet Cénévol*). In 2002, flash floods killed 23 people in parts of Gard, Hérault and Vaucluse; in the town of Sommières near Nîmes (30), six months' worth of rain fell in just a few hours.

The Languedoc-Roussillon region has typically hot, dry summers and much colder winters than the Côte d'Azur, where Nice probably has the smallest variation in temperatures throughout the year (never a sustained heat-wave and mild in the winter months), although it's the French city worst affected by flooding (see page 247). The high land in the Luberon area of

Vaucluse also experiences much colder temperatures in winter than the Var coast and the Riviera. In Gard, the wettest month is October, with around 135mm of rain, followed by January (75mm) and the driest July (28mm). Hérault is somewhat drier (20mm in July and 100mm in October) and Pyrénées-Orientales drier still (14mm in July and 68mm in October), while Aude has a different rainfall pattern, April being the wettest month (74mm). Inland Lozère is driest in March (38mm) and July (52mm) and wettest in May (100mm); it's also cooler than the coastal *départements*. The coastal *départements* of PACA (and Vaucluse) have a similar rainfall pattern to those of Languedoc-Roussillon, the wettest month being October (between 86mm and 106mm), the driest July (8-30mm), but the mountainous areas Alpes-de-Hautes-Provence and Hautes-Alpes have more evenly spread rain, with a high of around 95mm in October and a low of 40-50mm in July; Var has the highest average mid-winter temperature (6C).

In recent years there has been no pattern to the arrival and departure of snow on the ski slopes and other medium to high-altitude areas. In 1999 there was heavy snow at the beginning of November on land around 400m (1,300ft) in the Bouches-du-Rhône and Var *départements*, and in May 2002 there were heavy snowfalls (after the winter snow had melted) in some areas above 800m (2,600ft) in Languedoc-Roussillon. Nevertheless, these areas are inevitably colder in winter and milder in summer than lower-lying parts.

The Mediterranean coast also experiences the strong *Tramontane* and *Mistral* winds, and the PACA region is occasionally visited (usually overnight) by the warm and gentler sand-bearing *Scirocco* wind from the Sahara. The frequency of the *Mistral* is variable; it's particularly strong in February, March and April and less so in July and August. The Nice area, in summer, is often a few degrees cooler than the rest of the coast on account of a partially clouded sky: there's no *Mistral* here to chase the clouds away. Three *départements* – Aude, Pyrénées-Orientales and western parts of Hérault – are affected by another unpleasant wind, the westerly Cers, which is said to drive people mad. Buyers of west-facing properties beware.

Average daytime temperatures in summer vary little between the towns along the Mediterranean coast. In June they're around 26C (79F), in July and August, around 28C (82F), and in September around 25C (77F), although slightly cooler around Nice and hotter inland, away from sea breezes. In the winter, from January to March, average temperatures are noticeably lower in the Montpellier area, just off the coast, than in the areas around Nice, Perpignan and Toulon. Toulon is France's sunniest city and one of the sunniest spots on the Mediterranean coast, with an average of around 2,900 hours' sunshine per year. The table below shows the number of hours' sunshine and number of days' rainfall in selected towns in the area.

Town	Sunshine Hours	Days' Rainfall
Gap (05)	2,506	83
Antibes (06)	2,694	63
Cannes (06)	2,694	64
Nice (06)	2,694	63
Carcassonne (11)	2,506	94
Aix-en-Provence (13)	2,836	60
Arles (13)	2,836	57
Marseille (13)	2,836	57
Nîmes (30)	2,669	67
Béziers (34)	2,687	57
Montpellier (34)	2,687	59
Sète (34)	2,687	57
Perpignan (66)	2,506	56
Toulon (83)	2,899	60
Avignon (84)	2,595	68

Average summer sea temperatures in Centigrade (and Fahrenheit in brackets) for the eastern and western coasts are shown below:

	May	June	July	Aug	Sep	Oct
Montpellier to Toulon	15 (59)	19 (66)	19 (66)	20 (68)	20 (68)	17 (62)
Hyères to Menton	17 (62)	19 (66)	20 (68)	22 (72)	22 (72)	19 (66)

Corsica

Not surprisingly, Corsica has a Mediterranean climate, with sudden storms in mountain areas. Ajaccio enjoys 2,735 hours of sunshine per year (Bastia around 2,655) and the island is often the hottest place in France, although temperatures rarely exceed 30C (86F) even in high summer. The sea temperature in July and August may reach 25C (77F). Average daytime January temperatures in both Ajaccio and Bastia are 9C (48F) and average annual rainfall is 645mm (25in) on 75 days in Ajaccio and 750mm (29in) on just 67 days in Bastia.

CRIME RATE & SECURITY

The PACA and Languedoc-Roussillon regions are numbers two and three respectively (after Ile-de-France) in the crime-rate charts and include all but 5 of the 13 towns with the highest (reported) crime rates in the country. On the other hand, Lozère in Languedoc-Roussillon is the French *département* with the lowest crime rate, due no doubt to its predominantly rural nature. On the other hand, the town of Gap (05) enjoys the lowest (reported) crime rate of any major town in France.

Here, as in France generally, drug-associated crimes, including physical attacks, have increased markedly over the last ten years while (detected) financial skulduggery, despite publicity suggesting the contrary, has diminished. Marseille retains a (largely undeserved) unsavoury international reputation (its crime rate is only the 23rd-highest of the 100 major towns in France), and the city centre doesn't attract tourists or foreign homebuyers. Its most dangerous neighbourhoods are the 13th, 14th and 15th *arrondissements* to the north of the centre and the 4th in the city centre, where violent crime and the burning of parked vehicles aren't uncommon. To a lesser extent, Nice and Toulon have earned unfavourable reputations through political (financial) scandals since the '90s.

Thefts from cars stopped at traffic lights and motorway toll booths and rest areas are common, particularly in the Nice-Antibes-Cannes area and in Marseille; thieves are usually on motorcycles and particularly target foreign-registered and hired cars. Parked cars are also broken into, and purse-snatching and pickpocketing are common throughout the Côte d'Azur. There has also recently been an increasing number of crimes on trains between Marseille and Nice, but by far the most common crime is burglary, which is rife in resort towns such as Cannes (where people have been burgled while having dinner on the terrace!).

Car thefts are frequent throughout the area (as reflected in car insurance premiums), and driving standards are poor – even for France (see page 290). Forest fires are another hazard and are prevalent in the dry summer months, and you should ensure that the grass and vegetation surrounding your house surrounding your house are trimmed back at least to the statutory minimum distance of 50m (165ft) from the building (local regulations can increase this to 100m). It should also be noted that there are no fewer than six high-risk factories in and around Sète (34).

Despite all this, the Mediterranean coastal area remains a fairly safe (and extremely healthy) place to live, provided you exercise care and take the usual precautions – don't let the sun 'go to your head'!

AMENITIES

Sports

Both PACA and Languedoc-Roussillon are popular with sportspeople. It goes without saying that the whole of the Mediterranean coast is a paradise for watersports lovers – Languedoc is one of Europe's premier sailing and windsurfing centres, with some 25 marinas and over 22,000 moorings (Port Camargue is Europe's largest marina, with 4,500 berths) – and there's also a wealth of other sporting facilities in resort and main town areas, although facilities are lacking in some rural areas. Traditional community sports centres, housing several activities together where you walk in, pay and play, are rare. Public swimming pools (usually overheated) and well maintained tennis courts are, on the other hand, quite common. They're usually good value and you can often purchase a coupon of tickets (*carnet*) reducing the unit entrance price. *Complexes sportives* or *halles/palais/salles des sports* are municipal gymnasiums providing a court for the local basketball, handball or volleyball team. Local town halls (*mairies* or *hôtels de ville*) should be able to provide you with a list of sports clubs and associations in their area, and the local Office des Clubs sportifs publishes an annual directory.

6

Golf

Despite the high cost of playing golf regularly, due partly perhaps to the water bills incurred in maintaining the lush greens and fairways, golf is one of the fastest growing sports in the area. The PACA region has around 45 18-hole courses and 25 schools with nine-hole and practice courses. The greatest concentration of courses is to be found around Cannes (06), where there are six. For more information contact the Ligue Golf PACA, domaine Riquetti, chemin départemental 9, 13290 Les Milles (☎ 04 42 24 20 41). The Languedoc-Roussillon region also has several first-class courses, near to the main towns, several of which offer both 9 and 18-hole rounds. For more information contact the CRT, 20 rue de la République, 34000 Montpellier

(☎ 04 67 22 81 00, 💻 contact.crtlr@sunfrance.com). The table below lists the number of courses in each *département* (there's also an 18-hole course in Monaco).

Département	**No. of Courses**
Alpes-de-Haute-Provence	3 x 18 holes
Alpes-Maritimes	2 x 9 holes, 9 x 18 holes, 1 x 27 holes
Aude	1 x 18 holes
Bouches-du-Rhône	3 x 9 holes, 5 x 18 holes
Gard	1 x 9 holes, 2 x 18 holes
Hérault	1 x 9 holes, 5 x 18 holes, 1 x 36 holes
Lozère	3 x 9 holes
Pyrénées-Orientales	2 x 9 holes, 1 x 18 holes, 1 x 27 holes
Var	1 x 9 holes, 11 x 18 holes
Vaucluse	1 x 9 holes, 4 x 18 holes

Information (in both French and English) on how to find courses, the cost of a round (which varies between €15 and €50), etc. is available via the internet (💻 www.backspin.com). Another useful website for golfers is 💻 www.golf.com.fr.

In property advertisements in French, watch out for the word '*golfe*', which means bay or gulf, as opposed to '*golf*', which means golf. (Watch out for the prices as well!)

Skiing

The *départements* of Alpes-Maritimes and Alpes-de-Hautes-Provence are within a short drive of the Alps and their incomparable ski resorts (see page 304), while Pyrénées-Occidentales has its own resorts, at Font-Romeu, Les Angles, Porté-Puymorens and Pyrénées 2000, and is close to those of Ariège and Andorra (see page 207). Although not as famous or challenging as the Alps, the Pyrenees offer a good selection of downhill runs as well as plenty of cross-country skiing.

Other Sports

Languedoc-Roussillon is a stronghold of French rugby, whereas soccer fans have two first-class professional teams to idolise in PACA – those of Marseille and Monaco. In high season, the lakes of Castillon, Esparron-Gréoux and Quinson near the Grand Canyon du Verdon in Var have first-class aquatic facilities (such as white-water rafting and canoeing) with qualified staff.

Leisure

Few areas of France can match the Mediterranean coast for the excellence and variety of its attractions, many of which are available all year round. Apart from the simple pleasures of beaches for sun-worshippers, beautiful and spectacular countryside for nature lovers, and mountains and seas for sports enthusiasts, the natural light and contrasting colours of the sea and landscapes are ideal for would-be artists. (The area was home to Cézanne, Picasso and Van Gogh.) Contact the cultural services *département* of your town hall for details of workshops or associations. The *Officiel des Arts* (💻 www.od-arts.com) publishes a weekly list of major art exhibitions taking place throughout France. English-language newspapers (see **English-language Media** on page 277) should also be consulted.

6

English-language Cinema & Theatre

All major towns with a large university student population, such as Aix-en-Provence (13) (Cinémas Renoir), Avignon (84), Montpellier (34), Nice (06) and Toulon (83) (Cinéma le Royal), have at least one cinema dedicated to showing foreign films (mainly American and British) in their original language version (*version originale/VO*). Programmes and further information are available from local newspapers and tourist offices. There's an English-language Cinema Club in Pézensas (34). A useful website for finding out what films are on in a given area, which also indicates whether the films are being shown in the original language is 💻 www.cinefil.com. Don't expect always to see the latest commercial blockbuster; *VO* films may be avant-garde or offbeat. Also, although cinemas are being modernised, they don't generally offer grandiose comfort and large screens with stunning sound systems. Municipal cultural centres (*maisons de la culture*) may also show films in *VO* at a subsidised price of around €5. All films are shown in *VO* at the annual Film Festival Cannes (whose citizens visit the cinema more frequently than those of any other major town in France), but unless you're involved in the film industry you're unlikely to be able to obtain tickets. (Incidentally, La Ciotat, in Bouches-du-Rhône (13) is recognised as the birthplace of motion pictures.)

The Limelight Theatre Company in Antibes (Alpes-Maritimes, 💻 www.limelighttheatrecompany.com) presents plays in English.

Festivals

The area is renowned for its festivities, which include carnivals in Nice (06) for three weeks in February and in Limoux (11) every weekend from mid-January to the end of March, and the famous Cannes (06) Film Festival in May, to gain admission to which, however, you must be able to show a 'professional interest' in the cinema. The *département* of Var is known for its summer jazz festivals, including those at Brignolles, Ramatuelle and Tourves. One of the oldest festivals in the area is the annual sausage fair in Le Val (83), which has been taking place every August/September for over 370 years and attracts gourmands from all over France.

Among the oddest festivals is the Fête de l'Ours (Bear Festival) in the pretty Catalan village of Prats-de-Mollo-la-Preste (66), where every February villagers don bear suits and paint their faces in celebration of the once-feared creature.

Museums & Cultural Events

If you're a culture vulture, the area is rich in historical (particularly naval) museums. For example, on Mount Faron, near Toulon, there's a museum commemorating the liberation of Provence in 1944, and there's a museum of prehistory just over the departmental border from the Grand Canyon du Verdon, at Quinson (04) in Alpes-de-Haute-Provence (☎ 04 92 74 09 59, 💻 www.museeprehistoire.com). Nice (06) boasts 12 museums (the largest number in any French town other than Paris) and Marseille ten; Aix-en-Provence (13) has over 60 historical monuments.

Many local French newspapers publish weekly magazines or supplements containing a detailed programme of local events and entertainment. The CityVox website (💻 www.cityvox.com) has lively information in English on what's going on in Aix-en-Provence, Avignon, Marseille, Montpellier and Nice and in French for Nîmes and Perpignan.

Casinos

Not surprisingly, there are more casinos in this area than in almost any other part of France – over 35 in the two regions, including one in Alpes-de-Provence (04), ten in Alpes-Maritimes (06), two in Aude (11), four in Bouches-du-Rhône (13), one in Gard (30), seven in Hérault (34), one in Mende (48), seven in Pyrénées-Orientales (66) and five in Var (83). Details of all casinos and what they offer are available via the internet (e.g. 💻 www.journaldescasinos.com – partly in English).

Theme Parks

There's a number of theme parks in the area (mostly open between the middle of June and early September, weather permitting), including:

- Aqualand in Port-Leucate (11), Cap-d'Agde (34) and Saint-Cyprien (66): water parks;
- Aquatic park at Saint-Cyprien (66);
- Aquarium de Bagnuls-sur-Mer (66): Mediterranean sea life;
- Aquarium de Cannet in Cannet-en-Roussillon (66): tropical fish;
- Aquarium du Cap-d'Agde (34): sea life;
- Aquatica in Fréjus (83): water park;
- Atlantide Parc in Saint-Jean-du-Gard (30): sea life;
- La Bambouseraie in Anduze (30): tropical gardens;
- Le Catalan in Casteil (66): wildlife park;
- El Dorado City in Ensuès-la-Redonne (13): Wild West theme park;
- Géospace in Montpellier (34): observatory and botanical institute;
- L'Ile des Embiez in Six-Fours-les-Pins (83): sea life;
- Kiddy Parc in Port d'Hyères (83): farm animals;
- Les Loups du Gévaudan near Marvejols (48): wolves in a 'natural' environment;
- Marineland at Biot near Antibes (06): featuring killer whale and dolphin acts – one of France's leading aquariums, attracting over a million visitors per year;

- Musée océanographique de Monaco: marine and maritime museum;
- OK-Corral in Cuges-les-Pin (13): Wild West park – the largest theme park in southern France, attracting half a million visitors per year;
- Parc animalier des Angles (66): Pyrenean wildlife in 'natural' environment;
- Parc ornithologique de Pont-de-Gau in Les Saintes-Maries-de-la-Mer (13): bird park;
- Réserve de Sigean (11): 'African' game park;
- Seaquarium in Le Grau-du-Roi (30): fish and aquatic mammals;
- Le Village des Tortues in Gonfaron (83): 2,500 turtles and tortoises;
- Zoo du Cap-Ferrat (06): 300 animals;
- Zoo et Jardin exotique in Sanary-sur-Mer (83): zoo and garden.

Shopping Centres & Markets

On the outskirts of large towns (and also in the centres of Marseille, Nice and Toulon) there are huge shopping centres (*centres commerciaux*) with hypermarkets and accompanying open-air or underground parking, attractive boutique shopping galleries (*galeries marchandes*), DIY stores, furniture stores, garden centres and sports equipment and sportswear stores. The main hypermarket chains are Auchan, Carrefour and Géant Casino, with an exception at the out-of-town Nice site of Cap 3000, where there's a Lafayette Gourmet (part of the Groupe Galeries Lafayette) hypermarket. The Grand Littoral and Grand Var regional centres, to the west of Marseille and the east of Toulon respectively, are particularly large. The Auchan hypermarket at Le Pontet (next to Avignon) is the largest hypermarket in the area.

While buying food in shopping centres is more a necessity than a pleasure, markets – whether for fresh meat, fruit, vegetables, fish, cheese and bread or flowers, artisans' products or bric-a-brac – are colourful, entertaining and an experience not to be missed. Food is generally more expensive than in hyper and supermarkets, but is better quality, especially local and in season produce, e.g. Cavaillon cantaloupe melons from May to September, and wild strawberries (*fraises des bois*) in the spring. Good bargains are to be had for clothes and shoes, particularly if you become a regular customer with the same stall-holder. Montpellier has a renowned *marché paysan* on Sunday mornings selling only local products (*produits du terroir*) and the Marché du Plan Cabanes, a bazaar with a distinctive African and Arabic flavour. The Cours Lafayette in Toulon has a daily provençal market offering almost everything under the sun (and normally under the sun). The fish market on the old port (le Vieux Port) at Marseille and the flower market near the old part of Nice are also recommended. Active participation in the truffle market in Aups (83) between mid-December and mid-March, on the other hand, isn't wise unless you have money to burn, with prices between €300 and €600 per kilogram!

Foreign Food & Products

Supermarkets sell few foreign foods with the exception of biscuits, cereals (including Weetabix), confectionery, preserves, smoked salmon, Chinese and Vietnamese foods, delicatessen foods and some cheeses. However, there are a few specialist shops in PACA where foreign 'delicacies' can be found, e.g. the Comptoir Irlandais in Toulon (83), which sells British and Irish food, including cheddar, chutney, Marmite and smoked salmon.

There are specialist English and Chinese furniture shops in most cities, including Habitat stores, which can be found in Montpellier, Marseille, Toulon, Nice and Vallauris (06). IKEA furniture stores are located at Vitrolles (13) near Marseille-Provence airport and at Toulon. If you live near Carcassonne, a trip to Toulouse, where there's an IKEA and a Habitat, is worth considering.

There are English-language book shops in Nice, Cannes, Marseille and Aix-en-Provence – Heidi's English Bookshop (☎ 04 93 34 74 11) in Antibes boasts the largest stock of English-language books on the Côte d'Azur – and from around May to October paperback display units with English, German and Dutch bestsellers appear in book shops, newsagents and supermarkets along the Mediterranean coast and inland as far as Avignon (84). You will also find, all year round, pictorial guides and souvenir books with English text which describe particular areas, and possibly books by local-interest authors such as Peter Mayle.

Restaurants & Bars

There's an almost infinite variety of restaurants offering authentic languedocien and provençal regional dishes (fish and *produits du terroir*), gastronomic French cuisine, international hotel cuisine, Arab stews (*couscous*), Greek salads, Italian pasta, Spanish paella and Chinese and

Vietnamese specialities. Establishments vary from seasonal beach shacks and attractive terraces and pedestrian-area town and village brasseries and bistros to Michelin-starred gourmet restaurants, of which there are no fewer than five in Avignon (84). The two regions offer beautiful country and sea views, which contribute to the enjoyment of the meal and, of course, influence the price. If you're dining out, the best value and quality cuisine is more readily found in the hinterland of Provence and not on the coast.

On a day-to-day basis, self-service cafeterias such as Flunch and Casino offer a variety of hot and cold dishes as a quality three-course meal for around €8. If you have a young family, McDonald's and Quick (the French fast-food chain) offer the usual hamburger menus, complemented by regional salad dishes, and if you're really in a hurry all large towns have pavement kiosks selling substantial hot and cold half-baguette sandwiches.

Regional specialities include sea fish and molluscs, e.g. octopus salad (*salade de poulpe*), freshwater fish, especially in the Tarn valley streams, and anchovies (*anchois*) from the Mediterranean, hams and cheeses from Cévennes area, herbs and red vegetables from Languedoc, lamb from the mountains, notably around Sisteron in Alpes-de-Hautes-Provence, and locally reared ostrich, which provides an alternative to a traditional roast. Italy is the overriding foreign influence on the regional dishes in PACA, particularly along the Côte d'Azur, including salads, fish and meat dishes plus pastas – a somewhat lighter diet than that of Languedoc-Roussillon, which is nevertheless regarded as 'healthier'. Local speciality dishes include Carcassonne *cassoulet* of white beans, mutton and sausage, *salade niçoise* (Nice salad), *bouillabaisse* (also a Nice speciality) and wild boar (*sanglier*) stew. Blanquette de Limoux is a sparkling white wine produced using champagne methods, but don't expect the taste to compare with that of a quality champagne. Local sweet white wines (*vins doux naturels*) are often drunk as an *apéritif*, which is an acquired taste for northern palates.

A wide selection of coffees, ranging from light *arabica* to stronger *robusta* flavours, can be enjoyed in coffee shops, usually found in *galeries marchandes* (see **Shopping Centres & Markets** on page 272).

SERVICES

International & Private Schools

International schools in the PACA and Languedoc-Roussillon regions are concentrated in the Riviera area, although the International School at Toulouse (see page 218), which is under two hours' drive from Carcassonne

(11), is a possibility if you're planning to live in that area. Details of the principal schools in the area (including Monaco) are given below.

- Centre international privé pour l'Education et la Culture (☎ 04 42 60 84 25, 💻 www.c-i-p-e-c.com) in Luynes (06);
- The International Bilingual School of Provence (☎ 04 42 24 03 40, 💻 www.ibsolfprovence.com) in Aix-en-Provence (13);
- The International School of Monaco (☎ 0377-9325 6820, 💻 www.ismonaco.org);
- The International School of Nice (☎ 04 93 21 04 00, 💻 www.isn-nice.org);
- The International School of Sophia Antipolis (ASEICA, ☎ 04 97 23 92 30, 💻 www.aseica.org);
- Mougins School (☎ 04 93 90 15 47, 💻 http://mougins-school.com) in Sophia Antipolis (06).

There are many private schools (*écoles privées*), mostly Roman Catholic but also Jewish and Protestant (the Nîmes area is a Protestant stronghold), from primary (*écoles primaires*) to secondary (*collèges* and *lycées*) level, providing study courses up to the French *baccalauréat* examination with all its options. There are also two private primary schools catering specifically for English-speaking students:

6

- Ecole privée active bilingue 'Le Pain de Sucre' (☎ 04 93 73 70 41, 💻 www.ecoledupaindesucre.com) in Cagnes-sur-Mer (06);
- Ecole privée internationale 'Le Pain d'Epice' (☎ 04 93 44 75 44, 💻 www.ecoledupaindesucre.com) in Nice (06);

Language Schools

The Côte d'Azur area has the greatest concentration of language schools in France outside Paris; Nice (06) and Montpellier (34) between them offer over 40 schools, including the Alliance française, which also has a branch in Marseille. There are other schools in Manosque and Moustiers-Sainte-Marie (04), two in Antibes, three in Cannes, one each in Cap d'Ail, La Napoule, Le Rouret, Menton, Sophia-Antipolis, Villefranche-sur-Mer and Villeneuve-Loubet (06), two in Aix-en-Provence and one each in Istres and Noves (13), one each in Saint-Bonnet-du-Gard, Saint-Geniès-de-Comolas (30), Béziers and Loupian (34), two in Sète (34), two in Perpignan (66), one each in Hyères, La Seyne-sur-Mer and Toulon (83), and three in Avignon and one each in Castellet and Morières-les-Avignons (84), as well as two schools in Monaco. Details of the above schools can be found on 💻 www.europa-pages.com. The French Consulate in London (see **Appendix A**) publishes a booklet called *Cours de français Langue étrangère et Stages pédagogiques du français Langue étrangère en France*, which includes a comprehensive list of schools, organisations and institutes providing French language courses throughout France. Language courses are also offered by local Chambres de Commerce et d'Industrie and Centres culturels.

Hospitals & Clinics

The majority of towns have at least one public hospital, and cities such as Marseille, Montpellier, Nice and Toulon have several that are particularly well equipped. Marseille, Montpellier and Nice have teaching hospitals (*CHU*) and many of their graduate specialists remain on the Mediterranean coast as hospital consultants. Insomniacs should note that the Montpellier *CHU* has a specialist unit devoted to (lack of) sleep and sleep-related problems.

As well as *cliniques chirurgicales*, there are also *cliniques-polycliniques*, the equivalent of private general hospitals, in the large towns in the two regions. *Cliniques chirurgicales* should not be confused with *cliniques chirurgicales esthétiques* (cosmetic surgery clinics), which aren't lacking along the Riviera! In coastal towns, you should find at least one doctor in each hospital service who speaks good enough English to understand and converse with you.

If you're planning to live in a remote village in the mountains, e.g. in Alpes-de-Haute-Provence (04), take into account that the nearest hospital and maternity unit may be up to an hour's drive away on a winding road, which for part of the winter may be snowbound.

Tradesmen

There are a number of English-speaking and other foreign tradesmen in the major resorts and towns. Consult the advertisements in English-language newspapers and magazines and English magazines covering French property (see **English-language Media** on page 277, **Useful Publications** on page 291 and **Appendix B**). The British Consulate in Marseille (☎ 04 91 15 72 10) may be able to provide a list of officially registered builders (whose work is automatically guaranteed by insurance cover) in your area, although this will include French and foreign tradesmen, who may speak little English.

English-language Media

Riviera Radio (FM 106.5), based at Monte Carlo, can be received from the Italian border to Saint-Tropez and in summer (for some climatic reason) as far as Toulon, but not, for example, on the Var coast around Le Lavandou. Radio International (FM 100.5, 110.7, 100.9 and 101.90), also based in Monaco, can be received in an even smaller area. It's possible to receive BBC Radio 1, 2, 3, and 4 on your television via the Astra satellite, and you can listen to recordings of radio programmes on Radio 1, 2, 3, 4, 5, 6 and 1Extra on your computer via the internet (go to 💻 www.bbc.co.uk/radio/aod/index.shtml). The World Service can be received on short wave (for frequency details, go to 💻 www.bbc.co.uk/worldservice/schedules/frequencies/eurwfreq.shtml) and via the Astra satellite. Local music stations usually broadcast 60 per cent non-French language songs, most of which are in English.

The *International Herald Tribune* is widely available on the day of publication and the *Guardian* is available in some areas the same day. Cosmopolitan cities such as Nice, Aix-en-Provence and Montpellier have other English-language daily newspapers available the day after publication; although they may also be sold in some other towns and coastal villages throughout the low season, they're more extensively available in the high season. The *Guardian Weekly* and the *Weekly Telegraph* are available all year round, in certain areas, and are a good way to keep abreast (almost) with British news. Alternatively, they can be airmailed to you directly at reduced rates on subscription.

6

Certain newsagents sell English-language magazines, ranging from *Women's Day* to the *National Geographic Magazine*. Local publications in English include the following:

- *Le Eleven* – a classified ads review published in Aude and available online (💻 www.eleven.fr);
- *Languedoc Sun* – a free bi-monthly paper distributed throughout Aude, Gard and Hérault and also available online (💻 www.languedocsun.com);
- *The Riviera Reporter* – a monthly magazine covering the Côte d'Azur (💻 www.riviera-reporter.com;
- *The Riviera Times* (incorporating *The Monaco Times*) – a monthly newspaper covering the Côte d'Azur (💻 www.rivieratimes.com);
- *Le Sixty Six* – a classified ads review published in Pyrénées-Orientales.

Nice-Matin publishes a weekly leisure guide in English called, somewhat unidiomatically, *Let's Go Riviera*. Also monthly are the newspapers *The*

Connexion and *The News*, which cover the whole of France (see **Appendix B**).

The English Yellow Pages is a directory of English-speaking businesses in the south of France, covering mainly the Mediterranean coast between Monaco and Saint-Tropez; although aimed at customers, it may be helpful to those looking for employment. Copies are available from English Yellow Pages, 1 avenue Saint-Roch, 06600 Antibes (☎ 04 92 90 49 34, 💻 www.yellowpages.fr).

Embassies & Consulates

The list below includes the American and British Consulates General and Honorary Consulates in the area. For Austria, Finland, Germany, Italy, the Netherlands, Norway and Sweden, the Consulates General are in Marseille, for Canada in Nice, and for Ireland in Antibes (see the yellow pages under 'Ambassades, consulats et autres représentations diplomatiques'). For details of embassies and consulates for other nations, consult the yellow pages for Marseille, Nice or Paris.

- British Consulate General, 24 avenue du Prado, 13006 Marseille (☎ 04 91 15 72 10);
- Honorary British Consul, 26 avenue Notre Dame, 06000 Nice (☎ 04 93 62 13 56);
- Honorary British Consul, 33 boulevard Princesse Charlotte, BP 205, MC 98005 Monaco (☎ 0377-9350 9966);
- United States Consulate General, 12 boulevard Paul Peytral, 13286 Marseille Cedex 6 (☎ 04 91 54 92 00);
- United States Consulate, 7 avenue Gustav V, 06000 Nice (☎ 04 93 88 89 55).

Places of Worship

Evangelical, Orthodox, Protestant and other churches and Jewish synagogues, offering regular services, are well represented throughout the area, and the Gard (30) *département* is a stronghold of the French Reformed (Protestant) Church (*Eglise réformée*). There are churches in the following towns which hold regular services in English:

- Aix-en-Provence (13);
- Beaulieu-sur-Mer (06) – Saint Michael;
- Cannes (06) – Holy Trinity;
- Grasse (06) – Saint John the Evangelist;
- Marseille (13) – All Saints;
- Menton (06) – Saint John;
- Montauroux (83) – The Community of the Glorious Ascension;
- Nice (06) – Holy Trinity & International Baptist Church;
- Saint-Paul-de-Vence (06) – International Baptist Church;
- Saint-Raphaël (83) – Saint John the Evangelist;
- Toulon (83) – Babptist Church and Eglise Evangélique;
- Vence (06) – Saint Hugh.

Monaco also has an Anglican church. Contact the Holy Trinity (Church of England) in Nice (☎ 04 93 87 19 83) for information regarding Anglican services in English. For further information on finding churches and English-language services in France, see page 86.

There are numerous mosques in the area: Briançon (05), Cagnes-sur-Mer, Cannes, Menton and Nice (06), Carcassonne (11), Arles and Marseille (13), Beaucaire and Nîmes (30), Béziers and Lunel (34), Perpignan (66), Fréjus and Toulon (83), Sorgues and Valreas (84); details can be found on 🖳 http://mosquee.free.fr. There are also several synagogues in Marseille and three in Montpellier (34), details of which can be found on 🖳 www.feujcity.com (where there's also information about Kosher food shops and restaurants, Jewish clubs, associations and schools, etc.) as well as one each in Narbonne (11), Fréjus, Toulon (83), Avignon and Carpentras (84), details of which can be found on 🖳 www.pagesjaunes.fr (enter 'Synagogues' in the first box and the name of the town).

Clubs

The generally fine weather throughout the two regions means that there's a wealth of clubs for outdoor activities. These include hunting (*chasse*), *boules*, which is marginally safer, and sailing (*clubs nautiques*), in addition to the usual indoor and outdoor games, sports and activities. Town halls have details, and the France Télécom directory website (💻 www.pagesjaunes.fr) is a rapid means of finding clubs in a particular area.

International clubs and associations such as Lions also exist, with branches in major towns. If you want to join an expatriate club, Alpes-Maritimes (06), Bouches-du-Rhône (13), Hérault (34) and Var (83) are the places to be, and your consulate (see **Consulates** on page 278) will have details. For example, there's an American Association in Marseille at 3 avenue Parc Borely, 13008 Marseille (☎ 04 91 77 18 83), the Alliance Franco-Anglaise du Languedoc in Narbonne, Aude (💻 www.afal.fr) and *French Scene* in Fitou, also in Aude. Ask at English-speaking churches and see also the local press and articles in English-language newspapers and magazines such as *The News*, *The Riviera Times* and *The Riviera Reporter* (see **Useful Publications** on page 291).

For French speakers, the Accueil des Villes Françaises (AVF), a French organisation designed to welcome newcomers to an area, is an option (there's often at least one fluent English-speaker in each group). There are 15 AVF groups in Languedoc-Roussillon – in Carcassonne, Castelnaudary, Limoux (11), Alès, Bagnols-sur-Cèze, Beaucaire, Nîmes, Uzès, Villeneuve-lèz-Angles (30), Béziers, Clermont-l'Hérault, Lunel, Montpellier (34), Mende (48), and Perpignan (66) – and 35 in PACA: in Digne, Forcalquier, Manosque, Sisteron (04), Antibes/Juan-les-Pins, Cagnes-sur-Mer, Cannes, Le Cannet, Grasse, Mandelieu, Nice, Sophia Antipolis, Vence (06), Aix-en-Provence, Carry-le-Rouet, Châteaurenard, La Ciotat, Eguilles, Martigues, Salon-de-Provence, Tarascon, Le Tholonet, Vitrolles (13), Cavalaire, Draguignan, Hyères, Le Luc, Saint-Cyr-sur-Mer, Saint-Raphaël, Sainte-Maxime, Toulon (83), Avignon, Carpentras, Cavaillon and Le Pontet (84). The website (💻 www.avf.asso.fr) includes a directory (*annuaire*) of local groups by *département* as well as an online form for contacting your local AVF before you move to the area. Listings indicate whether information and services are available in English or other languages.

PROPERTY

Most properties in the Mediterranean coastal area are purchased by French people (around 25 per cent of French executives have a second home), and permanent foreign residents account for only 6 to 7 per cent of the total population, although in some parts (e.g. Cannes) British buyers make up a significant proportion of homebuyers. Following a long period of stagnation, and at times regression, in the early and middle '90s, property prices on the

Mediterranean coast escalated towards the end of the decade. There was a slow-down at the beginning of the new century, but since then prices have begun to rise again.

In Languedoc-Roussillon, the Hérault *département* accounts for approximately 50 per cent of all property sales and developments. There have been steep price rises in one or two parts of the region, notably in and around Nîmes (30), where prices rose by up to 30 per cent in the year following the arrival of the *TGV*. Cheaper properties are to be found in Gard. Marseille is also enjoying something of a property boom, with luxury, two or three-bedroom waterfront apartments selling for over €200,000 and any good quality properties being snapped up within a day or two of coming on the market. Cheaper properties are to be found in Gard.

If you're physically prospecting the *départements*, you will find no shortage of estate agents (over 350 in Cannes, 300 in Nice and 270 in Cap d'Antibes, for example). The free magazines *Logic-Immo* and *Mag Immo*, published fortnightly, are full of property advertisements, with colour photographs and are widely available from stands outside bakers and estate agents. The English-language *French Property News* (see **Appendix B**) also has some advertisements. Recently built or off-plan luxury apartments and villas are available from property development companies such as Kaufman Broad (💻 www.KetB.com), FDI Promotion in Montpellier (💻 www.fdi.fr), George V Provence Languedoc (☎ 04 95 09 33 83), Meunier Méditerranée in Nice (☎ 04 92 29 25 30, 💻 www.meunier-habitat.fr), Bouygues Immobilier (💻 www.bouygues-immobilier.com) and Marignan Immobilier (💻 www.bouwfounds-marignan.com), but prices are well above the averages given below. Coast & Country is an English estate agent based in Nice (25 boulevard Carnot, 06300 Nice, ☎ 04 92 04 99 99, 💻 http://coast-country.com) with an office in Mougins (La Palombière, 71 avenue de Tournamy, 06250 Mougins, ☎ 04 92 92 47 50).

Typical Homes

In both the PACA and Languedoc-Roussillon regions, newer houses (i.e. those up to around 25 years old) normally follow a set regional style as regards façades (and their stucco colouring) and roofs. If you're seeking a property with distinctive character and, for example, open stone-work, you should visit older properties, which have usually been built in the traditional way (*construction traditionnelle*) with solid interior brick, (i.e. not partition) walls. (Estate agents' descriptions specify *construction traditionnelle* when it features in a newer property, as it's a selling point.) Houses in all categories often have small north-facing windows and larger, but not enormous, south-facing windows. A basement (*sous-sol*) running under the entire ground floor is often a feature of new properties.

In **Languedoc-Roussillon**, apart from the blocks of unattractive apartments and properties that were constructed around 20 years ago in the purpose-built coastal resorts, there's perhaps a greater variety of property types than in PACA. The new and recent 'Mediterranean' style house, which is similiar to the provençal style (see below) is prevalent, as are solidly built terraced *maisons de village* in village centres. Mountain areas have heavier built properties than those on the coast and stone is a much favoured building material.

In Montpellier and the Hérault *département*, there's the usual mix of luxury apartment developments and new and recent villas, many of which are built on one level, bungalow style. You may still find genuine fishermen's cottages (*maisons de pêcheur/cabanons*) in the Camargues conservation area – long, single-storey buildings (*longères*) similar to those found in Normandy and Brittany. Exposed stone-work Catalan properties are sought after on the *Côte Rocheuse* (Rocky Coast) near the Spanish border. There are many vineyard properties in this region with pink or ochre walls and slate tiled roofs (*toits de lauzes*), features shared by their smaller *mazet* 'cousins' – rectangular, stone built one-room lodges. In the sheep-rearing areas there are traditional stone or wooden converted sheep shelters (*bergeries*), built to resist the strong winds.

Along the coast of **PACA**, the major resort towns have relatively few large properties: just 24 per cent of homes in Cannes and Nice (06) consist of four rooms or more, and 28 per cent in Antibes (06). There's a concentration of modern provençal houses and villas, with red or ochre stucco facades and terracotta roof tiles. There are also Italianate villas, which feature pyramid-shaped roofs. New blocks of apartments, often having a 'Florentine' flavour, are more visually attractive than their heavier-looking predecessors, built around 20 years ago. Deluxe apartment blocks often feature magnificently landscaped gardens, with a private swimming pool and tennis courts. You may find an old fisherman's cottage for sale from time to time.

The town centres of Aix-en-Provence, Marseille and Nice feature bourgeois town houses (*hotel particulier/maison de maître*), usually converted into elegant, self-contained apartments. All villages have solidly built old houses, often terraced, which may have substantial accommodation on two or three floors. Rural specialities in the old property category are small farmhouses (*mas*), large houses (*bastides*), converted oil mills, Camargue reed-matted *cabanes* and (in the southern Alps) houses with long sloping roofs. If you want a property with a large plot, look inland and don't even consider the coastline of Alpes-Maritimes.

Cost of Property

The table below gives the average selling price of houses in 2006. Note, however, that house sizes vary from area to area, which can distort average figures.

Town/Area	Average House Price			
	2-bed	3-bed	4-bed	5+-bed
Languedoc-Roussillon				
Béziers/Narbonne	€150,000	€205,000	€260,000	€320,000
Carcassonne	€190,000	€275,000	€440,000	€540,000
Montpellier	€210,000	€260,000	€405,000	€595,000
Perpignan	€180,000	€235,000	€285,000	€445,000
PACA				
Aix-en-Provence	€365,000	€510,000	€595,000	€835,000
Antibes	€475,000	€540,000	€680,000	€980,000
Avignon	€185,000	€245,000	€420,000	€615,000
Briançon	€280,000	€310,000	€480,000	€650,000
Cannes	€440,000	€770,000	€1.75m	€2.2m
Marseille	€295,000	€420,000	€495,000	€715,000
Nice	€430,000	€570,000	€720,000	€980,000
Saint-Tropez	€710,000	€1.3m	€2.2m	€3.3m
Toulon	€285,000	€340,000	€385,000	€530,000
Corsica				
Porto Vecchio	€335,000	€470,000	€655,000	€695,000

6

The average price of a period property in 2006 in Languedoc-Roussillon as a whole was around €124,400 (national average of €102,250), the average for a new house €129,000 (national average €117,650) and for a building plot €33,000 (average €23,000). The equivalent prices in PACA were

€224,000, €200,000 and €35,000. Prices in Languedoc-Roussillon are around average for France and comparable with those in neighbouring Midi-Pyrénées (see page 225) and in Brittany and Upper Normandy (see page 89). The PACA region is the second most expensive for property in France, marginally behind Ile-de-France. However, away from the coastal strip, prices fall dramatically, although there are other expensive pockets, such as the area around the Grand Canyon du Verdon. Béziers (34) boasts the lowest average prices for older properties in the area (and the third-lowest in France), while the area's highest average prices are to be found in Cannes and Antibes (06), where the average home is more expensive than anywhere else in the country outside Ile-de-France and where prices for waterfront properties have doubled in the last two or three years.

In Corsica, two-bedroom apartments (both new and older) by the sea vary between 40 and 80m² while older two-bedroom apartments in a historic town measure between 60 and 75m². Three-bedroom apartments (both categories) tend to be much larger, from 90 to 105m². Corsica tends to offer larger (three- and four-bedroom) houses (both categories) with average plots around 1,500m².

Land

In Languedoc-Roussillon, the coastal area of Pyrénés-Orientales around Canet Plage, Saint-Cyprien and Argelès has been heavily developed over the last 25 years, resulting in a scarcity of available building land. Permission to build near Collioure is difficult to obtain. Little private building land is available in Nîmes either, partly because of archaeological excavation work and partly because of municipal development. In Montpellier and its suburbs, most private building land is in the area around Port Marianne. The municipality has its own property company, which controls around 60 per cent of this land. There's virtually no land available to the north of the city.

In PACA, it's becoming increasingly difficult to find building land for houses in the narrow strip between the coast and the mountains in Alpes-Maritimes, partly because of coastal construction regulations (*la loi littoral*) and partly because of the topography of the terrain. Apartment block developers tend to snap up what is available. Urbanisation in Var is causing concern (even among local *notaires*!), as an increasing amount of agricultural land is being built on. There are plenty of plots available in towns throughout the region, although most of them are too small for a reasonable-size house and certainly wouldn't accommodate a swimming pool.

A plot of around 600m² (6,000ft²) is a good size, although if you're planning to build a large swimming pool with paved surrounding area, up to 1,000m²

(10,000ft²) may be a more sensible size. Care should be taken not to buy or build a property in a riverside area which is liable to flooding even if a building permit has been granted, as this is no guarantee that it's safe to do so! Bear in mind also the *Tramontane* and *Mistral* wind factors (see page 264). For example, an exposed situation on level ground with a beautiful view of the western Pyrenees means you receive the brunt of the *Tramontane*.

Average prices for building land are shown below:

	up to 600m²	**600 to 1,000m²**	**1,000 to 2,500m²**
Languedoc-Roussillon (Coast)			
Perpignan (66) area	€48,000	€76,000	€77,000
Narbonne (11) area	€42,000	€59,000	€42,000*
Béziers (34) town	€42,000	€67,000	€50,000*
Montpellier (34) area	€90,000	€105,000	€132,000
Mende (48) area	€35,000	€36,000	€38,000
Carcassonne (11) area	€32,000	€33,000	€36,000
Nîmes (30) area	€51,000	€59,000	€58,000*
PACA (Coast)			
Aix (13) town	€108,000	€142,000	€162,000
Aix (13) area	€66,000	€90,000	€105,000
Marseille (13) area	€96,000	€124,000	€120,000*
Toulon (83) town	€81,000	€129,000	€134,000
Hyères (83) town	€108,000	€145,000	€228,000
Nice (06) town	€70,000	€178,000	€168,000*
Avignon (84) area	€51,000	€60,000	€60,000*
Dignes (04) area	€25,000	€38,000	€35,000*
PACA (Inland)			
Gap (town)	€45,000	€67,000	€85,000

* Prices reflect the availability and relative unpopularity of large plots.

6

Corsica has few plots under $600m^2$ for sale. The average price of plots between 800 and $1,000m^2$ is around €45,000. There's a wide variation in price according to situation (e.g. sea view) for plots between 1,000 and $2,500m^2$, but the average is around €90,000.

Rental Accommodation

There's a shortage of properties for rent in the Mediterranean coastal area generally, where it's almost impossible to find a furnished (*meublé*) apartment or house. Rental properties are particularly scarce in the Pyrénées-Orientales (66) and Aude (11) *départements* of Languedoc-Roussillon. Although you may find a property through French property magazines, such as *Les Annonces Immobilières*, published monthly, or via the internet (e.g. 💻 www.123immo.com), it's best to deal with a reputable local estate agent that specialises in rental properties (check the agent's window to see if it features *biens à louer* or *locations habitations*). Contact the National Federation of Estate Agents (FNAIM, 129 rue du Faubourg St Honoré, 75008 Paris, ☎ 01 44 20 77 00, 💻 www.fnaim.com) for a list of members in your *département*.

The rates listed below are approximate average monthly rates, exclusive of maintenance and standing charges, for long-term lets. You may find quite respectable properties below these figures and there are certainly luxury properties far above them. Holiday or short-term lets, for one to four-week periods, particularly at the peak of high season, i.e. July to mid-August, can cost three or four times these rates or even more in the purpose-built coastal resorts of Argelès-sur-Mer, Gruissan, Saint-Cyprien, Port-Bacarès, Port-Leucate and Cap-d'Agde in Languedoc-Roussillon, as well as in Saint-Tropez and other exclusive spots on the Riviera. An apartment in Cannes, for example, can cost up to €3,000 per week (more during the Film Festival), which means of course that, if you own a property there, you can let it for that amount.

The number of rooms in a property (expressed in advertisements by F or T, followed by a number) includes living rooms and bedrooms, but excludes the kitchen, bathroom, WC and any other utility rooms.

	One-bed Apartment	Three-bed House
Avignon (84)	€400	€900
Aix-en-Provence (13)	€450	€1,000

Cannes (06)	€650	€1,200
Carcassonne (66)	€500	€850
Hyères (83)	€450	€900
Marseille (13)	€450	€900
Montpellier (34)	€450	€770
Nice (06)	€475	€1,100
Nîmes (30)	€350	€1,000
Perpignan (11)	€425	€850
Toulon (83)	€400	€900

Corsica generally offers rental prices between those of the Côte d'Azur and Alsace (see page 286).

If you're renting a substantial house (*villa*) with garden, it normally has a swimming pool. If it doesn't, you should check whether you will have the use of one.

COMMUNICATIONS

Air

The Mediterranean coastal area is easily accessible by air from most countries. The main international airports are Marseille-Provence at Marignane, 25km (16mi) from the coast at Marseille, and Nice-Côte d'Azur (France's second busiest airport) to the west of Nice. There are also good air connections for Languedoc-Roussillon (particularly if you're living or staying in the Aude or Pyrénées-Orientales *départements*) via Toulouse international airport, which is in the adjacent region of Midi-Pyrénées (see page 287). Flying times from London airports are around 90 minutes. Transatlantic flights operate mainly to and from Nice. The area has several other airports which boast international flights: Carcassonne, Montpellier, Nîmes, Perpignan and Toulon/Saint-Tropez (formerly Toulon/Hyères).

Direct flights from British and Irish airports are listed in **Appendix F**. Airports are shown on the maps at the beginning of the chapter. Details of all French airports and their services can be found on 💻 www.aeroport.fr.

Corsica

There are no direct flights to Bastia or Calvi (Haute-Corse) from London or other European cities, but you must change at Marseille or Nice, the latter airport also being the transit point for flights from the USA.

Sea

Apart from numerous yachting and motorboat marinas along the coast and companies offering deep-sea fishing and pleasure boat trips, there are regular ferry boat services for passengers and their cars. Between them, the Société nationale maritime Corse-Méditerranée (SNCM) and Corsica Sardinia Ferries offer sailings from Marseille, Toulon and Nice to Corsica, Sardinia, Algeria and Tunisia. There are also ferries from Sète (34) to Tangiers, Morocco. There's a plan to introduce a ferry service from the small fishing port of Port-Vendres (near Collioure in Pyrénées-Orientales) to Barcelona in Spain. Mediterranean cruise ships have ports of call (depending on the route) at Sète, Marseille, Toulon and Nice. Sète, Marseille and Nice are major cargo ports, and Toulon is the French navy's Mediterranean base.

Public Transport

The *TGV* calls at the main towns and cities in the northern Alps and at Gap, but not Briançon, in the southern Alps. High-speed trains (*TGV*) now take just three hours from Paris to Marseille and under five hours to Perpignan. Other towns in the area served by *TGV* include Nîmes and Montpellier. (These services have proved so popular that Air France has cut the cost of its flights to Montpellier and pulled out of Nîmes altogether.) Marseille is only one hour from Lyon by *TGV*. In addition, there's a summer service, between late July and early September, direct from London to Avignon. (For details of the *TGV* network, see map in **Appendix E**.) The state run rail network (SNCF), which provides services to all sizeable towns in the two regions, has first-class safety and punctuality records. Train fares are extremely reasonable, and inexpensive season tickets are available to salaried employees living in 'dormitory' towns and commuting, for example, to major towns such as Montpellier, Marseille and Nice. Local trains (*omnibus*) stop at most stations but don't have timetables! If you work late, you must commute by car. If you want to savour the blue sea and the sandy beaches, take a semi-fast train between the main towns along the coast or the The Nice to Digne narrow gauge railway (*chemin de fer de Provence/train de pignes*), which offers a picturesque winding journey of 153km (95mi) taking around three hours.

All major towns and cities have at least one local bus company providing a frequent and usually punctual service, at reasonable prices, up to around 10pm throughout the week. From major towns to smaller nearby towns, there's usually a half-hourly service from Mondays to Saturdays (hourly on Sundays), terminating around 8pm. So, if you're spending an evening out in a major town but live outside the town, a car or taxi is essential. Taxi fares are reasonable and strictly regulated, but not all taxi drivers speak English. Buses to rural villages and outlying areas may run only once a day, or less frequently. There are school bus services in rural areas.

Public transport (usually privately operated) in some of the major towns in Languedoc-Roussillon and PACA is as follows:

- **Carcassonne (11)** – there's a free shuttle service, every 15 minutes in high season, to the fortified old town.
- **Marseille (13)** – there are single-decker buses and also, in central areas, trolley buses and trams, as well as an underground (métro) service – the only one in the Mediterranean area in France – with two lines, from the town centre to the suburbs; a tourist train runs around the old port (Vieux Port) area, and you can cross the old port with a frequent ferry service.
- **Montpellier (34)** – a two-line tram system is currently in operation, with plans for a third (linking the city with the airport) under consideration; the TAM bus company operates throughout the town and suburbs; the Petibus minibus service runs in the pedestrian area of the old town (cars are banned from almost the whole town centre), as does a sightseeing train; open four-wheeled carriages ply the tourist trade along the esplanade and in the Place de la Comédie.
- **Toulon (83)** – a frequent passenger ferry service from the adjacent town of La Seyne, ideal for people working in the centre of Toulon, takes around 10 minutes; there's also a tourist train in the pleasure port and old town area.
- **Corsica** – public transport in Corsica is comprehensive but there's often only one service per day. Detailed information can be found on a website run by a British expatriate, Rosalind Fiamma (💻 www.cosicabus.org).

Roads

If you're driving down from Paris to the PACA region, it's difficult to avoid the notorious bottleneck at Lyon, particularly in holiday periods, but the 'Wily Bison' website (💻 www.bison-fute.equipement.gouv.fr) provides invaluable forecasts and up-to-the-minute reports. If, on the other hand, you're driving from Paris to the Roussillon area, you can pick up the A20, 80km (50mi) south of Orléans, for Toulouse and at Toulouse take the A61 for Carcassonne and Narbonne. Michelin (💻 www.viamichelin.fr) suggests a route from Paris to Perpignan of around 900km (550mi) with motorway toll charges of around €45, and another route, from Paris to Nice, of a similar distance with toll charges of around €65. The A51 from Marseille to Grenoble is as yet incomplete but the A75/750 from Clermont-Ferrand (in Auvergne) to Montpellier, via the spectacular Millau Viaduct, is now finished.

All towns along the Mediterranean coast, from Perpignan to Nice, are linked by the A9, A54, A50, A52 and A8 motorways. If you're driving directly from Perpignan to Nice and wish to avoid the conurbations of Marseille and Toulon, Michelin's proposes a motorway route, via Nîmes and Aix-en-Provence, of 470km (290mi) taking just four hours (if you're very lucky!) and costing around €40 in tolls. If you wish to drive from Nice to Dignes-les-Bains (04) reasonably quickly, take the motorway route via Aix-en-Provence.

Needless to say, roads along the Côte d'Azur become hopelessly clogged in the summer months, when it can take three hours to drive from Cannes to Saint-Tropez (or vice versa) – a distance of around 75km (45mi).

Main roads and motorways are, almost without exception, in excellent condition. Departmental roads are also well maintained, while smaller local roads (*chemins vicinaux*) vary in quality according to the state of the local community's coffers. The condition of mountain roads often depends on the severity of the previous winter or last period of heavy rain. For private country roads leading to isolated properties, you may need a four-wheel drive vehicle.

Road users should note that drivers on the Mediterranean coast are among France's worst (which is saying something!): Antibes (06) has the dubious distinction of being France's most dangerous town in terms of your likelihood of being killed or injured on the roads, with over nine deaths or serious injuries per 1,000 inhabitants in the year 2000 – over ten times as many as in Béziers (34), one of France's safest driving towns – and Cannes, Nice (06), Nîmes (30) and Avignon (84) aren't far behind.

FURTHER INFORMATION

Useful Addresses

- Comité régional du Tourisme du **Languedoc-Roussillon**, 20 rue de la République, 34000 Montpellier (☎ 04 67 22 81 00, 🖳 www.cr-languedoc roussillon.fr or 🖳 www.sunfrance.com)
- Comité régional du Tourisme (**PACA**), 10, place de la Joliette, 13002 Marseille (☎ 04 91 56 47 00, 🖳 www.decouverte-paca.fr or 🖳 www.discover-southoffrance.com)
- Comité départemental du Tourisme des **Alpes-Maritimes**, 55, promenade des Anglais, 06000 Nice (☎ 04 93 37 78 78, 🖳 www.cgob.fr/tourisme/tourisem-crt.hml)
- Comité départemental du Tourisme des **Hautes-Alpes**, 8 bis rue Capitaine de Bresson, 05000 Gap (☎ 04 92 53 62 00, 🖳 www.hautes-alpes.net) ;
- Comité départemental du Tourisme des **Alpes-de-Haute-Provence**, 19 rue Docteur Honnorat, 04000 Dignes (☎ 04 92 31 57 29, 🖳 www.alpes-de-haute-provence.com)
- Comité départemental du Tourisme de l'**Aude** rue Moulin-de-la-Seigne, 11000 Carcassonne (☎ 04 68 11 66 00, 🖳 www.audetourisme.com) ;
- Comité départemental du Tourisme des **Bouches-du-Rhône**, Le Montesquieu, 13 rue Roux de Brignoles, 13006 Marseille (☎ 04 91 13 84 13 and ☎ 04 91 33 01 82, 🖳 www.visitprovence.com)
- Agence de Tourisme de **Corse**, 17 boulevard Roi Jérôme, BP 19, 20176 Ajaccio (☎ 04 95 51 00 00, 🖳 www.visit-corsica.com)
- Comité départemental du Tourisme du **Gard**, 3, place des Arènes, BP 122, 30010 Nîmes (☎ 04 66 36 96 30, 🖳 www.cdt-gard.fr)
- Comité départemental du Tourisme de l'**Hérault**, avenue des Moulins, 34184 Montpellier Cedex 4 (☎ 04 67 22 81 00, 🖳 www.tourisme-herault.com)
- Comité départemental du Tourisme du **Lozère**, 14 boulevard Nenri-Bourillon, BP 4, 48002 Mende (☎ 04 66 65 60 00, 🖳 www.lozere-tourisme.com)

- Comité départemental du Tourisme des **Pyrénées-Orientales**, 16 avenue des Palmiers, 66000 Perpignan (No office for visitors; write or phone: ☎ 04 68 51 52 53, 💻 www.pyreneesorientalestourisme.com)
- Comité départemental du Tourisme du **Var**, 1 boulevard Foch, BP99, 83300 Draguignan (☎ 04 94 50 55 50, 💻 www.tourismevar.com)
- Comité départemental du Tourisme du **Vaucluse**, 12 rue Collège da la Croix, 84000 Avignon (☎ 04 90 80 47 00, 💻 www.tourisme-en-vaucluse.com)

Useful Publications

- *Corse Matin* (💻 www.corsematin.com)
- *The Riviera Reporter*, 56, chemin de Provence, 06250 Mougins (☎ 04 93 45 77 19, 💻 www.riviera-reporter.com)
- *The Riviera Times*, 8 avenue Jean Moulin, 06340 Drap (☎ 04 93 27 60 00, 💻 www.rivieratimes.com)
- *Spirit of Place Provence*, Russell Ash and Bernard Higton (Pavilion Books)

Useful Websites

💻 www.adaptinfrance.org – information and help with settling on the Côte d'Azur

💻 www.alpillesnews.com – news and information in English for residents of the Alpilles area (including Les Baux, Eygalières and Saint-Rémy)

💻 www.camargue.fr – information about the Camargue

💻 www.creme-de-languedoc.com – information about Languedoc and a property listing

💻 www.europe.anglican.org – details of Anglican services throughout France

💻 www.guideriviera.com – information about the Côte d'Azur

💻 www.languedocliving.com/languedoc-directory – a 'yellow pages' directory of services in Languedoc

💻 www.provenceweb.fr – tourist information about Provence

GARRET
FOR SALE
APPLY:
QUASIMODO

Aiguille du Midi
cable car – The Alps

7

THE ALPS

The Alps cover an area extending from Lac Léman ('Lake Geneva'), the largest lake in western Europe, southwards almost to the Mediterranean and are bounded by the Italian border to the east and the Rhône to the west. They include part of the regions of Rhône-Alpes and Provence-Alpes-Côte d'Azur and part or all of the following *départements*: Hautes-Alpes (05), Drôme (26), Isère (38), Savoie (73) and Haute-Savoie (74). It's the most mountainous area of France, the Alps being Europe's biggest mountain range, 'shared' between France, Italy and Switzerland. The average altitude of the mountains in the Alps is 1,150m (3,772ft); the eastern area of the Alps has the highest peaks and forms a natural barrier with Italy. The most mountainous *département* is Isère, followed by Hautes-Alpes, Savoie, Haute-Savoie and Drôme. Mont Blanc, altitude 4,807m (15,767ft) in Haute-Savoie is the highest peak in Europe (excluding the mountains of Georgia). The Mont Blanc road tunnel and the Tunnel du Fréjus road and rail tunnel cut through the Alps, from Haute-Savoie and Savoie respectively, linking France to Italy.

The Alps are, of course, noted for their majestic mountain scenery, which is unrivalled at most times of the year, and are probably France's most picturesque region with its dense forests, lush pasture land, fast-flowing

7

rivers, huge lakes and deep gorges. It's a paradise for sports fans and nature lovers with superb summer sports, such as rock-climbing and canyoning (abseiling and water-chute descents), hiking and walking, all-terrain cycling, hang-gliding and paragliding, and white-water sports, while winter sports and ski resorts offer some of the best facilities in Europe for downhill (Alpine) and cross-country (Nordic) skiing and snowboarding (see **Sports** on page 304). Albertville (73), Chamonix (74) and Grenoble (38) have all been venues for the Winter Olympic Games. Top ski resorts include Chamonix, France's mountaineering capital, Courchevel, Megève, Méribel and Val d'Isère. The Alps therefore have two high seasons: the usual summer period, and the winter skiing season (December to April), the two peaks within the latter being the school holidays at Christmas and Easter (see **Sports** on page 304 and **Skiing** on page 304).

The Alps are the third most popular tourist area in France, after Paris and the Côte d'Azur, and Annecy is one of the most popular tourist towns in France after Paris, but property prices are well below those of Paris and prestigious towns on the Riviera. Lower property prices than neighbouring Switzerland attract many Swiss who live in the area and commute to work in Geneva and other Swiss cities.

ADVANTAGES & DISADVANTAGES

One of the principal attractions of the Alps is the breathtaking, picture post-card scenery: in summer, lush green mountain slopes, with the highest mountain peaks permanently snow-capped, overlooking beautiful lakes; and, in winter, Christmassy snow-covered landscapes on high land everywhere. Healthy, sleep-inducing mountain air is a pleasant contrast to increasingly congested and polluted large cities in France, such as Marseille and Strasbourg. On the other hand, the higher you live, the colder it gets – and it can get **very** cold.

The Alps is possibly the leading area in France for the variety and quality of outdoor activities available (see **Sports** on page 304 and **Leisure** on page 306). With over 1,200km^2 (465mi^2) of ski slopes, the French Alps have more skiing than Switzerland (840km^2/326mi^2) or Austria (790km^2/306mi^2). A disadvantage is that the ski slopes are often crowded, especially during school holidays. Around 15 per cent of French families take regular skiing holidays and 80 per cent of French skiers go to the Alps every winter (the other 20 per cent choose the Jura, Massif Central, Pyrenees and Vosges – and the same percentages apply to foreigners taking skiing holidays in France).

Low-cost international flights (see **Air** on page 319) to Geneva and Grenoble make the northern Alps (Isère and the Savoy *départements*) readily accessible. If you're considering the southern Alps for residence or holidays, however, bear in mind that there's no major airport in or near the Hautes-Alpes *département*. Traffic congestion means that Marseille-Marignane airport can be two hours' drive from Gap (05), and there's no motorway link from Grenoble (38) to Briançon (05) and Gap. The *TGV* runs from Paris to Lyon (Rhône) and to Valence (26), from where Chambéry (73), Grenoble (38), and Annecy (74) are readily accessible (see **Public Transport** on page 319), although getting to a small town or village high in the Alps by public transport may not be so easy.

Property prices in the Alps are above the national average, with especially high prices in and around top tourist areas such as Annecy. Nevertheless, even here prices are well below those of Paris and major resorts on the Côte d'Azur, and properties in or near ski resorts are generally considered to be an excellent investment. Establishing social contacts and making friends with French people native to the area is easier, for example, than with the French Mediterraneans, who are more reserved (despite outward appearances). All this is good news if you're considering a property purchase, whether as an investment or as a permanent or holiday home, or for letting.

The following points may help you to decide whether to choose an area in the northern Alps (*départements* 26, 38, 73 and 74) or the southern Alps (05) – note that Drôme (26) is considered part of the northern Alps, although it's west of Hautes-Alpes (05):

- The northern Alps area has an international feeling, the four university sites at Grenoble attracting the largest number of foreign students in France outside Paris. The Geneva urban area spills into France here. Lyon is just one hour from Grenoble and Valence, and Grenoble itself is an important, dynamic city.

- The southern Alps is quieter, rural and more laid-back, with smaller, local businesses. (You might consider working and living in the northern Alps, and retiring to the southern Alps.)

- It's drier, sunnier and warmer in the southern Alps.

- Good road and rail links between the northern Alps *départements* provide the opportunity to sample the numerous ski resorts, whereas communications are more limited in the southern Alps, where there are also fewer ski resorts.

- Property prices are generally lower in the southern Alps (see **Cost of Housing** on page 315).

Those in search of a town with plenty of green space should favour Gap (05) and Annecy (74), the former having more green space per inhabitant (over 156m^2) than any other major town in France except Besançon (although curiously Gap makes no provision for cyclists – there's no cycle track). Note also that there are nuclear power stations in Saint-Paul-Trois-Châteaux south of Drôme (26), and in Saint-Alban-du-Rhône/Saint-Maurice-l'Exil around 50km (30mi) south of Lyon in Isère, as well as one in neighbouring Ardèche near Montélimar, Privas, Le Teil and Valence.

MAJOR TOWNS & PLACES OF INTEREST

The major towns and other places of interest, including ski resorts, are listed below by *département*. The altitude given for each of the main ski resorts is the lowest at which skiing is normally possible. Note that there are sometimes considerable altitude differences between the highest and lowest slopes, so the highest slopes in each *département* are also indicated.

There are two national conservation areas in the Alps, each with around 800,000 visitors annually: the Parc national de la Vanoise, extending approximately between Méribel, Les Arcs and Val d'Isère (73) and covering some 2,000km^2 (780mi^2) with over 100 mountain peaks exceeding 3,000m (9,840ft), and the Parc national des Ecrins, extending approximately between Les Deux-Alpes (38) and the northern part of Hautes-Alpes, an area of 2,700km^2 (1,040mi^2). The parks are divided into 'inner zones', where there are strict regulations to protect all wildlife, and 'outer zones', where skiing and walking are permitted.

There are also four regional conservation areas (*parcs naturels régionaux*): Queyras, in the eastern part of Hautes-Alpes, covering 1,600km^2 (615mi^2); Vercros, in the area approximately between Die (26) and Grenoble, covering 1,780km^2 (685mi^2); le Massif des Bauges, forming a triangle roughly between Chambéry, Annecy and Albertville and covering 8,100km^2 (3,125mi^2); and Chartreuse, approximately between Chambéry, Grenoble and the valley of the Isère river, covering 6,900km^2 (2,655mi^2). Building regulations and permits in these areas are strictly controlled. If you really want to get away from it all, you should consider the Parc naturel régional du Queyras in Hautes-Alpes, whose population is only around 3,000.

Hautes-Alpes (05)

Gap (pop. 38,200), at 735m (2,411ft), is the highest departmental capital in France, but Briançon (pop. 10,700), in the centre of the *département*, is more interesting historically, with its fortified medieval upper town area. At an altitude of 1,310m (4,300ft) it rivals Davros (Switzerland) as the highest town in Europe. There are around 25 ski resorts, of which approximately half are classed Nordic (for cross country skiing). The main resorts are Serre-Chevalier at 1,350m (4,428ft) and Montgenèvre at 1,829m (6,000ft), both just a few miles from Briançon. The upper slopes at La Grave-La-Meije are the highest, at 3,550m (11,644ft).

Drôme (26)

The departmental capital, Valence (pop. 65,000), which marks the start of Provence, is around one hour's drive from both Lyon and Grenoble. There are five ski resorts in the *département*, the main one being Col de Rousset at 1,367m (4,484ft) in the Parc naturel de Vercors in the *Préalpes* (lower Alpine slopes) in the north-east of the *département*. The upper slopes at Valdrôme are the highest in the *département*, at 1,300m (4,264ft). Névache and Saint-Véran are reckoned to be among France's most beautiful villages.

Isère (38)

Grenoble, the administrative capital of the Alps region, is a progressive city (pop. 160,000) with four university campuses attracting many foreign students. The capital of the former Dauphiné province, it's spectacularly situated amid surrounding mountains and is around 100km (60mi) from both Annecy (74) and Gap (04). Isère has no fewer than 40 ski resorts, principally Alpe d'Huez at 1,860m (6,100ft) and Les Deux-Alpes at 1,650m (5,412ft). The upper slopes at Les Deux-Alpes are the highest, at 3,600m (11,808ft).

Savoie (73)

Chambéry (pop. 56,000) is the *département*'s capital and a university town, with an interesting *château*, the residence of the former Dukes of Savoy; according to a 2005 survey conducted by *Le Point* magazine, Chambéry is the 'best' town in France to live in (see **Appendix F**). Aix-les-Bains (26,000),

20km (13m) north of Chambéry on the Lac du Bourget, is the Alps' spa town *par excellence*.

PROPERTY CHECK – AIX-LES-BAINS

This pretty town in the heart of Savoie, on the western edge of the Alps near the Swiss and Italian borders as well as to medieval Chambéry and picturesque Annecy, is known for its thermal baths but has much else to offer. It overlooks France's largest natural lake, the Lac du Bourget, where watersports of all kinds can be enjoyed; in fact, every sport available in France (except surfing) can be done in or near Aix. The town is 20 minutes from the ski resorts of La Feclaz and Le Revard, although these are mainly for cross-country skiing; and the major downhill ski resorts, including those of the Trois Vallées, are just over an hour's drive away. Property prices range from around €175,000 for a two-bedroom apartment to around €600,000 for a six-bedroom house with a swimming pool.

Attic Immobilier (www.attic-immobilier.com)

Bonneval-sur-Arc is reckoned to be one of France's most beautiful villages. Albertville (18,000), to the east of the Parc régional du massif des Bauges conservation area, was the venue for the 1992 Winter Olympic Games. Savoie has around 20 ski resorts, including several of the best known in France: Courchevel at 1,850m (6,068ft), Méribel at 1,450m (4,756ft), one of the most beautiful Alpine ski resorts, and Pralognan la Vanoise at 1,410m (4,625ft) – together the three comprise the so-called Trois Vallées; Les Arcs at 1,600m (5,248ft), Les Menuires at 1,850m (6,068ft), Val d'Isère at 1,850m (6,068ft), Tignes at 2,100m (6,888ft) and Val Thorens at 2,300m (7,544ft) – one of the highest Savoie resorts (its upper slopes are the highest, at 3,300m (10,725ft)).

Haute-Savoie (74)

The capital Annecy (pop. 51,000), on the northern tip of the Lac d'Annecy, is one of France's most visited towns and has a delightful historic town centre built along canals (Annecy is known as the 'Venice of the Alps'), although it's usually crowded with tourists (the area around Annecy and the Lac d'Annecy is to be avoided at weekends and in the peak of the summer season). On the French (south) side of Lac Léman are Thonon-les-Bains, rich in Italian architecture, and Evian-les-Bains (almost adjacent – the combined population is 29,000), famous for its mineral water. There are around 25 ski resorts in the *département*, the largest, oldest and one of the most exclusive being Chamonix-Mont Blanc (pop. 10,000) at 1,050m (3,444ft), the starting point for the thousands of walkers every year who climb Mont Blanc. (If you've set your heart on this, you must be fit and suitably equipped; there are around 150 rescues every year and several fatalities, and some people experience mountain 'sickness' at over 3,000m (9,840ft). Ski guides can be obtained from the tourist office, 85, place du Triangle de l'Amitié, BP 25, 74400 Chamonix, ☎ 04 50 53 00 24, 💻 www.chamonix.com.) Other ski resorts include Avoriaz at 1,280m (4,200ft) and Megève at 1,113m (3,650ft). The upper slopes at Chamonix are the highest, at 3,842m (12,600ft).

POPULATION

With a total population of around 2.7m, the *départements* of Drôme, Hautes-Alpes, Isère, Savoie and Haute-Savoie have a population slightly higher than Languedoc-Roussillon (see **Chapter 6**), which covers a similar area. The population has increased by around 6 per cent over the last ten years, compared with the national average of 4 per cent. Isère is one of the most densely populated *départements* in France, while Hautes-Alpes, with under eight people per km^2 (20 people per mi^2), is one of the least. The proportion of students among the population of the major towns is generally low; Grenoble (38) has the highest proportion of students (12 per cent). The total and official foreign populations of each *département* are given below.

Hautes-Alpes (05): Population 132,000, of which 800 are Italians, 700 Algerians, 350 Moroccans and just over 100 Britons.

Drôme (26): Population 440,000, of which 6,000 are Moroccans, 5,000 Algerians, 2,700 Portuguese, 2,500 Tunisians and around 275 Britons.

Isère (38): Population 1.1m, of which 15,500 are Algerians, 12,000 Italians and 12,000 Portuguese, 5,500 Turks and 1,500 Britons.

Savoie (73): Population 373,000 of which 6,000 are Algerians, 6,000 Italians, 4,500 Portuguese, 3,300 Moroccans and 650 Britons.

Haute-Savoie (74): Population 632,000, of which 7,500 are Algerians and 7,500 Italians, 6,500 Portuguese, 6,000 Turks and 1,100 Britons.

For the populations of main towns, see **Major Towns & Places of Interest** above.

LANGUAGE

Occitan or the *Langue d'Oc* is spoken in southern parts of the area (see page 262), although it isn't necessary to learn it, as French is universally spoken.

CLIMATE

The Alps is noted for its extremes of temperature, with heavy snow (on high ground) throughout the winter months and hot sunshine in summer, although cool summer evenings are usual high in the Alps. The climate is most pleasant in spring and autumn. The higher and further north you go, the colder and more humid it becomes. The southern Alps (Hautes-Alpes) have more sun and less rain – a generally milder climate than the northern Alps. However, the natural barrier of the Alps disrupts normal weather patterns and there are often significant local climatic variations. For example, while the average annual rainfall in the mountains is over 800mm (30in) it sometimes exceeds 2,000mm (80in) in the Grande Chartreuse area in Isère. Annual rainfall at Embun (05) and Bourg-Saint-Maurice (73), both of which are at around 870m (2,850ft), is 716mm (28.5in) and 971mm (38in) respectively.

In Grenoble, rainfall is spread more or less evenly throughout the year, with between 50mm (2in) and 100mm (4in) per month and an annual total of around 980mm (38.5in). In summer, daytime temperatures throughout the Alps are generally between 20C (67F) and 30C (86F), although Grenoble can be like a cauldron with temperatures frequently exceeding 30C. Grenoble Bourg-Saint-Maurice enjoy around 2,030 hours of sunshine per year, compared with 2,505 hours in Embrun. The table below shows the number of hours' sunshine and number of days' rainfall in selected towns in the area.

Town	Sunshine Hours	Days' Rainfall
Valence (26)	2,026	81
Grenoble (38)	2,031	110
Chambéry (73)	2,027	110
Annecy (74)	2,027	110

CRIME RATE & SECURITY

The Rhône-Alpes region is fourth in the French crime league table (a respectable distance behind Ile-de-France, Provence-Alpes-Côte d'Azur and Languedoc-Roussillon), although it should be noted that the region includes the city of Lyon, where the crime rate is relatively high, as well as the Alps, where (particularly in rural areas) crime is uncommon. In fact, the town of Gap (05) enjoys the lowest (reported) crime rate of any major town in France. Chambéry (73), on the other hand, is among the 20 towns with the highest crime rates; Valence (26), Grenoble (38) and Annecy (74) also have higher than average crime rates. On average in the area, there are around 62 reported crimes annually per 1,000 inhabitants. If you're absent from a property for a prolonged period, advise the local police, who may keep an eye on it for you.

AMENITIES

Sports

Multi-sports complexes are rare in the Alps, but the municipal *salle des sports* usually houses a gym and perhaps a separate room for table tennis and is home to the local basketball, handball and volleyball teams. Municipal tennis courts (normally well maintained) and municipal swimming pools (usually overheated) are reasonably priced. Swimming pools often operate a *carnet* system, reducing the entrance price. Private sports clubs may include swimming, rowing, cycling, rugby, sailing, skiing, gymnastics, volleyball and judo. You can also swim in mountain lakes in the summer (check with a local guide beforehand) and in designated beach areas alongside lakes such as the Lac d'Annecy (74) and Lac de Serre Ponçon (05). The water temperature is around 20C (68F) in July and August. Avoid the areas at the eastern ends of both these lakes, Le Bout du Lac (73) and Embrun (05), unless you like crowds or want to take place in a water activity.

Skiing

Skiing is, of course, the sport the region is best known for, and it includes many of the world's top resorts (see **Major Towns & Places of Interest** on page 299). Their international popularity, however, means that resorts are often crowded, particularly during school holidays at Christmas and Easter.

French state schools are divided between three 'zones', each of which has a different holiday period, in order to minimise crowding on the ski slopes, but there are still traffic jams around Lyon at peak times. Grenoble, for example, is in Zone A, Marseille in Zone B and Paris in Zone C. Holiday dates can be checked with your town hall or a French diary.

Information to help you choose the most suitable ski resort can be obtained from Ski-France (61 boulevard Haussmann, 75008 Paris, ☎ 01 47 42 23 32, 💻 www.skifrance.fr), who provide details of access, ski slopes, accommodation and après-ski activities, as well as advice on the best destinations for family skiing, the latest snowboard activities, Nordic skiing, club stations (those providing a range of après-ski entertainments and local amenities) and traditional style Alpine ski villages. Altitudes are given, the state of the snow and the number of skiing slopes by grade of difficulty (from green, the easiest, through blue and red to black, the most difficult). Around 45 of the Alpine ski resorts have a '*Les p'tits Montagnards d'Hiver*' club for young children. This guarantees a kindergarten for children from 18 months old, ski schools (with sleigh areas and separate ski slopes) for three to four year olds with qualified instructors, initiation in the latest snow sports for older children, and free ski lifts for the under fours, with reductions for those aged 5 to 12.

Snowboarding facilities are available in many ski resorts, and Avoriaz (74) and Chamonix (74) have especially well adapted sites. Half-pipe snowboarding (like dry land skateboarding on 180° concave slopes) is well catered for at Chamrousse (38), Val d'Isère (73), Avoriaz, Chamonix and Flaine (74). Almost half the skiers at Risoul, at 1,850m (6,068ft), near Vars and the Italian border in Hautes-Alpes, are snowboard enthusiasts. Val d'Isère (73) is particularly well suited for acrobatic mogul skiing (*ski sur bosses*).

A useful website for winter sports enthusiasts is that of the Fédération française des Sports de Glace (💻 www.ffsg.org), which offers information on all sports practised on ice, e.g. skating, bobsleighing, sledging, skeleton (sledging face down!), ice-hockey and curling.

White-water Sports

Various white-water sports are available near Thonon-les-Bains (74) in the Dranse canyon, in the torrents around Chamonix (74), on the Durance river (05) and along the Isère river (several *départements*) and can be great fun, provided you like waves and fresh (i.e. cold!) water. If you're really brave, you can even try white-water swimming!

Hiking

Walking is popular in the area's national and regional parks, e.g. the Vanoise national park and the Queyras regional park (see **Major Towns & Places of Interest** on page 299). There's a tremendous variety of Alpine flowers, and animal wildlife includes marmots, chamois and ibex goats. Details are available from the Fédération française de Randonnée pédestre, 14 rue Riquet, 75019 Paris (☎ 01 44 89 93 93, 💻 www.ffrandonnee.fr).

Fishing

Fishing is another popular sport in the area; salmon and pike are found in the rivers of Isère (38) and trout and turbot in Savoy's lakes.

Golf

There are nine 18-hole golf courses in Haute-Savoie: prestigious courses at Chamonix and Evian-les-Bains, three in Savoie, three in Isère in the area around Grenoble, and one in Hautes-Alpes (in Gap). There are also several 'compact' courses, i.e. those with nine holes or under. Not all golf courses are open all year round. Contact the Ligue Rhône-Alpes de Golf, 7, quai Général Sarrail, 69006 Lyon (☎ 04 78 24 76 61, 💻 www.liguegolf rhonealpes.org) for details. Information (in both French and English) on how to find courses, the cost of a round (which varies between €15 and €50), etc. is available via the internet (💻 www.backspin.com). Another useful website for golfers is 💻 www.golf. com.fr.

Spectator Sports

As far as spectator sports are concerned, there are no major professional football teams in the Alps, but there's a fine athletics stadium at Annecy, with beautiful views of surrounding mountains, where international meetings are held. The Olympic rink at Albertville has ice hockey and ice-skating events.

Leisure

The Alps is a particularly rich area for culture. There are many historical museums relating to the Franco-Italian history of the Alps, a museum devoted to the novelist Stendhal, who was born in Grenoble, and a fine-arts museum in the same city. The Abbey of Hautecombe (burial place of the princes of Savoy) and the remains of Roman baths at Aix-les-Bains are of particular historical interest, as are the ramparts by Vauban in the old fortified town of Briançon, the Château de Menthon-Saint-Bernard (near the Lac d'Annecy) and the secluded monastery of the Grande Chartreuse near Cambéry.

Major towns have theatres, occasionally staging opera. Both Albertville and Grenoble have large indoor stadiums/entertainment centres which stage international shows such as Holiday on Ice and the Lord of the Dance (for information see 💻 www.albertville.com and 💻 www.ville-grenoble.fr). The CityVox website (💻 www.cityvox.com) also has regularly updated information, in several languages including English, on current and future events in Annecy, Chambéry, Gap, Grenoble and Valence. Information is also provided by regional newspapers, including *L'Essor savoyard*, *La Maurienne* (every Friday) and *Le Dauphiné libéré* (💻 www.ledauphine.com), which has local editions.

English-language Cinema & Theatre

The university towns of Chambéry and Grenoble each have one cinema dedicated to showing foreign films (mainly American and British) in their original languages (*version originale/VO*). In Chambéry, it's the Curial (☎ 04 79 85 63 16) and in Grenoble, the Club (☎ 04 76 43 36 36). Films tend to be avant-garde or offbeat – not commercial block-busters. Don't expect deluxe seats, a panoramic screen and popcorn! Some municipal cultural centres (*maisons de la culture*) regularly show *VO* films at subsidised prices. A useful website for finding out what films are on in a given area, which also indicates whether the films are being shown in the original language is 💻 www.cinefil.com. There are no regular English-language theatre performances in the area.

7

Spas & Casinos

The region boasts a number of spa towns, each with a casino (casinos were originally permitted only in spa towns), including Allevard, Urage-les-Bains, Villard-de-Lens (38), Aix-les-Bains (two), Brides-les-Bains, Challes-les-Eaux (73), Annecy, Annemasse, Chamonix-Mont-Blanc, Evian and Saint-Gervais-les-Bains (74). Details of all casinos and what they offer are available via the internet (e.g. 💻 www.journaldescasinos.com – partly in English).

Theme Parks

There are a number of theme parks and attractions in the region, including:

- Aquarium d'Aix-les-Bains (73): fish and bird park;
- Aquarium tropical du Val-de-Drôme in Allex (26): sea life;
- Aventure Parcs in Autrans and Les Deux-Alpes (38) and Les Gets (74): activity parks;
- Ferme aux Crocodiles in Pierrelatte (26): 500 crocodiles;
- Forêt aux Champignons et Insectes géants in Saint-Antoine-l'Abbaye (38): giant insects and mushrooms;
- Le Jardin des Découvertes in Die (26): butterflies;
- Parc Animalier de Merlet in Les Houches (74): wildlife park;
- Vivarium d'Yvoire (74): reptile park;
- Walibi Rhône-Alpes at Les Avenières near Grenoble (38): amusement park which attracts over 400,000 visitors annually.

In the adjoining *départements* of Rhône are a bird park in Villars-les-Dombes (01), 'Aero City' in Aubenas and a safari park in Peaugres (07), a zoo at Saint-Martin-de-la-Plaine (42) and a wolf and bird park in Courzieu (69).

Other interesting places to visit include the Evian water-bottling plant (by appointment between mid-June and mid-September only) and the Caves et Distillerie de la Chartreuse in Voiron (38), where the famous liqueur has been distilled by the monks since 1605.

Shopping Centres & Markets

The principal regional shopping centre (*centre commercial*) is the Grande Place in Grenoble, with a Carrefour hypermarket, shopping mall (*galerie marchande*) and major DIY, garden centre, furniture and sportswear stores. There are area shopping centres throughout the Alps, some with hypermarkets, including Albertville, Annecy, Bourg-de-Péage (26), Briançon and Valence. The major hyper and supermarket companies are Auchan, Carrefour, Casino, Géant Casino and Leclerc.

Local specialities include a variety of dry and smoked hams (from Savoy *départements*), sausages and sausage meat, dried and salted goats' legs (*cuisses de bouc*), cow and goat cheese (including the strong-tasting *reblochon*), *fondue savoyarde* (made with a mixture of cheeses) and Montélimar nougat. The area around Nyons in southern Drôme (strictly speaking in Provence) is renowned for its olive oil, and Grenoble is famous for its walnuts and walnut products. Although the Alps isn't known for its wines, Savoy's white wines are agreeable. Local craftsmen's products, such as woodcarvings, can be found in boutiques throughout the region.

Most towns and villages have daily or weekly markets. The major markets in the area are in Annecy, which specialises in handicraft products, Rumilly and Saint-Gervais-les-Bains (all in 74). General markets offer local dairy produce, fruit and vegetables. Especially appetising are local cheeses and fruit such as bilberries, raspberries and strawberries (particularly in the Chambéry area).

Foreign Food & Products

Hyper and supermarkets sell few foreign foods, with the exception of biscuits, cereals, preserves, Norwegian and Scottish smoked salmon, Chinese and Vietnamese foods, Italian pasta, delicatessen foods and some cheeses. From time to time Guinness and British beers are stocked (Kronenbourg, a French brewer, brews an English-style beer; packs are marked '*tradition anglaise*').

Specialist English and Chinese furniture shops are found in most large towns and cities. IKEA, the Swedish furniture manufacturer, whose good quality pine furniture is ideal for holiday chalets, have a large store in Lyon (Rhône), around one hour's drive from Grenoble or Valence. Gift shops sell pictorial guides and souvenir books with English text describing local and regional beauty spots, and in high season some book shops stock a selection of English-language paperbacks.

Restaurants & Bars

There's a tremendous variety of restaurants offering international cuisine and regional dishes. They're generally good value, especially in low season. You may find a comfortable restaurant, or *brasserie*, with a fine mountain view, offering a three-course lunch, without wine, for around €15. (At the opposite end of the scale is the three-Michelin-star Auberge de l'Eridan in Annecy, where the 11-course (!) menu will set you back almost €200 per head.) Local specialities include *fondue* and *raclette* (melted cheese – *you* melt the cheese – with boiled potatoes and cold meats), *gratin Dauphinois* (potatoes, cheese and cream) and *tartiflette* (a diced-bacon flan). In bars, large coffees with milk or cream (*café crème*) are popular at breakfast time. Expect to pay at least €2. If you want a beer like brown ale, try Pelforth *brune* bottled beer: around €3. If you're on a full day's shopping binge in a shopping centre, self-service cafeterias such as Casino's offer good quality three-course meals at reasonable prices.

SERVICES

International & Private Schools

There are no international schools in this area, but the Collège privé international Sainte-Croix des Neiges (☎ 04 50 73 01 20, 💻 www.ste-croix-des-neiges.com) in Abondance (74) caters specifically for English-speaking students.

Language Schools

Language lessons are offered by a number of public and private bodies in the area, including those listed below. Language courses are also offered by local Chambres de Commerce et d'Industrie and Centres culturels.

- Logos in Gières (38);
- Centre Universitaire d'Etudes françaises in Grenoble (38);
- Centre international de Formation et d'Echanges linguistiques in Albertville (73);
- IFALPES Chambéry in Chambéry (73);
- Institut Savoisien d'Etudes françaises in Chambéry (73);
- Alp'lingua – Institut Alpins des Langues in Hauteluce (73);
- IFALPES d'Annecy in Annecy (74);
- CILFA in Annecy-le-Vieux (74);
- Altiplano in Chamonix (74);
- INSTEAD – Institute of Foreign Education in Chamonix (74).

Details of the above schools can be found on 💻 www.europa-pages.com. The French Consulate in London (see **Appendix A**) publishes a booklet called *Cours de français Langue étrangère et Stages pédagogiques du français Langue étrangère en France*, which includes a comprehensive list of schools and organisations providing French language courses throughout France.

Hospitals & Clinics

All cities, large towns and major ski resorts (such as Chamonix) have at least one public hospital. Grenoble, with 2,500 medical students, has a teaching hospital (*CHU*) with the widest range of equipment and specialists. In large hospitals you should find at least one doctor in each *département* who speaks English, although the only general hospitals included in the US Embassy's list of hospitals where English is spoken are the Debrousse (for children), du Parc, Eugène André, la Sauvegarde, Protestant, Sainte-Anne Lumière and Saint-Louis hospitals in Lyon. If you're buying property in a rural, mountainous area, take into account access time to the nearest hospital, especially in the event of an emergency in winter when there's heavy snow. If you have an accident on the ski slopes, the mountain ambulance (helicopter) service is extremely well organised.

Balneology centres (consult the yellow pages under 'Cures' or 'Thermalisme') with saunas and thermal baths are concentrated in the two Savoy *départements* and also near Briançon in Hautes-Alpes. Establishments cater for those merely seeking relaxation as well as for the infirm.

English-language Media

There's no local radio in English, but it's possible to receive BBC Radio 1, 2, 3, and 4 on your television via the Astra satellite, and you can listen to recordings of radio programmes on Radio 1, 2, 3, 4, 5, 6 and 1Extra on your computer via the internet (go to 💻 www.bbc.co.uk/radio/aod/index.shtml). The World Service can be received on on short wave (for frequency details, go to 💻 www.bbc.co.uk/worldservice/schedules/frequencies/eurwfreq.shtml) and via the Astra satellite. Note, however, that positioning a satellite dish correctly in a mountainous area may be tricky, or perhaps impossible, for proper reception. Local music stations usually broadcast 60 per cent non-French language songs, most of which are in English.

The *International Herald Tribune*, published in Paris, is widely available on the day of publication, and the *Guardian*, printed in Frankfurt, is available, also on the day of publication in some areas. Large towns and cities, such as Annecy and Grenoble, have other English-language daily newspapers available the day after publication, and other towns and mountain resorts have these in the high seasons. The *Guardian Weekly* and *Weekly Telegraph* are available all year round in certain areas or can be ordered on subscription. The *International Herald Tribune* is available on subscription but is often delivered the day after publication. Certain Maisons de la Presse newsagents sell English-language magazines, ranging from popular women's household magazines to *The Economist* and *Time Magazine*. *The Connexion* and *The News* are English-language monthly newspapers covering the whole of France (see **Appendix B**).

Embassies & Consulates

There are no foreign embassies or consulates in the Alps area, except two Italian Honorary Consuls in Chambéry and Grenoble. Austria, Belgium, Canada, Denmark, Finland, Greece, Ireland, Italy, Luxemburg, the Netherlands, Portugal, Sweden, the UK and USA have consulates in Lyon (69), Norway in Francheville (69) and Spain and Switzerland in Villeurbanne (69). The British Consulate General is at 24 rue Childebert, 69288 Lyon Cedex 1 (☎ 04 72 77 81 70) and the United States Consulate General at 16 rue de la République, 69002 Lyon Cedex 02 (☎ 04 78 38 36 88 and ☎ 04 78 38 33 03). For contact details of other consulates refer to the local yellow pages under 'Ambassades, consulats et autres représentations diplomatiques'. For details of consulates and embassies of other nations consult the yellow pages for Lyon or Paris.

Places of Worship

Regular services in English are held in the following towns:

- Annecy (74) – Notre-Dame de Liesse;
- Evian (74) – Notre-Dame;
- Grenoble (38) – Centre Oecuménique Saint-Marc.

There's also an Anglican church with services in English in Lyon (at Le Foyer l'Escale Lyonnaise) in the *département* of Rhône.

There are mosques in Briançon (05), Valence (26), Grenoble (38), Albertville (73) and Bonneville (74); details can be found on 💻 http://mosquee.free.fr. There are also four synagogues in Grenoble (for details, go to 💻 www.feujcity.com, where there's also information about Kosher food shops and restaurants, Jewish clubs, associations and schools, etc.) and one in Valence (as well as five in Lyon), details of which can be found on 💻 www. pagesjaunes.fr (enter 'Synagogues' in the first box and the name of the town).

Clubs

There are clubs for numerous indoor and outdoor activities, ranging from archery (*tir à l'arc*), bridge (*bridge*), board games (*jeux de société*) including chess (*échecs*), and computing (*informatique*), to paint-ball (*paintball*), paragliding (parapente) and parachuting (*parachute*). If you're a keen skier or walker, joining a skiing or walking club, particularly if you live all year round in the Alps, is strongly recommended. You benefit from the experience of others, visit other areas and possibly enjoy group reductions on lifts as well as making a new circle of friends. Consult the yellow pages under 'Clubs, associations de loisirs', local and departmental tourist offices and the Office des Clubs sportifs at your town hall.

The International Rotary Club has several branches in Annecy, Chambéry and Grenoble and also branches in Aix-les-Bains, Albertville, Chamonix and Valence. Consult the website (💻 www.rotary-francophone.org) and click on 1780 for the full list.

For French speakers, the Accueil des Villes françaises (AVF), a French organisation designed to welcome newcomers to an area, is an option (there's often at least one fluent English-speaker in each group). There are around 20 AVF groups in the Alps – in Crest, Montélimar, Romans, Valence (26), Bourgoin-Jallieu, Claix, Grenoble, Meylan-Grésivaudan, Vienne, Voiron (38), Aix-les-Bains, Chamonix-Mont-Blanc, Chambéry, Saint-Jean-de-Maurienne (73), Annecy, Annemasse, Bonneville and Saint-Julien-en-Genevois (74). The website (💻 www.avf.asso.fr) includes a directory (*annuaire*) of local groups by *département* as well as an online form for contacting your local AVF before you move to the area. Listings indicate whether information and services are available in English or other languages. Other sources for clubs in the area are *The News* (see **Appendix B**) and the English-speaking church (see above).

PROPERTY

Property prices are above the national average in the Alps with especially high prices in and around tourist towns such as Annecy (74), although even here prices are well below those of Paris and top resorts on the Riviera. Typical village houses (see below) are much sought after and are rarely for sale in or near ski resorts. Properties in or near ski resorts are usually an excellent investment and there are currently tax advantages to be gained from buying new property and letting it out. Demand for new property is particularly strong in Isère and the two Savoy *départements*.

Valence (26) boasts the lowest average prices for older properties in the Alps, while the area's highest average prices are to be found in Annecy (74). The table below gives average prices per m² for older properties in major towns in the area:

Town	Average Price per m²
Valence (26)	€750
Grenoble (38)	€1,145
Annecy (74)	€1,835

Finding Property

Several property search companies such as Alpine Angels (UK ☎ 01225-442128, 💻 www.alpineangels.co.uk) specialise in Alpine properties. Consult also the articles and advertisements in *French Property News* and *Focus on France* (see **Appendix B**). The French property magazine, *Logic-Immo*, has editions for Drôme, Savoie and Haute-Savoie, published every three weeks and full of advertisements, many in colour (💻 www.logic-immo.com). You will find these in stands in front of estate agents' offices (look for the FNAIM member sign: a yellow diamond) and bakers (*boulangeries*).

Typical Homes

These include elegant traditional farmhouses (*mas*) in their own grounds in Isère, detached Swiss-style lakeside and mountain chalets, stone village houses (rarely on the market), even rarer barn-type sloping-roof Alpine valley houses, probably requiring renovation or conversion, and modern provençal houses (see **Typical Homes** on page 281) in and around Valence. *Construction traditionnelle*, which means with solid (brick) interior walls, is a strong selling point for new and recent houses, and estate agents' descriptions, normally scanty on details, emphasise this. Note that small chalets or apartments which are large enough for holidays may be cramped, even if there are only two of you, as a main residence. A room or rooms with an attractive, sunny outlook should be a priority.

Cost of Property

Generally speaking, the higher the resort (and therefore the more reliable the snow), the more expensive the property, though of course some resorts also have more 'cachet' than others and property is snapped up despite astronomical prices. Property in linked resorts (e.g. those in the so-called Trois Vallées, the Espace Killy, Paradiski and, in the northern Alps, Les Aravis) is also sought after. It's possible, however, to buy in a village further down the mountain, at correspondingly lower prices, from where it's just a short drive to the resort proper – for example, Aime and Peisey below La Plagne and Les Arcs, and Saint-Martin-de-Belleville below Les Menuires (in the Trois Vallées). Such properties have the added advantage, if you're buying to let, since they're more attractive to summer tourists (some of the higher resorts, such as Courchevel, are more or less shut in summer) though they're less easy to let in the ski season. A specialist in 'off-piste' property is French Mountain Property (🖳 www.frenchmountainproperty.com).

PROPERTY CHECK – THE ALPS

An increasing number of people (particularly foreigners) are looking for quality chalets and apartments, while building land is becoming harder to find and planning permission harder to obtain. This means that potential buyers outnumber good properties for sale and properties purchased off plan can take up to two years to be completed. The *Loi de Montagne* ('Mountain Law') of 2002 banned new building in open spaces in Savoie, though 'infilling' in villages is still allowed, and some resorts, such as Méribel and Les Gets in Les Portes du Soleil, have banned all new building owing to a shortage of … water. Studio apartments have been increasing in price by around 7 per cent per year and now start at around €90,000, while a chalet at the foot of the slopes in a main resort will set you back over €2.5m. Megève and Courchevel 1850 are among the most expensive resorts, where luxury chalets go for upwards of €10m. In lesser resorts, such as Argentière, a de luxe four-bedroom chalet with panoramic views is a snip at €1.5m. High in demand are Samoens, with its new lift, and Morillon, linking to Les Carroz and Flaine.

There are, however, more affordable new developments, such as Les Fermes des Granges, between Chamonix and Les Houches, where characterful chalets and apartments in traditional style range from €240,000 to €900,000. In Chatel, on the Swiss border, new apartments are selling for between €375,000 and €630,000 and new chalets nearby for €450,000 – around a third cheaper than Morzine and Les Gets.

The major property developer in the French Alps is MGM French Properties (UK ☎ 020-7494, 💻 www.mgm-immobilier.fr), which is currently building new homes in the established resorts of Les Arcs, Chamonix, Courchevel, Les Menuires, Méribel, La Plagne, Tignes and Val d'Isère, as well as in new, purpose-built resorts such as Sainte-Foy-en-Tarantaise and Vallandry, with prices ranging from €150,000 to €2.5m. Most of these properties, however, as sold as leasebacks on an 11-year contract and at a maximum yield of just 2.5 per cent.

Most properties in top resorts have good rental possibilities; as a rule, a three-week let in high season (February) will cover your annual running costs. For example, a four-bedroom chalet can be let for between €500 and €750 per week in high season and almost as much in mid-summer. Various leaseback schemes are available but the properties have to rented for between 9 and 18 years.

Alpine Apartments Agency (UK ☎ 01544-388234, 💻 www.alpineapartmentsagency.com or 💻 www.allalps.com); Erna Low Property (UK ☎ 020-7590 1624, 💻 www.ernalowproperty.co.uk)

7

The table below gives the average selling price of houses in 2006. Note, however, that house sizes vary from area to area, which can distort average figures.

Town/Area	Average House Price/Apartment Price			
	2-bed	3-bed	4-bed	5+-bed
Alps				
Chamonix	€340,000	€575,000	€680,000	€1.1m

Courchevel	€295,000	€425,000	€495,000	€1m
Lac d'Annecy	€230,000	€365,000	€420,000	€575,000
Les Menuires	€185,000	€335,000	€345,000	€470,000
Méribel	€265,000	€460,000	€595,000	€800,000
Val d'Isère	€330,000	€475,000	€800,000	€1.1m

The average prices per m² in various resorts listed below are taken from a 2006 survey by *Living France* magazine:

Resort	Price per m²
La Plagne	€4,000 to €4,500
Sept Laux (nr Grenoble)	€4,000 to €4,500
La Rossière	€5,000
Valloire	€5,000
Samoëns	€5,000 to €6,000
Morzine	€5,000 to €6,000
Chamonix	€7,000 to €8,000
Méribel	€8,000 to €10,000
Val d'Isère	€10,000 to €15,000
Courchevel	€15,000 to €20,000

According to the Alpine Apartments Agency (UK ☎ 01544-388234, 💻 www.alpineapartmentsagency.com or 💻 www.allalps.com) the following developments were available or coming on stream in May 2007; although they may no longer be available, they will give an idea of prices in various resorts:

- **Macot-la-Plagne** – near La Plagne, 'Crête Côté Village' is a new construction of seven apartments from one-bedroom at €189,000 to two-bedroom at €349,000;

- **Morzine** – two traditional-style four-bedroom chalets to be built in Morzine village less than a kilometre from the main ski lift, costing €850,000;
- **Peisey-Nancroix** – in the centre of the Paradiski region, 'La Maison d'Olga' is a large building being renovated into five apartments in Savoyard style, with prices ranging from €205,000 for a studio to €540,000 for a three-bedroom apartment;
- **Samoëns** – 'Les Chalets Plein Soleil' is a new complex comprising six four- and five-bedroom chalets and 46 apartments close to the village, with prices including €123,400 for a studio, €307,700 for a two-bedroom apartment and €367,100 for a three-bed.

Rental Accommodation

Unfurnished property for rent is difficult to find, although you may find something through the French property magazines such as *Le Journal des Particuliers* (💻 www.journaldesparticuliers.com) and *Les Annonces Immobilières* (💻 www.entreparticuliers.com); go to the section 'Locations'. You can also try the website 💻 www.123immo.com. The FONCIA group are the leading property rental specialists in France. They have over ten offices throughout the Alps, including Annecy, Bourg-Saint-Maurice, Grenoble, Thonon-les-Bains and Valence. Consult their website (💻 www.foncia.fr) for full details. The National Federation of Estate Agents (FNAIM), 12 rue du Faubourg Saint Honoré, 75008 Paris (☎ 01 44 20 77 00, 💻 www. fnaim.com) can also provide a list of its members specialising in property rentals. Check to see if '*Locations*' is displayed in the windows of these agents.

The table below is an indication of average monthly rents for four-room properties, i.e. two-bedroom in most cases.

Location	Studio Apt	4-room Property
Annecy	€450	€1,200
Chambéry	€400	€800
Grenoble	€400	€950
Valence	€350	€600

Holiday apartments and flatlets are usually let on a weekly basis. The two weeks just before, during and after Christmas are the most expensive, with another peak in February. For example, a 30m^2 apartment in Chamonix (not the cheapest of ski resorts) sleeping up to four people costs between €400 and €500 per week in the summer months, between €500 and €700 per week in the period January to March, and around €900 a week over Christmas. Interhome, 15 avenue Jean Aicard, 75011 Paris (☎ 08 05 65 03 50, 🖳 www.interhome.fr) is one of the chalet apartment specialists. Their website has an English option and you can quickly access the resort that interests you, the type of accommodation, current availability and weekly rental price.

COMMUNICATIONS

Air

The two main airports in the area are Grenoble Saint-Geoirs (☎ 04 76 65 48 48), served by Air France from Paris Orly and by direct flights from the UK (see **Appendix F**), and Annecy-Haute-Savoie (☎ 04 50 27 30 06), which handles four flights a day from Paris (flying time around 75 minutes) but receives no international flights.

The nearest major airports are Geneva (☎ +41 4122-717 7105/7111, 🖳 www.gva.ch), on the Swiss-French border, and Lyon-Saint-Exupéry (☎ 08 26 80 08 26, 🖳 www.lyon.aeroport.fr) in Rhône, both of which handle flights from many European countries, including several airports in the UK and, of course, flights from Paris. (Lyon has a second airport, Lyon-Bron, which handles mainly business flights within France.)

Other nearby airports are Chambéry/Aix-les-Bains, served by flights from Paris (flying time around 55 minutes), and Marseille-Marignane (see page 287) in Bouches-du-Rhône (13), which is some two hours' drive from Hautes-Alpes. The website 🖳 www.aeroport.fr gives all flight schedules to and from French airports, details of airports and their proximity to main towns, and on-going transport links.

Public Transport

The *TGV* calls at the main towns and cities in the northern Alps and at Gap, but not Briançon, in the southern Alps. Lyon (Rhône) is just two hours from Paris, and Valence (26) can be reached in 2 hours 25 minutes. The *TGV* continues (on normal track, at present) to Chambéry (3h), Grenoble (3h 10m), and

Annecy (3h 45m) and there's even a direct service to Moutiers (from London Waterloo!) near the Trois Vallées. For details of the *TGV* network, see map in **Appendix E**. There's also an excellent rail service between cities and main towns, and weekly season tickets are excellent value for commuters, although mid-evening timetables for suburban commuters tend not to exist. If you work late or irregular hours, or live outside a main town, you need to travel by car.

The major towns and cities have frequent, and usually punctual, bus services, reasonably priced, running up to around 10pm during the week. The service from major towns to smaller nearby towns is less frequent and tends to terminate around 8pm, with perhaps a bus every hour on Sundays. If you live in a semi-rural area, a car is essential. School bus services exist in semi-rural and rural areas.

There's a number of other local public transport services that are mainly for tourists, including a cable car from the centre of Grenoble to the Fort de la Bastille, offering a superb view over the city; four-wheeled open carriages running around the Lac d'Annecy; *le petit train de Chambéry*, offering a 40-minute tour of the pedestrian streets (one of the largest pedestrian town centres in France); and the *train de Montenvers*, the highest cog railway in France at 2,400m (7,870ft), which will take you (and around 900,000 other visitors annually) from Chamonix to the largest glacier in France (40km²/16mi²). There are also pleasure boats on the four largest lakes in the Alps, Lac de Serre Ponçon (05), Lac du Bourget (73) – the largest natural lake in France, Lac d'Annecy (74) and Lac Léman/Lake Geneva (74). Some lakes have restaurant boats on which you can enjoy gastronomic dining at night with superb views of the lake and surrounding mountains.

Roads

The Alps region has a denser motorway network than any other part of France, so communications by road are generally excellent, at least between major towns. For example, Grenoble can be reached (at the legal speed limit) in just over five hours from Paris via Lyon, only 8km (5mi) of the journey not being on motorways (the motorway toll cost is around €40 for a car). If your destination is Haute-Savoie, you can avoid Lyon by leaving the A6 at Mâcon and taking the A40. The recently-completed A51 links Grenoble with Marseille.

Within the Alps, Isère, Savoie and Haute-Savoie are well linked by motorways (*autoroutes*) and major dual-carriageways. For example, Grenoble is linked to Chambéry (55km/34mi) by motorway, Chambéry to Annecy (45km/28mi) is mostly motorway, and Annecy to Chamonix is also mostly motorway, with dual-carriageway terminating just before the Mont Blanc tunnel. Chambéry to Albertville (around 45km/28mi) is mostly

▲ *Strasbourg, Bas-Rhin*
© felinda (www.bigstockphoto.com)

▲ *Château de Chenonceau, Val-de-Loire*
© bparren (www.istockphoto.com)

▲ *Port Grimaud, Var © Ewan Scutcher*

▲ *© Ogen (www.istockphoto.com)*

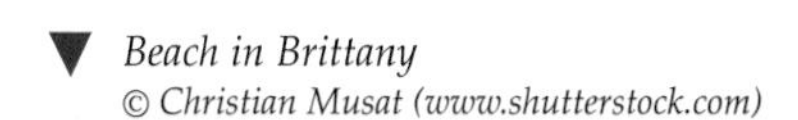

▼ *Beach in Brittany*
© Christian Musat (www.shutterstock.com)

▲ *Strasbourg Cathedral, Bas-Rhin*
© Claudio Giovanni Colombo (www.123rf.com)

▶ *Villefranche-Sur-Mer, Alpes-Maritimes*
© Le Walton (www.istockphoto.com)

▲ *Collioure, Pyrénées-Orientales*
© Dubassy (www.shutterstock.com)

▼ *© Dianne Maine (www.shutterstock.com)*

▼ *© Darren Baker (www.shutterstock.com)*

▲ © Sean Nel (www.shutterstock.com))

▲ *Château de Chambord, Loir-et-Cher*
© ItalianStyle (www.bigstockphoto.com)

▼ *Vogüé, Ardèche*
© boyatlantis (www.bigstockphoto.com)

▼ *Marseille*
© dubassy (www.shutterstock.com)

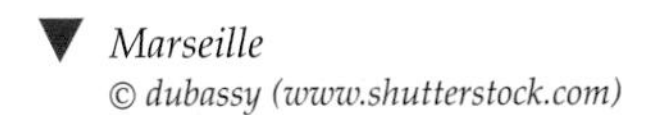

▼ © Val Gascoyne

▲ *Mont St Victoire, Provence*
© Giscard Gabriel (www.123rf.com)

▼ *Coursegoules, Alpes-Maritimes*
© Uolir (www.istockphoto.com)

▲ *© Survival Books*

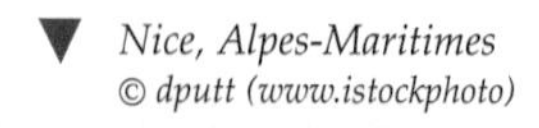

▼ *Nice, Alpes-Maritimes*
© dputt (www.istockphoto)

▼ *Honfleur, Calvados*
© Cyrille Lips (www.123rf.com)

motorway, but there are only main roads (*routes nationales*) between Albertville and Annecy, (around 50km/31mi). To reach Briançon in the southern Alps from Grenoble can take over two hours, with just 25km (15mi) of motorway out of a total distance of 160km (100mi).

Local mountain roads vary in condition. If they're access roads to ski resorts, they will be well maintained and kept open throughout the winter. Other mountain passes may be closed during periods of heavy snow. If you drive in winter, make sure you have snow tyres (*pneus-neige*).

FURTHER INFORMATION

Useful Addresses

- Comité régional du Tourisme **Rhône-Alpes**, 104, route de Paris, 69260 Charbonniéres les Bains (☎ 04 72 59 21 59, 💻 www.rhonealpes-tourisme.com)
- Comité départemental du Tourisme de la **Drôme**, 8 rue Baudin, BP531, 26005 Valence (☎ 04 75 82 19 26, 💻 www.drometourisme.com)
- Comité départemental du Tourisme d'**Isèr**e, 14 rue de la République, 38000 Grenoble (☎ 04 76 54 34 36, 💻 www.isere-tourisme.com)
- Agence touristique départementale de **Savoie**, 24 boulevard Colonne, 73000 Chambéry (☎ 04 79 85 12 45, 💻 www.savoiehautesavoie.com)
- Comité départemental du Tourisme de **Haute-Savoie**, 56 rue Sommeiller, 74000 Annecy (☎ 04 50 51 32 31, 💻 www.savoiehautesavoie.com)

Useful Websites

💻 www.europe.anglican.org – details of Anglican services throughout France

The Sacré-Coeur — Paris

8

CITIES

This chapter comprises detailed information about the French capital and the surrounding region and an overview of the property market in a number of other French cities. Information about cities and towns not included here can be found in the relevant chapter.

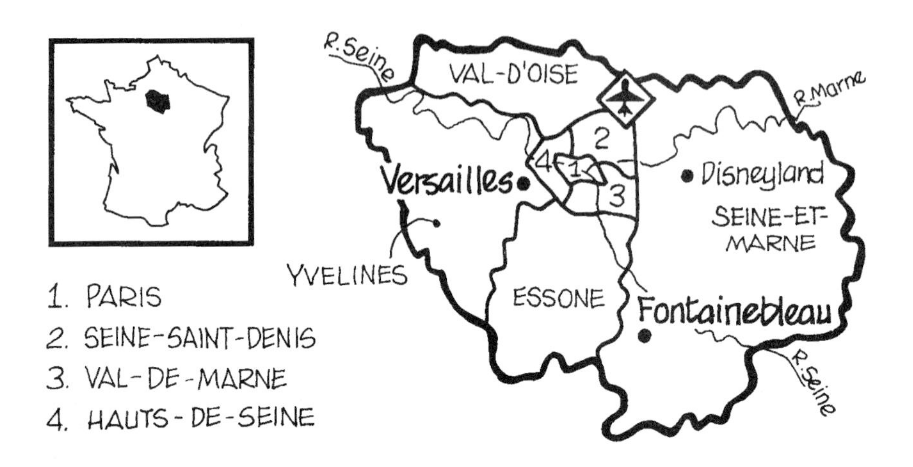

Two recent surveys of French cities – those of *Le Nouvel Observateur* and *Le Point* magazines – draw different conclusions, based on different criteria of evaluation, as to which is the 'best' city in France to live in. According to the former publication, it's Nancy, followed by Dijon, Angers, Toulouse and Strasbourg; of the other major cities, Bordeaux comes ninth, Montpellier 12th, Lyon 16th, Paris 17th, Marseille/Aix-en-Provence 22nd and Nice 23rd. According to *Le Point*, on the other hand, Chambéry is France's top city, followed by Lyon, Niort, Toulouse and Tours, with Bordeaux sixth, Nice 37th, Montpellier 42nd, Paris 51st and Marseille a lowly 65th. Details of the results of each survey can be found in **Appendix G**.

PARIS

Paris is one of eight *départements* comprising the region of Ile-de-France, in northern central France. By far France's most populous *département*, Paris is the heart and soul of Ile-de-France, which is sometimes referred to as the *région Parisienne*. The three *départements* immediately adjacent to Paris, which make up the so-called *petit couronne* ('small crown' or 'small wreath') are Hauts-de-Seine (92), Seine-Saint-Denis (93) and Val-de-Marne (94). The outer circle of *départements* is called the *grand couronne* ('large crown' or 'large wreath') and consists of Seine-et-Marne (77), Yvelines (78), Essonne (91) and Val-d'Oise (95). Ile-de France means 'island of France' and, although the region isn't literally an island, it's more or less surrounded by rivers and was therefore considered an island through much of French history.

Ile-de-France covers 12,070km^2 (around 4,700mi^2), a little over 2 per cent of France's land mass, but houses over 15 per cent of France's population. (Those who live in Ile-de-France are called *Franciliens* or *Franciliennes*.) As these figures indicate, Ile-de-France is the most densely populated region in France, with an average of around 900 inhabitants per km^2 overall. Paris is Europe's most crowded capital, with over 20,000 people per km^2 (over 50,000 per mi^2), almost five times the population density of London, compared with a mere 200 inhabitants per km^2 (around 500 per mi^2) in relatively rural Seine-et-Marne.

Ile-de-France is also, not surprisingly, the wealthiest region in the country in terms of the number of people with high incomes. Of the 100 main cities and towns in France, Ile-de-France contains six of the seven wealthiest – Saint-Germain-en-Laye and Versailles (78), Boulogne-Billancourt, Neuilly-sur-Seine and Rueil-Malamison (92) and Paris itself (the other is Cannes in Alpes-Maritimes). Together, these are home to almost 37 per cent of the country's richest people (almost 17 per cent of French people liable to wealth tax live in Neuilly!).

Ile-de-France region offers a wide range of living environments and types of accommodation, as do the various districts (*arrondissements*) and neighbourhoods of the city of Paris. Each *département* and each district has

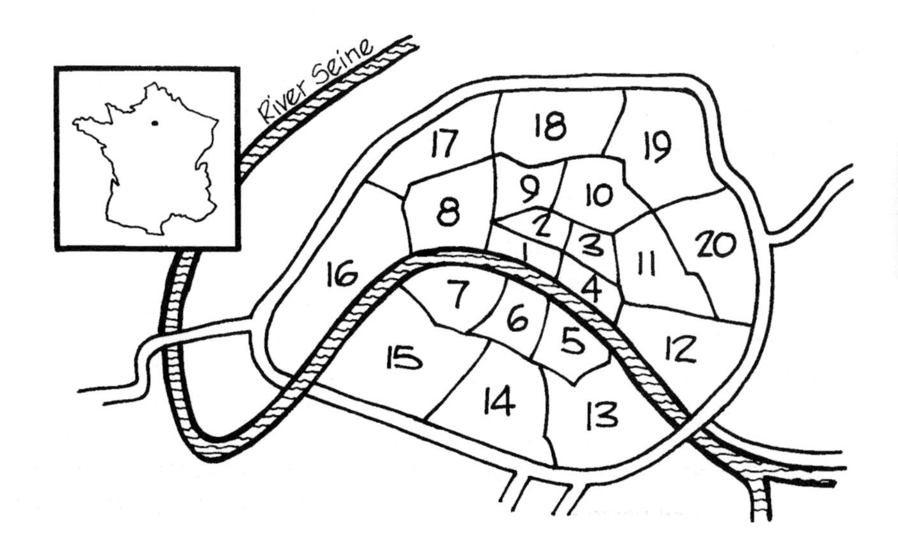

8

a general character and reputation, although there are exceptions and 'atypical' towns and districts in each area.

The 'City of Light' is the most popular tourist destination in the world. Named after the Parisii tribe, which settled on the Ile de la Cité in the third century BC, it's also the capital of France and the political centre of a highly centralised (most would add highly bureaucratic) system of government. One in three French companies with 100 or more employees make Paris their headquarters, as do two-thirds of all companies in France with over 500 employees, and Paris is Europe's third-largest financial market (after London and Frankfurt). Paris is also well known as a cultural capital, with many of the world's great museums and galleries, as well as world renowned restaurants, cafés and *bistrots*, and enjoys a deserved reputation for fashion, romance and passion. The city is divided into 20 *arrondissements*, each of which is a distinct political unit with its own town hall (*mairie*), mayor (*maire*) and police headquarters (*préfecture*) handling day-to-day administrative matters for local residents, including marriages, birth records, death certificates and voting. (The Mairie de Paris is an administrative centre for the 20 district governments and not normally open to the public.)

The numbering system for the *arrondissements* starts at the Palais du Louvre, formerly the French king's primary residence located roughly at the centre of the city, and proceeds in a clockwise spiral out to the city limits (see map below). Almost all addresses and directions in Paris include the relevant *arrondissement* number (as well as the nearest underground station). For example, the post code 75016 indicates the 16th *arrondissement*.

In an effort to lessen dependence on Paris, the government established five satellite towns in the mid-'60s, with the intention of making these 'new towns' (*villes nouvelles*) self-sufficient in terms of employment, local commerce and public services. The *villes nouvelles* are Cergy-Pontoise in Val-d'Oise to the north, Saint-Quentin-en-Yvelines to the west, Evry in Essonne to the south, and Marne-la-Vallée and Sénart in Seine-et-Marne to the east. Although the experiment wasn't entirely successful, the *villes nouvelles* have managed to dilute the concentration of jobs, people and services in the capital to a certain extent and offer a less frenetic alternative to the urban intensity of Paris itself.

West

To the west of Paris lie the *départements* of Hauts-de-Seine and Yvelines, a favourite residential area for corporate executives, including a large number of expatriates. Their popularity is due mainly to the easy access to the cluster of corporate offices at La Défense, a modern, high-rise development on the western edge of Paris. Hauts-de-Seine is home to 1.4m residents, while the much larger Yvelines has 1.35m inhabitants. The western suburbs have the reputation of being rather well-to-do, expensive and *chic*, although there are also pockets of council housing. The *ville nouvelle* of Saint-Quentin-en-Yvelines, just to the south of Versailles, houses the police headquarters for the *département*.

North

The *départements* to the north of Paris are Seine-Saint-Denis and Val-d'Oise, home to 1.4 and 1.1m residents respectively. Both *départements* are highly industrialised, many commercial enterprises taking advantage of their proximity to Paris' major airport, Roissy-Charles de Gaulle, which straddles the border between Val-d'Oise and Seine-et-Marne. They're also the location of the largest and most troubled of the *banlieues* (the French for 'suburb', which has in recent years acquired a connotation of 'socially undesirable'), with a concentration of immigrants (particularly from North Africa) and high unemployment. However, there are also many charming areas and small towns with excellent public services and direct access into Paris. Val-d'Oise is home to the *ville nouvelle* of Cergy-Pontoise, situated along a northward bend in the river Seine. Some people (mainly estate agents) include the neighbouring *département* of Oise (60), or at least its southern sector, in Ile-de-France, as more and more people now choose to live there (in a rural setting) and commute into Paris.

East

To the east of Paris are the *départements* of Val-de-Marne and Seine-et-Marne. This area has long been rather ignored by trendy (some might say 'snooty') Parisians, in much the same way as the east end of Paris itself (like that of London) is considered '*déclassé*', but this is starting to change. Thanks to the location of the Bibliothèque de France (the so-called 'Mitterand Library') on the east side of the city and a general push towards redevelopment around the Gare de l'Est, Gare de Lyon and Bastille, there has been a resurgence of interest in the eastern suburbs. As in many other urban areas of the world, young professionals are starting to take advantage of lower property prices and contributing to an overall 'gentrification' of formerly run-down neighbourhoods. Seine-et-Marne is a largely rural *département* that curls around to the south of Paris as far as Fontainebleau and Nemours. It's home to two of the *villes nouvelles*, Marne-la-Vallée (best known as the site of Disneyland Paris – see page 343) and Sénart to the south near Melun. The eastern and southern edges of Seine-et-Marne have a distinctly rural character, which is no surprise since its neighbouring regions are Champagne and Burgundy, with their vineyards and villages.

South

Between Seine-et-Marne and Yvelines, the *département* of Essonne stretches from the southern edge of Orly airport (part of which is in Val-de-Marne) past Etampes. The northern part of Essonne is heavily built-up, the *ville nouvelle* of Evry housing its police headquarters. Evry is the site of the newest cathedral in France, completed in 1995 (in fact France's only 20th century cathedral) – a stark modern building with large stained glass panels and a rooftop garden, complete with trees. Further south, the *département* rapidly becomes more rural as it approaches the large agricultural region of Centre-Val-de-Loire (see page 399). Essonne is also home to the scientific research centre at Saclay, which attracts students and research personnel from around the world (see page 332).

Advantages & Disadvantages

Most of the advantages of living in Ile-de-France come from being near Paris, which is the focus for all aspects of French life, including government, education, culture, entertainment and transport, and it isn't far from the country's geographical centre. You're most likely to be able to find a job in the Paris region, irrespective of your profession, particularly if you're interested in working for a large international company. Wages are the highest in France (although so are taxes, property prices and the cost of living).

Paris and its environs are home to the largest number of English-speaking foreigners in France, and there are many expatriate resources available, from clubs and associations to schools, language classes, English-speaking professionals and services and Anglophone publications and publishers. There are well established British and American communities, which enjoy a rapport with their embassy and consular officials. Officials often work with expatriate groups to plan and host receptions, meetings and events for the respective community members. While the embassies concentrate on serving the business and diplomatic communities, the consulates have services available to individuals, such as renewing passports and other documents, and providing lists of local clubs, events and English-speaking professionals in the Paris area.

The large foreign population means that there's the widest selection of 'exotic' (i.e. imported) products in France. It isn't usually difficult to find a source of food and goods you miss from 'back home', whether you're from the UK, the USA, Australia or any other part of the world. There are shops and restaurants offering food and other products from China, Thailand, Africa, the Caribbean, Mexico, Algeria, Morocco and a host of other foreign goods that can be difficult or impossible to find in other regions of France. The specialities and delicacies of almost all the French regions are also on offer at restaurants and shops throughout Ile-de-France.

Even if you aren't a 'city person', Ile-de-France offers a variety of non-urban living environments, including the wide open spaces of southern Essonne and the lush forests surrounding Fontainebleau and Rambouillet. There are many small towns in the region, and even the larger towns tend to be divided into communes and neighbourhoods with distinctive characteristics and a sense of community. Not surprisingly, Paris and the surrounding towns are largely built-up and have relatively little green space. Most spacious is Sarcelles (95) with over $35m^2$ of green space per inhabitant, followed closely by Rueil-Malamaison (92); at the other end of the scale are Neuilly-sur-Seine (92) and Corbeil-Essonnes (91), the latter with a mere $0.2m^2$ of green space per inhabitant. (Even Paris itself has $14m^2$ per inhabitant.) Nevertheless, Ile-de-France is a relatively healthy place to live, the mortality rate (from all causes) being lower than the national average (Neuilly-sur-Seine is apparently the healthiest place in all of France, with a mortality rate less than half that of Valenciennes in Nord, although it may have something to do with the average wealth of the inhabitants!).

Of course, life in Ile-de-France also has its disadvantages. Paris, and much of the urbanised area immediately surrounding the city, can be crowded, noisy, dirty, and maddeningly bureaucratic. Everyone who has visited Paris seems to want to live there, and many are sorely disappointed to discover that taking up residence can be very different from living as a tourist. Like many city dwellers, Parisians tend to be busy people in a hurry, and it can be difficult to develop friendships in the local community, particularly if your French isn't fluent.

If you're planning to live in the suburbs, bear in mind that, depending on the wind direction, you may be affected by the noise of aircraft landing at and (especially) taking off from Paris' two airports.

The region as a whole is the most expensive in France, although costs are lower the further you are from the centre of Paris. Competition for well paid, desirable jobs is intense, thanks to the perceived 'glamour' of working in or near Paris. For those without job qualifications, particularly those who don't speak fluent French, there simply are no jobs, unless you're willing to work illegally, which is risky. Bosses in Paris (as in much of France) are expected to be authoritarian taskmasters whose prime directive is to get the most work possible out of employees during their working week. That is starting to change, particularly in international companies headquartered in Paris, but employees still tend to be suspicious of bosses who show more than a modicum of interest in members of staff and may be quick to complain of any violation of the numerous and sometimes petty labour laws.

Outside the city, access to jobs, transport and resources may be limited. Not all parts of Ile-de-France are equally well served by the regional transport network. In some areas, owning a car (or two, in the case of a family) is a necessity when shops, schools and public transport aren't within walking distance or where rural roads have turned pedestrians into an endangered species. Rush hour traffic can be a nightmare when entering and leaving Paris. The same is true at the start and end of school holiday periods, when everyone in Paris seems determined to leave or return on the same day. Strikes, demonstrations and other 'man made' disturbances often wreak further havoc on traffic and public transport, although most locals have managed to develop a philosophical attitude towards the situation.

In the large, semi-rural areas of Essonne and Seine-et-Marne, it can be impossible to find local doctors, dentists or any professional person willing to admit to speaking or understanding English or even to explain procedures clearly in French, which can be frightening in an emergency situation. Another (unexpected) drawback to living in or near Paris is that long-lost friends and family members have a tendency to 'drop by' and will of course gratefully accept your offer to show them around the city. Although this can be fun for a while, some expatriates quickly tire of acting as tour guides and having their spare bedrooms constantly occupied by visitors.

Nevertheless, Paris is a city like no other in the world, and the vast majority of its inhabitants and those of the surrounding region feel that the advantages of living there greatly outweigh the disadvantages.

Places of Interest

Paris is a big city, and some *arrondissements* are of greater interest to foreign buyers than others. Like London, it's divided by the river, and there's much debate as to whether it's preferable to live to the north (known as the *rive droite* or 'right bank') or to the south (*rive gauche* or 'left bank') of the Seine. Generally, the lower numbered *arrondissements* are considered the most desirable by Parisians, although in typical French fashion there are exceptions and you may well find that your criteria for evaluation are rather different from those of the natives.

North of the river, the 1st to 4th *arrondissements* (usually referred to simply as 'the first' 'the second' etc.) make up what many regard as the heart of the city, not to mention its historic centre. The 1st contains the royal residences of the Palais du Louvre and the Palais Royal, as well as the former marketplace of Les Halles, now converted into an enormous underground shopping centre. The 2nd *arrondissement* includes the historic Bourse (stock market), the garment district and many banks and insurance offices, while the 3rd and 4th include the Marais ('marsh') district, the centre of Paris' Jewish community and a trendy residential area complete with alternative lifestyle bars, discos and late night hang-outs.

Across the Seine is the 5th *arrondissement*, the Latin Quarter (so called because its student population once conversed in Latin), which is home to the Sorbonne and a plethora of student (as well as tourist) shops and restaurants. The 6th is something of a transition zone between the Latin Quarter and the considerably more upmarket 7th and includes the Luxembourg Garden and Palace, now home to the French National Senate. The 7th, referred to as the Saint-Germain-des-Prés district, is dominated by the Eiffel Tower and the Champs de Mars, the Ecole militaire, the Hôtel des Invalides (not a hotel but a former hospital and now a military museum) and numerous government buildings (including the Assemblée nationale in the Palais Bourbon) and embassies. It's a highly sought-after (and therefore expensive) *arrondissement*, although some Parisians find it too austere and cold for their liking (a case of sour grapes perhaps?).

Back on the north side (*rive droite*) of the Seine is the 8th *arrondissement*, Paris' most expensive, which includes the Champs-Elysées, some of Paris' top hotels (including the Georges V), the Elysée Palace (the President's home), and the designer shops on and near the Avenue Montaigne. The 9th is known as a 'lively' *arrondissement*, in both the positive and the negative senses. Many of the large Paris department stores are here, as well as the Opéra Garnier and a host of theatres, cinemas and restaurants, which means that it tends to be crowded and noisy until late into the evening.

The 10th is best known for its railway stations (the Gare de l'Est and the Gare du Nord) and hospitals, while the 11th and 12th are part of the long-neglected eastern side of Paris that's starting to come into its own, thanks to a number of urban renewal projects. The old Bastille district, which spans the two *arrondissements*, is beginning to attract artists, musicians and other creative people.

Back on the left bank, the 13th, 14th and 15th are largely residential areas, with many small neighbourhoods and shops and a proliferation of parks, as well as the Tour Montparnasse, Paris' second-highest building. The 16th, on the right bank and with the Bois de Boulogne as its western border, is alleged to be the preferred *arrondissement* for Paris' 'new money' crowd (as opposed to the 'old money' residing in the 7th). It's a popular area for diplomats and their families, as a number of embassies are located there, as well as the Organisation for Economic Cooperation and Development (OECD).

The 17th is largely residential, although not as fashionable (or expensive) as the 16th. The 18th is Paris' 'hilly' district, and includes the Sacré Coeur church perched on Montmartre and overlooking the rest of Paris – a beautiful spot but hopelessly crowded with tourists almost year round. The 18th generally has the reputation of being rather run-down, and the Montmartre, Barbès and Pigalle areas, which comprise Paris' red-light district, are considered seedy, if not dangerous, by most Parisians (see **Crime Rate & Security** on page 336).

The 19th and 20th are working-class districts, traditionally looked down upon by most Parisians, but there has been considerable renovation and redevelopment in recent years. The Parc de la Villette, with its museums and exhibition and concert halls is located in the 19th, while the famous Père Lachaise cemetery (see **Leisure** on page 341) is in the 20th.

Villes Nouvelles

The so-called *villes nouvelles* (see page 326) were established in the mid-'60s in an attempt to draw some of the congestion away from Paris and into the relatively sparsely populated countryside (and unofficially to move a large amount of council housing out of central Paris). Since then, local government officials have generally made great strides in developing local industry, shopping and other resources. Although the term *ville nouvelle* is often used by the French as a pejorative to indicate the proliferation of ugly high-rise buildings and the artificiality of government attempts to create new communities, each of these 'agglomerations' of towns and communes has developed its own character, aided by public investment in local schools, attractions, activities and events. For those who prefer modern living (e.g. lifts that can take more than two people at a time) and clean, simple lines to the ornate style of Parisian apartments, the *villes nouvelles* offer new construction and many of the advantages of planned urban development.

Saclay & Fontainebleau

More recently, the French government has devoted much time and money to the development of a scientific research centre at Saclay, a town in Yvelines just off the N118 trunk road (*route nationale*) south-west of Paris. The research centre and nearby university *département* attract large numbers of visiting scientists from around the world, and the area around

Saclay has developed clusters of both employment and residential areas, including Massy, Palaiseau, Orsay, Les Ulis and Gif-sur-Yvette. The area is well served by public transport into Paris and offers a range of housing and shopping comfortably outside the city limits.

Another major centre of learning is at Fontainebleau, to the south of the city in Seine-et-Marne. Fontainebleau is the site of INSEAD, Europe's most prestigious graduate business school. Like Versailles, Fontainebleau was once a royal holiday retreat and the surrounding area is lush and dense with trees, thanks to the national forest that used to form part of the royal hunting grounds. INSEAD lends the town a distinctly international flavour, attracting a constant flow of teachers and students from around the world. Most residents find Paris a bit too far to commute daily, although there are frequent trains and direct access via the A6 motorway for those who want the best of both worlds.

Western Suburbs

The area stretching from the city limits to the town of Versailles has long been regarded as Paris' most desirable suburban area (the prevailing westerly winds blew the smoke and other pollution from the city centre towards the east, where the poorer folk lived!) and is extremely popular with English-speaking expatriates and corporate executives on secondment. For English-speakers, the west side has obvious advantages, from the availability of resources (international and private schools, English-speaking doctors, dentists and hospitals, etc.) to the proximity of other Anglophones. Particularly popular, on account of their proximity to Paris and pleasant ambiance, are the towns of Boulogne-Billancourt, Neuilly, Saint-Cloud and Saint-Germain-en-Laye, but there are numerous smaller towns throughout the area with large concentrations of English-speaking expatriates.

Population

According to the latest census (taken in 2004), the population of Ile-de-France is almost exactly 11.5m, over a sixth of the population of France, including almost 40 per cent of all foreigners living in France. In all, there are around 1.3m foreigners, accounting for almost 12 per cent of the region's population, more than double the overall average for France (5.6 per cent), although there has been a gradual decline in the number of foreigners over the last decade, due both to the naturalisation of older immigrants and to migration away from the Paris area to other regions of France.

Traditionally, Paris and Ile-de-France region have been a magnet for young French people, drawing population from the countryside. Indeed, Ile-de-France has the lowest average age of any French region, 20 per cent of the population being under 15 and only 12 per cent over 65. This pattern is most marked in some of the towns surrounding Paris, particularly Evry (91) and Rueil-Malmaison (92), the former also boasting the lowest population ageing rate of any major town in France. In recent years, however, this trend seems to have reversed, thanks largely to government-sponsored development of industry and employment in the regions. More and more *Franciliens* are moving elsewhere to escape crowded living conditions, traffic congestion, pollution and the high cost of living in and around Paris. Saint-Germain-en-Laye and Versailles (78), Corbeil-Essonnes (91), Saint-Denis (93) and Paris itself are particularly affected by this trend.

The population of Ile-de-France is growing at around the average rate for the country as a whole (0.7 per cent per year), yet this statistic disguises a massive inflow and outflow of people. Every year, some 20,000 people leave the city, 60 per cent of them to the suburbs and the remainder further afield. Most of them are families in search of larger but affordable accommodation, as housing in the capital tends to be small: less than 45 per cent of homes have more than one bedroom compared with almost 70 per cent in the suburbs and over 80 per cent in the rest of the country.

The populations of the eight *départements* are as follows: Essonne (1.19m), Hauts-de-Seine (1.52m), Paris (2.15m), Seine-et-Marne (1.26m), Seine-Saint-Denis (1.46m), Val-de-Marne (1.28m), Val-d'Oise (1.15m) and Yvelines (1.4m). The populations of Créteil (94) and Evry (91) comprise a high proportion of students (around 20 per cent), compared with 3 per cent in Neuilly-sur-Seine (92) and a mere 1 per cent in Corbeil-Essonnes (91), Rueil-Malmaison (92) and Sarcelles (95).

By far the most numerous foreign nationals in Ile-de-France are the Portuguese, with over 270,000 official residents. Algerians and Moroccans number 190,000 and 145,000 respectively. Completing the top ten foreign nationalities are (in order): Tunisians, Turks, Spanish, Italians, Malians, Yugoslavians and Congolese, accounting in total for a further 285,000 people. Contrary to the fears of those on the political far right, recent percentage increases in the foreign population have been virtually identical to those in the native population, although there have been some shifts in the immigrants' countries of origin over the past decade (notably increases in immigrants from the former Yugoslavia and other conflict-torn regions of the world).

The greatest concentration of foreigners is in Seine-Saint-Denis, where there are many immigrants of Algerian, North African and sub-Saharan

African origin. *Immigrés* make up almost 20 per cent of the population in this *département*, often living in high-rise *HLM* (council flats or subsidised housing blocks). Yvelines and Hauts-de-Seine to the west contain concentrations of Moroccans, particularly in the towns of Mantes-la-Jolie, Canteloup-les-Vignes and Les Mureaux (in Yvelines) and Gennevilliers, Clichy and Villeneuve-la-Garenne in Hauts-de-Seine. Val-de-Marne is home to many Portuguese immigrants and is increasingly popular with Asians seeking to move out of Paris. The *départements* of the *grand couronne* generally have much lower proportions of foreigners, except for Val-d'Oise, whose foreign population of around 11 per cent includes many Turkish immigrants. Within Paris, the proportion of foreigners is around 15 per cent, with distinct communities of Asians in the 1st, 2nd and 10th *arrondissements* and a concentration of African immigrants in the 18th and 19th.

There are relatively few Britons and Americans living in Ile-de-France, and their numbers tend to rise and fall according to the needs of the multinational corporations headquartered in the Paris area. It's estimated that there are between 5,000 and 10,000 Britons and 5,000 to 8,000 Americans living in and around Paris (the French statistical institute, INSEE, doesn't publish these figures). Paris is hardly a popular retirement destination, and many English-speaking expatriates in the area are 'transient' executive families making a two to five-year tour of duty with an international company or students enjoying a 'Paris experience' as part of their studies. The few permanent residents of British or American background include those married to French nationals.

Climate

The climate in Paris, as in much of the north of France, is temperate, with cool winters and warm summers. Average temperatures in January range from just above freezing to 5 or 6C. Winters tend to be damp and gloomy, as in much of northern Europe, although the temperature only rarely dips below freezing and heavy snow and severe frosts are extremely rare. In July, average temperatures range from night time lows of 15C (62F) to daytime highs of around 25C (77F). Summer temperatures over 30C (85F) are rare events and normally last only for a few days. The region enjoys an average of around 1,800 hours' sunshine per year and average rainfall is between 600 and 700mm per year (similar to that of London) on around 112 days per year. Although 'Paris in the spring' conjures up idyllic images, rainfall is generally heaviest in May (with around 65mm), with October not far behind, while August is the driest month (around 45mm). Winter is slightly wetter than summer (although there are occasionally impressive thunderstorms during July and August), but otherwise rainfall varies little across the seasons. Thick fog is a common phenomenon in spring and autumn in the open fields and woodlands of the *grand couronne*.

The greater Paris area tends to create its own micro-climate, due to the concentration of industry, vehicles and people (the French government in particular generates a lot of hot air, or so some residents contend). This means that temperatures in Paris are generally a degree or two warmer at all times of the year than in the region overall. In summer, a layer of cool air and cloud sometimes traps the warmer air in the river basin (a phenomenon known as temperature inversion), and the whole city becomes smoggy, hot and unpleasant until a thunderstorm breaks or the high cloud layer dissipates or is blown away to the east. (This is one reason Parisians are more than happy to leave the city to the tourists in July and August, when temperature inversions are most likely to occur.) Various anti-smog procedures are then put into effect, including the reduction of speed limits and the banning of certain vehicles from the *boulevard périphérique*, the city's ring road.

Crime Rate & Security

Like any big city, Paris has a higher level of crime than the country as a whole, including pick pocketing and bag snatching (particularly on the underground and from cars by thieves on motorcycles), burglary (especially when flats and houses are obviously vacant for weeks at a time during the summer holidays), and more serious forms of urban crime (not to mention allegations of corruption and misuse of public funds by local politicians!).

Particular areas where high levels of crime have been reported include:

- the rail link between Charles de Gaulle airport and central Paris, where thieves distract tired travellers in order to steal their luggage;
- near the Eiffel Tower at night, where there have been a number of armed robberies;
- on the no.1 underground line, through the centre of the city, especially during the summer;
- in the Gare du Nord;
- at the major department stores, such as Galeries Lafayette, Printemps and Samaritaine ;

- in hotel foyers and from hotel rooms (many older hotels have inadequate door locks);
- in restaurants (particularly of handbags put on the floor);
- at ATMs.

There has been a steady increase in the number of violent crimes recorded in the last few years, although this may be partly due to a change in reporting style among the French media, which used to more or less ignore local crime stories. Violent crime occurs mainly in the 18th, 19th and 20th *arrondissements* and in the suburban areas of Essonne and Seine-Saint-Denis. Most gang activity takes place in the latter region, and the town of Saint-Denis. Paris itself has the fifth-highest crime rate among France's major towns, but the only other town in the Ile-de-France with a particularly high crime rate is Créteil (94.

On the other hand, Saint-Germain-en-Laye and Versailles (78), and Neuilly-sur-Seine and Rueil-Malmaison (92) enjoy some of the country's lowest crime rates. Note also that most violent crimes (e.g. armed robbery) are directed at 'anonymous' targets – banks, jewellers' and armoured cars – rather than against individuals and you're far less likely to be a victim of violent crime than to be injured crossing the street.

There are a few areas of Paris that most people advise avoiding, at least late at night – primarily the Pigalle 'red light' district and Barbès in the Montmartre district, which has a reputation for more serious crimes against unwitting tourists. The Bois de Boulogne and, to a lesser extent, the Bois de Vincennes also have a reputation for late night crimes involving drug dealers and prostitutes, although during the day these are popular public parks, considered safe for all. Commercial Area 13 of the Défense business district is also a favourite haunt of thieves.

Terrorism has been a threat in Paris in the past, mostly in the form of bombings of public areas, including the underground. However, the government's programme of raising public awareness and encouraging people to report suspicious packages left unattended seems to have been successful. Large department stores may hire security guards to check bags and packages when you enter, which can be annoying, although most residents find it reassuring and it seems to be effective. At times of 'high alert', it isn't unusual to see heavily armed police, *gendarmes* and even the *CNS* (national security service) on the streets of Paris, particularly in the underground and around national monuments, embassies and consulates.

Amenities

Sports

Thanks to the 1998 football World Cup, Paris now has an 80,000-seat sports stadium, the Stade de France, located in La-Plaine-Saint-Denis, just north of the city. The stadium was built with public funds in order for France to have an appropriate venue for international sporting events, such as the World Cup, the Olympic Games (Paris lost its bids in 2008 and 2012), and various European and world athletic championships. After the 1998 World Cup, management of the Stade de France was turned over to a concession of private companies, although the facility is still under the direction of the Ministry for Sports and Youth, which has promised to find a resident first division football team for the stadium in order to assure a minimum of 20 games per year. Currently the Stade de France is used for a variety of sporting events, concerts, performances and trade shows, although these take up only a handful of dates each year. Information about the stadium and scheduled events there can be found on the Stade de France website (💻 www.stadefrance.fr).

Outside Paris, most communes have a variety of sporting facilities and sports clubs, which often hold exercise and fitness classes open to local residents and their families. Many towns have a small stadium for matches and events and some towns offer tennis clubs, swimming pools and other sports facilities at nominal prices to local residents. Non-residents may be able to use the facilities by paying a higher fee.

Football: For football fans, the 'home team' for all of Ile-de-France is Paris Saint-Germain. PSG, as it's known, plays its home matches at the Stade Parc des Princes, which is part of the sports complex at the southern end of the Bois de Boulogne. The stadium holds around 48,000 spectators and houses the administrative offices of the team, as well as a shop selling team regalia. Tickets for matches can be purchased online at the PSG website (💻 www.psg.fr) or at various ticket outlets throughout Ile-de-France. PSG is a first division team, normally ranked in the top 20 to 25 in Europe.

Tennis: Tennis is the other major sporting passion in the Paris region, with considerable attention devoted each June to the international tournament held at Roland Garros. (Foreigners refer to this as the 'French Open', but the locals speak only of 'Roland Garros,' the French tennis champion after whom the tennis facility in the Bois de Boulogne sports complex is named.) Tickets to any of the matches are highly prized and obtainable only from the Fédération française de Tennis (FFT), which gives priority to its own members.

For those who want to play rather than watch, there are tennis clubs throughout Ile-de-France region, most of which are affiliated to the FFT. Membership of a local FFT tennis club not only entitles you to advance Roland Garros tickets, but also offers other benefits (e.g. reduced court fees, insurance and reciprocal privileges at other FFT tennis clubs throughout France). The cost of family membership of a tennis club varies from around €150 to €750 per year, depending on the size of your family and whether or not the annual fee includes court time, lessons or other benefits. Nearly all tennis clubs in Ile-de-France include FFT membership in their annual fees. Generally speaking, the most expensive clubs are those in the city of Paris or in the inner western suburbs. Clubs on the fringes of Ile-de-France may charge as little as €75 per year for membership, with fewer additional charges or even free use of the courts on a first-come-first-served basis.

Fitness clubs: American-style gyms have opened in the city of Paris and in the more fashionable suburbs. Many are operated as franchises, often within larger hotels. These include Vit'Halles, Gymnase Club, Forest Hill (part of the hotel chain of the same name) and others, all offering a dizzying assortment of fitness programmes – everything from weight training and standard fitness machines to nutritional counselling, squash and racquetball, billiards, dance exercise and even (at the Forest Hill chain) 'aqua-sports' parks with wave machines and hydrotherapy. Many hotels offer health club facilities, which may be open to the public on a membership or per-visit basis.

It's difficult to compare prices for fitness facilities, as the services offered vary greatly and most clubs have trial offers and off-peak or long-term membership discounts. If you're working for a French company with a *comité d'entreprise* (a sort of employees' activity organisation), check whether there's a group membership you can take advantage of – usually for a fitness centre near your place of work. It's normally possible to negotiate a one or two-month trial membership for as little as €10 to €20, although you may be restricted to odd hours or certain facilities or have to pay an additional fee per visit. For €8,000 to €10,000 per year, you may be entitled to all the services and features of a well equipped club, including a personal fitness evaluation and nutritional counselling or time with a personal trainer. However, most memberships are negotiable if you're prepared to bargain for the services you want or need.

Golf: Golf has become very popular in France in recent years, and there are over 65 golf courses in Ile-de-France region, mostly in the outer *départements*: one each in Seine-Saint-Denis and Val-de-Marne, five in Hauts-de-Seine, nine in Val-d'Oise, 13 in Essonne, 16 in Seine-et-Marne and no fewer than 24 in Yvelines, including five 36-hole and two 45-hole courses (the latter among five courses near Versailles). Parisian residents tend to favour the courses in the western suburbs, although there are also several popular courses near Disneyland Paris (in Marne-la-Vallée) to the east. One of the best resources for information regarding the location, fees and terms of golf courses in Ile-de-France is the *Pariscope* website (💻 www.premiere.fr), better known for cinema and theatre reviews (see below). Under the 'Sport' section, golf clubs are listed by *département*, complete with directions, maps, number of holes and green fees. Information (in both French and English) on how to find courses, the cost of a round, etc. is also available from 💻 www.backspin.com. Another useful website for golfers is 💻 www.golf.com.fr.

Most golf courses are open to the public year round, although the more 'exclusive' clubs (e.g. in Versailles and Fontainebleau) may restrict non-members to the low season or certain days of the week or require the invitation of a club member. Some clubs require a qualifying handicap. Green fees for most courses are around €25 to €60 during the week, and €35 to €90 at weekends.

Horse racing & riding: The French, particularly the Parisians, are well known as fans of horse racing, and there's a number of racecourses (*hippodromes*) in Ile-de-France, including the Hippodrome d'Auteuil in the Bois de Boulogne on the western edge of Paris. Off-track betting is popular in the many PMU shops and bars throughout the area (identifiable by the green PMU signs in the windows) where bets can be made and races followed on television. Horse riding as a participant sport is also popular, and there are many stables (*écuries*) and riding schools (*écoles d'équitation*) throughout the region.

Cycling: Cycling is another popular sport in France, for both spectators and participants. The *Tour de France* takes place every year in July, and the final stage on the last Sunday of the month winds its way along the back roads of Ile-de-France, usually through Essonne or Seine-et-Marne, before culminating in a sprint up the Champs-Elysées. There are numerous cycling clubs in the area, whose members can be seen most Sundays (when the weather permits and sometimes even when it doesn't!) in their brightly coloured club outfits. The French Cycling Federation (Fédération française de Cyclisme) is the main cycling organisation in France and its website (💻 www.ffc.fr) contains information about local clubs and all kinds of cycling, from off-road to indoor racing and stunt riding. Alternatively, contact either your *mairie* (many cycling clubs are sponsored by the town officials) or ask at a local bicycle shop.

Other sports: There are, of course, numerous other sporting facilities and clubs in Ile-de-France, including a few English-speaking sports clubs (see **Clubs** on page 357).

Leisure

There's no shortage of leisure opportunities in Ile-de-France region, whether cultural, physical or purely fun.

English-language cinema & theatre: The multi-screen cinemas along the Champs-Elysées and the Boulevard Montparnasse show all the latest films, with foreign films in their original language with French subtitles (*version originale/VO*) or dubbed into French (*version française/VF*). *VO* films are also shown at many other cinemas throughout Paris and in the inner suburbs, particularly to the west of the city, although the suburbs generally suffer from a dearth of cinemas and most residents travel into the capital to watch the latest films. In the outer suburbs, the availability of *VO* films varies. In Seine-Saint-Denis, for example, you're likely to find Indian, Tunisian and Iranian films in *VO*. In Seine-et-Marne, where many Asians have settled, Japanese films (including Manga cartoon films, popular with young people) are often shown in *VO*. Fontainebleau cinemas offer a wide selection of films in *VO*, thanks to the large international population. In Essonne, where the foreign population is small and scattered, English-language films in *VO* may be shown only in the larger towns close to Paris (i.e. Massy, Chilly Mazarin and Bretigny-sur-Orge) and in a few small community cinemas that specialise in 'art' films (e.g. the community centres in Orsay and Dourdan).

Cinema listings are published in local newspapers and magazines, as well as in a number of Paris-based activity magazines, such as *Pariscope*. There are a number of online cinema listings for Ile-de-France (e.g. *Pariscope* 💻 www.pariscope.fr and *Allociné* 💻 www.allocine.fr), where you can search by *département* and even book tickets online. *Allociné* is also available on television, if you have digital cable or satellite service, offering previews and reviews of current films, behind the scenes reporting and show business news, although, like *Pariscope*, it's mainly in French. A useful website for finding out which films are on in a given area, which also indicates whether the films are being shown in the original language is 💻 www.cinefil.com.

Plays are seldom performed in English in the professional theatres in Paris, which often present plays by Shakespeare and other English-language writers in French translation. However, Les Amis du Jardin Shakespeare du Pré Catelan (in the 16th) present a Shakespeare play in

English at least once a year and the Dear Conjunction Theatre Company performs plays in English as well as in French at various venues.

There's a number of amateur English-language theatre groups in the inner western suburbs, notably The International Players in Saint-Germain-en-Laye (78). Performances are generally advertised in expatriate newsletters, on lampposts or in local shop windows. Several of the towns sponsor French amateur theatre clubs, which may occasionally perform in public but almost always in French (participating in one of these productions is an enjoyable way to improve your language skills). The local *mairie* may organise evening outings to attend plays, operas or concerts in Paris or elsewhere, including transport by coach.

Festivals: During the spring and summer months, Paris hosts a variety of street festivals, fairs and special events, the best known of which is probably the Fête de la Musique on 21st June. Designed as a midsummer's night party, this features open air concerts and performances in all the *arrondissements,* including appearances by famous popular musicians and groups, all free of charge. Paris's Parc Floral is the site of the Festival Classique au Vert, an *al fresco* classical music festival that takes place every weekend during August and September. Every August, the banks of the Seine are closed to traffic and transformed (at vast expense) into 'Paris Plage', complete with sand, palm trees and deck chairs; a temporary swimming pool, floating on the Seine, is to be added in 2008.

Museums & monuments: Not surprisingly, Paris has more museums and monuments than any other city or town in France; there are over 400 historical monuments and almost 70 national museums within the city, from the Louvre, spectacularly housed in the former royal palace, to specialist galleries such as the Musée Picasso, the Musée Rodin and the Musée Grévin, Paris' answer to Madame Tussaud's. If you aren't an art lover, there are plenty of other kinds of museum, from the historic (e.g. the Musée Carnavalet, dedicated to the history of the city of Paris, and the Musée de l'Histoire de France, located in the Hôtel de Soubise complex where the National Archives are also housed) to the scientific (e.g. the Palais de la Découverte, just off the Champs-Elysées, and the Cité des Sciences et de l'Industrie at the Porte de la Villette). There are also museums dedicated to textiles, natural history, coins and medals, music and musical instruments and even individual performers (e.g. Edith Piaf and Georges Brassens). Most museums and monuments in Paris are owned and operated by the national government, and tourist offices throughout the city carry information about these and other attractions.

As well as Paris' most famous buildings – the Eiffel Tower and Arc de Triomphe, Notre Dame and the Sacré-Coeur – there are numerous less well known places to visit, including the Pompidou Centre, *Les Invalides* and Napoleon's tomb, and the Montparnasse and Père Lachaise cemeteries. These are both surprisingly popular tourist attractions, as many famous people are buried there. Père Lachaise is the final resting place of Chopin, Molière, Oscar Wilde, Edith Piaf and Jim Morrison (whose grave is often littered with hashish offerings from devoted fans) among numerous others, while in Montparnasse lie the remains of Jean-Paul Sartre, Samuel Beckett, Man Ray and Jean Seberg.

Parks & gardens: Although one of the world's most densely populated cities, Paris has a wealth of attractive parks and gardens, including the Jardin du Luxembourg, the Jardin des Tuileries, the Parc Monceau (all of which offer playgrounds for children and entertainment including puppet shows and concerts during the summer months) and the Parc de la Villette in the 19th, which incorporates an open-air cinema and number of 'futuristic' attractions. On the outskirts of the city are the Bois de Vincennes and the Bois de Boulogne, which despite its popular image as a trawling ground for prostitutes of the most outlandish varieties also offers camping grounds, sports fields, hiking trails and picnic and restaurant facilities. Further information can be obtained from guidebooks and from the Paris *Office de Tourisme* on the Champs-Elysées or one of its branch offices in the main railway stations or at the base of the Eiffel Tower. Tourist information is also available online (💻 www.paris.org). Many expatriate clubs and organisations organise outings to local museums and monuments or sights that may not be open to the general public, e.g. the Hôtel de Ville, the main city hall of Paris, which is open only to group tours.

Theme parks: Ile-de-France is home to the biggest (and, for many French people, the most controversial) of all French theme parks, **Disneyland Paris**. Originally opened as Euro-Disney, the park has been blamed for everything from contributing to the destruction of European culture to gross violation of workers' rights (e.g. by requiring female employees to shave their legs and underarms and banning all facial hair on male workers). While still considered something of a threat to local culture, Disneyland Paris is now more or less accepted as a feature of the landscape (and is more popular with the locals than many would care to admit). Located just outside Marne-la-Vallée, Disneyland includes not only the theme park itself but also Walt Disney Studios Park (an attraction dedicated to the art of film making, a topic near and dear to the hearts of the French), Disney Village (containing shops, restaurants, bars, discos and a Wild West show), Disney Hotels, and Golf Disneyland. The hotels and golf courses do a booming business in seminars and meetings, particularly for large corporations, and it isn't uncommon for a business meeting at one of the nearby hotels to include an afternoon or evening admission to Disneyland. There's a direct *RER* line (A) from Paris, the station being located in the centre of the Disney complex. For those travelling by car, the park is well sign-posted from the A4 motorway.

A single admission to the parks for one day costs €46 for an adult, €38 for a child. Various combination tickets are available for multiple days, admission with parking or in conjunction with other services (golf or hotel accommodation, transit passes, etc.). Tickets are available in Disney stores throughout Europe, in many Paris underground stations, ticket outlets and travel agencies and from the Disney website (💻 www.disneylandparis.com). There's even a variety of discounted season tickets for Ile-de-France residents who can't get enough of the place (you must present proof of residence in one of the eight *départements* of Ile-de-France region). Some season tickets are restricted to non-peak times or dates, but many cost no more than two or three days' worth of single admissions. See the website for details.

Those who prefer a more 'traditional' French theme park (or who find Disneyland too expensive or too crowded) head for **Parc Astérix**, at Plailly (60) just outside Ile-de-France region on the A1 motorway towards Lille. Parc Astérix is France's second-most popular theme park, where rides, shows and the general décor are themed on the plucky little Gaul and his friends, made famous by the comic book series. Unlike Disneyland Paris, Parc Astérix isn't open year-round and opens roughly from Easter until the end of October, and only at weekends during school terms. Single admissions are €35 for adults, €25 for children for the day. Tickets for Parc Astérix are available online at their website (💻 www.parcasterix.com) and at most *RER* and SNCF (railway) stations and travel agencies in Ile-de-France region, often packaged with train tickets and/or hotel accommodation.

Other theme parks and attractions of note in and around Paris include:

- Aquaboulevard (15th *arrondissement*): Europe's largest aquatic park;
- Le Château et Parc de Thoiry (78): wildlife park where visitors are caged and the animals roam 'free';
- Famiparc in Nonville (77): amusement park;
- France miniature in Elancourt (78): as the name suggests, scale models of famous places in France;
- Le Jardin des Plantes (5th): botanical gardens;
- Le Parc aux Etoiles in Triel-sur-Seine (78): space theme park;

- Parc de l'Emprunt in Souppes-sur-Long (77): animal and amusement park;
- Zoo de Vincennes (12th): 1,200 animals.

There are also leisure parks at Jablines-Annet (77), Saint-Quentin-en-Yvelines, Trappes, Verneuil-sur-Seine, Villennes-sur-Mer (78) and Draveil (91). Just north of Ile-de-France region is La Mer de Sable ('The Sea of Sand') in Ermenonville near Senlis in the *département* of Oise, which celebrates the American Wild West, with spectacular horse riding displays.

Châteaux: Outside the city limits, there are many attractions and activities to occupy your leisure time. For example, there are literally hundreds of *châteaux* in the area, from the world famous Versailles to lesser known royal estates such as Vaux-le-Vicomte (near Melun south of Paris), Sceaux (just outside Paris to the south), Saint Jean de Beauregard (near Les Ulis in Essonne) and Chantilly (just north of Ile-de-France in the *département* of Oise). Many towns have their own *châteaux* open to the public, which can be located by following the brown and white road signs on main roads. There are also the forests (*forêts*) of Rambouillet, Vincennes, Fontainebleau, Saint-Germain and Montmorency.

Other attractions: Many of the *villes nouvelles* have concert venues which attract popular local performers, singers and comedians, and most sports arenas and stadiums host short-run concerts and shows from time to time. Many communities organise local fairs and festivals, street dances (common on or around 14th July – National Day), and 'music and light' shows (*son et lumière*) celebrating historical events. Strangely, however, there are no casinos in Paris or anywhere else in Ile-de-France.

Each of the *départements* has its own tourist office, providing information about local leisure opportunities, and almost all the *départements* publish monthly or quarterly guides to local events.

As Paris is the transport hub of France, it's possible to get to almost every other part of France and to many other parts of Europe within a few hours, whether by car, train or plane. For example, the region is within comfortable day-trip distance of Giverny (Monet's house and garden) in Eure (see page 50) and Chartres (with its magnificent cathedral) in Eure-et-Loire. Thanks to the *TGV* line, even Marseille is a mere three hours away by high-speed train.

Shopping Centres & Markets

The boulevard Haussmann, at the southern end of the 9th *arrondissement*, is often considered the shopping 'centre' of Paris, thanks mainly to the two large and well known department stores (*grand magasins*), Galeries Lafayette and Au Printemps, but also to a concentration of shops and boutiques of all kinds. Many of the stores in this area attract tourists at all times of the year, and the area is generally crowded. Both Galeries Lafayette and Au Printemps carry a wide selection of clothing, household goods, electronics and furnishings for the home, and you can enjoy a snack, meal or simply a drink in their many cafés and restaurants. The same is true of the other *grands magasins* in Paris: Samaritaine in the 1st, the Bazar de l'Hôtel de Ville (BHV) in the 4th and Bon Marché in the 7th, although each has its own character and specialities. All the *grands magasins* offer their own credit cards, which entitle you to rebates, credits and discounts throughout the year.

Other major shopping areas in Paris include the Montparnasse Shopping Centre at the Tour Montparnasse (in the 14th) and the adjacent neighbourhood, particularly the Rue de Rennes, the Forum des Halles and surrounding neighbourhood, and the Champs-Elysées and the area along the Rue Montaigne with its chic designer shops. Virtually every residential neighbourhood, however, has its own shops, at least for food.

Outside Paris, most towns have a cluster of smaller shops, including at least one bakery (*boulangerie/pâtisserie*), butcher's (*boucherie*) and shops selling sausages and processed meats (*charcuterie*) and prepared foods (*traiteur*). In smaller towns, the bakery or butcher's generally carries a small assortment of tinned vegetables, packaged items (rice or noodles), drinks, including alcohol, and other essential foodstuffs. Shops are normally open from 10am to 7pm, Mondays to Saturdays, smaller shops (particularly those outside Paris) closing for an hour or two at lunchtime. In some areas, smaller shops are closed all day on Mondays or, in a few cases, on Monday mornings. Those food shops (bakers', butchers', cheese shops and *traiteurs*) that are open Sunday mornings are, in most cases, closed all day on Mondays. Many small shops close for a month's holiday during the summer, but in the case of bakers' and butchers', they must display an advance notice of their closing dates, indicating what provision has been made for supplying bread and meat to their loyal customers, either at a nearby shop or with the help of a van making the rounds at a specified time each day.

Most towns (and many neighbourhoods in Paris) also have open-air street markets, usually at least once a week, and in a few places daily. In the towns, there are often signs prohibiting parking in the town centre or main square on market days. Most open-air markets are open from early morning (7 or 7.30am) to around 12.30 or 1pm, although a few markets stay open until 4 or even 5pm. For staple items or between market days, there are grocery shops (*supermarchés* or *superettes*), most of which are open six days a week until the early evening (although most local shops still close for an hour or two at lunchtimes).

For 'mass' shopping, there are shopping centres with a supermarket or hypermarket (over 2,500m^2/27,000ft^2) and a variety of other stores (for garden supplies, hardware, clothing and shoes) on the outskirts of larger towns in *Zones d'Industries* or *Zones d'Activités* (*Z.I.* or *Z.A.* on most street signs). The major hypermarkets in Ile-de-France are Auchan, Carrefour and Cora. In some areas you'll also find Champion, Intermarché, Leclerc and Shoppi as well as other chain stores, although generally these are smaller and concentrate on food and household products. The shopping centres and *zones* in and around Paris often include large, international stores, such as IKEA, Office Depot, Pier Import and Toys 'R' Us, as well as French DIY and garden chains such as Bricorama, Mr. Bricolage and Truffaut. Shopping centres are usually named after the nearby town, with the designation II ('two'), e.g. *Parly II*, *Les Ulis II*, *Velizy II*. The *Parinor* centre is on the way to Roissy-Charles de Gaulle airport, and the *Belle Epine* centre is near Orly. Some of these centres are permitted to stay open on Sundays, as they're considered part of the 'tourist trade' and thus eligible for exemption from normal retailing regulations. Centres offer large, usually free, car parks, but these can be full to overflowing on Saturday afternoons, especially in the weeks before Christmas. Most larger shops and chain stores are open continuously throughout the day (i.e. without closing at lunchtimes).

Foreign Food & Products

In the city of Paris, and increasingly in the western suburbs, there's a number of shops that specialise in imported foods, both British and American as well as from many other countries. These shops advertise in English-language publications as well as in expatriate club newsletters and frequently online. Galeries Lafayette features a British Food Hall in the old Marks & Spencer building in boulevard Haussman. The Grande Epicerie de Paris is an international grocery store, owned by Le Bon Marché (which is in turn owned by Harrods) offering foods from Britain, the USA and other countries around the world. There's also a number of small British shops throughout Paris, often owned and run by expatriates. Among the American community in Paris, Thanksgiving (in the 4th *arrondissement*) and The Real McCoy (in the 7th) are probably the best known specialist food shops, featuring many popular brands and items not normally obtainable in France.

Although the French are notoriously reluctant to import anything, many supermarkets and hypermarkets have recently established 'exotic' (i.e. foreign) food sections that offer items from Britain and the USA, as well as many Italian, North African, Chinese, Spanish and Portuguese foods.

Nevertheless, the selection of items is usually small and sometimes provides a startling (or amusing) insight into the French view of 'typical' foreign fare. For example, British food shelves often contain little more than marmalade, Heinz soups, biscuits and tea, while American 'delicacies' usually consist of microwave popcorn, cake and muffin mixes and barbecue sauce. A few imported items are also starting to appear on the shelves of some grocery shops in the Paris area, notably muffins and crumpets, American-style hamburger buns and some Australian wines and beers.

Restaurants & Bars

It goes without saying that Paris is chock full of restaurants (including over 70 Michelin-starred restaurants), bars, cafés, *bistrots* and every other sort of eating and drinking establishment. Restaurants are generally open only during meal times, i.e. from around noon to 2pm and from 7 until 11pm or midnight. Cafés, *bistrots*, *brasseries*, bars and *salons de thé* are generally open all day and offer simpler fare (salads, sandwiches and grilled dishes) at any time. It's still true that in most cafés and *bistrots* you can 'occupy' a table all day for the price of a cup of coffee or a drink while you read your newspaper, sort through your mail or chat with friends. (Generous tips help.) Most restaurants accept major credit cards, although a few of the fancier Parisian establishments still refuse to accept credit cards or cheques.

The Paris area hasn't produced any distinctive local cuisine, but it does benefit by attracting excellent bakers and chefs from all the other regions of France. The *Michelin Red* guide and the *Gault Millau* are still considered the authorities on rating (and sometimes berating) the restaurants of Paris. Dining at Michelin favourites such as the Tour d'Argent, Lasserre and Taillevent can require booking up to three months in advance (not to mention having a small fortune to burn!). But you don't need to push the boat out to dine well in Paris, and most neighbourhoods have several restaurants, often tiny establishments that may seat only a handful of people. Thanks to the immigrants and the tourists, there's a growing number of 'ethnic' restaurants in and around Paris, including a wide range of Asian restaurants (Chinese, Japanese, Thai, Cambodian, Indian and Vietnamese), Algerian and Moroccan restaurants and a small but growing selection of Mexican, South American and Caribbean establishments. In the 18th and 19th *arrondissements*, you can find Senegalese, Cameroon and other sub-Saharan African specialities. Couscous (an assortment of meats and vegetables cooked as a sort of spicy stew and served on steamed semolina) has practically become a French national dish and is very popular as a 'fast food' option for lunch.

Outside the city, almost every small town has at least one bar or restaurant, usually within walking distance of the church. The menu may vary from *sandwichs* and *steak frites* to various local and regional dishes, like *cassoulet* or *pot au feu* or the ever-popular *moules* (steamed mussels). The variety of ethnic foods may depend on the local foreign population, but most towns, even in the farthest reaches of the region, can claim at least a pizza restaurant and possibly a Chinese restaurant or take-away. Chinese *traiteurs* are becoming increasingly common in shopping centres, usually with seating available for consuming your purchases on site. There are also some surprisingly good classic French restaurants tucked away in the outer suburbs, usually with prices that are a fraction of those charged in the centre of Paris. Unfortunately, these establishments tend to close or change ownership with amazing frequency, so it isn't wise to base your choice of area on the presence of a particular restaurant! Nevertheless, sharing, comparing and debating the relative merits of newly discovered restaurants is a good (not to mention enjoyable) way to assimilate yourself into French life.

Despite their philosophical objection to *le fast food* (dubbed *le néfaste food* meaning 'unhealthy food') in general and McDonald's (*McDo's* in local parlance) in particular, the French have developed some chain restaurants of their own. *La Crée* is a chain of seafood restaurants offering reasonably priced fish and seafood (*fruits de mer*), including oysters, in a pleasant although functional setting. *La Courte Paille* ('the short straw'), whose restaurants are easily recognisable by their round, thatched roofs, offers dishes grilled over an open flame in the dining room and is popular with families, no doubt because of its basic, simply prepared meats, served with salad and *frites*, and reasonable prices. Buffalo Grill is a steak house *à la française*, complete with 'cowboys' and 'cowgirls' as waiters and waitresses. Most chain restaurants are located in or near shopping centres or industrial estates or just off busy motorway exits.

Services

International & Private Schools

For families with children, the availability of suitable schools plays a crucial role in determining the choice of area in which to live. Although many schools provide transport, this may be along specific routes only, and it may not be practical for children to travel from the outer reaches of Seine-et-Marne or Essonne, where there are few, if any, international schools or private schools with international programmes. Most international schools with English-language curricula are located in the city of Paris or in nearby towns to the west. Private schools include:

- American School of Paris (in Hauts-de-Seine at 41 rue Pasteur, BP 82, 92216 Saint-Cloud, ☎ 01 41 12 82 82, 💻 www. asparis.org);
- The British School of Paris (in Yvelines at 38 quai de l'Ecluse, 78290 Croissy-sur-Seine, ☎ 01 34 80 45 90, 💻 www.britishschool.fr);
- Marymount International (an independent Catholic school in Hauts-de-Seine at 72 boulevard de la Saussaye, 92200 Neuilly-sur-Seine, ☎ 01 46 24 10 51, 💻 www.ecole-marymount.fr);
- International School of Paris (in the 16th *arrondissement* at 6 rue Beethoven, 75016 Paris, ☎ 01 42 24 09 54, 💻 www.isparis.edu).

There's also a number of private bilingual or trilingual schools, such as the Ecole active bilingue (70 rue du Théâtre, 75015 Paris, ☎ 01 44 37 00 80, 💻 www.eabjm.com) with three locations in Paris (in the 7th and 15th), according to age group) and Eurécole (in the 16th at 5 rue de Lübeck, 75116 Paris, ☎ 01 40 70 12 81, 💻 www.eurecole.com), which teaches sports in English, art in German and other subjects in French for primary students (up to around age ten). Other schools in the region which cater for English-speaking students are the Ecole nouvelle privée Emilie-Brandt (12 rue du Parc, 92300 LEvallois-Perret, ☎ 01 47 58 53 40, 💻 www.emiliebrandt.fr) in Levallois-Perret and the Lycée (☎ 01 46 26 60 10) in Sèvre (both in 92).

Both the British and American Embassies maintain lists of international and bilingual schools on their websites, and every other year the Association of American Wives of Europeans (AAWE, 34 avenue de New York, 75116 Paris, 💻 www.aaweparis.org) holds an 'open house' where local private schools promote their services to prospective students and their parents.

Admission to international, private and multi-lingual schools is usually on a competitive basis, involving entrance exams and interviews of the prospective student and family members. Private schools can be expensive (costing €2,000 to €5,000 or more per term), and many have an ever-changing student population, as they cater for the itinerant expatriate executive community.

A few French state schools offer international programmes, bilingual tracks or special language sections, which can be ideal for children (as well as for their parents, who don't have to pay tuition fees!). Being a native speaker of English doesn't guarantee a student a place in the English section of a state-sponsored international programme, although it certainly helps. The French school system favours students who demonstrate particular aptitudes in maths and the sciences and will look favourably upon English-speaking students who excel in these areas.

At kindergarten and nursery school level, there are many English-language and bilingual programmes available throughout Paris, including Montessori schools, which are particularly popular with the French. Many expatriate clubs run or arrange play-groups and informal day activities in English for pre-school children.

As far as post-secondary education or further education for adults is concerned, there are university level programmes conducted in English in and around Paris, e.g. at the American University in Paris, New York University in France, Schiller International University and at several business schools offering joint French/American programmes. The UK's Open University (OU) maintains an office in Neuilly-sur-Seine (92), where you can obtain information about its distance learning courses and degree programmes and attend tutoring sessions for the courses once you're enrolled. Details can be found on the OU website (💻 www.open.ac.uk).

Language Schools

There's a wide variety of classes, courses and language learning programmes available in the Paris area, and your choice will depend largely on how much time and money you have or want to spend. The world-famous and highly regarded Sorbonne Language and Culture programme offers all levels and intensities of French lessons for prices ranging from €2,500 for a beginner's summer course to nearly €20,000 for a year's intensive instruction in both the language and culture of France. The Alliance française (AF, 💻 www.alliancefr.org) is popular with many expatriates, as they can start language training in their home countries and continue the same programme on arrival in France. The AF in Paris offers a variety of courses costing from €45 per week (for six hours' tuition) to €200 (for 20 hours in a single week). Individual tuition at the AF costs from €45 per hour. The AF school is on the boulevard Raspail in the 6th *arrondissement*.

Both the Alliance française and the Sorbonne are part of the French government's *francophonie* mission to promote and encourage the study and use of the French language throughout the world. Teaching methods used draw heavily upon the standard teaching of foreign languages in French schools and tend to focus on grammar, translation and written language skills. While both programmes have excellent reputations for teaching French, students who are primarily interested in conversational fluency may prefer other types of programme.

There are around 30 private language schools in Paris, each specialising in a particular approach to language learning. Berlitz offers three-hour per day intensive sessions with no more than three students per class for around €550 per week and puts more emphasis on conversational skills than the Sorbonne or AF programmes. Other private schools offer four-week courses for between €200 and €500, depending on how many hours per week you can stand – usually 10 to 20. Class sizes can vary from 6 to 20 and the programme may also offer tours or lectures on French culture and history. The most popular of the private language schools include the Institut Parisien (operated by the Nouvelles Frontières travel group), Ecole Eiffel and Ecole des Roches, but there are many others. Language schools advertise heavily in expatriate newsletters and often in the travel sections of British and American newspapers. Most language schools offer 'degressive' fee scales, meaning that the hourly rates go down if you're willing to commit to a longer course, in some cases dropping as low as €3 to €4 per hour.

Language classes are also offered by the Collège franco-britannique, the British Council and the British Institute in Paris, the Open University (based in Neuilly-sur-Seine in Hauts-de-Seine) and the British School of Paris (see **International & Private Schools** above). The Anglophone Parents' Association in Chantilly in the *département* of Oise just north of Ile-de-France region organises classes for the children of English-speaking families.

Outside Paris, Berlitz and Inlingua have offices and classrooms throughout Ile-de-France and there are also the following private schools in Yvelines and Hauts-de-Seine:

- Institut international de Rambouillet in Rambouillet (78);
- Ecole Yvelines Langues in Saint-Germain-en-Laye (78);
- Ecole de la Tournelle in Septeuil (78);
- Metropolitan Languages in Boulogne (92);
- Citylangues in La Défense (92);
- France Campus in La Défense (92);
- Linguarama in Puteaux (92);
- Centre international d'Etudes in Sèvres (92).

Details of the language schools can be found on 💻 www.europa-pages.com. The French Consulate in London (see **Appendix A**) publishes a booklet called *Cours de français Langue étrangère et Stages pédagogiques du* *français Langue étrangère en France*, which includes a comprehensive list of schools, organisations and institutes providing French language courses throughout France.

There are advertisements for private tutors in most expatriate publications and newsletters, ranging from offers to swap French tuition for English practice (i.e. basically free) up to around €50 or €60 per hour for a qualified teacher. There are also a number of conversation groups, where you can practise your French under the guidance of native speakers or trained instructors. Some groups charge €8 or €10 per session (usually an hour or two), while some expatriate organisations make conversation groups or other French practice sessions a benefit of membership. It's often possible to find a local student or public school teacher who's willing to give French lessons in exchange for help with their English if you post a small card or sign in the window of your local bakery or butcher's shop.

Language training may be offered by your employer (who can count its cost towards the annual 'continuing education' levy every employer is obliged to pay).

Hospitals & Clinics

Paris is the centre of the health care and hospital industry in France and boasts the most prestigious and best-equipped hospitals in the country, although there are acknowledged shortages of some advanced technical equipment, such as CAT scanners and MRI machines. There are over 100 hospitals and clinics serving Paris and the surrounding area. Specialist facilities include maternity centres, eye and ear facilities and the world-renowned Neckar Hospital for Sick Children. Outside the *petit couronne*, there's usually a choice of at least two hospitals within a radius of 25km (15mi), wherever you live.

In Paris you can find English-speaking staff at many of the larger hospitals, but that isn't always the case outside the city, especially in the *grand couronne*. There are two private English-speaking hospitals in the Paris region: The Hertford British Hospital (also known as the Hôpital franco-britannique) in Levallois-Perret (92), and the American Hospital of Paris, which is actually in Neuilly (92). Both hospitals offer English-speaking staff and British and American-trained doctors. Fees and charges at both hospitals can usually be reclaimed through the French social security system and most complementary insurance providers (*mutuelles*). For those with private expatriate insurance, some forms of treatment or extended stay may require pre-approval from your insurance company. The American Hospital also serves as something of a social centre for the English-speaking community in Paris and the western suburbs, hosting lectures and discussions on a variety of health care topics.

Tradesmen

The main source for English-speaking workers and tradesmen is *France-USA Contacts* (*FUSAC*), a free bi-weekly magazine consisting of small advertisements (see **English-language Media** below). You can also locate handymen, computer repair technicians, satellite installers, etc. through the various expatriate clubs (see **Clubs** on page 357), as this sort of work is popular with expatriates whose residence status is still 'undetermined'. Note, however, that it's strictly illegal in France to hire undocumented or unlicensed workers, although cases against individuals aren't often prosecuted. Magazines such as *French Property News* and newspapers such as *The News* (see **Appendix B**) carry advertisements by English-speaking tradesmen. French tradesmen are unlikely to speak much English but are generally reliable – and have the advantage that they often take several months to submit an invoice!

English-language Media

Radio France internationale (RFI) broadcasts in English for three-and-a-half hours every day in the Paris region on 738MW: a one-hour news and magazine programme at 7am, including a French lesson; a one-hour news programme at 2pm (replaced on Sundays by a report on cultural events in France); and a one-and-a-half hour news and magazine programme at 4.30pm. Long-awaited but still not 'live' is Paris Live Radio (💻 www.parislive.fm), billed as France's first English-language radio station; perhaps the Académie française is sabotaging it ...

You may be able to receive BBC Radio 4 on long wave (198) in some parts of the region. BBC Radio 1, 2, 3, and 4 can be received on your television via the Astra satellite, and you can listen to recordings of radio programmes on Radio 1, 2, 3, 4, 5, 6 and 1Extra on your computer via the internet (go to 💻 www.bbc.co.uk/radio/aod/index.shtml). The World Service can be received on 648MW in some parts, as well as on short wave in all areas (for frequency details, go to 💻 www.bbc.co.uk/worldservice/schedules/frequencies/ eurwfreq.shtml) and via the Astra satellite. Local music stations usually broadcast 60 per cent non-French language songs, most of which are in English.

English language newspapers are generally available at many of the larger newsstands and kiosks in Paris and much of the surrounding area. The *International Herald Tribune* is published in Paris and is considered by many to be the leading journal for the expatriate community. *The Financial Times* and *USA Today* are also available throughout the region on a same-day basis. In the city, it's often possible to find same-day copies of the London *Times* or the *Guardian* at 'international' newsstands. In addition, many newsstands carry the *Economist* and the international editions of American news weeklies such as *Time* and *Newsweek*. Home delivery of newspapers, including English-language dailies, is sometimes available, but outside Paris receipt on the day of publication isn't always guaranteed.

In the Paris region, there are a number of locally published English-language magazines and guides, including *Paris Voice*, *France-USA Contacts* (*FUSAC*), and *Irish Eyes*. These are available on subscription or free at pick-up points around the city, including shops, schools, most English-language clubs and many 'ethnic' restaurants with a large English-speaking clientele. (Mexican restaurants seem to be a particularly popular distribution point.) *FUSAC* is a collection of advertisements, including ads for jobs, apartments, dating services, classes, and even personal ads. *Paris Voice* and *Irish Eyes* are general interest magazines, geared towards the American and Irish communities respectively.

Paris has several English-language bookshops, including WH Smith for British books and Brentano's for American publications. There are several shops specialising in buying and selling used books in English, such as Tea and Tattered Pages, which also boasts its own café. Outside Paris, it can be difficult to find English-language titles in local shops, although in the western suburbs, boot and rummage sales organised by international schools and expatriate organisations are a popular way of picking up (and disposing of) used books. Some expatriate clubs also maintain 'swapping libraries' to share titles among their members.

Embassies & Consulates

Being the national capital, Paris is home to the embassies and consulates of every country that has diplomatic relations with France. Addresses and phone numbers can be found in telephone directories under 'Ambassades'. Both Britain and the USA have separate embassies and consulates (see **Useful Addresses** on page 373), although they aren't far apart. Generally speaking, for matters relating to individuals living in France, you'll need to contact the consulate; embassies tend to deal with political and business matters. Both the British and American embassies maintain websites (www.britishembassy.gov.uk and www.amb-usa.fr) containing a considerable amount of information for their expatriates living in France. Be sure to check your embassy or consulate's opening hours before making a trip into Paris, as many (including the British and American embassies) have very limited public office hours. Strict security measures at all diplomatic missions mean that foreign nationals living in or around Paris are encouraged to conduct most business (including registration and passport renewal) by post.

Places of Worship

There are places of worship for most religions in Paris, including many offering English-language services. For example, there's a number of Anglican churches, including Saint Michael's (in the 8th *arrondissement* opposite the British Embassy) and Saint George's in the 16th, Saint Joseph's Roman Catholic Church in the 8th, a Church of Scotland (Presbyterian), an American Church (7th) and the American Cathedral (8th). Several of the English-speaking churches in Paris also serve as community centres, offering meeting rooms and social programmes for the Anglophone community.

Outside Paris, there are churches in the following towns which hold regular services in English:

- Fontainebleau (77) – Chapelle du Lycée Saint-Aspais;
- Versailles (78) – Saint Mark's;
- Gif-sur-Yvette near Chevry (91) – Eglise Saint-Paul;
- Maisons-Lafitte (78) – Holy Trinity Church;
- Rueil-Malmaison (92) – Emmanuel Baptist Church.

Saint Peter's Anglican church in Chantilly (in Oise, just outside Ile-de-France) also holds English-language services.

There are also English services for Jews, Buddhists, Jehovah's Witnesses and Latter Day Saints (Mormons), although some may be held in the church hall of another denomination or in rented premises. There are mosques in every *arrondissement* of Paris as well as at least a dozen in each of the other *départements* of Ile-de-France (over 30 in Seine-Saint-Denis); details can be found on http://mosquee.free.fr. There are also numerous synagogues in Paris (for details, go to 💻 www.feujcity.com, where there's also information about Kosher food shops and restaurants, Jewish clubs, associations and schools, etc.), one in Yvelines, two each in Seine-et-Marne and Essonne, four in Val-d'Oise, five in Seine-Saint-Denis, six in Hauts-de-Seine and eight in Val-de-Marne, details of which can be found on 💻 www.pagesjaunes.fr (enter 'Synagogues' in the first box and the name of the *département* or town).

Clubs

The Paris area is home to a huge number of clubs and societies founded and run by groups of expatriates. In fact, the choice can be literally overwhelming (one of the biggest problems for many expatriate clubs is scheduling their events so as not to conflict with each other!). Clubs include:

- Arts groups, including The English Cathedral Choir of Paris, The International Players (an amateur drama group), the Paris Decorative and Fine Arts Society and The Royal Scottish Country Dance Society;
- English-speaking sports clubs in the region, including the British Rugby Club of Paris in Saint-Cyr-l'Ecole (78), the Standard Athletic Club in Meudon-la-Forêt (92) and the Thoiry Cricket Club in Château-de-Thoiry (78);
- Miscellaneous – e.g. the Association France Grande-Bretagne, The British Freemasons in France, the French branches of British Guides and Scouts in Foreign Countries, The English-speaking Union France, The Royal British Legion for ex-servicemen, The Salvation Army and the TOC H Association for elderly people;
- National groups – e.g. the Association franco-écossaise, The Clan MacLeod society of France, The Caledonian Society of France, The Paris Welsh Society and The Royal Society of Saint George;
- Professional associations – e.g. The Association of British Accountants in France, The Chartered Management Institute, The Institute of Directors, The Institution of Civil Engineers and The Institution of Electrical Engineers;
- University-based groups – e.g. The Alumnae Club of Paris, the Alumni of the University of Edinburgh in France, The Cambridge Society of Paris and The Oxford University Club;

- Women's clubs – e.g. American Women's Group of Paris, The British and Commonwealth Women's Association, the International Women's Club and MESSAGE – the Mother Support Group.

There's also an English Language Library for the blind in the 17th *arrondissement*. A list of the most popular organisations is available from the American Consulate (see page 373) or through the British Consulate's British Community Committee (💻 www.britishinfrance.com). Both lists are included in the consulates' websites and are updated regularly. The British Consulate also publishes a free *Digest of British and Franco-British Clubs, Societies and Institutions*, most of which are in Ile-de-France.

During October, many organisations hold 'open houses' or other events to welcome new expatriates, and the popular 'Bloom Where You Are Planted' programme, organised by and at the American Church in Paris, invites representatives from the various clubs and expatriate associations in Paris to speak at its orientation sessions. Participants in the 'Bloom' programme receive a copy of the guidebook published for use in the sessions. If you can't attend in person, copies of the programme handbook are on sale at WH Smith and other English-language bookshops in Paris. Most clubs and associations in Paris shut during July and August, when many members join the Parisian exodus to the countryside or head home, so if you arrive in the summer don't be discouraged at the lack of activity; by October, there will be more than you can handle.

On the fringes of Ile-de-France, there may not be many groups accessible to non-French speakers unless you're in an area with a concentration of foreigners, such as Fontainebleau or Versailles. Private and international schools (see page 349) generally have an active parents' association and often need volunteers to help organise and run after-school activities for students.

For French speakers, the Accueil des Villes françaises (AVF), a French organisation designed to welcome newcomers to an area, is an option (there's often at least one fluent English-speaker in each group). There are over 65 AVF groups in Ile-de-France region, including 19 in Hauts-de-Seine and 24 in Yvelines, although there are only two in Paris itself. The website (💻 www.avf.asso.fr) includes a directory (*annuaire*) of local groups by *département* as well as an online form for contacting your local AVF before you move to the area. Listings indicate whether information and services are available in English or other languages. Other sources for clubs in the area are *The News* (see **Appendix B**) and English-speaking churches (see above).

Property

Although Paris itself is the world's most visited city, the residents of Ile-de-France don't spend their holidays there, abandoning it almost totally to foreign tourists in July and August. Therefore, there's little in the way of holiday homes, timeshares or tourist communities, such as can be found in mountain or coastal resort areas of France. Residential property in Ile-de-France is automatically considered to be a 'primary residence' (*résidence principale*). You're also far less likely than in almost any other area of France to find a tumble-down farm or *château* going for a song that you can 'fix up' as a second home. Even virtual ruins can command top prices, in accordance with the property value mantra: 'location, location, location'.

Not surprisingly, the rate of new building in Paris and the major surrounding towns is low or – in the case of Evry (91), Rueil-Malmaison (92) and Sarcelles (95) – virtually non-existent. However, many areas on the edges of Ile-de-France are undergoing something of a construction boom, as land previously held for agriculture is gradually being converted to housing estates. Along the *routes nationales* of Seine-et-Marne, Essonne, Yvelines, and at the outer limits of Val-d'Oise, you're likely to see signs directing you to housing estates in the process of construction, with countdowns of the number of homes or plots left to sell.

Given an average property price per m^2 of €5,500, meaning that a 100m^2 apartment costs in excess of €500,000, it's also little surprise that fewer than 30 per cent of properties are owned, compared to well over 50 per cent in the rest of France.

There are at least half a dozen weekly publications, costing between €2 and €5 and available at newsstands throughout the region, which are dedicated to property advertisements, both for rent and for sale. *De Particulier à Particulier*, one such journal that carries only direct ads (i.e. where sellers are trying to avoid an estate agent's hefty commission), devotes almost half of its 300 to 400 pages each week to properties in Ile-de-France region. Other property advertising journals concentrate on new properties or focus on 'luxury' properties. There are also many estate agents throughout the region, including the American franchise, Century 21, which handles both purchases and rentals as well as land, commercial property and property management, although most estate agents cover limited areas of the city and it can be worthwhile using a foreign-based buying agent, who will deal with several local agencies to find suitable properties for you to view. Many estate agencies and property publications have websites, with search functions to help you narrow your choice by specifying a price range, size, location or other criteria (see also **Appendix C**).

Typical Homes

Homes in and around Paris tend to be small by British and (particularly) American standards, whether apartments or houses. In fact, they're small even by French standards: the average Parisian home consists of 3.18 rooms compared with the national average of 3.86, and only just over 20 per cent of Parisian homes have four rooms or more (the lowest percentage of any major town in France). In the centre of Paris, it's possible to find single room lodgings as small as $9m^2$ ($90ft^2$) where you share toilet and shower facilities with your neighbours. A house or apartment of 85 to $100m^2$ is considered standard for a small family, i.e. with up to two children. Any residence over $100m^2$ is considered large – even luxurious – and may be priced accordingly.

Most residential buildings are made of stone or concrete block and are sturdily built. Older buildings in the centre of Paris and the surrounding towns are highly sought after, even though their architecture may limit the modern conveniences that can be installed. Many Parisians, in particular, prefer 'authenticity' to sleek, modern architecture and the latest gadgets. Many older buildings of six or seven floors have no passenger lift simply because there isn't enough space in which to install one. Even apartment blocks that boast of an *ascenseur* may have only a one or two-passenger cage-style lift tucked into a corner of the spiral staircase, sometimes only available to upper floor residents by means of a key or code.

Not surprisingly, Paris has the highest proportion of old properties of any major town in France: over 65 per cent of buildings date from before 1950 (compared with less than 20 per cent in Montpellier, for example), and in certain areas (e.g. the 2nd *arrondissement*), over 90 per cent of properties were built before the first world war. Paris also has the highest proportion of homes without a bath or shower and a high percentage (10 per cent) of vacant properties. Saint-Denis (93) has the lowest percentage of property owners (22 per cent) of any major town in France.

Apartment buildings, whether new or old, tend to have rather plain, boxy exteriors, architectural niceties being saved for the interiors. It's possible to find some spectacular apartments – featuring ornately carved mouldings, high ceilings and wooden flooring that creaks when you walk on it – concealed in apparently unremarkable buildings. *Franciliens* tend to create their own privacy zone within and around their homes. Windows are usually small, particularly those looking onto the street, and most homes have shutters (*volets*) to exclude the outside world when appropriate, both at night and when the family is away. Larger windows and balconies or terraces are reserved for the side of the home that faces away from the street, whether into a communal courtyard or a private garden. Most houses are protected by walls, tall fences or hedgerows, with high gates (often locked) at the entrances to the front door and drive or garage.

In older buildings, many apartments have long, narrow, airless corridors, with small rooms leading off on both sides. Floor plans are often haphazard, as large single residences have been split into individual flats and space made for electrical wiring, plumbing and telephone services not in existence when the buildings were first constructed. Tiny toilets are often sandwiched between rooms wherever plumbing connections are convenient, and traditional French 'bathrooms' (sometimes referred to as *salles d'eau*) normally contain only a basin and bathtub or shower – no toilet. Kitchens tend to be small and may come fully equipped or with just basic appliances (sink, cooker and maybe a refrigerator). In some cases, you must install your own cupboards or shelving. The water heater and gas or electricity meters may be simply hung on the wall or contained in a utility box, usually in the kitchen.

Apartments in newer buildings are more likely to boast a '*cuisine américaine*', which means that the kitchen is open to the adjoining room (usually the lounge or dining room) or separated only by a counter. Newer apartment blocks are more likely to have spacious lifts and may even have a garage, usually directly underneath the building. Houses, both detached and semi-detached, still exist in a few areas of Paris, although they don't come onto the market very often.

Apartments can also be found outside the centres of Paris and other large towns. These may be above shops or in newly constructed apartment blocks, complete with parking facilities and nearby shops. However, the ideal for many *Franciliens* is to have their own house with a (sometimes very small) piece of land, and in most cases detached houses are the norm. Older houses are solidly built and often meticulously fitted out and decorated inside. However, there are also many older properties that are falling into disrepair. New homes are mostly built to standard designs and may or may not include kitchen appliances and other fittings. *Franciliens* tend to be traditional in their decorating tastes, and it's rare to find a house decked out with state-of-the-art appliances or with a highly unusual layout or styling. Most interior walls are built in cement block, so modifications are difficult or impossible to make, particularly if they involve knocking through a supporting wall.

Houses in estates or in the centre of even the smallest town must usually conform to a particular style, and there are numerous restrictions on house design: distance from property boundaries, location of windows (so as not to disturb the neighbours' privacy), maximum height, etc. Houses located near restricted land (agricultural or forest) may be subject to special land use regulations. If you buy an existing house, you may not be permitted to cut down trees, add additional rooms or even build a terrace or garage unless your plans can be justified to the local and regional officials, irrespective of much of the surrounding land you own.

Cost of Property

Not surprisingly, property prices in Ile-de-France are the highest in France. The five French towns and cities with the highest average property prices are all in Ile-de-France, the average home in Neuilly-sur-Seine (92) costing on average almost ten times as much as the average house in Montluçon in Auvergne, five times as much as in Toulouse, twice as much as in Cannes and Antibes and over 60 per cent more even than in Paris. (A small consolation is that property taxes in Neuilly are the lowest in France!) Ile-de-France's lowest average property prices are to be found in Sarcelles (95), where property taxes are also relatively low.

Property prices in Paris are similar to those in other international cities (e.g. London). In central Paris, €200,000 barely buys a one-bedroom apartment in some areas and it isn't unusual to pay €2m for a luxury apartment in a fashionable area. Prices are calculated per m², ranging from around €3,500 in the cheaper areas to €8,000 or more for a luxury property in the chic 8th and 16th districts (*arrondissement*). The average price of property in each district in August 2006 is given below. (For comparison, the average price of apartments in most other cities is between €1,000 and €1,500 per m².)

Arrondissement	Average Price per m²
1	€6,600
2	€5,600
3	€6,000
4	€7,300
5	€6,800
6	€8,000
7	€7,300
8	€6,600

9	€5,200
10	€4,500
11	€4,900
12	€4,900
13	€5,100
14	€5,500
15	€5,600
16	€6,100
17	€5,300
18	€4,000
19	€3,900
20	€4,300

The table below gives the average selling price of houses in 2006. Note, however, that house sizes vary from area to area, which can distort average figures.

Arrondissement	Average House Price			
	2-bed	3-bed	4-bed	5+-bed
1	€600,000	€835,000	€1.2m	€2m
2	€510,000	€1m	€1.25m	€2.65m
3	€480,000	€830,000	€1.15m	€1.5m
4	€520,000	€800,000	€1.6m	€2m
6	€520,000	€785,000	€1.2m	€2.1m
7	€610,000	€945,000	€1.1m	€1.6m
8	€400,000	€910,000	€1.25m	€2.2m
16	€660,000	€1.05m	€1.6m	€2.9m
17	€600,000	€865,000	€1.25m	€2.3m

The following is a guide to the property market in each *arrondissement* in late 2006, by courtesy of Intransit International (💻 www.intransit-international.com):

- **1st** – the geographical centre of the city, including the touristy Ile de la Cité (site of Notre Dame cathedral) and the 'quiet' residential Ile Saint-Louis, where property is among the capital's most expensive at up to €17,500 per m^2; apartments on the Place Vendôme rue de Rivoli and rue Saint-Honoré, rubbing shoulders with glitzy hotels and exclusive jewellers', cost a 'mere' €7,000 per m^2; more modest prices (below €6,000 per m^2) are to be found around Les Halles, the former fruit and vegetable market regenerated into the city's largest shopping precinct; most properties are small (between around 50 and 75m^2).
- **2nd** – prices in the lively pedestrianised Montorgueil district, with its 17th-century buildings divided into small apartments, start at an affordable €5,000 per m^2.
- **3rd & 4th** – also incorporating part of the Ile de la Cité and Ile Saint-Louis (see above), the 3rd and 4th *arrondissements* include the medieval Marais district, where there's a large Orthodox Jewish community and an 'alternative lifestyle' scene; the cheapest property is to be found in the 3rd (from €5,000 per m^2); the Marais' main feature is the Place des Vosges, the capital's oldest square, where a three-bedroom apartment will cost at least €2.5m.
- **5th** – south of the river (i.e. on the left bank), the area known as the Latin Quarter features desirable riverside residences (along the Quai de Tournelle) and vast apartments in the Place Panthéon costing well over €10,000 per m^2 but also more modest abodes in medieval buildings with small courtyards, where a fully renovated apartment costs from around €6,000m^2.
- **6th** – an expensive district, especially so along the river (Quai de Conti and Quai Voltaire), where a three-bedroom house costs around €2.5m, in chic Saint-Germain-des-Prés, where top-floor apartments can cost €2m, and overlooking the Jardins du Luxembourg (€8,500 per m^2).
- **7th** – among the museums, galleries and other tourist attractions (principally the Eiffel Tower and Invalides) are leafy residential areas of impressive early 20th-century buildings; a river view costs upwards of €8,000 per m^2, an apartment overlooking the Invalides at least €8,500 per m^2 and a three-bedroom top-floor apartment facing the Champ de

Mars and the Eiffel Tower up to €2m; even a parking space can cost €40,000.

- **8th** – the few residential properties on the Champs-Elysées cost at least €8,000 per m^2, while those between the famous avenue and the river start at €10,000; if you have to ask the price of an apartment on the Rue du Faubourg-Saint-Honoré, where foreign embassies and fashion houses vie for attention, you cannot afford it.
- **9th** – a predominantly (and relatively) downmarket district, the 9th boasts some grand properties along the Boulevard Haussmann, site of the major department stores, where a two-bedroom apartment can set you back €800,000.
- **10th** – a multi-cultural neighbourhood dominated by the Gare de l'Est and the Gare du Nord but also including the attractive Canal Saint-Martin, which has become a trendy and somewhat bohemian area; a two-bedroom apartment facing the canal can cost around €800,000, while a three-bedroom apartment elsewhere can be had for €650,000 and a two-bedroom near the Gare du Nord for as little as €250,000.
- **13th** – next to the 5th *arrondissement* but with much lower prices, the 13th includes the Gobelins area (famed for its tapestry works) and is generally green and quiet; renovation projects can be found for under €4,000 per m^2 and few properties exceed €6,000.
- **15th** – the area between the Eiffel Tower and the Montparnasse Tower, the 15th is being regenerated and offers good investment potential, with one-bedroom apartments starting at €375,000.
- **16th** – away from the tourists (apart from those who venture as far as the Arc de Triomphe and Trocadéro), this smart district bordering the Bois de Boulogne and close to the Défense business area is nevertheless relatively affordable, apartments starting around €6,000 per m^2, though the most sought-after addresses (e.g. on avenue Victor Hugo) cost up to €10,000.
- **18th** – the famous Montmartre area offers a mixture of upmarket townhouses near the Sacré-Coeur and seedy apartments in the red light districts of Clichy and Pigalle (although these have been 'cleaned up' considerably in recent years); a hilltop studio apartment costs from around €125,000.

- **20th** – Paris's cheapest district, famous for the Père Lachaise cemetery, still offers properties for renovation costing under €4,000 per m², though the area is becoming 'gentrified'.

Potential buyers should also keep an eye on the run-down Batignolles district, in line for renovation under Mayor Delanoë, who plans to create a park in north-west Paris – no doubt with appealing adjacent property. The business district of La Défense just west of the city is to be further developed with a 2km 'corridor' of green space lined with 290,000m² of residential property and 205,000m² of retail and amenity property. Outside the city, property 'hotspots' include the area beyond Versailles to the west, where there are four-bedroom detached properties in villages such as Montfort-l'Amaury and Thoiry costing as little as €375,000, and the former industrial areas to the east, due for regeneration and therefore ripe for investment; the Domaine du Golf, near Disneyland, is a new estate where three-bedroom townhouses start at around €300,000.

Features and factors that increase prices include proximity to shops and restaurants, nearby access to public transport, a 'quiet' neighbourhood or nearby parks, availability of parking, a terrace, balcony or courtyard, a lift, and location in a building of '*grand standing*' (which can mean either a luxury building or one of established reputation).

Most apartments are part of a 'community property' (*co-propriété*) arrangement, where residents share common costs (e.g. lighting in hallways, maintenance of lifts, *gardien*'s (caretaker's – salary, etc.) and building maintenance charges. When it's time to paint or sandblast the exterior of the building, mend the roof or substitute a digi-code system for the *gardien* who's retiring, you'll be summoned to a meeting to vote on the work, and then be assessed your share of the costs. *Co-propriété* meetings can become very heated and 'political', and of course the proceedings are governed by an entire body of rules and regulations decreed by the state.

If a Parisian house comes onto the market, you should expect to pay €250,000 to €300,000 for a mere 60 or 70m² in an outer *arrondissement* (e.g. the 18th and 19th). In more desirable districts (e.g. the 12th, 13th and 17th), a house priced under €500,000 is liable to need 'some work' (i.e. be virtually uninhabitable without major renovation).

Outside Paris there's a wide range of apartments and houses on offer, with prices starting at around €150,000 and depending on factors such as location and ease of access to Paris (by motorway or public transport) as well as size and amount of land, restrictions on building or renovation, and general condition of the property. Prices for properties just outside the city limits are often virtually identical to those in Paris itself, particularly in upmarket parts of Neuilly-sur-Seine, Boulogne-Billancourt and Issy-les-Moulineaux. Generally speaking, the farther away from Paris, the lower the prices, except for homes in and around Versailles, a highly desirable residential area having large homes with spacious grounds. To a lesser extent, residential property in or very close to a town centre with shops and access to public transport and other services is more expensive than property in the countryside, some distance from town services and conveniences.

If you have money to burn, you can always splash out on a *château*, *manoir*, or other *propriété de caractère*, complete with extensive grounds, woods, equestrian facilities or other special features, starting at around €750,000. This sort of property is generally to be found in the outer reaches of the region, although now and then a spectacular *maison de ville* or other unusual residence comes up for sale in the *petit couronne*. There are entire publications dedicated to larger and more elegant residences, such as Demeures de Charme, produced by the publishers of De Particulier à Particulier (see **Appendix B**).

Land

Close to Paris, not surprisingly, most building land is already built upon. However, many areas on the edges of Ile-de-France are undergoing something of a construction boom, as land previously held for agriculture is gradually being converted to housing estates. Where large tracts of land have been reclassified for residential use, plots are normally sold to builders, who then package them with a house built to one of their standard designs. The advantage of this arrangement is that the builder has already secured the necessary permits, although you won't obtain an individually designed home. Within a housing estate, there may be several builders offering similar land-plus-building options, costing around €300,000 for a finished home.

In the western suburbs of Paris, a plot ready to build on (not part of a housing estate) and with access to all mains services costs between €250 and €500 per m^2. As with housing costs, the further out you go, the lower the costs. In the outer reaches of Essonne or Seine-et-Marne, for example, land prices are between €100 and €200 per m^2.

If you're considering building your own home, note that houses in the suburbs must conform closely to local standards, which are carefully monitored by town officials. There are strict rules regarding the placement of a house on a plot, as well as restrictions on the positioning of windows, so as not to invade the privacy of neighbours. It's unlikely that you will be able to obtain building permission for a radically styled house that clashes with the general ambiance of your town or village. In fact, in most towns, you're limited to a prescribed choice of colours if you choose to paint the exterior.

If you hire an architect and independent construction company to design and build a house on your own piece of land, expect to pay at least €200,000 over and above the cost of the land. 'Mass-market' construction companies normally offer a range of standard house plans that can be built for as little as €100,000 for a small, basic home. This type of standardised home will meet most communes' requirements, although it may not be the last word in originality.

Rental Accommodation

In Paris itself, monthly rents start at around €500 for a studio apartment (which can be as small as 20m²/200ft²), to which you normally need to add 10 to 20 per cent for charges such as water, rubbish collection and communal costs (e.g. maintenance of common areas or the services of a *gardien*). Even smaller flats (called *studettes* in the adverts) can be found for as 'little' as €350 per month, fully furnished (how much furniture can you fit in a 10m² room?). These tiny units, often converted maid's quarters in older buildings and sometimes with shared bathrooms or toilets, are highly sought-after by students and others on a limited budget.

Three-room apartments (i.e. two bedrooms and a living room) are the standard rental accommodation, prices ranging from around €1,000 per month to €2,000 or more, depending on the size of the apartment, equipment included and, of course, location. Charges are sometimes included in the quoted price, but you should usually allow an additional €75 to €200 per month if they aren't part of the basic rent. Apartments in older buildings (sometimes centuries old) are highly sought after and rents can be sky high (as much as €10,000 per month) in buildings of 'character' in desirable districts, such as along the Champs-Elysées (where there are still a few private apartments), in certain neighbourhoods in the 16th and nestled among the designer shops in parts of the 8th.

Outside Paris, you can find both apartments and houses for rent, costs generally declining as you move away from the city. It's possible to rent a three-room apartment with 75m² of living space for less than €1,000 per month in many areas of the *grand couronne*. There's a premium to be paid, of course, for flats that include parking space and those located close to shopping, public transport and other amenities. Monthly rents for detached houses start at around €1,000 for a house of around 70 to 85m² with a small garden (e.g. 300 to 500m²), prices varying according to similar factors as for an apartment (see above).

For an overview of rents throughout Ile-de-France region, consult the publication *De Particulier à Particulier* (see **Appendix B**), which is also available online in searchable form and in English (🖳 www.pap.fr).

Communications

Air

Both of France's major international airports are located in Ile-de-France. Charles de Gaulle (CDG), also known as Roissy-Charles de Gaulle or simply Roissy, after the town in which the airport is located, is 27km (17mi) north of the city, just off the A1 motorway, while Orly, in the town of Antony, is 16km (10mi) south of the city, just off the N186. Between them, they handle flights from almost every part of the world. Around 25m passengers use Orly every year, and twice as many pass through CDG. Most long-haul flights arrive and depart from CDG, while Orly handles many inter-European flights and all flights of a few smaller airlines not accorded gate space at CDG.

Both airports offer taxi, private coach and public transport connections to Paris, and there's a *TGV* station at CDG, which is handy for those making connections to the farthest corners of France. The B line of the *RER* (see below) runs out to CDG, where there are two stations, one for each of the main terminals. At the southern end of the same line, a special rail connection, called the *Orlyval*, takes you from the Antony stop directly to the airport terminals at Orly. There are frequent shuttle buses between the two airports for those making connections (or for those who live closer to the 'wrong' airport for their travel needs). Most local taxis outside Paris have special rates for passengers going to either of the two airports, and you can often arrange with your local taxi service to pick you up at the airport on your return. For those who drive to the airport, there are long-term car parks at both CDG and Orly, which charge a flat fee per day (currently €10.70) irrespective of how long you leave your car. Even for short periods, this can be cheaper than taking a taxi from your home to the airport and saves you the inconvenience of having to carry heavy luggage on buses or trains.

Plans to construct a third 'Paris' airport to the north of the city in the town of Soissons, well outside Ile-de-France region (actually some 120km/75mi from the centre of Paris!) have raised considerable controversy, over both the location and the question of whether a third airport is actually needed in the light of expansion plans for Roissy-Charles de Gaulle. In mid-2002, the government rejected the plan, which in any case would take at least ten years to realise.

Details of all French airports and their services can be found on 💻 www.aeroport.fr.

Public Transport

Paris is easily accessible from Brussels and London. Paris is easily accessible by *TGV* from Brussels and London. The Eurostar from London takes around two hours and 40 minutes (the journey time will be reduced by around 20 minutes on 14th November 2007, when the terminal moves from Waterloo to St Pancras station). Those wishing to escape Paris can reach the furthest parts of France within a few hours (Marseille is just over three hours away). For details of the *TGV* network, see map in **Appendix E**.

Travellers within the Paris area are blessed with one of the best public transport systems in the world. Fares (which are heavily subsidised by the government) are very reasonable, the network is extensive and services are frequent and generally reliable. Those who need to commute into and out of Paris from other parts of Ile-de-France are particularly well served. Within the city and in much of the surrounding area, there's usually a choice of modes of transport, including the underground (*métro*), the *RER* (*réseau express régional* – an express commuter railway, which runs underground through the centre of Paris), traditional suburban commuter trains, buses and, in a few areas, trams.

Two-zone tickets (covering the city of Paris and all *métro* lines) cost €1.40 each or €10 for a book (*carnet*) of ten. There's a variety of reduced fares offered on both single tickets and *carnets* to students, children and senior citizens. There are also day passes covering all travel within certain zones (e.g. the *Mobicarte*), multi-day passes designed for tourists (incorporating discounts for museum and other site admission fees) and weekly and monthly passes for commuters. Employers in Ile-de-France are required to pay half of the cost of a monthly commuter pass (*carte orange*) for all employees who choose to travel to work by public transport, and the passes allow you unlimited travel within the specified zones even when you aren't commuting. Monthly *cartes oranges* range from €52.50 for the Paris two-zone area to €142.70 for an eight-zone pass that will take you beyond Ile-de-France borders.

The popularity of the Paris area public transport system has its down side, however. Transport workers (*cheminots*) are prone to strike for a day or for a few hours, on one or more lines or routes, whenever the government proposes any change to their cushy pay and benefits packages. Oddly enough (at least to most foreigners) the *Franciliens* tend to sympathise with the strikers and their cause, despite the massive inconvenience transport strikes cause. Morning news broadcasts include the extent of any strikes called for that day, and traffic reports mention routes to avoid where demonstrations (*manifestations*) are planned.

Public transport between suburbs can be much less efficient, as local bus routes are often designed primarily to feed commuters to the major railway stations or employment centres, mostly at morning and evening rush hour periods. Bus services are sometimes available during the day to nearby shopping centres or between larger cities and towns, but schedules and routes change frequently according to demand. Outside the *petit couronne*, most residents agree that a car is almost a necessity unless you live in the centre of a substantial town or within walking distance of a regional rail or bus route.

Roads

In France, and particularly in Ile-de-France region, almost all roads lead to Paris (in fact much of the French road system is based on a 'hub and spoke' pattern with roads radiating from major cities and towns). Most of the major motorways in the area fan out from the *boulevard périphérique*, the main ring road that defines the city's perimeter and connects its various 'gateways' (*portes*). Major motorways include the A1 to the north, the A13 to the west, the A4 to the east and the A6 and A10 heading south-east and south-west respectively. All of these are wide, well maintained highways, which become toll roads once you leave the metropolitan region (i.e. roughly at the outer edges of Ile-de-France) and are the main thoroughfares used by office workers and executives commuting into and out of Paris. Many residents of the outer reaches of Ile-de-France leave for work as early as 5.30 or 6.30am each morning to beat the rush, as a journey that takes 30 or 45 minutes in light traffic can easily stretch to two hours in 'normal' rush hour congestion (make that three hours if there's a strike on the underground or railways, a serious accident or heavy rain or snow!). In bad weather, at the start and end of a holiday period, and whenever there has been an accident, traffic can soon come to a standstill, with queues stretching for several kilometres.

Perhaps surprisingly, Paris doesn't have the worst road accident record among French towns, although there's a fatal accident every day on average on the *périphérique*. In fact, your chance of being killed or injured on the roads in the capital is no greater than it would be in a provincial town such as Annecy, Bayonne, Bordeaux or Clermont-Ferrand and far less than in many towns on the Mediterranean coast (see page 290). Outside Paris, Neuilly-sur-Seine (92) and Sarcelles (95) are among France's safest driving towns and Hauts-de-Seine has the lowest accident record of any *département* in France, with a 'mere' 31 deaths per million inhabitants per year. Nevertheless, driving in Paris isn't for the faint-hearted and resembles a continuous ride on the 'dodgems' at the funfair, particularly around the Place de la Concorde and the infamous Etoile! Parking is another problem in the city, where it's considered acceptable to shove other cars out of the way in order to create a space for your own (many residents leave their handbrakes off to minimise damage). To Parisians, a car is a tool rather than an ornament and is treated accordingly!

A number of 'peripheral' roads have been built to link the *villes nouvelles*. The N104 (known as the *Francilienne*) runs east-west across Essonne from near Les Ulis to Evry, where it turns northward to join the A1 close to Roissy-Charles de Gaulle airport. The N186 connects the west side of Paris to the research centre at Saclay and continues to the south of Palaiseau where it turns east, running past Orly airport. The A86 is a ring road that starts north of Paris, running out to Versailles and then forming an east-west corridor connecting Versailles with Créteil to the south; links between Versailles and Vancresson and between Rueil and Bailly (and the A12) are due to be completed in 2009 and 2012 respectively. These newer ring roads offer alternative routes to the main *autoroutes* in and out of Paris, although often they can be as congested as the *périphérique*.

By contrast, roads connecting the various suburbs, particularly between *départements* (road construction is a departmental matter), are generally smaller, not always well maintained and often lined with trees. When departmental roads pass through small towns or villages, they often narrow to one lane in each direction or even less, thanks to the placement of historic buildings and the careless parking habits of local citizens. The French love of fast driving makes town officials keen to place speed bumps and other obstacles (large cement planters are popular) on roads running through residential areas or past schools. Speed traps are fairly common in some areas, although 'helpful' French drivers generally warn oncoming traffic by flashing their headlights!

The French tradition of taking holidays for the whole of July or August means that traffic jams on the first and last weekend of these two months are nothing short of horrendous, with the very worst traffic on the weekend that marks the return of the July vacationers and the departure of those with August holidays. Jams are almost as bad during the school holidays in February or March, when many Parisian families head for the mountain regions of the Alps, the Jura, the Massif Central or the Pyrenees to take advantage of state-sponsored ski schools. Friday weather reports on radio and television generally include traffic forecasts from an agency known as *Bison futé* ('Wily Bison'), which gives predicted levels of traffic congestion using a series of colour codes: green for moderate traffic, yellow for congestion, red for severe congestion and every now and then black for 'you'd be better off walking'.

Further Information

Useful Addresses

- American Citizen Services (US Consulate), 2 rue Saint-Florentin, 75001 Paris (☎ 01 43 12 22 22)
- British Consulate, 18bis rue d'Anjou, 75008 Paris (☎ 01 44 51 31 00);
- British Community Committee, 68 quai Lois Blériot, 75016 Paris (☎ 01 45 25 28 34);
- The British Council, 9 rue Constantine, 75007 Paris (☎ 01 49 55 73 00)
- British Embassy, 35 rue du Faubourg St. Honoré, 75383 Paris Cedex 08 (☎ 01 44 51 31 00)
- US Embassy, 2 avenue Gabriel, Paris 75008 (☎ 01 43 12 22 22, 💻 www.amb-usa.fr)

Useful Publications

- *At Home in Paris* (Junior Service League of Paris)
- *Bloom Where You Are Planted* (Women of the American Church) – the handbook accompanying the annual programme at the American Church in Paris (see page 356)
- *FUSAC* (France-USA Connections) – a free fortnightly publication containing advertisements published for and by the Anglophone community in Paris
- *Paris Voice* – a free monthly journal published in English

Useful Websites

Websites for departmental *Conseils généraux* (see the following list??) are normally the best starting point for basic information on each *département* in the region and usually include links to many other services and features in the area. However, there's little or no information available in English:

- www.essonne.fr (Essonne)
- www.hauts-de-seine.net (Hauts-de-Seine – this site is actually a portal linking the *Conseil général* site and many other official sites within the *département*)
- www.seine-et-marne.fr (Seine-et-Marne)
- www.cg93.fr (Seine-Saint-Denis)
- www.cg94.net (Val-de-Marne)
- www.valdoise.fr (Val-d'Oise)
- www.cg78.fr (Yvelines)

Miscellaneous

- www.aaweparis.org – Association of American Wives of Europeans; a source for *Guide to Education*, *Vital Issues* and other publications
- www.adp.fr – ADP, the Paris airport authority; includes an English-language section
- www.amb-grandbretagne.fr – British Embassy and Consulate;
- www.amb-usa.fr – US Embassy and Consulate
- www.britishinfrance.com – British Community Committee
- www.fusac.fr – FUSAC, a free bi-weekly magazine consisting of small advertisements
- www.iledefrance.fr – information on the Ile-de-France; includes an English-language section, although not all information is available in English
- www.paris-france.org – official Paris website, with many links to city government offices and useful addresses and phone numbers; English-language version available
- www.paris-link.com – 'news, blogs, podcasts and more'
- www.parisvoice.com – site of the *Paris Voice* journal
- www.pidf.com – information on Paris and Ile-de-France

BORDEAUX

France's sixth-largest city, with around 230,000 inhabitants (750,000 including suburbs), Bordeaux is currently undergoing a transformation in a bid to achieve UNESCO World Heritage status; almost 1,000 city-centre buildings have been renovated (another 1,000 are due for renovation by 2010), some 4,000 new homes have been built since 2002 (and a further 7,000 are to be built by 2010, mostly in suburban areas), and the city's infamous traffic congestion has been relieved with a new tramway, pedestrian areas, underground car parks and a north-south road bypass (and 550km of cycle lanes). In fact, on the first Sunday of every month, cars are banned from the city centre.

Bordeaux's central 'old districts' area, where property has been listed since 1967, covers almost 150ha (375 acres) and includes 17th-, 18th- and 19th-century buildings. Each district has a distinct character: for example, Saint Michel, with its bustling markets, is cosmopolitan; Saint Pierre (known as Vieux Bordeaux) has narrow, winding streets; the Grands Hommes district boasts elegant townhouses and expensive shops; Chartrons, the former wine trading district, is being restored to its former glory. The area along the river Garonne is gradually being refurbished, through quayside property renovation, the creation of parks and gardens, annual events such as the Fête du Vin and the Fête du Fleuve (River), and the regular docking of cruise ships.

PROPERTY CHECK – BORDEAUX

Property values doubled in the first five years of the century but stabilised in 2006 and remain better value than in Nantes or Toulouse (Bordeaux's two main western rivals), though new planning regulations restrict the extension (particularly upwards) of the typical old stone houses. A basic, one-bedroom apartment in a modern block can be had for as little as €60,000, a three-bedroom apartment in a more prestigious building costs from around €200,000 and a townhouse in the city centre from €250,000. Just outside Bordeaux, for example in the market town of Libourne, country houses are available from around €300,000.

Bordeaux & Beyond (🖳 www.bordeauxbeyond.co.uk)

LYON

Voted by *Le Point* magazine in 2005 as the second-best city or town in France to live in, Lyon is second only in size to Paris, with almost half a million inhabitants in the city itself and over 3m including suburban areas. Its crime rate is the lowest of all France's major cities, the cost of living is far lower than in the capital, and it has an excellent public transport system (including four underground lines, four tram lines, three funiculars and 100 bus routes). Lyon is also famous for its gastronomy and boasts some of the world's finest restaurants, which include many offering foreign cuisine. It's a cosmopolitan city (though with a large Swiss and German population) and the various nationalities are well integrated, with no 'ghettos'. Most property is owner-occupied, the city having only around 8,000 second homes.

PROPERTY CHECK – LYON

Property values have doubled in the last five years and prices now range from €1,500 to €6,000 per m², the most expensive homes being in Bellecour, Les Brotteaux, Tête-d'Or and the old town, with Croix-Rousse and Saxe-Préfecture not far behind, and the cheapest in Charlemagne, La Guillotière and Les Terreaux. While property at the lower end of the market is selling well, however, homes over €350,000 aren't. Some areas, including Carré-de-Soie, Confluence and La Duchère, have recently been regenerated but there has been little new building owing to planning restrictions. Over half of property sales are to investors, though rents are being outstripped by property prices, making letting less and less viable. Studios in the city centre start at around €50,000, a loft-style apartment costs up to €200,000 and a three-bedroom apartment in a good area up to €500,000. A studio apartment can be let for around €10.50 per m², a one-bedroom apartment for around €9.50 and a two-bedroom for less than €9.

The city's main residential areas include the following (the numbers in brackets indicate the *arrondissement*):

- Croix Rousse (4) – a collection of 19th-century buildings on a steep hill formerly housing Lyon's silk workers and containing high-ceilinged workshops; most buildings have lifts but parking is limited; prices

8

start at around €2,750 per m² and rise to €3,750 for properties with a view over the city.

- **Monts d'Or (9)** – the 'golden mountains' are hills north-west of the city, where the upper classes used to go to escape the summer heat; some areas, such as Ecully and Saint-Foy-lès-Lyon, are popular with foreign buyers, while others, such as Saint-Cyr and Saint-Didier, house the rich and famous; apartment blocks are still being constructed and prices vary according to the area and property type.
- **Part-Dieu (3)** – Lyon's largest *arrondissement*, the 3rd is centred on the Part-Dieu business district, where some 20,000 people work; 19th-century apartments on the wide boulevards cost around €3,000 per m², while newer properties cost up to €4,000 per m².
- **Presqu'île (1 & 2)** – the 'peninsula' is a residential and business district between the rivers Rhône and Saône with narrow medieval streets in the 1st *arrondissement* and broad (largely residential) avenues with open spaces in the 2nd; period properties (from 16th to 19th century) abound, some divided into luxury apartments (which can cost up to €1m); the more commercial end of the peninsula is being regenerated, with the creation of more residential property as well as shops and leisure facilities, including a watersports lake and museum, so prices should rise significantly over the next decade; prices range from €2,000 per m² (e.g. in Perrache) to €4,000 per m² (e.g. in Ainay).
- **Tête d'Or (6)** – the sixth *arrondissement* contains some of Lyon's most exclusive property, including elegant late 19th-century Haussmann-style, Belle Epoque and post-War buildings, surrounding the vast Tête d'Or park (one of France's finest urban parks); apartments overlooking the park are highly sought after, with prices around €4,000 per m², though elsewhere in the district property costs nearer €3,000 per m².
- **Vieux-Lyon (5)** – with its cobbled streets and antiquated shop signs, this is one the largest areas of Renaissance buildings in Europe, around two-thirds of which have been restored in a long-term project; it's also Lyon's tourist centre, with 'secret' passageways and steep hills, restaurants and nightclubs; property is old, lacking modern amenities such as lifts, and, if well restored, expensive – a four-bedroom apartment costing up to €1m – though less so at the top of the Fourvière hillside and in buildings awaiting renovation.

The former industrial areas of the 7th, 8th and 9th arrondissements are being regenerated or due for regeneration; renovation projects start at around €2,000 per m², but restored properties cost up to €3,500.

Cabinet Majoux Virieux (💻 www.majoux-virieux.com); Guy Hoquet Immobilier (💻 www.guyhoquet-immobilier-lyon-5.com)

MARSEILLE

Bustling and cosmopolitan, Marseille has a generally poor reputation (even the French denigrate both the city and its inhabitants, who they say are 'mean') but it has much to offer: a growing population (currently around 800,000), a dynamic business district in the former docks, La Défense au Bord de la Mer, which, as its name suggests, is right by the sea; a sophisticated shopping and cultural scene; an attractive old town and over 30km of sandy beaches. Nearby is the Port Saint-Louis seaside development, and the popular resorts of Bandol, Cassis and La Ciotat are only a short drive away. The city's Euromediterranean project, which was launched in the mid-'90s, is France's biggest urban regeneration programme since the Défense development in western Paris in the '70s, aiming to create 20,000 jobs by attracting major businesses to the city. It involves the extension of the underground railway network and the introduction of a tram system (from 2007) to reduce traffic congestion as well as the improvement of the *TGV* service to Paris, now only three-and-a-quarter hours away. And Marseille boasts France's first purpose-built budget airline airport, opened in September 2006 in an old warehouse: MP2, where passengers carry their own luggage to the plane. Ryanair has already started 13 routes into MP2 and aims to bring a million people a year into the city.

All this development has attracted foreign and French buyers; even Parisians are starting to snap up holiday homes here.

PROPERTY CHECK – MARSEILLE

As in many other French cities, prices almost doubled in the first five years of the 21st century but slowed markedly in 2006 as buyers bide their time, particularly in the middle price range (around €3,500 per m²). New apartments in the city start at €150,000 (and garages sell for between €15,000 and €35,000

depending on the area), while near the beach apartments start at €175,000 and villas with a pool at €350,000. The main residential areas of interest to foreign buyers include the following (the numbers in brackets indicate the *arrondissement*):

- **Belle de Mai (1 & 3)** – formerly a working-class area but now a fashionable part of town, served by both the underground and tram networks, its tobacco factories converted to film studios; almost all homes are apartments, some early 19th century (costing between €1,500 and €2,000 per m²), some new (costing around €2,500 per m²); though prices are rising fast, affordable properties can still be found.
- **Bompard, Endoume & Roucas Blanc (6 & 7)** – quiet areas popular with British and American buyers on account of their sea views (which can carry a 30 per cent premium) and proximity to the beach, they offer a variety of property, mostly early 20th century but modernised, starting at €3,000 and rising to €7,500 per m²; Endoume has a mixture of houses and apartments, while most property in Roucas Blanc is houses; none of the areas is on the underground or tram network and parking space is in short supply (garages sell for between €30,000 and €35,000).
- **Les Hauteurs de Perier (8)** – a highly (literally) desirable neighbourhood with views over the Mediterranean, where property prices range between €3,000 and €6,000 per m².
- **Le Panier (2)** – Marseille's most famous *quartier*, with its maze of narrow streets (setting of the TV soap opera *Plus Belle la Vie*) lined with three-storey buildings, some dating back to the 18th century, others recently rebuilt in similar style, Le Panier is favoured by young professionals and foreign buyers who don't want to be overrun by tourists, as they would be in the centre of Nice, Cannes or even Montpellier; prices start at €2,000 per m² for renovation projects and €2,500 for renovated and modern properties, a small terraced townhouse in reasonable condition costing at least €250,000.
- **La Plaine (several)** – near the university and with a lively nightlife, this area is popular with young professionals as well as students; most property is small apartments in buildings dating from the '60s, '70s and '80s and is cheap by Marseille standards.

- **Vieux Port (1)** – mostly not as old as its name suggests – most property dates from after the Second World War, though built in traditional style – the Vieux Port is the heart of the city and prices are high: between €5,000 and €7,000 per m² for an attractive apartment overlooking the port.

Latitudes (💻 www.latitudes.co.uk); Recouly Immobilier (💻 www.immobilier-recouly.com)

MONTPELLIER

This university town has doubled in size in the last two decades, now housing some 230,000 people (over twice as many including its suburbs), and offers a wealth of attractions – including an Olympic-size swimming pool, several theatres and an opera house, and a *TGV* link with Paris – which bring some 10,000 people (including many wealthy Parisians) to the town every year in search of jobs and housing. The opening of a second tram line in December 2006 has eased congestion and there are plans for a third (linking the city with the airport); the TAM bus company operates throughout the town and suburbs; the Petibus minibus service runs in the pedestrian area of the old town (cars are banned from almost the whole town centre), as does a sightseeing train.

PROPERTY CHECK – MONTPELLIER

After a decade in which property of all types sold at practically any price almost before it had come on the market, 'For Sale' signs are becoming a more common sight in Montpellier and prices are once again negotiable – by as much as 15 per cent, though foreign buyers (who represent around half of the market) often fail to do so. Nevertheless, building continues (especially in new *quartiers* spreading towards the sea) and the letting market is buoyant, especially at the lower end of the market. A studio apartment in the city centre costs from around €70,000, a three-bedroom apartment in a 19th-century block from €300,000 and a nearby villa from €250,000.

Montpellier's residential districts include the following:

- **Aiguelongue** – Montpellier's most sought-after district, with huge mansions with up to 1,200m² of garden that sell for between €2,500 and €5,000 per m².
- **Les Arceaux** – a former working-class area, around the 'arches' of the Saint-Clément aqueduct, but now the main shopping district; ornate 1930s stone townhouses sell for up to €3,500 per m² and there are a few large detached houses with gardens.
- **Beaux-Arts & Boutonnet** – just north of the city centre, these districts have a 'village' atmosphere, their elegant late 19th-century buildings popular with foreign buyers and housing a significant Jewish community; prices start at around €1,500 per m² for a ground-floor apartment (where street noise can be invasive) and rise to around €3,500 for a top-floor apartment (most buildings have lifts).
- **Les Cévennes** – an area of affordable terraced houses costing between €1,000 and €1,500 per m² and attracting mostly young couples and families.
- **La Chamberte & Figuerolles** – predominantly working class districts with a high proportion of North African immigrants and a poor reputation but some desirable terraced houses costing between €1,000 and €2,500 per m².
- **L'Ecusson** – the pedestrianised tourist centre and oldest part of Montpellier, with diverse architecture, including 17th-19th-century buildings on the central Place de la Comédie and along the Esplanade Charles de Gaulle; renovation projects can be found for as little as €1,500 per m², while well restored apartments with a view cost up to €4,000.
- **Quartier des Hôpitaux** – a student area, studios and one-bedroom apartments costing between €1,750 and €3,000 per m².
- **Satin-Clément-de-Rivière** – a leafy 'village' featuring mansions with swimming pools, costing between €2,000 and €3,000 per m².

The new districts of Antigone, Les Aubes, Marianne Gauche and Richter, which have been created in the last two decades to accommodate university students and workers, are close to the city, the motorway, the beach, out-of-town shopping centres and

the vast new Odysseum leisure complex. Prices start at around €2,000 per m², the most expensive properties, along the river Lez, costing around €3,000 per m²; particularly sought after are Antigone's neo-classical apartments.

Laforet Immobilier (💻 www.laforet.com); Poncet & Poncet (💻 www.poncet-poncet.com)

NICE

The largest city on the Côte d'Azur, with a population of around 350,000 (1m, including its suburbs), Nice offers quick access to the Alps as well as instant access to the Mediterranean. Nice-Côte d'Azur airport is France's busiest after Paris Charles-de-Gaulle, and a new tramway is due to open in 2007, improving access to the Place Massena in the city centre. Nice is also one of the cheapest places to buy property in Alpes-Maritimes (where in mid-2006, the average price of property wan't far short of €5,000 per m²), though lack of building land and strict building controls ensure that demand outstrips supply and prices remain buoyant – which is good news for those who wish to let.

PROPERTY CHECK – NICE

Homes in the city itself start at around €2,000 per m² and a small studio apartment can be bought in the north of the city for under €100,000, though in a desirable area such as the Carré d'Or studios start at around €150,000; an attractive view can double the price. The principal residential areas are as follows:

- **Carré d'Or** – near the city centre and the beach, apartments start at around €200,000; some older buildings don't have lifts and parking is limited, though season tickets for local car parks are available.
- **Cimiez** – a quiet but chic residential area with Belle Epoque villas on tree-lined streets; a fair distance from the city centre, but with good parking; prices start at €4,000 per m² so a villa will cost at least €750,000, though there are some affordable apartments with parking in the north, starting at €150,000.

- **Massena** – bordering the old town and the seafront and containing the city's main shopping area, Massena offers a range of properties from affordable renovation projects (around €2,000 per m²) and one-bedroom apartments for €150,000 to luxurious properties with prices to match, especially those on the Place Massena itself, where a penthouse with terrace can cost €2m; the impending arrival of the tramway could push prices even higher.
- **Les Musiciens** – elegant Art Deco buildings in this upmarket central area are understandably sought after; ground floor apartments at the station end start at €150,000, while a three-bedroom property on the Boulevard Victor Hugo would cost at least three times as much; there are plenty of shops and restaurants but parking is limited.
- **Mont-Alban** – just behind Mont-Boron (see below) and with prices from €5,000 per m², this is one of Nice's most exclusive areas, where most property is less than 40 years old and therefore has modern facilities.
- **Mont-Boron** – high above the town with prices starting at €3,500 per m² and a lot higher for property with a good view; all developments have modern facilities such as lifts, parking is good and almost all apartments have balconies.
- **North** – recently regenerated to provide affordable family housing, the area is set to be boosted further by the arrival of the tramway in 2007, which could raise prices by as much as 20 per cent; there are many modern buildings, with lifts, cellars and parking facilities.
- **Old town** – Vieux Nice, nestling at the foot of the chateau and home to the city's famous flower market, has buildings dating back to medieval times, most of them lacking lifts and some having rather scruffy exteriors; the cheapest property is in the backstreets, the most expensive on the main squares, such as the Cours Saleya.
- **Port area** – partly regenerated and due to be renovated by the city council at great expense, which will no doubt be reflected in property prices, already high on the port itself; the area includes antique shops and chic restaurants and nightclubs (though there are also a large number of homeless people) and is close to the town centre; most property is old, though there are some 1970s buildings near the sea,

and renovation projects at reasonable prices can be found in the backstreets, mostly in buildings without lifts.

- **Seafront** – If you want to live on the famous Promenade des Anglais, especially between the Hotels Méridien and Negresco, you will need to spend at least €1.5m; beware of apartments advertised as 'on the promenade' at low prices – they're almost certainly several streets back from the front.

- **West** – a mostly modern residential area, including the *quartiers* of Arenas, Fabron, La Lanterne, Madeleine and Sainte-Marguerite, mostly quiet except areas bordering main roads (including the A8) and the airport; most property is in tower blocks, though all have car parks (public transport services are limited) and many have communal pools and tennis courts; prices start at around €150,000 for a small apartment, which can be let (e.g. to students) for around €750 per month; there are also some villas, costing around €500,000 upwards.

Attika International (🖳 www.attikainternational.com); Azur Assistance (🖳 www.azurassistance.com)

TOULOUSE

The capital of the Midi-Pyrénées region and unofficial economic capital of the south-west of France, Toulouse is a dynamic city. Its population of over 700,000 is growing by around 18,000 per year, as French people and foreigners flock to the city in search of jobs and a life in the sun, and the city council has pledged to build up to 3,500 new homes per year to cope with the influx. The AeroConstellation site to the east of the city, where the Aibus A380 super-jumbo is being constructed, is the area's biggest employer, but the site of the disastrous AZF factory explosion of 2001 is being redeveloped as a biotechnology centre dedicated to the fight against cancer (Canceropôle). To cope with this rapid expansion, public transport and other infrastructure is being improved, with a recent extension to Line A of the underground railway system and the building of a north-south Line B, as well as plans to build a tramway between the city and the AeroConstellation site.

PROPERTY CHECK – TOULOUSE

Known as the pink city, on account of its red brick buildings with terracotta roof tiles, Toulouse has a small centre, its focal points being the vast Place du Capitole with its monumental Hôtel de Ville (the Capitole itself) and adjoining narrow shopping streets of the Old Quarter and the Garonne river, with its island, on which is a huge outdoor swimming pool. New apartments cost around €3,250 per m^2 in the city and around €2,900 in the suburbs. Being such an industrious city, Toulouse is also an attractive place for property investment; apartments are being built near the Airbus factory and start at €150,000, with monthly rents of around €500.

Green Acres (🖳 www.green-acres.com)

Autlin ~ Burgundy

9

OTHER REGIONS

The preceding chapters have examined the most popular regions of France with foreign homebuyers. The remaining mainland regions, in the centre, east and north-east of the country are summarised below (roughly anti-clockwise). Although these are less popular with foreign buyers, all have their attractions.

Did you know?

Many of the *départements* in the areas in this chapter have borders with other countries: Nord (in Nord-Pas-de-Calais), Aisne (Picardie), Ardennes (Champagne-Ardenne), Meuse and Meurthe-et-Moselle (Lorraine) with Belgium; Meurthe-et-Moselle and Moselle (Lorraine) with Luxembourg; Moselle (Lorraine), Bas-Rhin and Haut-Rhin (Alsace) with Germany; Doubs, Jura (Franche-Comté) and Haute-Savoie (Rhône-Alpes) with Switzerland; and Savoie (Rhône-Alpes) with Italy. (Hautes-Alpes, Alpes-de-Haute-Provence and Alpes-Maritimes also border Italy – see page 242) In fact, some of these areas were, until relatively recently, part of another country. Savoie was an independent state until 1860, when it chose to become part of France rather than Italy, Alsace was occupied by the Germans in 1936 and not returned to France until after the war, and a tiny part of Alpes-Maritimes – La Brigue, just north of Nice – was under Italian control until 1947. Living near a border can give you the best of two (or more) worlds, with the option to savour a 'foreign' culture, cuisine and architecture whenever the fancy takes you without even having to change currency (except in the case of Switzerland, which obstinately refuses to join the EU). In fact, in most cases, the frontier is 'blurred' by an overlap of culture, cuisine and architecture, creating a fascinating mix of experiences. Those living near Belgium, Luxembourg, Switzerland and Germany will find that the inhabitants of those countries are generally more ready to speak English (and speak it better) than the French (many Belgians would rather speak English than French). Border-crossing can have other advantages: cheaper clothes and cigarettes and Sunday shop opening in Belgium, and cheaper alcohol, fuel and tobacco in Luxembourg. The downside is that, as French property is cheaper than that in neighbouring countries (with the possible exception of Belgium), a lot of foreigners buy holiday or permanent homes in France while continuing to work in their own country, causing an excess of demand over supply and pushing property prices up in border areas.

9 NORD-PAS-DE-CALAIS

The Nord-Pas-de-Calais region in the far north of France contains the *départements* of Nord (59) and Pas-de-Calais (62). It's one of France's smallest regions and shares a border with Belgium, from where it derives its Flemish influence and beer-producing traditions. The region was (along with

Picardy – see below) the birthplace of 19th century manufacturing in France and contains the country's only major conurbation outside Paris. Although derided as industrialised, over-populated and one of France's least attractive regions, it has many beautiful areas and is noted for its clean beaches, undulating countryside, secluded woods, scenic river valleys (particularly the Canche and Authie), colourful market gardens, fine golf courses and many pretty, peaceful villages.

Beginning in the northernmost *département*, Nord's rivers include the Aa, Escaut, Sambre, Scarpe and Yser, while in Pas-de-Calais, *Les Sept Vallées* is, as its name suggests, an area crisscrossed by rivers: the Authie, Bras de Brosne, Canche, Créquoise, Lys, Planquette and Ternoise. The region of Picardy is crossed by the Oise and the Somme, as well as the Aisne and Oise canals etc.

The region's main towns include Amiens, Arras, Calais, Cambrai, Dunkerque, Lille (the regional capital), Montreuil, Roubaix, Saint-Omer, Tourcoing and Valenciennes (see **Major Towns & Places of Interest** on page 410). The region's coastline, known as the *Côte opale* ('Opal Coast'), has a number of pleasant resorts, including Berck, Boulogne, Etaples, Hardelot, Le Touquet (the most fashionable) and Wimereux. There wasn't the expected surge in property prices after the opening of the Channel Tunnel, although prices are now rising quite quickly, particularly at the lower end of the market and there are few small farmhouses left for renovation. Nevertheless, homes in the region remain relatively inexpensive, although coastal areas are naturally more expensive than the interior. As well as frequent ferry services to the UK via Calais and the Channel Tunnel (*Tunnel sous la Manche*), the area has excellent road connections with Paris and the rest of France via the A26 and A25 motorways, and with Belgium and northern Europe, and is also linked with Brussels, London, Paris and the rest of France by *TGV* and Eurostar trains (see map in **Appendix E**).

PROPERTY CHECK – NORD-PAS-DE-CALAIS

Boasting some of France's widest and sandiest beaches, the coast of Nord-Pas-de-Calais includes a number of resorts, from upmarket Le Touquet (which caters for virtually every activity) and nearby Hardelot, Merlimont and Stella Plage (where prices are a third lower than in Le Touquet) to older resorts such as Wimereux and Berck, while inland are pretty villages set in rolling countryside, especially in the 'Trois Vallées' area (main town Hesdin). Traditional properties in this region are long, single-storey farmhouses (*fermettes*), often in an L shape, and double-fronted *maisons bourgeoises*, mostly built of brick, sometimes painted white; there are also plenty of new developments, usually sold off plan. Needless to say, property inland is cheaper (up to 60 per cent cheaper) than coastal property. For example, in picturesque Montreuil-sur-Mer a modern four-bedroom house costs over €350,000, whereas in Saint-Omer, a few miles inland, a restored four-bedroom farmhouse with outbuildings can be bought for under €325,000. A three-bedroom townhouse in Boulogne costs from around €150,000, while in nearby villages such as Embry and Maninghem *fermettes* in need of renovation can be found for under €100,000 and a restored three-bedroom *fermette* can be yours for under €175,000. In Le Touquet, a modern two-bedroom apartment costs around €300,000, while in Wimereux the same money can buy a four-bedroom townhouse and a one-bedroom apartment can be had for just €75,000.

L'Abri-Tanique (🖳 www.labri-tanique.com); En France (🖳 www.enfrance.co.uk); Immobilier Montreuil (🖳 www.immobilier-montreuil.com); Latitudes (🖳 www.latitudes.co.uk); Select Homes in France (🖳 www.selecthomesinfrance.com)

9

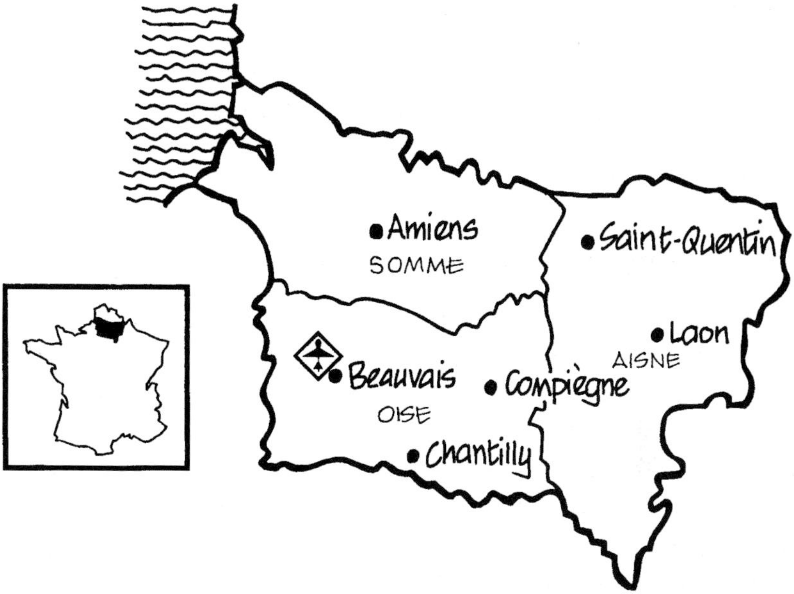

PICARDY (PICARDIE)

The region of Picardy contains the *départements* of Aisne (02), Oise (60) and Somme (80) and is one of the least known regions of France. It's mainly famous for its battlegrounds from the first and second world wars, particularly the Somme, although the region is rich in earlier history and architecture. Picardy has a generally flat and uninteresting agricultural landscape, with just a 37km (23mi) coastal strip around the mouth of the river Somme near Abbeville, although this is one of a number of attractive areas, including the valleys of the Aisne, Oise and Somme rivers. The region's main towns include the regional capital Amiens (80), Beauvais, Compiègne, Chantilly, Saint-Omer and Saint-Quentin. Picardy has some of the lowest property prices in France, although it isn't popular with foreign buyers. The Oise *département* is the most expensive of the three on account of its proximity to Paris. Picardy is crossed by the *TGV* line from Paris to Lille (see map in **Appendix E**) as well as by the A1, A16, A28 and A29 motorways and is within easy reach of England, via the Channel Tunnel or Calais ferries.

PROPERTY CHECK – PICARDY

Picardy is a region of contrasts: dubbed 'the Camargue of the north', the Somme estuary – Picardy's only bit of coast – is a wild and windswept area dotted with fishing hamlets; inland are First World War battlegrounds and quarries, and the city of Amiens, with its gothic cathedral; the *département* of Aisne is predominantly agricultural (and includes champagne vineyards), with the Ardennes mountains to the north-east; and Oise in the south reaches almost to Paris, whose ancient rulers used to hunt here. Property in Picardy is among the cheapest in France, cottages costing from as little as €60,000 and impressive *maisons de maître* to be found for under €300,000, though prices are higher near the coast and close to the capital (the area around Pierrefonds is a commuter zone and therefore attractive for investors). In the Bay de Somme, for example, fisherman's cottages sell for around €150,000, and new studio apartments for over €125,000. In chic Chantilly, a four-bedroom property can cost €450,000 and in classic Compiègne a half-timbered (*colombage*) house in good condition over €500,000. Older, rural properties often come with lots of land as well as outbuildings, tempting many foreign buyers (there's an established British community in the Albert-Arras-Péronne area – there's even a cricket club in Montbard) to run bed and breakfast and *gîte* accommodation, and predominantly rural Aisne attracts retirees looking for peace and quiet, with *fermettes* starting at just €150,000. In Somme, on the other hand, most property is post-war, although there are some 1920s brick-built houses; 18th-century farmhouses such as are common in other areas are few and far between and therefore expensive (€300,000+).

JSD Property Liaison (🖳 www.jsdpropertyliaison.com); Picardy Property (🖳 www.picardyproperty.co.uk or 🖳 www.picardyproperty.fr)

CHAMPAGNE-ARDENNE

The Champagne-Ardenne region (often called simply Champagne) contains the *départements* of Ardennes (08), Aube (10), Marne (51) and Haute-

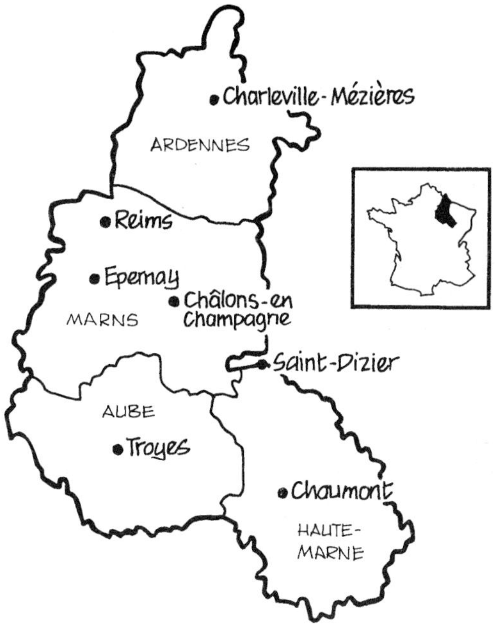

Marne (52). The region is celebrated for the sparkling wine after which it's named, and the production of champagne dominates most aspects of life in the region. Its main towns include Charleville-Mézières, Épernay, Reims, and Troyes (10), the regional capital. Reims is home to the *Grandes Marques* of champagne, such as Veuve Cliquot and Charles Heidsieck, although Épernay is the centre of champagne production. Reims cathedral is one of the most beautiful in France as well as historically the most important, being where the country's kings were crowned.

The region is highly cultivated and, although not one of France's most attractive areas, it's noted for its rolling landscape, immense forests (Verzy forest contains beech trees that are over 1,000 years old), deep gorges and vast rivers. Champagne-Ardenne also contains one of Europe's largest artificial lakes, the Lac du Der-Chantecoq near Saint-Dizier. Ardennes (which shares a border with Belgium) is the region's most picturesque *département* and its rolling, wooded landscape is dotted with ramparts, fortified castles and farmhouses. The Champagne-Ardenne region isn't popular with foreign homebuyers, despite property being relatively inexpensive, particularly in Ardennes. However, it becomes more expensive the nearer you get to Brussels in the north and Paris in the west (the western Aube is the most expensive area). The area has good road connections and is served by the A4 and A26 motorways.

PROPERTY CHECK – CHAMPAGNE-ARDENNE

Bordering Belgium, this region is popular with buyers from the Benelux countries, less so with the British (though there are a number of Britons in the Vallée de l'Ardre north-west of Reims), but improved access thanks to a *TGV* link from Paris to Reims (journey time 45 minutes) opening in 2007 may increase its attractiveness, particularly among investors. Property prices are low (reckoned to be five years behind those of Normandy and Brittany), with bargains to be found in Ardennes and Haute-Marne especially – the *départements* furthest from Paris. The area's many lakes can make attractive buys for those wishing to run a fishing or watersports business. Local investment in tourism in the town of Sedan could boost the property market, while prices in the Grand Pré-Rethel-Vouziers triangle (including, of course, Reims itself) are expected to rise sharply with the advent of the new *TGV* service. Current prices in Reims are around €150,000 for a two-bedroom townhouse with garage. Epernay (the other 'champagne town') boasts impressive three-storey townhouses and smart apartments and there are attractive village houses in nearby Condé-en-Brie, Dormans and Montmort, where prices are around a fifth lower than in Epernay and start at around €100,000. Still in Champagne country, Bar-sur-Aube (Aube) is a pretty town where two-bedroom apartments cost under €100,000 and nearby renovation projects only a little more. Elsewhere, Langres (in Haute-Marne) is something of a tourist town though the surrounding villages are largely unspoilt (and home to an expanding expatriate community); here a large country house to renovate can be bought for under €300,000, a renovated farm with outbuildings from €500,000. In Ardennes, the busy market town of Vouziers offers traditional stone houses and modern 'pavilions', the former starting at around €150,000 for three bedrooms.

Actif Immobilier (💻 www.actif-immobilier.fr); CAIG (💻 www.caig.fr); Currie French Properties (💻 www.curriefrenchproperties.com); First for French Property (💻 www.1st-for-french-property.com); French Homes (💻 www.frenchhomes.com)

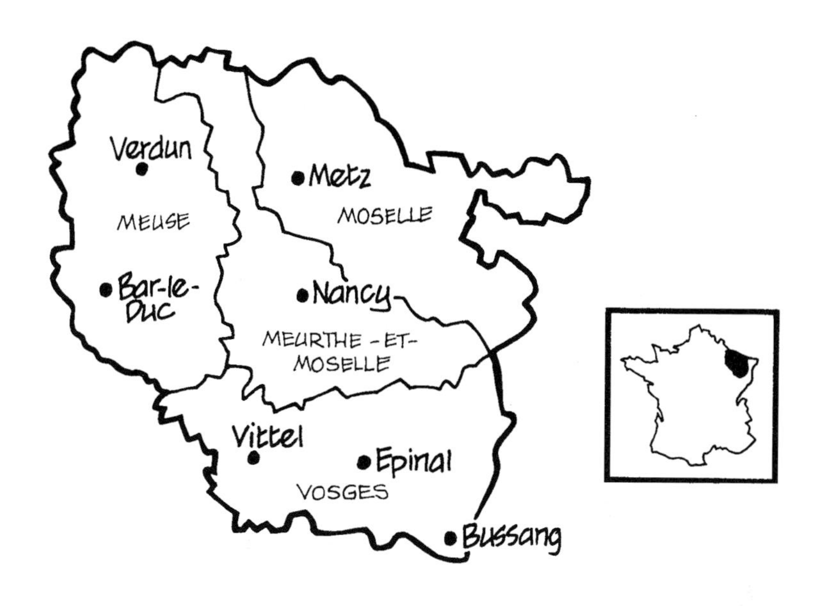

LORRAINE

Lorraine (or Lorraine-Vosges as it's also called) is situated in the north-eastern corner of France bordering Germany, Belgium and Luxembourg, and contains the *départements* of Meuse (55), Meurthe-et-Moselle (54), Moselle (57) and Vosges (88). Like Alsace (see below), Lorraine has been fought over for centuries by France and Germany, between whom it has frequently swapped ownership (the region retains a strong Germanic influence). Although mainly an industrial area, Lorraine is largely unspoiled and is popular with nature lovers and hikers. It's noted for its meandering rivers, rolling hills, wooded valleys, and delightful medieval towns and villages. Lorraine is famous for its Moselle wines and *quiche*, but regional cuisine also includes mouthwatering fruit tarts (clafoutis), soufflés and gratins, and the local beer is highly regarded. Glass and crystal making are ancient traditions. Lorraine's main towns include Nancy (54), the regional capital, and Metz, and there's a wealth of picturesque villages, including Bussang, Ferrette, Le Hohwald, Saint-Amerin and Schirmeck, plus resort towns such as Masevaux and Plimbières-les-Bains. Lorraine has few foreign residents and is largely ignored by tourists and second homebuyers despite the relatively low cost of living and reasonable property prices. The region has good road access via the A4 and A31 motorways.

PROPERTY CHECK – LORRAINE

If there's still a 'forgotten corner' of France, Lorraine must be it; many foreign property hunters don't even know where it is. Yet it offers scenic and architectural variety, historic and cultural richness and surprisingly low property prices. Although Lorraine is a major industrial region, some 87 per cent of its area is unspoiled forest (Lorraine has France's largest woodland, incorporating three national parks) or farmland, and the countryside is crisscrossed with rivers and canals. There are plains in the west, rolling hills in the north and mountains (the Vosges) in the east. The region's major towns are Metz (the elegant capital, known as 'the garden city') and Nancy (one of France's most attractive towns, due to be linked to the *TGV* network in 2007), as well as Verdun (renowned for its First World War battles but now a pretty town) and Vittel (the most famous of Lorraine's several spa towns). Germany and Switzerland are next-door. The traditional Lorraine farmhouse was built of stone (honey-coloured in Meuse, pink in Vosges) with a slate roof and adjoining stables plus a huge barn; these can be bought for under €200,000, while *maisons de maître* can cost only €50,000 or so more. There are also half-timbered properties in Meuse and tall, 18th-century townhouses in the cities and towns. Prices in Vosges tend to be higher, as many Germans have holiday homes there, and prices near Nancy are expected to rise dramatically with the arrival of the *TGV*.

French Homes (www.frenchhomes.com)

ALSACE

9

Alsace is one of France's smallest regions containing just two *départements*: Bas-Rhin (67) and Haut-Rhin (68) – Lower and Upper Rhine. It's located in the extreme east of France bordering Germany, to which it has belonged at various times in its colourful history. Not surprisingly it has a Germanic feel, which is reflected in its architecture, cuisine, dress, dialects (German is still widely spoken), names and people (called Alsatians). Sandwiched between the Vosges mountains and the Rhine, Alsace is gloriously scenic and largely unspoiled, with delightful hills (cross-country skiing is a popular winter sport), dense forests, rich farmland and pretty vineyards. It's noted for its many picturesque villages, particularly on the Wine Route (*Route du Vin*) stretching from Marlenheim west of Strasbourg down to Thann beyond Mulhouse. Alsace is famous for its beer (such as Kronenbourg) and white wines. Perhaps surprisingly, Alsace has more Michelin restaurant stars than any other region of France!

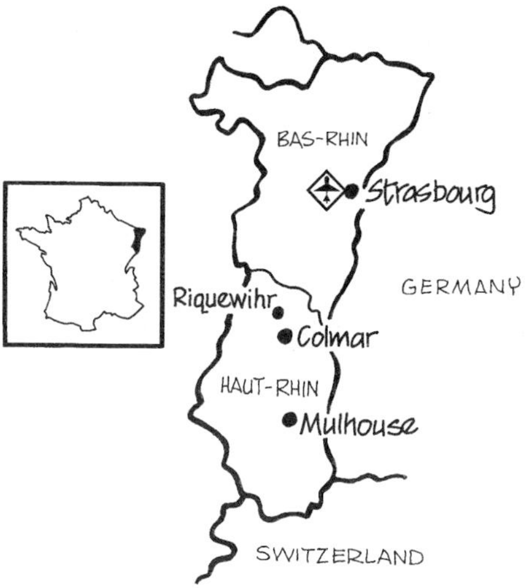

The regional capital is Strasbourg (67), home of the European Parliament, the European Court and the European Commission on Human Rights. Other notable towns include Colmar and Mulhouse, a prominent industrial city. Property prices are higher than the average for France and there are few bargains to be found. Rundown or derelict rural properties for sale are rare in Alsace, where (unlike many other regions) there hasn't been a mass exodus from the farms and countryside. The region has excellent road connections with Paris, the south of France, Germany and Switzerland.

FRANCHE-COMTE

Franche-Comté (literally 'free country') contains the *départements* of Doubs (25), Jura (39), Haute-Saône (70) and the Territoire-de-Belfort (90). It's a little-known region in eastern France bordering Switzerland, with which it shares much of its architecture, cuisine and culture. It's known for cheeses such as Comté and Morbier, Jura wines, and Morteau and Montbéliard sausages. Franche-Comté is acclaimed for its beautiful, unspoiled scenery (more Swiss in appearance than French) and recalls a fairy-tale land where time has almost stood still. It's reputed to be the greenest region in France. Sandwiched between the Vosges range to the north and the Jura mountains to the south, the landscape consists of rolling cultivated fields, dense pine forests and rampart-like mountains. Although not as majestic as the Alps, the Jura mountains are more accessible and are a Mecca for nature lovers and winter sports fans; the linked resorts of Bois d'Amont, Lamoura, Prémanon and Les Rousses offer over 40 downhill skiing pistes and 400km of cross-country skiing trails. The Doubs and Loue valleys (noted for their timbered houses perched on stilts in the river) and the high valley of Ain are popular areas. The region's main towns include Belfort and Besançon (25), the regional capital on the river Doubs.

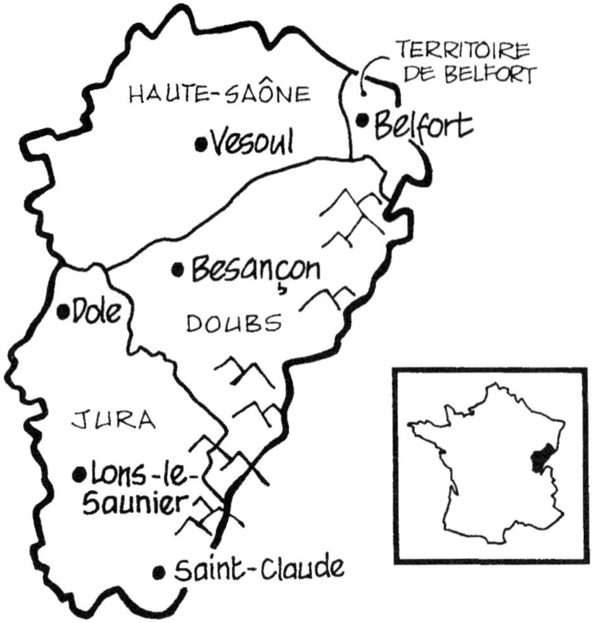

Franche-Comté is largely ignored by foreign tourists and homebuyers, although it has many attractions. Property prices are higher than the French average, although bargains can be found, particularly if you're seeking a winter holiday home. Besançon is served by the A36 motorway and has good connections with the centre and south of France, Germany and Switzerland via *TGV* (see map in **Appendix E**).

PROPERTY CHECK – FRANCHE-COMTE

With just a million inhabitants, this region is predominantly rural, though with easy access to Paris, Lyon and Geneva. Lying between the wine-producing areas of Alsace, Burgundy and Champagne, Franche-Comté itself is largely wooded, with rolling countryside in Bresse, plateaux and lakes in Haut Doubs and the mountains of Jura, which cover much of the region. Attractive villages include Baume-les-Messieurs and Château-Chalon, where properties for renovation can be found at under €125,000. Medieval grey-stone buildings are characteristic of the towns of Besançon and Dôle. Traditionally attracting Dutch and Swiss buyers (there are hardly any Britons in the region), Franche-Comté is now appealing to French people who want a mountain retreat but can no longer afford to buy in the Alps. Prices are therefore rising, especially for building land. Nevertheless, renovation projects cost as little as €50,000, small village homes can be bought for €125,000, renovated farmhouses in 4,000m² (1 acre) of land for less than €200,000 and four- or five-bedroom properties for around €350,000 – prices around 50 per cent of those for equivalent properties in neighbouring Burgundy.

The French Property Shop (www.frenchpropertyshop.com); Leapfrog Properties Europe (www.leapfrog-properties.com)

CENTRE-VAL-DE-LA-LOIRE

The central region of France contains the *départements* of Cher (18), Eure-et-Loir (28), Indre (36), Indre-et-Loire (37), Loir-et-Cher (41) and Loiret (45), the Loire and its tributary, the Loir, giving their names to several of the *départements*. The Loire is France's longest river (1,020km/628mi), with its source in the Vivarais mountains (south of Saint-Etienne) and its outlet at Saint-Nazaire in the Pays de la Loire (see **Chapter 3**). It's considered to be the dividing line between the colder regions of northern France and the warmer south, although the change is gradual. The Loire valley is noted for its natural beauty and fertility, consisting of pleasant undulating woodland, lakes, rivers, orchards, and fields of maize and sunflowers (it's the market garden of France), as well as for its *châteaux*, widely considered to be among the most beautiful in the world. The principal *châteaux* are in Loir-et-

Cher (Chambord, Chaumont and Chéverny) and neighbouring Indre-et-Loire (Azay-le-Rideau, Chenonceaux and Villandry, with its magnificent gardens).

The region's main towns include Blois, Bourges, Chartres, Orléans and Tours (37), the regional capital. One of its most attractive areas is the old province of Berry (comprising the *départements* of Cher and Indre), whose ancient capital was the majestic city of Bourges.

The Loire valley is unspoiled by industry, mass tourism or a surfeit of holiday homes, although it's quite popular with retirees and second homeowners. The region has excellent road connections via the A10, A11 and A71 motorways, which converge on Paris, as well as via the *TGV* from Paris to Poitiers and Bordeaux (see map in **Appendix E**).

9

PROPERTY CHECK – CENTRE-VAL-DE-LOIRE

Known as the Garden of France, this central region has much more to offer than its famous *châteaux*. It has been described by UNESCO (which designated the central and western Loire valley a World Heritage Site in 2000) as 'an exceptional cultural landscape, of great beauty, comprising historic cities and villages, great architectural monuments and lands that have been cultivated and shaped by centuries of interaction between the local population and their physical environment' – though much the same could be said of almost every region of France! Its scenery varies from rolling in the north to flattish in the south. The two southernmost *départements*, Cher and Indre, correspond roughly to the ancient province of Berry, once tied to Scotland, with its many picturesque villages and lively towns. Indre is also home to the Brenne Regional Park, known as the 'land of a thousand lakes' (in fact there are some 1,200). West of Tours, the Loire is wide and shallow, meandering past vineyards, orchards, woods and fields of fruit and sunflowers. Tours itself (where the purest French is said to be spoken) is a beautiful and lively city with a thriving bio-technology industry (and supposedly the best range of fashion boutiques outside Paris), the surrounding area (known unofficially as Touraine) popular with foreigners and the French. Property prices vary considerably according to the proximity to major towns (especially Paris), but bargains can still be found: for example, 'ruins' for €50,000, habitable properties from €100,000, and three-bedroom detached houses for under €250,000, while building plots start as low as €20,000.

Properties in France (💻 www.propertiesinfrance.com); RMS Property in France (💻 www.rmsproperty.com); Touraine Berry Immobilier (💻 www.agencetbi.com); VEF Indre (💻 www.vefuk.com)

BURGUNDY (BOURGOGNE)

Burgundy contains the *départements* of Côte d'Or (21), Nièvre (58), Saône-et-Loire (71) and Yonne (89). The region has few industries, which means it's almost totally unspoiled and one of France's most beautiful and fertile areas (it has been dubbed the 'rural soul' of France). It's a timeless land where little has changed over the centuries and a haven of peace and serenity (particularly the Parc du Morvan at its heart). The name Burgundy is synonymous with magnificent wines such as Nuits-Saint-Georges, Meursault, Beaune, Puligny-Montrachet, Gevrey-Chambertin and Pouilly-Fuissé, grown on the 60km (37mi) Côte d'Or hillside, as well as fine cuisine, including *boeuf bourgignon* (made with Charollais beef), *coq au vin* (with Bresse chicken), Morvan ham and snails, generally served with rich sauces, as well as *pain d'épices* ('spicy' bread) and *kir* (white wine with a dash of blackcurrant liqueur).

PROPERTY CHECK – COTE D'OR

The north-eastern *département* of Burgundy, Côte d'Or, offers forests as well as vineyards (whose grapes produce famous wines such as Aloxe Corton, Gevrey-Chambertin and Nuits Saint-George), its capital, Dijon, boasting museums and medieval mansions. Popular with Parisians for second homes but also with Americans and Swiss, Côte d'Or nevertheless has competitive property prices (well below the national average and around 25 per cent lower than those in nearby Beaune). A small village house to renovate costs around €80,000, while €600,000 can buy you a wine estate. Away from the vineyards, in the rolling farmland of the Auxois area, with its lively small towns of Pouilly-en-Auxois and Semur-en-Auxois, a three-bedroom farmhouse costs under €300,000. In the market town of Châtillon-sur-Seine, largely rebuilt after the second world war but featuring some older buildings, including the impressive castle set on a rocky promontory overlooking the famous river, a three-bedroom townhouse is a similar price.

Bourgogne Homes (💻 www.bourgognehomes.com); Propriétés en Bourgogne (💻 www.proprietes-en-bourgogne.com); BIP Bourgogne Immobilier (💻 www.vip-bourgogne-immobilier.com)

The region is also renowned for its many canals and canal boats, and has some 1,200km (750mi) of navigable waterways, including the Burgundy Canal and the rivers Saône and Yonne. Burgundy has a rich and colourful history (it was an independent kingdom for some 600 years), celebrated in numerous colourful festivals and pageants, and a wealth of Romanesque churches, cathedrals, medieval villages and historic towns. Its most important towns include Autun, Auxerre, Beaune, Chalon-sur-Saône, Dijon (21) – famous for its mustard and the regional capital (and recently rated the second-best town to live in France by *Le Nouvel Observateur* magazine – see **Appendix F**), Fontenay, Mâcon, Nevers, Paray-le-Monial and Vézelay.

PROPERTY CHECK – BEAUJOLAIS

There's a lot more to Beaujolais than the grape-juice-masquerading-as-wine that flashes through the shops at the end of November each year. Not only are proper Beaujolais wines among France's finest, but the area is picturesque and unspoiled, with pretty villages such as Vaux-en-Beaujolais perched above the Saône river, its golden stone cottages lending it a Tuscan look. Yet it's within easy reach of Lyon and only 90 minutes from the nearest ski resort. Beaujolais comprises three areas: the Saône valley to the east, the thickly wooded hills of Beaujolais Vert to the west, and the strip of granite hills in the centre on which some 22,000ha (55,000 acres) of vineyards are planted. For all its rural charm, however, Beaujolais is far from bargain basement territory, its recent eco-tourism drive also driving up property prices – while also increasing the market for bed and breakfast and self-catering accommodation. A renovated three- or four-bedroom village house costs from €300,000, a large country house with garden from €450,000, while a small stone house for renovation can be had for around €150,000. The principal town, Villefranche-sur-Saône (just half an hour from Lyon), with a vast covered market and varied shops, offers a range of property styles, with apartments in newly refurbished buildings starting at €100,000, while older studios can be had for under €75,000 (and let for between €300 and €600 per month) and four-bedroom townhouses can cost up to €400,000. The most sought-after part of Beaujolais is the so-called Pierres Dorées area ('the

Tuscany of Beaujolais' in estate agent-speak), where four-bedroom 'golden stone' houses in hilltop villages such as Oingt, Ternand and Theizé can cost up to €500,000. The most affordable area is also the largest, Beaujolais Vert, where farmhouses for renovation can be had for €100,000.

Home Attitudes (☎ 04 74 03 83 67); Leapfrog Properties (💻 www.leapfrog-properties.com); Leisure & Land (💻 www.leisure andland.com)

Somewhat surprisingly, Burgundy isn't popular with foreign property buyers, perhaps because of its relative isolation, and there are few holiday and retirement homes there. It rarely features in international property magazines and, although the region has a wealth of beautiful *châteaux*, manor houses and watermills, these (and vineyards) are rarely on the market. Burgundy is located just 100km (around 65mi) south of Paris and 80km (50mi) north of Lyon, and has excellent connections with both the north and south of France via the A6 and A31 motorways and the *TGV* (see map in **Appendix E**).

PROPERTY CHECK – BURGUNDY

With its world-famous wines, stunning and diverse countryside, including hills, forests, lakes, rivers and canals (a total of 1,400km of waterways), attractive towns, such as Autun, Beaune and Dijon, magnificent castles and excellent climate with clearly defined seasons, Burgundy ought to be overrun with foreign homeowners. One of its beauties is that it isn't, although there are Dutch, Italians and Swiss in the region. This is reflected in its house prices: renovation projects start at a mere €40,000 (though they're few and far between and can be very dilapidated), two-bedroom holiday homes at just €75,000 and four-bedroom detached properties at under €200,000. On the other hand, this traditionally wealthy region is popular with affluent French people, so there are also pricey properties at the top end of the market. Typical Burgundian properties are grand, brightly coloured and with intricately patterned roofs (slate in the north, canal or Roman tiles in the south). Ex-winemakers' houses, with their extensive cellars, are particularly sought after. However, it can be difficult to find properties with a large amount of land, which is at a premium for wine-growing purposes. Yonne in the north ('the gateway to Burgundy') boasts the historic towns of Auxerre, Pontigny and Sens as well as attractive villages such as Vézelay, Côte d'Or in the east is the heart of the wine-producing area (see above), Nièvre in the west is dominated by the 170,000ha Morvan park, with hills rising to 900m (3,000ft), in its centre, and Saône-et-Loire in the south offers rolling fields grazed by Charollais cows as well as architecture from Roman to modern times.

Burgundy4U (🖳 www.burgundy4U.com); Burgundy Property Specialists (🖳 www.burgundyproperty.com); Currie French Properties (🖳 www.curriefrenchproperties.com); Francophiles (🖳 www.francophiles.com); VEF (🖳 www.vefuk.com)

RHÔNE-ALPES

The Rhône-Alpes region contains the *départements* of Ain (01), Hautes-Alpes (05), Ardèche (07), Isère (38), Loire (42) and Drôme (26), Rhône (69), Savoie (73) and Haute-Savoie (74). Although largely unspoiled by development, the Rhône valley is one of France's major industrial regions. Lyon (69), which is the regional capital and France's second-largest city as well as reputedly its gastronomic capital, has a beautiful medieval quarter; it was recently rated the second-best town to live in France by *Le Point* magazine (see **Appendix F**). The Rhône river (whose source is high in the Swiss Alps) is a vital artery for river, road and rail traffic between the north and south of France.

Rhône-Alpes is one of France's most scenic and beautiful regions with dense forests, lush pasture land, fast-flowing rivers, huge lakes, deep gorges and spectacular mountains, although these are mostly in the eastern part of the region (see **Chapter 7**). It's a land made for sports fans and those with a love of the outdoors, with superb summer (e.g. climbing, hiking, biking, canoeing and white-water rafting) and winter sports facilities, including some of the best skiing in the world in the Alps. Apart from Lyon, Rhône's major towns include Bourg-en-Bresse, Privas and Saint-Etienne.

The price of property in the Rhône-Alpes region as a whole is well above the average, although the priciest areas are mostly in the Alps. Ardèche with its spectacular gorge is increasingly popular with foreign buyers and is consequently becoming more expensive. Like Franche-Comté, Rhône-

Alpes is popular with the Swiss, many of whom live in the region and commute to their workplaces in Geneva and other Swiss cities. The region is noted for its extremes of temperature and is usually freezing in winter and hot in summer, and most pleasant in spring and autumn. The Rhône-Alpes has excellent road, rail and air connections and Lyon is just two hours from Paris by *TGV* (see map in **Appendix E**).

For information about the Alps, see **Chapter 7**.

PROPERTY CHECK – RHONE-ALPES

The Rhône-Alpes region is famous for its mountains, the Alps, but its defining characteristic is water. From Lake Geneva (Lac Léman) in the north to the gorges of the Ardèche river in the south, there's literally water, water everywhere. As well as Lake Geneva, there's the Lac d'Aiguebelette, the Lac d'Annecy and the Lac de Bourget (France's largest natural lake); as well as the Ardèche, the rivers Ain, Drôme, Isère, Loire, Rhône and Saône are among the region's 15,000km of waterways. Many of these lakes and rivers form part of the region's two national parks, four regional parks and 28 nature reserves (more than any other region). Fishing is big business here – especially carp, though herring, salmon, monkfish, trout and pike can also be caught. The Dombes area, between the Ain and Saône rivers and reaching north to Bourg-en-Bresse and south almost to Lyon, comprises over 1,000 manmade ponds – part of the traditional method of agriculture. Lakeside properties naturally command a premium – especially when the lake in question is Geneva or Annecy. Nevertheless, a studio apartment near Lake Geneva can be had for as little as €80,000, while a three-bedroom chalet costs from €300,000.

Rhône-Alpes' most southerly *département*, Drôme offers a diversity of landscapes, from craggy mountains to orchard-covered hillsides and lavender-strewn Provençal fields as the river Drôme finds its way down from the Alps to the Rhône – sometimes calmly, sometimes wildly. Being adjacent to Provence and only two hours from Paris by *TGV*, Drôme is pricey, especially in and around the picture-postcard village of Mirmande, where a typical stone farmhouse with 1ha (2.5 acres) of land can cost up to €600,000 and even village houses start at €300,000 – if you can find one for sale. Slightly cheaper is Beaufort-sur-Gervanne, with its hilltop position above the town of Crest, and you might be lucky enough to find a remote house in need of restoration for under €100,000.

Neighbouring Ardèche also offers a mix of scenery, including volcanic mountains, rolling hills, forests and rushing rivers, its principal feature being the 85km (55mi) limestone gorges ground out over the millennia by the Ardèche river. There are few large towns, the capital, Privas, housing a mere 10,000 people, but many villages, with narrow streets and blue-and-white-stone houses, clinging to the mountains or nestling in the valleys. As Drôme borders PACA, Ardèche adjoins Languedoc-Roussillon and property prices are correspondingly lower, though highest in the south and around the towns of Annonay, Aubenas and Privas. The majority of foreign buyers are Dutch, though Belgians and Germans are also attracted to the area, as are the French themselves. Ruins for restoration are becoming rare but, when they turn up, sell for around €100,000, while small village houses start at around €150,000 and villas at €250,000.

Alpine Residences (💻 www.alpineresidences.com); Latitudes (💻 www.latitudes.co.uk); Sifex (💻 www.sifex.co.uk); VEF (💻 www.vefuk.com)

9

ADVANTAGES & DISADVANTAGES

Nord-Pas-de-Calais

Frequent ferry services from Calais and Dunkerque and the Channel Tunnel make the region convenient for those living in south-east England. The *TGV* also provides a rapid link to Paris and Brussels. The region boasts sandy beaches with nearby golf courses, but inland the flat landscape is less inspiring. The climate is among the worst in France, not unlike that of the UK or Belgium, and property prices aren't among the cheapest of the nine regions considered in this chapter, although older houses are relatively inexpensive (see **Cost of Property** on page 424). The region also suffers high unemployment and a high rate of new business failure.

Picardy

Along with Franche-Comté and Lorraine, Picardy is one of the cheapest regions in France for property. Both England in one direction and Paris in the other are accessible from most parts of the region, but it has little coastline and a rather featureless landscape. The climate is little better than in Nord-Pas-de-Calais.

Champagne-Ardenne

Conveniently placed for visiting Paris (and Disneyland), Champagne-Ardenne nevertheless offers reasonably priced property, but it suffers extremely cold winters and a large part of the region consists of monotonous chalk plains.

Lorraine

Lorraine is one of the cheapest regions in France, both for property and in terms of the cost of living, although the area around Metz is more expensive than the Nancy area. Like Alsace, it has many picturesque villages, but the weather is subject to sudden changes and extremes of temperature.

Alsace

Alsace boasts colourful towns and villages in the Germanic style and is one of the leading regions in France for economic growth. It enjoys (or suffers, depending on your point of view) hot summers and cold winters and is one of France's great wine regions. However, it's a long way from the sea and has poor air connections and is the most expensive of the nine regions considered here for property, although the Mulhouse area is considerably cheaper than Colmar and Strasbourg. The crime rate is particularly high in and around Strasbourg, where vehicle burning has become a traditional part of the New Year 'festivities', and the city is liable to flooding.

Franche-Comté

Franche-Comté is one of the cheapest areas in France for property. It has attractive forest and mountain scenery and there is some skiing in the Vosges and Jura (the northern Alps aren't far away either). It's generally quiet, which may be an advantage or a disadvantage, and is a long way from the sea, although it has around 80 lakes, where there's a variety of watersports.

Burgundy

One of the great wine regions of France, Burgundy is predominantly rural and offers reasonably priced property. Rail and road connections are good (the *TGV* runs through the region on its way from Paris to Lyon), though there are few direct international flights. Northern parts of the area are close to Paris and southern parts within reach of the Alps. It's widely tipped to be the most 'up-and-coming' region of France, although it may be rather unassuming for some.

Centre-Val-de-Loire

Architecturally one of the most interesting regions in France, with Chartres cathedral and the greatest of the Loire *châteaux*, Centre-Val-de-Loire also enjoys rapid *TGV* and motorway access from Paris and low-cost flights from London. Property is reasonably priced, except in the northern *départements* adjoining Ile-de-France, and the climate is mild. Like Burgundy, it isn't a major economic centre but has few disadvantages unless you want hot summers or quick access to the coast.

Rhône-Alpes

Strategically placed, just two hours from Paris and one hour from the Mediterranean coast and the northern Alps, Lyon is also a good place to find work, although the area may be too industrial for some tastes. The region is renowned for its food and includes Ardèche with its fabulous gorges and grottos. However, Lyon is relatively expensive and subject to horrendous traffic jams at holiday periods. The climate is mixed, although for some this will be an advantage.

MAJOR TOWNS & PLACES OF INTEREST

Nord-Pas-de-Calais

Lille (pop. 225,000, excluding suburbs), the capital of Nord and the Nord-Pas-de-Calais region, is the largest city in northern France after Paris; a stylish, prosperous and vibrant city, with a unique cultural identity and no fewer than five universities (mainly business and engineering faculties), it has a flamboyant old town and a revitalised city centre. It's the industrial and commercial hub of region, with excellent road and rail connections with the rest of France and the UK, Belgium and Holland (especially via the *TGV*, since becoming the network's hub. Lille also boasts France's biggest 'car boot sale'.

PROPERTY CHECK – LILLE

In recent years, the former 'capital' of north-east France's mining and textile industries has transformed itself into an IT, banking and administration centre and an international transport hub. At the centre of the London-Paris-Brussels triangle (in fact, Paris is furthest), Lille is the new *TGV* network hub as well as the crossroads of five inter-continental motorways and a major river port handling over a million tonnes of freight per year. The city itself has been regenerated with striking new buildings such as the Lille Europe station and Crédit Lyonnais tower, complementing its ancient architectural marvels, such as the Vieille Bourse and the Grand Place. European Capital of Culture in 2004, Lille has a vibrant cultural scene and boasts an extensive and efficient public transport system, which includes a tramway and the driverless VAL *métro* network covering some 60 stations, a pedestrianised shopping centre and a bike-hire scheme to discourage car users.

Property in the city starts at just €1,250 per m² for renovation projects in unfashionable areas, rising to around €3,000 for renovated property in the popular old town. Bargains can be found in the outskirts, though here as in the city itself you must compete with Belgian and French workers (including many who work in Paris), who choose to live in Lille because of its relatively low property prices.

Dunkerque (pop. 70,000), near the Belgian border in Nord, is the third-largest commercial shipping port in France with a ferry connection to the UK (Norfolk Line); it also has France's largest mining museum.

The capital of Pas-de-Calais, Arras (pop. 41,000; 80,000 including suburbs) is a historic and attractive town rich in museums, especially of fine arts. The *département*'s other major towns include Boulogne-sur-Mer (pop. 45,000), France's largest fishing port with 13th century ramparts around the upper town and a national sea life centre (Nausicaa) attracting 800,000 visitors; Saint-Omer (pop. 70,000 including suburbs), an attractive market town surrounded by the Audomarois Nature Reserve; Le Touquet-Paris-Plage (pop. 5,000), an upmarket seaside resort (with a sandy beach over 1.5km/1mi long and a beautiful promenade), a racecourse and several golf courses nearby; and the attractive nearby fishing village of Etaples.

Picardy

The major towns in Aisne are Laon (pop. 27,000), the departmental capital, with its new Center Parcs holiday resort, and Saint-Quentin (pop. 57,000), a historic city on the Somme river – originally a Roman settlement and boasting the 13th-century Collégiale Saint Quentin cathedral – with nearby First World War battlefields.

Beauvais (pop. 55,000) is the capital of Oise, dominated by its vast but unfinished cathedral and offering direct flights to the UK and Ireland from its airport. The capital of Somme is Amiens (pop. 136,000), which is a university town largely re-built after the Second World War but with one of the finest Gothic cathedrals in France; nearby is the picturesque Saint-Leu area, while the Somme estuary (Baie de Somme) is very much noted for its wildlife.

PROPERTY CHECK – AMIENS

Around 120km (75mi) north of Paris, on the Somme river, Picardy's capital is best known for its magnificent gothic cathedral (France's largest) but has many other attractions, including the cobbled Place du Don, with its 16th-century buildings; Les Hortillonnages ('floating gardens'), a 300ha (800-acre) area of canals and islands near the city centre; and the former textile-manufacturing district of Saint-Leu (known as 'the little Venice of the north'). With regular flea markets (every second Sunday on the Quai Parmentier) and a Christmas market, annual music and film festivals and a horse show, Amiens is also a lively town. A four-bedroom terraced house near the city centre can cost as little as €150,000, homes in a modern development on the outskirts between €200,000 and €300,000 and, just outside Amiens, a three-bedroom *fermette* for around €175,000 and a four-bedroom house for just over €200,000.

First For French Property (💻 www.1st-for-french-property.co.uk)

Champagne-Ardenne

Charleville-Mézières (pop. 55,000), with its attractive Place Ducale, is the capital of Ardennes. The capital of Aube is Troyes (pop. 61,000), a university town (attached to the University of Reims) and centre of the hosiery and mechanical industry. renowned for its *andouillette* (pig intestine) sausages.

The cathedral city of Châlons-en-Champagne (pop. 47,000) is the capital of Marne, where Epernay (pop. 26,000; 40,000 including suburbs) is the epicentre of the champagne area, boasting the Champagne Museum and the cellars (covering 14ha/35 acres) of Moët et Chandon among other famous champagne houses. Nearby Hautvilliers (pop. 900), with its Benedictine abbey, is famous as being the place where Pierre Pérignon, a 17th-century monk, discovered how to put a fizz into the local wine, thus creating champagne. The other famous 'champagne town' and Marne's largest city is Reims (pop. 190,000; 290,000 including suburbs), with a technological university and College of Art and Design as well as its magnificent 12th century cathedral.

Chaumont (pop. 26,000) is the capital of Haute-Marne and has a splendid 19th-century viaduct, 600m (2,000ft) long and over 50m (170ft) high. The region also features an extravagant basilica at l'Epine and two regional parks, Montagne de Reims and Forêt d'Orient.

Lorraine

Nancy (pop. 105,000), the capital of Meurthe-et-Moselle and former seat of the Dukes of Lorraine, features fine 17th-century architecture – especially in Place Stanislas, a World Heritage site – and was recently rated the 'best' town to live in France by *Le Nouvel Observateur* magazine (see **Appendix F**).

The capital of Meuse, Bar-le-Duc (pop. 17,000), is an industrial town (textiles, printing, machine tools, jam making, and food-research laboratories), while Verdun (pop. 21,000), where there's also light industry, is renowned for its nearby First World War battlefields, cemetery and war museum.

The Gothic cathedral of Metz (pop. 125,000), the capital of Moselle, boasts the world's largest stained-glass windows, designed by Chagall; it's a university town and the largest river port in France with substantial local industry, including the Peugeot/Citroën car factories.

In Vosges, Bussang (pop. 1,800), at the source of the Moselle river, offers the nearest ski resort to Paris, Domrémy-la-Pucelle (pop. 170 but over 50,000 visitors a year) is the birthplace of Joan of Arc, Epinal (pop. 35,000), the departmental, is the centre of both light and heavy (metallurgy) industry, Plombières-les-Bains (pop. 2,000) is a spa town, as is Vittel (pop. 6,200), with its renowned natural spring water.

Alsace

Strasbourg (pop. 270,000), the capital of Bas-Rhin and seat of the European Parliament, is a picturesque, animated, town with Germanic allure; a cathedral and university town, it's the second-largest river port in France (on the Ill and Rhine rivers) and the site of France's first urban 'eco-district'.

The capital of Haut-Rhin, Colmar (pop. 67,000) is an important artistic and cultural centre, with multi-coloured houses, an extremely picturesque old town and a 'Venetian area' traversed by the Lauch river. Mulhouse (pop. 110,00; 220,000 including suburbs) is much more industrial, with a Peugeot car factory and national car and railway museums. Riquewihr (pop. 1,200) features ancient houses and medieval walls while nearby Château de Haut-Koënigsburg (alt. 755m/2,475ft) offers magnificent views.

Franche-Comté

Besançon (pop. 115,000), the capital of Doubs and the birthplace of Victor Hugo, is a university town and the first official 'green' town in France; it boasts a beautiful *citadelle* and its Swiss influence (the border is nearby) is evident in its watch-making industry.

Lons-le-Saunier (pop. 19,000) is the capital of Jura and a spa town with some industry, including the manufacture of spectacles. The *département*'s ski resorts include Les Rousses (alt. 1,120m/3,675ft), dominated by La Dole mountain near the Swiss border, and Lamoura (alt. 1,100m/3,610ft). The regional conservation area of Haut-Jura (146,000ha/360,000 acres), at between 1,000 and 1,600m (3,280 and 5,250ft), is another major attraction.

Vesoul (pop. 18,000), the capital of Haute-Saône, is the site of another Peugeot car factory, with nearby ski resorts at La Planche-des-Belles-Filles (alt. 1,148m/3,765ft) and Belfahy (alt. 950m/3,115ft).

Belfort (pop. 50,000), the capital of Territoire-de-Belfort, is also an industrial town producing car components, railway equipment, electronic and computer goods.

The region's other attractions include Le Corbusier's chapel at Ronchamp and the Royal Saltworks at Arc-et-Senans.

Burgundy

Famous for its mustard, Dijon (pop. 142,000) is the capital of Côte d'Or and the industrial centre of a mainly rural region; a university and cathedral town and a major crossing point for motorway and rail routes, it was recently rated the second-best town to live in France by *Le Nouvel Observateur* magazine (see **Appendix F**). Beaune (pop. 21,000), at the centre of the famous wine region, boasts a History of Wine Museum and splendid Hôtel-Dieu (15th-century hospital).

Picturesque Nevers (pop. 37,000), on the Loire, is the capital of Nièvres boasting a Ducal Palace, cathedral and numerous churches.

The capital of Saône-et-Loire, Mâcon (pop. 33,000) is another cathedral town, on banks of the Saône river, and also a wine centre. In the same *département* are Autun (pop. 17,000), with its Roman remains and a remarkable 12th-century cathedral, and Chalon-sur-Saône (pop. 45,000), another town noted for its wines.

In Yonne, whose capital is Auxerre (pop. 35,000), are Avallon (pop. 8,000), whose medieval fortified town offers panoramic views of the Cousin valley, and Vézelay (pop. 500), a renowned medieval pilgrimage destination with a 12th-century basilica.

Centre-Val-de-Loire

Bourges (pop. 75,000) is the capital of Cher, with a splendid Gothic cathedral, medieval houses and cobbled streets in the centre; its many industries include armaments.

The capital of Eure-et-Loir, Chartres (pop. 40,000) boasts one of Christianity's great shrines, a magnificent Gothic cathedral with unique stained-glass windows, widely considered to be the most beautiful in Europe; local industries include cosmetics, electronics and mechanical engineering.

Châteauroux (pop. 50,000), the capital of Indre, is another industrious town, local products including biscuits, ceramics and textiles.

Tours (pop. 133,000) is the capital of Indre-et-Loire; a lively city with a Gothic cathedral – and a 'congestion charge' for cars entering the city centre – Tours is an industrial centre (aeronautics, electronics, mechanical and pharmaceutical products) and gateway to the Loire *châteaux*, including Chenonceau and Villandry.

Blois (pop. 50,000), the capital of Loir-et-Cher, has its own *château* and is close to the most famous of all, Chambord and Cheverny; local industries are similar to those of Tours.

Orléans (pop. 114,000), the capital of Loiret, is a lively cathedral town saved by Joan of Arc but heavily bombed in the Second World War and largely rebuilt; it too offers access to nearby châteaux and various industries.

Rhône-Alpes

Bourg-en-Bresse (pop. 41,000), the capital of Ain, has some heavy industry (metallurgy, mechanical and lorry manufacture) but nearby are cross-country skiing resorts such as Brénod (alt. 1,100m/3,610ft), Giron (alt. 1,078m/3,535ft), Hotonnes (alt. 1,350m/4,430ft), Le Poizat (alt. 1,300m/4,265ft) and Mijoux-la-Faucille-Lélex (alt. 1,320m/4,330ft).

Privas (pop. 9,000), the capital of Ardèche, is known for its *marrons glacés* (candied chestnuts); its industries include textiles and weighing machine equipment. The Ardèche river valley is a natural conservation area offering superb canoeing, and the *département*'s ski resorts include Areilladou (alt. 1,448m/4,750ft), Borée (alt. 1,132m/3,710ft), Croix-de-Bauzon (alt. 1,511m/4,955ft) and Sainte-Eulalie (alt. 1,230m/4,035ft).

Saint-Etienne (pop. 183,000) is the capital of Loire and the second-largest town in the area after Lyon, its great rival – not least in football; a university town (engineering and business faculties) and former mining area it has various heavy and light industries and nearby skiing at Le Bessat (alt. 1,170m/3,840ft) and Chalmazel (alt. 1,400m/4,590ft).

Lyon (pop. around 1m), on the Saône and Rhône rivers, is the capital of Rhône and the regional capital; a university and cathedral city and one of the great gastronomic centres of France, Lyon boasts a huge modern shopping centre and pedestrian area, important electronic, chemical and mechanical industries and a major exhibition centre; it was recently rated the second-best town to live in France by *Le Point* magazine (see **Appendix F**). Nearby Charbonnières-les-Bains (pop. 4,000) is a charming spa town.

POPULATION

Approximate regional and departmental population figures, including numbers of foreign nationals with residence permits are shown below. For populations of towns, see **Major Towns & Places of Interest** above.

Nord-Pas-de-Calais

4m, of which 45,500 Moroccans, 40,000 Algerians, 18,000 Portuguese, 15,500 Italians and 1,800 Britons. Also popular with Belgians and Dutch. The region's population is growing at well below the national average rate (0.16 per cent per annum compared with 0.66). While the city of Lille and the towns of Hénin-Beaumont, Marcq-en-Barouland Valenciennes are growing fast, Calais, Coudekerque-Branche, Grande-Synthe, Liévin, Maubeuge, Saint-Pol-sur-Mer and Villeneuve-d'Ascq are declining rapidly.

- **Nord (59)** – 2.58m, of which 36,000 Moroccans, 35,000 Algerians, 16,500 Portuguese, 12,500 Italians and 940 Britons.
- **Pas-de-Calais (62)** – 1.46m, of which 9,500 Moroccans, 5,000 Algerians, 3,000 Italians, 1,500 Portuguese and 870 Britons.

Picardy

1.9m, of which 18,500 Portuguese, 18,000 Moroccans, 9,000 Algerians and 1,100 Britons. In common with other northern regions, Picardy's population is growing at well below the national average rate (0.22 per cent per annum compared with 0.66 per cent), the *département* of Oise being the fastest-growing (at 0.61 per cent), while the population of Aisne is in gradual decline. The towns of Abbeville, Beauvais, Saint-Quentin and Soissons have decreasing populations, while Amiens, Compiègne, Creil and Laon are growing.

- **Aisne (02)** – 536,000, of which 4,000 Portuguese, 3,500 Moroccans, 1,500 Algerians, 1,000 Spaniards, 650 Turks and 100 Britons.
- **Oise (60)** – 786,000, of which 11,500 Portuguese, 11,000 Moroccans, 6,000 Algerians, 3,000 from other African countries and 750 Britons.
- **Somme (80)** – 559,000, of which 3,500 Moroccans, 3,000 Portuguese, 1,500 Algerians, 1,200 from other African countries and 250 Britons.

Champagne-Ardenne

1.34m, of which 15,000 Algerians, 14,000 Portuguese, 12,000 Moroccans and 375 Britons. The region has the dubious distinction of being the only one where the population is in decline; it has decreased by around 0.05 per cent per year since the turn of the century. The most notable decline has been in people in their 20s, resulting in an ageing population.

- **Ardennes (08)** – 287,000, of which 7,000 Algerians, 1,850 Italians, 1,850 Moroccans, 1,800 Portuguese and 45 Britons.
- **Aube (10)** – 298,000, of which 4,500 Portuguese, 4,000 Moroccans, 2,000 Algerians, 1,050 Spaniards, 1,000 Vietnamese, 900 Italians and 80 Britons.
- **Haute-Marne (52)** – 187,000, of which 1,800 Algerians, 1,200 Turks, 1,150 Portuguese, 1,150 Moroccans and 40 Britons.
- **Marne (51)** – 565,000, of which 6,550 Portuguese, 5,000 Moroccans, 4,200 Algerians, 1,500 from other African countries and 200 Britons.

Lorraine

2.34m, of which 34,500 Italians, 29,000 Algerians, 22,000 Moroccans and 700 Britons. The region's population is growing at a slow rate (0.17 per cent per annum compared with the national average of 0.66), mostly in the 50–59 age group and in the two largest *départements*, Meurthe-et-Moselle and Moselle (and especially in the town of Thionville, which has grown by 3 per cent to over 42,000 inhabitants since 1999). The region's two largest cities, Metz and Nancy, are also growing, unlike many other French cities, while

Epinal, Lunéville and Saint-Dié-des-Vosges have declining populations. There's high unemployment in the region, particularly among women.

- **Meurthe-et-Moselle (54)** – 722,000, of which 9,000 Algerians, 8,500 Italians, 7,000 Moroccans, 6,000 Portuguese and 300 Britons.
- **Meuse (55)** – 193,000, of which 1,200 Turks, 1,000 Italians, 950 Portuguese, 900 Moroccans and 40 Britons.
- **Moselle (57)** – 1.04m, of which 24,000 Italians, 18,500 Algerians, 10,900 Moroccans, 10,500 Turks and 280 Britons.
- **Vosges (88)** – 383,000, of which 5,000 Portuguese, 3,500 Turks, 3,200 Moroccans, 1,500 Algerians, 1,000 Italians and 100 Britons.

Alsace

1.8m, of which 27,000 Turks, 19,000 Moroccans, 17,000 Algerians and 1,460 Britons. Alsace's rapid growth between during the '90s, when it was France's second-fastest growing region, has slowed in the early part of the 21st century, though it's still just above the national average at 0.68 per cent per year and some 10 per cent of the population has moved to Alsace since 2000. Virtually all of this increase has been in the *département* of Haut-Rhin. In particular, the region has attracted young people and unemployment is lower than the national average, although the population is slowly ageing.

- **Bas-Rhin (67)** – 1m, of which 17,200 Turks, 11,400 Moroccans, 7,200 Portuguese, 5,700 Algerians and 930 Britons.
- **Haut-Rhin (68)** – 736,000, of which 9,800 Turks, 7,600 Moroccans, 11,300 Algerians and 530 Britons.

Franche-Comté

1.15m, of which 11,400 Moroccans, 9,800 Turks, 8,700 Algerians, 7,600 Portuguese and 420 Britons. The region's population is growing at below the national average rate (0.37 per cent per annum compared with 0.66 per cent) as the area attracts few foreigners and other French – except in Haute-Saône, where more people have moved to the *département* than from it. The fastest growth is in the *département* of Doubs (0.45 per cent), which, along with the Territoire-de-Belfort, has a predominantly young population, owing to the prevalence of urban areas.

- **Doubs (25)** – 513,000, of which 5,000 Moroccans, 4,800 Algerians, 4,000 Turks, 3,000 Portuguese, 2,000 Spaniards and 170 Britons.
- **Jura (39)** – 255,000, of which 3,000 Turks, 2,500 Moroccans, 2,400 Portuguese, 1,200 Algerians, 600 Italians and 90 Britons.
- **Haute-Saône (70)** – 234,000, of which 2,800 Moroccans, 1,500 Portuguese, 1,000 Turks, 700 Algerians and 60 Britons.
- **Territoire-de-Belfort (90)** – 140,000, of which 2,000 Algerians, 1,800 Turks, 1,100 Moroccans, 600 Italians, 600 Portuguese and 100 Britons.

Burgundy

1.62m, of which 22,000 Portuguese, 19,000 Moroccans, 9,550 Algerians and 900 Britons. The region's population is increasing by just 0.12 per cent per year, the country's second-slowest growth rate after Champagne-Ardenne. The fastest-growing *département* is Yonne (0.4 per cent annual growth), while Nièvre is decreasing in population (-0.25 per cent per annum). There has recently been a slight increase (around 1,000 per year) in the number of retirees in the region.

- **Côte d-Or (21)** – 513,000, of which 8,300 Moroccans, 6,300 Portuguese, 3,500 Algerians, 2,000 Italians and 340 Britons.
- **Nièvre (58)** – 222,000, of which 2,100 Portuguese, 1,000 Moroccans, 400 Spaniards, 300 Turks and 80 Britons.
- **Saône-et-Loire (71)** – 546,000, of which 8,300 Portuguese, 5,100 Algerians, 3,800 Italians, 3,700 Moroccans and 270 Britons.
- **Yonne (89)** – 341,000, of which 6,000 Moroccans, 5,300 Portuguese, 1,600 Turks, 950 Algerians and 210 Britons.

Centre-Val-de-Loire

2.45m, of which 43,000 Portuguese, 28,000 Moroccans, 12,000 Algerians, 12,000 Turks, 5,500 Spaniards, 3,200 Tunisians and 1,300 Britons. The region's population is growing at below the national average rate (0.38 per cent per annum compared with 0.66 per cent) and is losing over 2,500 people in their 20s every year, including students and people on work experience, with the result that almost one in ten of the population is now over 75. Almost half of those moving to the region come from Ile-de-France, many of them retirees. The fastest-growing *départements* are Eure-et-Loir, Indre-et-Loire and Loir-et-Cher, while the population of Indre is in decline.

- **Cher (18)** – 315,000, of which 4,800 Portuguese, 2,300 Moroccans, 2,000 Algerians, 950 Turks and 130 Britons.
- **Eure-et-Loir (28)** – 417,000, of which 8,200 Moroccans, 6,800 Portuguese, 2,500 Algerians, 2,500 Turks and 200 Britons.
- **Indre (36)** – 232,000, of which 1,100 Portuguese, 1,100 Moroccans, 500 Algerians and 110 Britons.
- **Indre-et-Loire (37)** – 569,000, of which 9,100 Portuguese, 3,600 Algerians, 2,800 Moroccans, 750 Spaniards and 420 Britons.
- **Loir-et-Cher (41)** – 322,000, of which 5,800 Portuguese, 2,700 Turks, 2,600 Moroccans, 700 Spaniards and 150 Britons.
- **Loiret (45)** – 620,000, of which 15,400 Portuguese, 11,000 Moroccans, 5,000 Turks, 3,200 Algerians and 280 Britons.

Rhône-Alpes

The population of Rhône-Alpes, France's second-most populous region after Ile-de-France, is growing at well above the national average rate (0.9 per cent per annum compared with 0.66 per cent) and reached 6m in 2006. The *départements* of Ain and Haute-Savoie have experienced the fastest increases in population (1.4 per cent per year); only Loire has a higher death than birth rate.

- **Ain (01)** – 559,000, of which 8,000 Moroccans, 6,800 Portuguese, 6,500 Turks, 4,200 Algerians and 1,300 Britons.
- **Ardèche (07)** – 302,000, of which 2,000 Moroccans, 1,800 Algerians, 1,600 Portuguese, 1,000 Spaniards and 200 Britons.
- **Drôme (26)** – population 463,000, of which 6,000 are Moroccans, 5,000 Algerians, 2,700 Portuguese, 2,500 Tunisians and around 275 Britons.
- **Isère (38)** – population 1.16m, of which 15,500 are Algerians, 12,000 Italians and 12,000 Portuguese, 5,500 Turks and 1,500 Britons.
- **Loire (42)** – 732,000, of which 16,500 Algerians, 8,500 Moroccans, 7,500 Portuguese, 6,000 Italians and 230 Britons.
- **Rhône (69)** – 1.65m, of which 45,000 Algerians, 20,000 Portuguese, 20,000 Tunisians, 11,000 Italians and 1,500 Britons.

- **Savoie (73)** – population 400,000 of which 6,000 are Algerians, 6,000 Italians, 4,500 Portuguese, 3,300 Moroccans and 650 Britons.
- **Haute-Savoie (74)** – population 686,000, of which 7,500 are Algerians and 7,500 Italians, 6,500 Portuguese, 6,000 Turks and 1,100 Britons.

CLIMATE

Nord-Pas-de-Calais

The region experiences no extremes of temperature on account of the influence of the warm Gulf Stream flowing up the Channel from the North Atlantic, but the weather is changeable and often cloudy and wet. In fact Nord-Pas-de-Calais has the least sunshine of any part of France, with only 1,600 hours per year and around 120 days' rain annually. Particularly rainy areas are Artois, Haut-Boulonnais and Avenois. The wettest month is November (with around 95mm of rain in Nord and 70mm in Pas-de-Calais), the driest February (40mm) and July (45-50mm). There's seldom snow or ice, although the hills of Ardennes, on the Belgian border, have some. The average for the region is 18 days of snow per year. Average maximum/minimum temperatures along the coast are around 20/14C (56/67F) in summer and 6/2C (43/36F) in winter.

Picardy

The climate of Picardy is similar to that of Nord-Pas-de-Calais (see above), although there's some continental influence, with greater variations in temperature between winter and summer in southern areas of the two inland *départements*, Aisne and Oise. Somme has a similar rainfall pattern to Nord and Pas-de-Calais, while Aisne's wettest month is June (68mm), its driest February (45mm) and in Oise the extremes come in December (70mm) and August (46mm). The region enjoys around 1,660 hours of sunshine per year and it rains on around 120 days.

Champagne-Ardenne

Champagne experiences a continental climate with severe winter temperatures, sometimes as low as -15C (5F). Average annual sunshine is around 1,730 hours and average annual rainfall 600mm (24in) on 113 days of the year. May, October and December are the wettest months, though rainfall varies considerably throughout the region (not surprisingly, it's highest in the Ardennes), though even in summer there's around 50mm of rain per month. Charleville-Mézières in Ardennes has the dubious distinction of having the least sunshine of any major town in France – a mere 1,440 hours annually.

Lorraine

Lorraine has a mixed continental and oceanic climate, the absence of high land around Ile-de-France region acting as a corridor for westerly winds bringing rain. Days are often warm and sunny, but nights can be cold. (There may be a 20C (36F) variation between day and night temperatures.) The region experiences distinct seasons, although the weather can be very changeable with hot or cold, dry weather giving way to heavy rain. Average annual sunshine hours are around 1,650 and rainfall 760mm (30in) on 125 days (as many as 135 in parts of Vosges).

Alsace

As the region is protected from westerly winds by the Vosges mountains, Alsace has a continental climate with cold winters (60 to 70 days of frost per year) and hot, dry summers, with occasional storms. Average maximum/minimum summer temperatures are 25/13C (77/55F) and average winter temperatures around 1 to 2C (34 to 36F). Average annual rainfall is between 600 and 700mm (23.5 and 27.5in) on between 104 days (Colmar) and 123 days (Mulhouse) with Strasbourg having around 112 days' rain. The region is one of France's least sunny, with just 1,637 hours' sunshine per year in Strasbourg, 1,724 in Colmar and 1,768 in Mulhouse.

Franche-Comté

The climate of Franche-Comté varies between the plains, where it's mild, and the mountains, where it's humid and cold. There are corresponding variations in rainfall: between 700mm (27in) on the plains and 1,700mm (67in) in the mountains. Belfort (90) and Besançon (25) have around 1,100mm (43in) of rain annually and around 1,870 hours of sunshine. Not surprisingly, rainfall is highest in the Jura mountains (up to 120mm in May and 80mm even in August) but elsewhere monthly rainfall rarely drops below

80mm. Average winter temperatures are around 2C (36F). Belfort has the dubious distinction of being the coldest and second-rainiest place in France: it rains on over 142 days in the year and the average annual temperature is a mere 9.3C (48F).

Burgundy

Despite its location, Burgundy's climate is predominantly oceanic with westerly winds bringing rain. Average annual rainfall is between 655mm (26in) on 115 days in Auxerre (89) and 815mm (32in) on 125 days in Nevers (58). Rainfall is fairly evenly spread throughout the year: the wettest month is May (with between 70 and 90mm of rainfall), followed by October, the driest February-March and July-August (around 60mm). Summers are usually hot (i.e. over 25C/77F during the day) and winters cold but sunny. The region enjoys between 1,758 (Auxerre) and 1,830 (Dijon) hours' sunshine per year. Not surprisingly, the mildest weather is in the most southern *département*, Saône-et-Loire (71). The Morvan mountains (in the centre of the region), which rise to over 600m (1,970ft) can experience sudden changes in weather.

Centre-Val-de-Loire

The climate of this region is similar to that of the Pays-de-la-Loire (see page 105), i.e. oceanic with moderate temperatures throughout the year and much less marked seasons than, for example, Alsace. Snow and ice are rare and the difference between average winter temperatures and average summer temperatures is just 14C (25F). Rainfall is between 580mm (23in) on 108 days in Chartres (28) and 725mm (28.5in) on 118 days in Bourges (18). May is the wettest month, with between 60 and 80mm of rain, the rest of the year having around 50mm per month, though August is generally the driest month. The region enjoys between 1,750 (Chartres) and 1,845 (Blois) hours' sunshine per year.

Rhône-Alpes

The lowlands of Rhône-Alpes have a mainly continental climate, with temperatures approaching those of the Mediterranean coast in southern Ardèche. (The *Mistral* occasionally blows up the Rhône valley.) Average annual rainfall for the two largest towns in the region is 710mm on 99 days in Saint-Etienne (42) and 825mm (32.5in) on 107 days in Lyon (69). Ardèche is the region's wettest *département*, with over 160mm of rain in October, though July is quite dry (50mm). Drôme's pattern is similar, with around 10mm less rain per month. Ain's wettest months are September (with 120mm) and May (115mm), but even its driest, July, has almost 80mm. Rhône is considerably drier, rainfall peaking in October (95mm), with February the driest month (50mm), while in Loire May is wettest (90mm) and July the driest (75mm). Bourg-en-Bresse (01) has as many as 126 days' rain and 1,787 hours' sunshine per year. Lyon has almost 2,000 hours of sunshine on average a year and average maximum/minimum summer temperatures of 27/15C (81/59F). In winter, Lyon averages 5/-1C (41/30F). Mountainous areas, not surprisingly, have a very different weather pattern, temperatures averaging -7C (20F) in winter in Haute-Savoie, with the most rain in June (130mm) and the least in March, April and August (80-85mm). Isère's weather falls between the two, with peak rainfall from September to November (100mm per month) and the least in July (70mm).

COST OF PROPERTY

The table below gives the average selling price of houses in 2006. Note, however, that house sizes vary from area to area, which can distort average figures.

Town/Area	**Average House Price**			
	2-bed	**3-bed**	**4-bed**	**5+-bed**
Nord-Pas-de-Calais				
Hesdin/Montreuil	€120,000	€170,000	€175,000	€365,000
Lille	€120,000	€195,000	€240,000	€380,000
Le Touquet	€255,000	€510,000	€635,000	€775,000

9

The average price of a period property in 2006 in Nord-Pas-de-Calais as a whole was around €92,500 (national average of €102,250), the average for a new house €125,800 (average €117,650) and for a building plot €22,400 (average €23,000). Note, however, that average property prices aren't always a reliable indication of the relative price of similar properties in different areas, as one may have a preponderance of cheaper or more expensive properties.

Town/Area	Average House Price			
	2-bed	3-bed	4-bed	5+-bed
Picardy				
Amiens	€130,000	€160,000	€285,000	€355,000
Somme Valley	€115,000	€150,000	€270,000	€310,000

The average price of a period property in 2006 in Picardy as a whole was around €93,000 (national average of €102,250), the average for a new house €120,600 (average €117,650) and for a building plot €6,500 (average €23,000). Note, however, that average property prices aren't always a reliable indication of the relative price of similar properties in different areas, as one may have a preponderance of cheaper or more expensive properties.

Town/Area	Average House Price			
	2-bed	3-bed	4-bed	5+-bed
Champagne-Ardenne				
Châlons	€155,000	€205,000	€225,000	€345,000
Charleville-Mézières	€105,000	€145,000	€205,000	€300,000
Epernay & Reims	€170,000	€200,000	€210,000	€300,000
Lorraine				
Metz & Nancy	€180,000	€220,000	€255,000	€355,000
Vosges area	€165,000	€200,000	€280,000	€385,000
Alsace				
Strasbourg	€190,000	€300,000	€395,000	€610,000
Franche-Comté				
Besançon	€185,000	€260,000	€370,000	€440,000
Lons-le-Saunier/ Vallée des Lacs	€90,000	€130,000	€200,000	€325,000

Burgundy				
Auxerre	€105,000	€175,000	€230,000	€300,000
Châtillon	€140,000	€235,000	€275,000	€470,000
Dijon	€145,000	€195,000	€350,000	€635,000
Mâcon	€130,000	€205,000	€255,000	€330,000
Nevers	€120,000	€180,000	€215,000	€330,000

The average price of a period property in 2006 in Burgundy as a whole was around €85,350 (national average of €102,250), the average for a new house €115,000 (average €117,650) and for a building plot €21,000 (average €23,000).

Town/Area	**Average House Price**			
	2-bed	**3-bed**	**4-bed**	**5+-bed**
Centre-Val-de-Loire				
Orléans	€225,000	€250,000	€300,000	€400,000
Tours	€200,000	€250,000	€350,000	€450,000

The average price of a period property in 2006 in Centre-Val-de-Loire as a whole was around €93,000 (national average of €102,250), the average for a new house €117,000 (average €117,650) and for a building plot €24,000 (average €23,000).

Town/Area	**Average House Price**			
	2-bed	**3-bed**	**4-bed**	**5+-bed**
Rhône-Alpes				
Beaujolais	€175,000	€245,000	€385,000	€500,000
Grenoble	€220,000	€350,000	€400,000	€615,000
Lac d'Annecy	€230,000	€365,000	€420,000	€575,000
Lyon	€265,000	€290,000	€465,000	€650,000

The average price of a period property in 2006 in Rhône-Alpes as a whole was around €147,000 (national average of €172,600), the average for a new house €100,000 (average €117,650). For prices in the ski resorts, see page 304.

Did you know?

The *département* of Ardèche has one of the highest concentrations of second homes in France and property prices have doubled in the last decade, though they're now falling, especially around the departmental capital, Privas, largely owing to the amount of building that has taken place recently. Generally, the further south you go, the higher the prices: the average property price in Privas in early 2007 was around €2,300 per m^2 and near the Gorges and Pont d'Arc around €2,900. It's still possible to find a 'ruin' with some land for around €160,000.

Ardèche Conseil (☎ 04 75 65 28 20, 💻 www.ardecheconseil.com)

COMMUNICATIONS

The information below details communications by air between regional airports and the UK and Europe (see also **Appendix F**). For details of sea links between England and France, see **Sea** on page 95.

The Paris airports (see page 369) are accessible from most of **Picardy**, **Champagne-Ardenne**, **Burgundy** and **Centre-Val-de-Loire** as well as southern parts of **Nord-Pas-de-Calais**, offering flights to most world-wide destinations. Lyon-Saint-Exupéry is the other international airport with direct flights to and from several European destinations and is accessible from the **Rhône** region as well as southern parts of **Burgundy** and **Franche-Comté**. There are no regular international flights to the airports at Amiens (**Picardy**), Reims and Troyes (**Champagne-Ardenne**) or Metz-Nancy (**Lorraine**). Details of all French airports and their services can be found on 💻 www.aeroport.fr.

Nord-Pas-de-Calais

Lille airport (59) offers flights throughout France, and to and from towns in Germany, Italy, Portugal, Spain and Switzerland, but no direct flights to and from the UK. There's a *TGV* connection to the city centre. Paris CDG is accessible from southern parts of the region.

Picardy

Beauvais airport (60) offers flights to Shannon (Ryanair) and towns in Italy and Sweden. Paris CDG is convenient for southern parts.

Alsace

Strasbourg airport (67) offers flights throughout France but no direct flights to the UK (change at Paris CDG for Heathrow and Stansted). Mulhouse-Basle airport (on the Swiss border) has direct flights, several times daily, to London Heathrow.

Franche-Comté

There are no major airports in Franche-Comté but Mulhouse-Basle (see above) and other airports in Switzerland are convenient for eastern parts of the *département*.

Burgundy

Dijon airport (21) currently offers no direct flights to the UK, but Paris Orly is convenient for northern parts (see above).

Centre-Val-de-Loire

There are currently no direct flights to the UK from local airports, but Paris Orly is accessible from Eure-et-Loir and Loiret, and Poitiers airport (in Vienne) from Indre and Indre-et-Loire.

Rhône-Alpes

Lyon-Saint-Exupéry airport offers direct flights to Birmingham, Dublin, Glasgow, Liverpool, London Heathrow and Stansted, Manchester and Nottingham-East Midlands.

FURTHER INFORMATION

Useful Addresses

- Comité régional du Tourisme de **Nord-Pas-de-Calais**, 6, place Mendès France, 59800 Lille (☎ 03 20 14 57 57, 🖳 www.crt-nordpasdecalais.fr and 🖳 www.northernfrance-tourism.com) ;
- Comité régional du Tourisme de **Picardie**, 3 rue Vincent Auriol, 80011 Amiens (☎ 03 22 22 33 66, 🖳 www.cr-picardie.fr and 🖳 www.picardietourisme.com);
- Comité régional du Tourisme de **Champagne-Ardenne**, 15 avenue du Maréchal Leclerc, BP 319, 51013 Châlons-en-Champagne (☎ 03 26 21 85 80, 🖳 www. tourisme-champagne-ardenne.com);
- Comité régional du Tourisme de **Lorraine**, Abbaye des Prémontrés, BP 97, 54704 Pont-à-Mousson (☎ 03 83 80 01 80, 🖳 www.crt-lorraine.fr);
- Comité régional du Tourisme d'**Alsace**, 20A rue Berthe Molly, 68000 Colmar (☎ 03 89 24 73 50, 🖳 www.tourisme-alsace.com);
- Comité régional du Tourisme de **Franche-Comt**é, La City, 4 rue Gabriel, Plançon, 25044 Besançon (☎ 08 10 10 11 13, 🖳 www.franche-comte.org);
- Comité régional du Tourisme du **Centre-Val-de-Loire**, 37 avenue de Paris, 45000 Orléans (☎ 02 38 79 95 00, 🖳 www.loirevalley tourism.com);
- Comité régional du Tourisme de **Bourgogne**, Conseil Régional, BP 1602, 21035 Dijon (☎ 03 80 28 02 80, 🖳 www.bourgogne-tourisme.com and 🖳 www.burgundy-tourism.com);
- Comité régional du Tourisme de **Rhône-Alpes**, 104, route de Paris, 69260 Charbonnières-les-Bains (☎ 04 72 59 21 59, 🖳 www.rhonealpes-tourisme.com).

Useful Publications

In addition to the national publications listed in **Appendix B**, the following regional and local publications will provide useful information:

- *La Voix du Nord*
- *Le Courrier picard*
- *Le Dauphiné libéré*
- *Le Journal de la Haute-Marne*
- *Le Populaire du Centre*
- *Le Républicain lorrain*

Useful Websites

- www.beaujolais.com – information on the Beaujolais area of Burgundy
- www.burgundyfriends.com – an English-language club aimed at helping new residents of Burgundy to integrate
- www.europe.anglican.org – details of Anglican services throughout France
- www.paysdesabbayes.com – information about Lorraine
- www.piedaterre.eu.com – property service business based in Pas-de-Calais
- www.somme-tourisme.com – information about the *département* of Somme in Picardy
- www.tourisme-hautemarne.com – information about the *département* of Haute-Marne in Champagne-Ardenne;
- www.tourismepierresdorees.com – information on the 'Golden Stone' part of Beaujolais (in Burgundy).

FOR
SALE

Montenvers – The Alps

APPENDICES

APPENDIX A: FURTHER INFORMATION

Embassies & Consulates

Foreign embassies are located in the capital Paris (those of selected English-speaking countries are listed below), and many countries also have consulates in other cities (British consulates are listed below). Embassies and consulates are listed in the yellow pages under *Ambassades, Consulats et Autres Représentations Diplomatiques*.

Australia: 4 rue Jean Rey, 15e (☎ 01 40 59 33 00).

Canada: 35 avenue Montaigne, 8e (☎ 01 44 43 29 00).

Ireland: 41 rue Rude, 16e (☎ 01 44 17 67 00).

Jamaica: 60 avenue Foch, 16e (☎ 01 45 00 62 25).

Malta: 92 avenue Champs Elysées, 8e (☎ 01 56 59 75 00).

New Zealand: 7ter rue Léonard de Vinci, 16e (☎ 01 45 01 43 43).

South Africa: 59 quai Orsay, 7e (☎ 01 53 59 23 23).

United Kingdom: see **British Consulates-general** below.

United States of America: 2 rue St Florentin, 1e (☎ 01 43 12 22 20) and 2, avenue Gabriel, 1e (☎ 08 10 26 46 26).

British Consulates-general

Consulates-general are permanently staffed during normal office hours.

Bordeaux: 353 boulevard du Président Wilson, BP 91, 33073 Bordeaux (☎ 05 57 22 21 10). Covers the departments of Ariège, Aveyron, Charente, Charente-Maritime, Corrèze, Creuse, Dordogne, Haute-Garonne, Gers, Gironde, Landes, Lot, Lot-et-Garonne, Pyrénées-Atlantiques, Hautes-Pyrénées, Deux-Sèvres, Tarn, Tarn-et-Garonne, Vienne and Haute-Vienne.

Lille: 11 square Dutilleul, 59800 Lille (☎ 03 20 12 82 72). Covers the departments of Aisne, Ardennes, Nord, Pas-de-Calais and Somme.

Lyon: 24 rue Childebert, 69288 Lyon Cedex 1 (☎ 04 72 77 81 70). Covers the departments of Ain, Allier, Ardèche, Cantal, Côte d'Or, Doubs, Drôme, Isère, Jura, Loire, Haute-Loire, Puy-de-Dôme, Rhône, Haute-Saône, Saône-et-Loire, Savoie, Haute-Savoie and the Territoire de Belfort.

Marseille: 24 avenue du Prado, 13006 Marseille (☎ 04 91 15 72 10). Covers the departments of Alpes-de-Haute-Provence, Hautes-Alpes, Alpes-Maritimes, Aude, Bouches-du-Rhône, Gard, Hérault, Lozère, Pyrénées-Orientales, Var and Vaucluse, as well as Corsica.

Paris: 35 rue du Faubourg Saint Honoré, 75008 Paris (☎ 01 44 51 31 00, 💻 http://www.amb-grandebretagne.fr – where there are links to the other Consulate-general sites). Covers the departments of Aube, Calvados, Cher, Côtes d'Armor, Eure, Eure-et-Loir, Finstère, Ille-et-Vilaine, Indre, Indre-et-Loire, Loir-et-Cher, Loire, Loire-Atlantique, Loiret, Maine-et-Loire, Manche, Marne, Haute-Marne, Mayenne, Meurthe-et-Moselle, Meuse, Morbihan, Moselle, Nièvre, Oise, Bas-Rhin, Sarthe and Vosges, as well as the whole of the Ile-de-France and the overseas departments and territories.

British Honorary Consulates

Honorary consulates aren't permanently staffed and should be contacted **in emergencies only** (e.g. for urgent passport renewals or replacements).

Boulogne-sur-Mer: c/o Cabinet Barron et Brun, 28, rue Saint Jean, 62200 Boulogne-sur-Mer (☎ 03 21 87 16 80).

Cherbourg-Octeville: c/o P&O Ferries, Gare Maritime, BP46, 50652 Cherbourg-Octeville (☎ 02 33 88 65 60).

Dunkerque: c/o Lemaire Frères & Fils, 30 rue de l'Hermitte, BP 2/100, 59376 Dunkerque (☎ 03 28 58 77 00).

Le Havre: c/o LD Lines, 124 boulevard de Strasbourg, 76600 Le Havre (☎ 02 35 19 78 88).

Montpellier: 271 Le Capitole, Bâtiment A, 64, rue Alcyone, 34000 Montpellier (☎ 04 67 15 52 07)

Nantes: 16 boulevard Gabriel Giust'hau, BP 22026, 44020 Nantes Cedex 1 (☎ 02 51 72 72 60).

Toulouse: c/o English Enterprises, 8 allée du Commingues, 317700 Colomiers, 31300 Toulouse (☎ 05 61 30 37 91).

Tours: 7 rue des Rosiers, 37510 Savonnières (☎ 02 47 43 57 97).

Miscellaneous

Alliance Française, 101 boulevard Raspail, 75270 Paris Cedex 06 (☎ 01 42 84 90 00, 💻 http://www.alliancefr.org). Famous language-teaching school.

Blevins Franks Tax Advisory Service (☎ 020-7015 2126, 💻 http://www.blevinsfranks.com). International tax planning experts.

Brit Consulting, 11 rue Félix Faure, 75015 Paris (☎ 06 23 86 30 21, 💻 http://www.britconsulting.com). A project management service for people building or renovating property in France.

British Association of Removers (BAR) Overseas, Tangent House, 62 Exchange Road, Watford, WD18 0TG, UK (☎ 01923-699480, 💻 http://www.removers.org.uk).

Centre des Impôts de Non-Résidents, 9 rue d'Uzès, 75094 Paris Cedex 02 (☎ 01 44 76 18 00).

Centre Renseignements Douaniers (💻 http://www.douane.gouv.fr). Customs information.

Chambre des Notaires, 12 avenue Victoria, 75001 Paris (☎ 01 44 82 24 00, 💻 http://www.paris.notaires.fr).

Compagnie Nationale des Experts Immobiliers, 18 rue Volney, 75002 Paris (☎ 01 42 96 18 46, 🖳 http://www.expert-cnei.com).

Conseil Supérieur du Notariat, 31 rue du Général Foy, 75383 Paris Cedex 08 (☎ 01 44 90 30 00, 🖳 http://www.notaires.fr).

Department for Environment, Food & Rural Affairs (DEFRA), Nobel House, 17 Smith Square, London SW1P 3JR, UK (☎ 020-7238 6951/0845-933 5577, 🖳 http://www.defra.gov.uk).

Fédération Nationale de l'Immobilier (FNAIM), 129 rue du Faubourg St Honoré, 75008 Paris (🖳 http://www.fnaim.fr).

Federation of Overseas Property Developers, Agents and Consultants (FOPDAC), First Floor, 618 Newmarket Road, Cambridge CB5 8LP (☎ 0870-350 1223, 🖳 http://www.fopdac.com).

Gîtes de France, 59 rue St Lazare, Paris 75439 Cedex 09 (☎ 01 49 70 75 75, 🖳 http://www.gites-de-france.fr).

Office du Tourisme, 25 rue des Pyramides, 75001 Paris (☎ 08 92 68 30 00, 🖳 http://www.parisinfo.com).

De Particulier à Particulier, 40 rue du docteur Roux, 75724 Cedex 15 (☎ 01 40 56 33 33, 🖳 http://www.pap.fr).

Société d'Aménagement Foncier et d'Etablissement Rural (SAFER), 91 rue du Faubourg St Honoré, 75008 Paris (☎ 01 44 69 86 00, 🖳 http://www.safer.fr).

Union Nationale des AVF (Accueils des Villes Françaises), 3 rue de Paradis, 75010 Paris (☎ 01 47 70 45 85, 🖳 http://www.avf.asso.fr).

Major Property Exhibitions

Below is a list of the main exhibition organisers in Britain and Ireland. Note that you may be charged a small admission fee.

Homes Overseas Exhibition (UK ☎ 020-7002 8300, 🖳 http://www.blendoncommunications.co.uk). The largest organisers of international property exhibitions, who stage over 30 exhibitions each year at a range of venues in the UK and Ireland.

International Property Show (UK ☎ 01252 720652, 🖳 http://www.internationalpropertyshow.com). Takes place several times a year in London and Manchester.

A Place in the Sun Exhibition (UK ☎ 0870-352 8888, 🖳 http://www.aplaceinthesunlive.com). A new annual show in London.

World Class Homes (UK ☎ 01582-832001/0800-731 4713, 🖳 http://www.worldclasshomes.co.uk). Exhibitions are held in small venues around the UK and include mainly British property developers.

World of Property Show (UK ☎ 01323-726040, 🖳 http://www.outboundpublishing.com). The *World of Property* magazine publishers (see **Appendix B**) organise three large property exhibitions a year, two in the south of England and one in the north.

Appendix B: Further Reading

English-language Newspapers & Magazines

The publications listed below are a selection of the dozens related to France and, in particular, French property. Most of these include advertisements by estate agents and companies offering other services for house hunters and buyers as well as an ordering service for books about France and the French.

The Connexion (France ☎ 04 93 32 16 59, 💻 http://www.connexionfrance.com). Monthly newspaper.

Everything France Magazine, Brooklands Magazines Ltd (UK ☎ 0870-403 0330, 💻 http://www.everythingfrancemag.co.uk). Bi-monthly lifestyle magazine.

Focus on France, Outbound Publishing (UK ☎ 01323-726040, 💻 http://www.outboundpublishing.com). Quarterly property magazine.

France Magazine, Archant Life (UK ☎ 01858-438832, 💻 http://www.francemag.co.uk). Monthly lifestyle magazine.

France-USA Contacts/FUSAC (France ☎ 01 56 53 54 54, 💻 http://www.fusac.fr). Free bi-weekly magazine.

French Magazine, Merricks Media Ltd (UK ☎ 01225-786840, 💻 http://www.frenchmagazine.co.uk). Monthly lifestyle and property magazine.

French News, SARL Brussac (France ☎ 05 53 06 84 40, 💻 http://www.french-news.com). Monthly newspaper.

French Property News, Archant Life (UK ☎ 020-8543 3113, 💻 http://www.french-property-news.com). Monthly property magazine.

Homes Overseas, Blendon Communications Ltd (UK ☎ 020-7002 8300, 💻 http://www.blendoncommunications.co.uk). Monthly international property magazine.

The Irish Eyes Magazine, The Eyes (France ☎ 01 41 74 93 03, 💻 http://www.irisheyes.fr). Monthly Paris cultural magazine.

Living France, Archant Life (UK ☎ 01858 438832, 💻 http://www.livingfrance.com). Monthly lifestyle/property magazine.

Normandie & South of England Magazine (France ☎ 02 33 77 32 70, 💻 http://www.normandie-magazine.fr). News and current affairs about Normandy and parts of southern England, published eight times a year mainly in French but with some English articles and translations.

Paris Voice/Paris Free Voice (France ☎ 01 47 70 45 05, 💻 http://www.parisvoice.com). Free weekly newspaper.

Property France, Outbound Publishing Ltd (UK ☎ 01323-726040, 💻 http://www.outboundpublishing.com). Bi-monthly magazine.

The Riviera Reporter (France ☎ 04 93 45 77 19, 💻 http://www.riviera-reporter.com). Bi-monthly free magazine covering the Côte d'Azur.

The Riviera Times (France ☎ 04 93 27 60 00, 💻 http://www.riviera times.com). Monthly free newspaper covering the Côte d'Azur and Italian Riviera.

World of Property, Outbound Publishing Ltd (UK ☎ 01323-726040, 💻 http://www.outboundpublishing.com). Bi-monthly magazine.

Books

The following books about France and the French are published by Survival Books and can be ordered using the forms at the back of the book.

The Alien's Guide to France, Jim Watson. A light-hearted look at life in France.

Brittany Lifeline, Val Gascoyne. A directory of services, amenities and facilities in Brittany for visitors and residents.

Dordogne/Lot Lifeline, Val Gascoyne. A directory of services, amenities and facilities in Dordogne, Lot and Lot-et-Garonne for visitors and residents.

Earning Money from Your French Home, Jo Taylor. How to make money from home, including bed & breakfast and *gîtes*.

Foreigners in France: Triumphs & Disasters, Joe & Kerry Laredo (eds). Real-life stories of people from all over the world who have moved to France.

Living & Working in France, David Hampshire. Everything you need to know about life and employment in France.

Making a Living in France, Joe Laredo. The ins and outs of self-employment and starting a business in France.

Normandy Lifeline, Val Gascoyne. A directory of services, amenities and facilities in Upper and Lower Normandy for visitors and residents.

Poitou-Charentes Lifeline, Val Gascoyne. A directory of services, amenities and facilities in Poitou-Charentes for visitors and residents.

Provence/Côte d'Azur Lifeline, Val Gascoyne. A directory of services, amenities and facilities in the Provence-Alpes-Côte-d'Azur region for visitors and residents.

Renovating & Maintaining Your French Home, Joe Laredo. How to realise the renovation dream and avoid nightmares.

Rural Living in France, Jeremy Hobson. Everything you need to know to create your very own French rural idyll.

Appendix C: Useful Websites

Below is a list of general websites that might be of interest and aren't mentioned elsewhere in this book; websites relevant to specific aspects of buying a home in France are given in the appropriate section. Websites generally offer free access, although some require a subscription or payment for services. Relocation and other companies specialising in expatriate services often have websites, although these may only provide information that a company is prepared to offer free of charge, which may be rather biased. However, there are plenty of volunteer sites run by expatriates providing practical information and tips.

A particularly useful section found on most expatriate websites is the 'message board' or 'forum', where expatriates answer questions based on their experience and knowledge and offer an insight into what living and working in France is **really** like; these are also offered by some magazine websites (see **Appendix B**). Websites are listed under headings in alphabetical order and the list is by no means definitive.

General Information About France

- http://adminet.com – information about selected towns in France.
- http://french-at-a-touch.com/index.html – general information on France and links to many other sites.
- http://nucleaire.edf.fr – information about nuclear power stations in France.
- www.abelcom.net – general information about France.
- www.actualinfo.com – news.
- www.admifrance.gouv.fr – includes links to all government ministry websites.
- www.afp.com – world news and information in English.
- www.all-about-france.com – general information about France.

- www.anglofrance.orgt – general information on France for English-speaking expatriates.
- www.culture.fr – information about cultural events and activities.
- www.expatica.com – practical information for English-speaking expatriates; mainly Paris-orientated, but lots of useful general information as well.
- www.finances.gouv.fr – economic information.
- www.diplomatie.gouv.fr – general information about France, including daily updated news.
- www.francealacarte.org.uk/education – information about education in France.
- www.franceguide.com – the French Tourist Office in London.
- www.franceguide.fr – tourist information.
- www.holidayfrance.org.uk – the British Association of Tour Operators to France.
- www.insee.fr – office of national statistics: population, unemployment, salaries, etc. (in English and French).
- www.legifrance.gouv.fr – legal information.
- www.lepoint.fr – articles and surveys on all aspects of French life from the consumer magazine *Le Point*.
- www.leprogres.fr – general information.
- www.letudiant.fr – information for students.
- www.meteofrance.com – weather and climate in France.
- www.pagesjaunes.fr – the French yellow pages.
- www.parisnotes.com – information about Paris.
- www.paris.alliancefr.fr – the site of the Alliance française.
- www.parisinfo.com – tourist information.
- www.pratique.fr – practical information.

- www.service-public.fr – French Public Services; includes links to most important French government websites.

Amenities

- www.amb-usa.fr/consul/acs/guide/doc.pdf – a list of English-speaking doctors and hospitals.
- www.backspin.com – excellent guide to golf courses in France.
- www.cinefil.com – information about films showing in each area, with an indication of which films are being shown in the original language.
- www.cityvox.com – information about eating out, accommodation, foreign food shops, etc. in selected towns in France.
- www.ffe.fr – Federation française d'Equitation for information on horse riding.
- www.equipyrene.com – Office of Pyrenean Equestrian Guides for information on horse riding.
- www.ffck.org – information on canoeing and kayaking.
- www.ffgolf.org – the French golfing federation.
- www.pavillonbleu.com – a list of 'blue flag' beaches in France (awarded by the Foundation for European Education and Environment).
- www.quechoisir.org – reports and articles from the consumer magazine *Que Choisir*.
- www.surfrider-europe.org – details of 'black flag' (i.e. polluted) beaches in France (awarded by the Surfrider Foundation Europe).
- www.thalasso-france.com – a list of balneology centres.

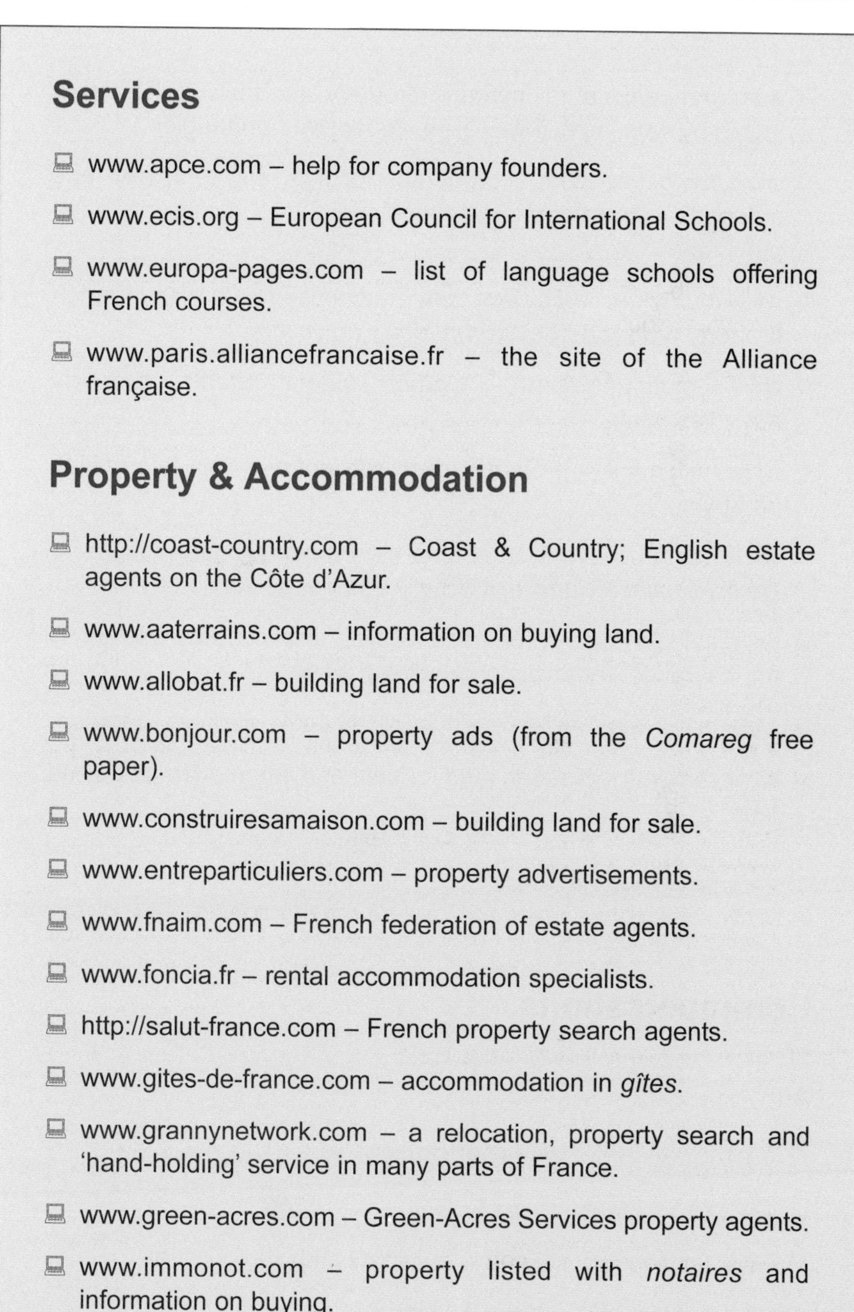

Services

- www.apce.com – help for company founders.
- www.ecis.org – European Council for International Schools.
- www.europa-pages.com – list of language schools offering French courses.
- www.paris.alliancefrancaise.fr – the site of the Alliance française.

Property & Accommodation

- http://coast-country.com – Coast & Country; English estate agents on the Côte d'Azur.
- www.aaterrains.com – information on buying land.
- www.allobat.fr – building land for sale.
- www.bonjour.com – property ads (from the *Comareg* free paper).
- www.construiresamaison.com – building land for sale.
- www.entreparticuliers.com – property advertisements.
- www.fnaim.com – French federation of estate agents.
- www.foncia.fr – rental accommodation specialists.
- http://salut-france.com – French property search agents.
- www.gites-de-france.com – accommodation in *gîtes*.
- www.grannynetwork.com – a relocation, property search and 'hand-holding' service in many parts of France.
- www.green-acres.com – Green-Acres Services property agents.
- www.immonot.com – property listed with *notaires* and information on buying.

- www.immoprix.com – average property and building land sale prices by type, size, town, area, department and region.
- www.immostreet.com – properties for sale and rent; also has automatic calculator showing repayment amounts for mortgage purchases.
- www.journaldesparticuliers.com – advertisements in the French property magazine *Le Journal des Particuliers*.
- www.logic-immo.com – French estate agents' property advertisements.
- www.notaires.fr – property listed with *notaires* and information on buying.
- www.pap.fr – advertisements in the French property magazine *De Particulier à Particulier* (English-language version available).
- www.seloger.com – properties for sale and rent plus quotations for insurance, removals and building work.
- www.southwestfrancepropertyservices.com – property agents.
- www.terrain.fr – building land for sale and information on buying land.
- www.terrains-a-batir.com – building land for sale.
- www.vefuk.com – Vivre en France property agents.

Communications

Air

- www.aeroport.fr – details of and links to all French airports.
- www.airfrance.com – Air France.
- www.britishairways.co.uk – British Airways.
- www.easyjet.com – EasyJet airline.

- www.flybe.com – Flybe airline.
- www.flybmi.com – Bmi airline.
- www.ryanair.com – Ryanair.

Sea

- www.brittanyferries.com – Brittany Ferries.
- www.condorferries.co.uk – Condor Ferries.
- www.norfolkline.com – Norfolkline ferries.
- www.poferries.com – P&O Ferries.
- www.seafrance.com – Sea France ferries.
- www.transmancheferries.com – Transmanche ferries.

Other Public Transport

- www.eurolines.com – Eurolines international coach services.
- www.eurostar.com – Eurostar rail services.
- www.eurotunnel.com – Eurotunnel.
- www.frenchmotorail.com – Motorail.
- www.gobycoach.com – National Express coaches.
- www.nationalexpress.com – National Express international coach services.
- www.raileurope.com – Eurostar/TGV link and Rail Europe.
- www.ratp.fr – Parisian regional transport authority.
- www.sncf.fr – French national railways.
- www.transbus.org – information about tramways in France.

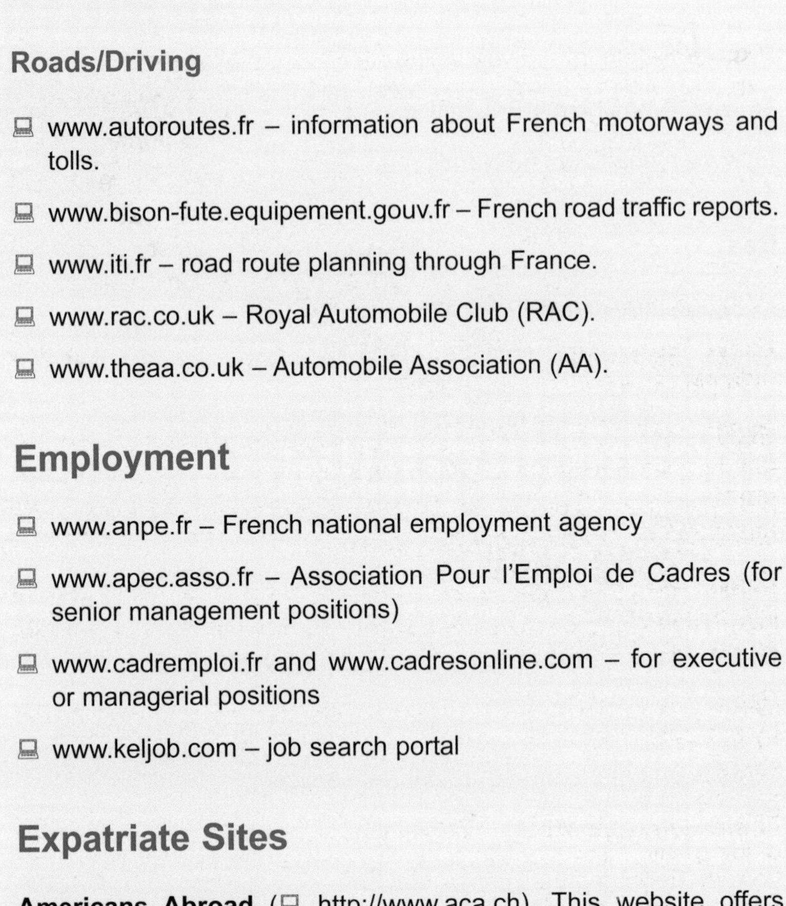

Roads/Driving

- www.autoroutes.fr – information about French motorways and tolls.
- www.bison-fute.equipement.gouv.fr – French road traffic reports.
- www.iti.fr – road route planning through France.
- www.rac.co.uk – Royal Automobile Club (RAC).
- www.theaa.co.uk – Automobile Association (AA).

Employment

- www.anpe.fr – French national employment agency
- www.apec.asso.fr – Association Pour l'Emploi de Cadres (for senior management positions)
- www.cadremploi.fr and www.cadresonline.com – for executive or managerial positions
- www.keljob.com – job search portal

Expatriate Sites

Americans Abroad (http://www.aca.ch). This website offers advice, information and services to Americans abroad.

Australians Abroad (http://www.australiansabroad.com). Information for Australians concerning relocating plus a forum to exchange information and advice.

British Expatriates (http://www.britishexpat.com). This website keeps British expatriates in touch with events and information about the UK.

Contact Expats (http://www.contactexpats.com). A worldwide forum for expatriates.

ExpatBoards (💻 http://www.expatboards.com). The mega site for expatriates, with popular discussion boards and special areas for Britons, Americans, expatriate taxes, and other important issues.

Escape Artist (💻 http://www.escapeartist.com). An excellent website and probably the most comprehensive, packed with resources, links and directories covering most expatriate destinations. You can also subscribe to the free monthly online expatriate magazine, *Escape from America*.

Expat Essentials (💻 http://www.expatessentials.com). Online ordering service for British food products.

Expat Exchange (💻 http://www.expatexchange.com). Reportedly the largest online community for English-speaking expatriates, provides a series of articles on relocation and also a question and answer facility through its expatriate network.

Expat World (💻 http://www.expatworld.net). 'The newsletter of international living.' Contains a wealth of information for American and British expatriates, including a subscription newsletter.

Expatriate Experts (💻 http://www.expatexpert.com). A website run by expatriate expert Robin Pascoe, providing invaluable advice and support.

Family Life Abroad (💻 http://www.familylifeabroad.com). A wealth of information and articles on coping with family life abroad.

Foreign Wives Club (💻 http://www.foreignwivesclub.com). An online community for women in bicultural marriages.

Francopats (💻 http://www.francopats.com). Online expatriate community.

Real Post Reports (💻 http://www.realpostreports.com). Includes relocation services and recommended reading lists for expatriates worldwide.

Third Culture Kids (💻 http://www.tckworld.com). A website designed for expatriate children living abroad.

Travel Documents (http://www.traveldocs.com). Useful information about travel, specific countries and documents needed to travel.

Travel for Kids (http://www.travelforkids.com). Advice on travelling with children around the world.

Women of the World (http://www.wow-net.org). A website designed for female expats anywhere in the world.

World Travel Guide (http://www.worldtravelguide.net.com). A general website for world travellers and expatriates.

Worldwise Directory (http://w01-0943.web.dircon.net/worldwise). This website run by the Suzy Lamplugh charity for personal safety, providing a useful directory of countries with practical information and special emphasis on safety, particularly for women.

APPENDIX D: WEIGHTS & MEASURES

France uses the metric system of measurement. Those who are more familiar with the imperial system will find the tables on the following pages useful. Some comparisons are approximate, but are close enough for most everyday uses. In addition to the variety of measurement systems used, clothes sizes often vary considerably with the manufacturer (as we all know only too well). Try all clothes on before buying and don't be afraid to return something if, when you try it on at home, you decide it doesn't fit.

Women's Clothes

Continental	34	36	38	40	42	44	46	48	50	52
UK	8	10	12	14	16	18	20	22	24	26
US	6	8	10	12	14	16	18	20	22	24

Pullovers

	Women's						Men's					
Continental	40	42	44	46	48	50	44	46	48	50	52	54
UK	34	36	38	40	42	44	34	36	38	40	42	44
US	34	36	38	40	42	44	sm	med	lar	xl		

Men's Shirts

Continental	36	37	38	39	40	41	42	43	44	46
UK/US	14	14	15	15	16	16	17	17	18	-

Men's Underwear

Continental	5	6	7	8	9	10
UK	34	36	38	40	42	44
US	sm	med		lar	xl	

Note: sm = small, med = medium, lar = large, xl = extra large

Children's Clothes

Continental	92	104	116	128	140	152
UK	16/18	20/22	24/26	28/30	32/34	36/38
US	2	4	6	8	10	12

Children's Shoes

Continental	18	19	20	21	22	23	24	25	26	27	28	29	30	31	32
UK/US	2	3	4	4	5	6	7	7	8	9	10	11	11	12	13

Continental	33	34	35	36	37	38
UK/US	1	2	2	3	4	5

Shoes (Women's and Men's)

Continental	35	36	37	37	38	39	40	41	42	42	43	44
UK	2	3	3	4	4	5	6	7	7	8	9	9
US	4	5	5	6	6	7	8	9	9	10	10	11

Weight

Imperial	Metric	Metric	Imperial
1oz	28.35g	1g	0.035oz
1lb*	454g	100g	3.5oz
1cwt	50.8kg	250g	9oz
1 ton	1,016kg	500g	18oz
2,205lb	1 tonne	1kg	2.2lb

Length

Imperial	Metric	Metric	Imperial
1in	2.54cm	1cm	0.39in
1ft	30.48cm	1m	3ft 3.25in
1yd	91.44cm	1km	0.62mi
1mi	1.6km	8km	5mi

Capacity

Imperial	Metric	Metric	Imperial
1 UK pint	0.57 litre	1 litre	1.75 UK pints
1 US pint	0.47 litre	1 litre	2.13 US pints
1 UK gallon	4.54 litres	1 litre	0.22 UK gallon
1 US gallon	3.78 litres	1 litre	0.26 US gallon

Note: An American 'cup' = around 250ml or 0.25 litre.

Area

Imperial	Metric	Metric	Imperial
1 sq. in	0.45 sq. cm	1 sq. cm	0.15 sq. in
1 sq. ft	0.09 sq. m	1 sq. m	10.76 sq. ft
1 sq. yd	0.84 sq. m	1 sq. m	1.2 sq. yds
1 acre	0.4 hectares	1 hectare	2.47 acres
1 sq. mile	2.56 sq. km	1 sq. km	0.39 sq. mile

Note: An *are* is one-hundredth of a hectare or $100m^2$.

Temperature

°Celsius	°Fahrenheit	°Celsius	°Fahrenheit
0	32	25	77
5	41	30	86
10	50	35	95
15	59	40	104
20	68		

Notes: The freezing point of water is 0C / 32F.
The boiling point of water is 100C / 212F.
Normal body temperature is 37C / 98.4F.

Oven Temperatures

Gas	Electric		Gas	Electric	
	°F	°C		°F	°C
-	225–250	110–120	5	375	190
1	275	140	6	400	200
2	300	150	7	425	220
3	325	160	8	450	230
4	350	180	9	475	240

Air Pressure

PSI	Bar
10	0.5
20	1.4
30	2
40	2.8

Appendix E: Maps

The map opposite shows the 22 regions and 96 departments of France (excluding overseas territories), which are listed below. Departments 91 to 95 come under the Ile-de-France region, which also includes Ville de Paris (75), Seine-et-Marne (77) and Yvelines (78), shown in detail opposite. The island of Corsica consists of two departments, 2A and 2B. The maps on the following pages show major airports and ports with cross-Channel ferry services, high-speed train (*TGV*) routes, and motorways and other major roads.

01 Ain
02 Aisne
2A Corse-du-Sud
2B Haute Corse
03 Allier
04 Alpes-de-Hte-Provence
05 Hautes-Alpes
06 Alpes-Maritimes
07 Ardèche
08 Ardennes
09 Ariège
10 Aube
11 Aude
12 Aveyron
13 Bouches-du-Rhône
14 Calvados
15 Cantal
16 Charente
17 Charente-Maritime
18 Cher
19 Corrèze
21 Côte-d'Or
22 Côte-d'Armor
23 Creuse
24 Dordogne
25 Doubs
26 Drôme
27 Eure
28 Eure-et-Loir
29 Finistère
30 Gard
31 Haute-Garonne
32 Gers
33 Gironde
34 Hérault
35 Ille-et-Vilaine
36 Indre
37 Indre-et-Loire
38 Isère
39 Jura
40 Landes
41 Loir-et-Cher
42 Loire
43 Haute-Loire
44 Loire-Atlantique
45 Loiret
46 Lot
47 Lot-et-Garonne
48 Lozère
49 Maine-et-Loire
50 Manche
51 Marne
52 Haute-Marne
53 Mayenne
54 Meurthe-et-Moselle
55 Meuse
56 Morbihan
57 Moselle
58 Nièvre
59 Nord
60 Oise
61 Orne
62 Pas-de-Calais
63 Puy-de-Dôme
64 Pyrénées-Atlantiques
65 Hautes-Pyrénées
66 Pyrénées-Orientales
67 Bas-Rhin
68 Haut-Rhin
69 Rhône
70 Haute-Saône
71 Saône-et-Loire
72 Sarthe
73 Savoie
74 Haute-Savoie
75 Paris
76 Seine-Maritime
77 Seine-et-Marne
78 Yvelines
79 Deux-Sèvres
80 Somme
81 Tarn
82 Tarn-et-Garonne
83 Var
84 Vaucluse
85 Vendée
86 Vienne
87 Haute-Vienne
88 Vosges
89 Yonne
90 Territoire de Belfort
91 Essonne
92 Hauts-de-Seine
93 Seine-Saint-Denis
94 Val-de-Marne
95 Val-d'Oise

REGIONS & DEPARTMENTS

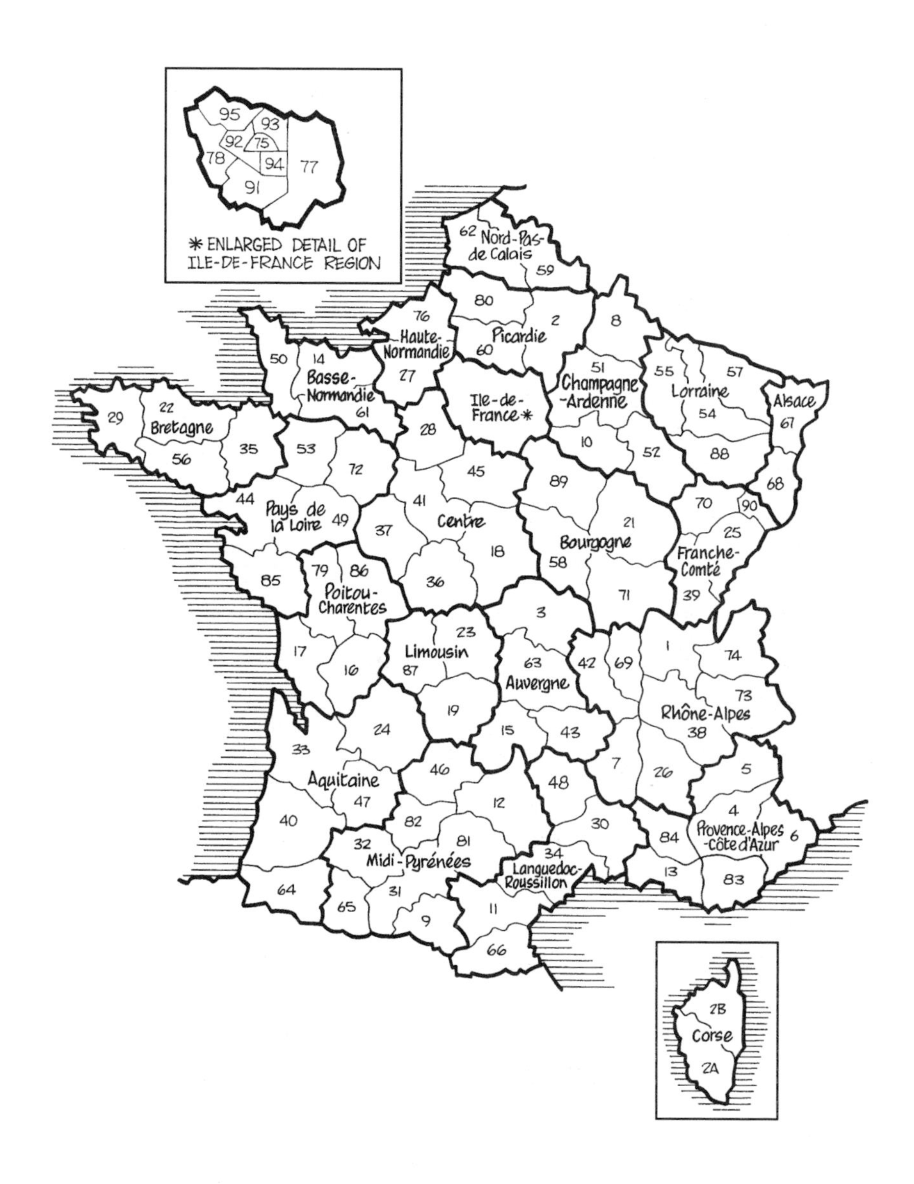

Airports & Ports

 Airports

 Ferry ports

TGV Network

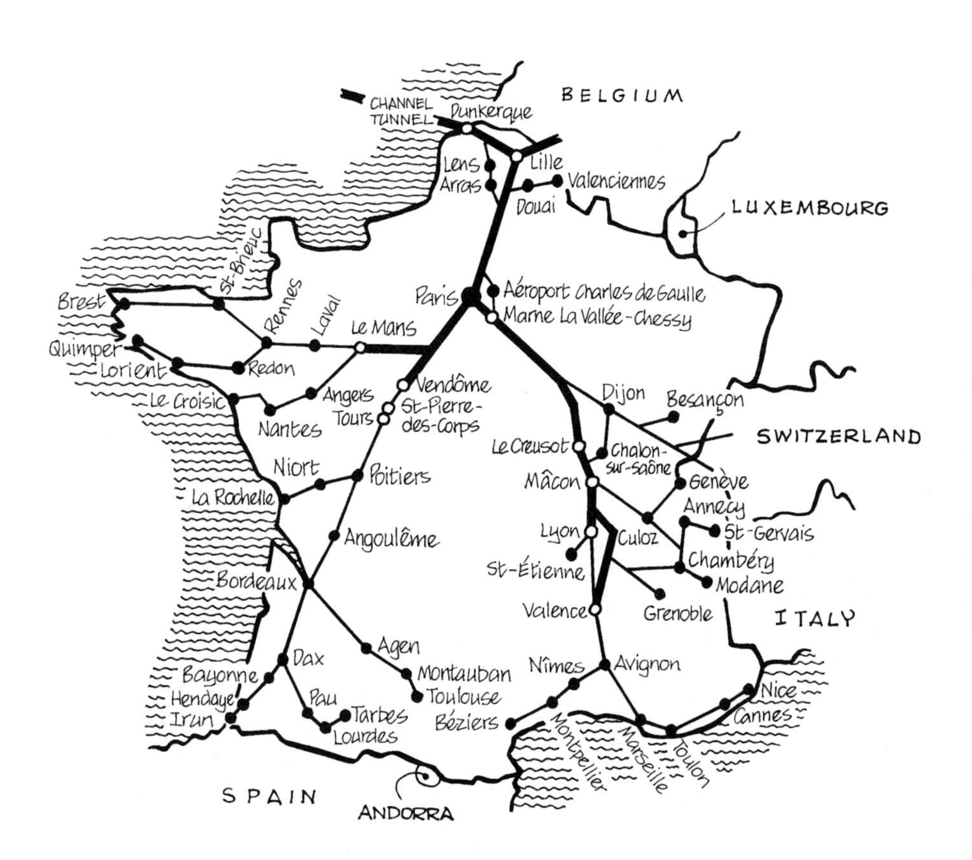

Special track, on which trains can run at up to 300kph (187mph).

Ordinary track, on which trains are restricted to around 200kph (122mph).

Motorways & Major Roads

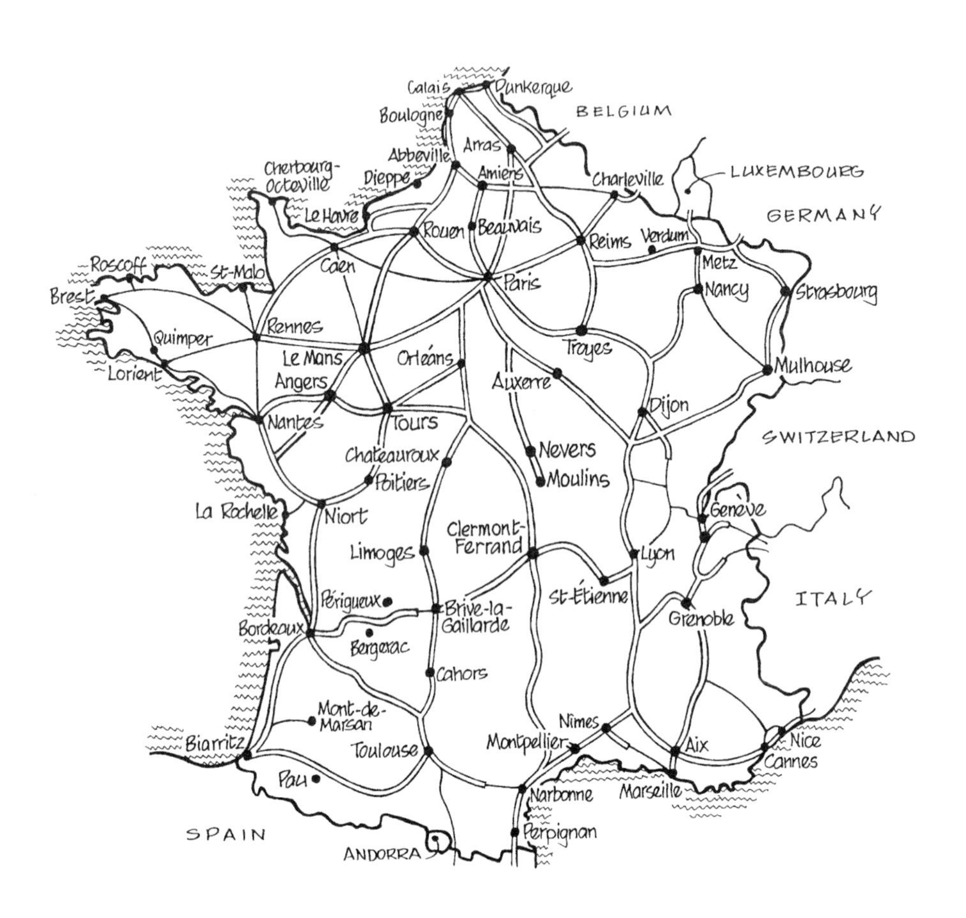

Motorways

Other main roads

MISTRAL CORNER
FOR SALE

Appendix F: Airline Services

The tables on the following pages indicate scheduled flights operating from UK and Irish airports to France. Details were current in April 2003. Airlines are coded as shown below (note that these aren't all official airline codes). Airport telephone numbers and website addresses are also shown below. Telephone numbers in italics are Irish numbers; all other numbers are UK numbers.

Code	Airline	Telephone/Website
AA	Aer Arann	0800-587 2324 http://www.aerarann.com
AF	Air France	0870-142 4343 http://www.airfrance.com
AL	Aer Lingus	*0813-365 000* http://www.aerlingus.com
AS	Air Scotland	0141-222 2363 http://www.air-scotland.com
BA	British Airways	0870-850 9850 http://www.ba.com
BB	BMIbaby	0890-710081 http://www.bmibaby.com
BM	BMI	0870-607 0555 http://www.flybmi.com
EJ	EasyJet	0871-750 0100 http://www.easyjet.com
FB	Flybe	0871-700 0123 http://www1.flybe.com
FG	Flyglobespan	0870-556 1522 http://www.flyglobespan.com
GB	GB Airways (British Airways)	0870-850 9850 http://www.gbairways.com
J2	Jet 2	0871-226 1737 http://www.jet2.com
RA	Ryanair	0871-246 0000 http://www.ryanair.com

Airport	Telephone/Website
Aberdeen	0870-040 0006 http://www.aberdeenairport.com
Belfast International	028-9448 4848/http://www.bial.co.uk
Birmingham	0870-733 5511/http://www.bhx.co.uk
Bristol	0870-121 2747 http://www.bristolairport.co.uk
Cork	*021-431 3131*/http://www.corkairport.ie
Dublin	*01-814 1111*/http://www.dublinairport.ie
Edinburgh	0870-040 0007 http://www.edinburghairport.com
Exeter	01392-367433/http://www.exeter-airport.co.uk
Glasgow Prestwick	0871-223 0800/http://www.gpia.co.uk
Liverpool	0870-129 8484/http://www.livairport.com
London City	020-7646 0088 http://www.londoncityairport.com
London Gatwick	0870-000 2468/http://www.gatwickairport.com
London Heathrow	0870-000 0123 http://www.heathrowairport.com
London Luton	01582-405100/http://www.london-luton.co.uk
London Stansted	0870-000 0303 http://www.stanstedairport.com
Manchester	0161-489 3000 http://www.manchesterairport.co.uk
Newcastle	0870-122 1488 http://www.newcastleairport.com
Norwich	01603-411923 http://www.norwichairport.co.uk
Nottingham/East Midlands	0871-919 9000 http://www.eastmidlandsairport.com
Shannon	*061-712000* http://www.shannonairport.com
Southampton	0870-040 0009 http://www.southamptonairport.com

	Aberdeen	Belfast International	Birmingham	Bristol	Cork	Dublin	Edinburgh	Exeter	Glasgow Prestwick	Liverpool
Ajaccio					AA					
Bordeaux				FB[1]		AF AL				
Brest			FB[1]							
Carcassonne						RA				
Chambéry			FB[1]					FB[1]		
Grenoble				EJ		RA			RA	RA
La Rochelle			FB[1]	EJ						
Limoges			BA							
Lyon			BA			AL RA			RA	RA
Marseille				EJ		AL RA			RA	EJ
Nice		EJ	BA	EJ	AL	AF				EJ
Paris CDG	AF	EJ	BA	BA EJ	AL	AL	BA	FB[1]	BA	EJ
Perpignan			FB[1]							
Rennes						AL			FB[1]	
Toulouse			FB[1]	EJ FB[1]		AF AL				

NOTES:

1. Flybe's schedules are planned only around six months in advance. All flights shown here were operating in winter 2006/07; summer 2007 schedules were to be fixed in December 2006.

Some tour operators, e.g. First Choice, Monarch, Thomas Cook and Thomson, sell seats on their 'charter' flights to Toulouse and other airports.

	London City	London Gatwick	London Heathrow	London Luton	London Stansted	Manchester	Newcastle	Norwich	Nottingham/East Midlands	Shannon	Southampton
Ajaccio		GB									
Angers						AA					FB[1]
Avignon											FB[1]
Bastia		BA GB									
Beauvais										RA	
Bergerac					RA						
Biarritz					RA						
Bordeaux	AF	AF BA	AF	EJ		BB		FB[1]			FB[1]
Brest				RA							FB[1]
Carcassonne										EJ	
Chambéry					RA			FB[1]			FB[1]
Cherbourg											FB[1]
Deauville				RA							
Dinard									RA		
Grenoble		BA EJ		EJ	EJ RA				RA		
La Rochelle					RA						FB[1]
Limoges					RA						FB[1]
Lyon			BA		RA	BA			RA		
Marseille		BA EJ			RA						
Montpellier		BA GB			RA						
Nantes		BA			RA					RA	
Nice		BA	BA BM	EJ	RA	BB	EJ		BB		FB[1]
Nîmes				RA	RA						
Paris CDG	AF		AF BA BM	EJ		BA		FB[1]	BB		
Pau					RA						
Perpignan					RA	BB					FB[1]
Poitiers					RA						
Rodez					RA						
Strasbourg		AF									
Toulon					RA						
Toulouse	AF	AF BA EJ	AF								

Appendix G: Major Town Rating

The table below is derived from a survey of 25 of France's major towns and cities published in November 2006 by *Le Nouvel Observateur* magazine. Ratings were in two sets of categories: economy/employment (including population growth, unemployment level, executive employment level, business creation rate, student population, wealth of inhabitants, cost of property and rental costs) and quality of life (including number of doctors, crime rate, number of museums, cinema attendance, air quality, traffic jams and rail links with Paris). Each town's ranking in each sub-category has been added to give a figure for each main category – the lower the figure the higher the overall ranking.

Note that, although the overall winner, Nancy wasn't top-ranked in any particular category, while Paris came top in executive employment, business creation and (not surprisingly) number of museums and wealth of inhabitants, Montpellier was top for population growth, number of doctors and cinema-going, and Saint-Etienne was top for cost of property and rents (i.e. both were the lowest of all the towns surveyed). Overall top for economy/employment was Nantes and for quality of life Dijon.

Rank & Town	Dept.	Economy	Quality of Life	Total
1 Nancy	54	80	72	152
2 Dijon	21	97	69	166
3 Angers	49	88	81	169
4 Toulouse	31	74	99	173
5 Strasbourg	67	81	95	176
6 Caen	14	102	83	185
7 Tours	37	112	75	186
8 Nantes	44	74	114	188
9 Bordeaux	33	78	112	190
10 Clermont	63	98	97	195
11 Rouen	76	118	77	195
12 Montpellier	34	97	100	197
13 Rennes	35	82	118	200
14 Grenoble	38	99	101	200
15 Orléans	45	91	111	202

16 Lyon	69	85	119	204
17 Paris	75	113	97	220
18 St-Etienne	42	125	96	221
19 Metz	57	99	122	221
20 Valenciennes	59	120	116	236
21 Lille	59	114	122	236
22 Marseille/Aix	13	141	109	250
23 Nice	06	134	126	260
24 Douai-Lens	59	149	113	262
25 Toulon	83	141	134	275

The table below is derived from a nationwide survey of 100 of the largest cities and towns in France published in January 2005 by *Le Point* magazine. Towns are rated in ten categories, each rating consisting of several criteria, as follows:

1. **Activity** – The 12 criteria were whether the city or town is served by the *TGV*, the level of rail, air and sea travel among inhabitants, the number of goods 'imported' and 'exported', the number of exhibitions, the proportion of skilled employment, the level of council spending, the average GDP per capita and the level of investment.
2. **Employment** – The 12 criteria were the level of unemployment (overall and in various sectors), the increase or decrease in employment since 2001, the number of jobs created, the percentage of the population in work (plus the percentage of women and the percentage working locally), the number of business bankruptcies and the percentage of people on short-term contracts.
3. **Wealth** – The four criteria were the proportion of income tax payers, the average amount of tax paid, the proportion of people subject to wealth tax and the average amount paid.
4. **Accommodation** – The nine criteria were the average price per m² of resale property, the percentages of homeowners, of owners of two or more bedroom homes, of detached house

owners, of insalubrious housing, of vacant properties and of social housing, and the number of homes under construction.

5. **Safety** – The six criteria were the current crime level and its increase or decrease since 2001, and the levels of imprisonment, crime against women, burglary and car theft.

6. **Road Safety** – The eight criteria were the number of road accidents and the increase or decrease since 2001, the number of drink-driving offences and the number of deaths in various categories.

7. **Education** – The five criteria were the percentage of students retaking a year, the proportion passing the *baccalauréat*, the number taking *classes préparatoires aux grandes écoles* and whether the town or city has a university.

8. **Spending** – The four criteria were total council spending per inhabitant, and spending on cleanliness, parks and gardens, and other 'environmental' amenities.

9. **Environment** – The 11 criteria were the proximity of the sea and ski resorts, whether there are boating facilities in the town or city, the amount of sunshine, the average temperature, the amount of rain, population density, the percentage of people who walk to work, the level of public transport services (including whether there's an underground (subway) and tram system), and the city or town's general attractiveness.

10. **Entertainment** – The 15 criteria were the number of cinemas (and screens), art galleries, sports clubs, dance groups, orchestras, opera companies, theatres, libraries, museums, historic monuments and Michelin-starred restaurants, the percentage of students and the number of tourists.

Rank/Town	Dept.	1	2	3	4	5	6	7	8	9	10	Total
1 Chambéry	73	22	30	15	53	59	12	22	12	25	42	292
2 Lyon	69	1	1	2	99	87	33	17	41	18	2	301
3 Niort	79	72	2	17	10	10	18	19	27	51	78	304
4 Toulouse	31	4	4	20	76	86	53	26	33	14	6	322
5 Tours	37	13	43	32	43	52	47	8	20	50	14	322
6 Bordeaux	33	6	29	4	95	69	75	17	4	37	3	339

Rank/Town	Dept.	1	2	3	4	5	6	7	8	9	10	Total
7 Nantes	44	9	19	13	28	68	61	42	46	53	5	344
8 Caen	14	18	70	14	75	50	14	12	14	77	9	353
9 Rennes	35	19	28	9	55	40	71	7	61	43	22	355
10 Vannes	56	54	23	18	18	11	39	2	76	52	67	360
11 Rodez	12	71	12	33	39	2	15	29	68	49	43	361
12 Quimper	29	63	13	54	9	23	4	28	53	72	46	365
13 Metz	57	17	33	30	61	64	41	9	23	77	13	368
14 Orléans	45	27	14	22	40	46	66	64	8	59	29	375
15 Grenoble	38	5	42	25	83	79	58	25	26	19	14	376
16 Aix-en-Provence	13	34	57	4	79	88	28	1	59	20	11	381
17 Annecy	74	40	24	19	64	75	77	4	19	28	32	382
18 Dijon	21	20	5	21	78	18	74	36	58	57	21	388
19 Cholet	49	95	36	64	1	1	17	16	44	32	92	398
20 La Roche-sur-Yon	85	75	9	42	3	8	46	10	89	39	79	400
21 Laval	53	58	7	44	12	17	13	72	86	40	53	402
22 Angers	49	23	79	59	47	22	86	6	24	33	24	403
23 Albi	81	78	41	77	8	35	6	21	64	30	55	415
24 Le Mans	72	44	11	39	7	27	93	44	31	66	61	423
25 La Rochelle	17	30	64	46	31	91	96	15	6	22	22	423
26 Limoges	87	67	25	24	41	3	65	83	8	80	28	424
27 Bourges	18	64	21	31	19	54	55	87	12	48	34	425
28 Rouen	76	10	37	26	86	48	45	30	51	82	12	427
29 Strasbourg	67	11	26	3	96	74	59	33	80	42	7	431
30 Colmar	68	41	15	37	57	39	52	62	62	30	39	434
31 Pau	64	26	77	52	80	12	5	62	10	71	41	436
32 Gap	5	87	8	41	42	7	31	48	66	29	82	441
33 Nancy	54	8	31	8	94	55	79	14	73	72	8	442
34 Besançon	25	30	39	39	69	58	72	37	51	41	26	462
35 Valence	26	32	71	62	61	83	20	54	35	6	38	462
36 Reims	51	15	51	26	70	61	26	27	74	81	37	468
37 Nice	6	14	35	16	98	94	95	49	54	4	17	476
38 Bourg-en-Bresse	1	38	16	71	36	56	36	73	44	64	48	482
39 Périgueux	24	83	27	60	50	16	38	54	15	68	71	482
40 Bayonne	64	73	55	79	82	32	81	3	5	43	30	483
41 Carcassonne	11	81	54	78	11	84	2	100	15	21	40	486
42 Montpellier	34	25	45	67	90	97	23	47	82	9	4	489
43 Clermont-Ferrand	63	48	47	56	71	13	91	32	83	34	18	493
44 Saint-Etienne	42	21	94	63	85	53	16	60	33	13	55	493
45 Avignon	84	16	65	73	34	100	97	61	18	15	16	495
46 Compiègne	60	86	56	6	72	76	1	58	38	60	49	502
47 Perpignan	66	60	74	81	65	92	10	50	30	8	33	503
48 Aurillac	15	98	3	80	29	5	21	86	32	79	73	506
49 Châteauroux	36	51	44	48	4	9	42	88	50	91	86	513
50 Epinal	88	49	48	23	33	20	62	20	92	70	96	513
51 Paris	75	2	6	1	100	93	87	40	41	69	75	514
52 Cannes	6	28	61	7	87	95	100	75	1	1	59	514
53 Blois	41	66	46	65	25	32	85	98	3	61	36	517

Rank/Town	Dept.	1	2	3	4	5	6	7	8	9	10	Total
54 Chartres	28	59	33	10	35	67	49	51	62	92	64	522
55 Dunkerque	59	45	96	71	22	21	27	66	11	89	75	523
56 Valenciennes	59	36	95	49	24	24	19	24	90	84	79	524
57 Thonon-les-Bains	74	91	18	12	60	71	32	90	20	46	85	525
58 Angoulême	16	52	58	69	44	30	48	79	46	24	77	527
59 Antibes	6	62	38	10	67	98	64	70	64	10	52	535
60 Arras	62	50	62	34	26	63	44	11	96	95	58	539
61 Beauvais	63	92	52	50	30	62	3	74	20	94	62	539
62 Chalon-sur-Saône	71	46	50	88	59	27	22	77	35	65	70	539
63 Brest	29	29	68	85	19	14	80	5	85	86	69	540
64 Lorient	56	33	78	88	15	31	66	41	56	67	66	541
65 Marseille	13	3	40	43	89	99	90	76	87	5	19	551
66 Saint-Brieuc	22	55	75	45	6	43	40	53	84	61	89	551
67 Nîmes	30	42	59	50	58	90	82	92	49	16	20	558
68 Auxerre	89	85	22	58	46	77	29	67	96	54	25	559
69 Poitiers	86	39	73	28	68	86	69	31	77	63	27	561
70 Castres	81	74	81	84	5	4	73	45	57	45	95	563
71 Saint-Nazaire	44	47	86	95	2	36	60	81	72	34	51	564
72 Evreux	27	70	10	68	23	73	35	96	41	92	57	565
73 Lille	59	6	89	35	97	81	56	71	46	75	10	566
74 Le Havre	76	24	93	87	32	60	70	35	27	98	44	570
75 Troyes	10	43	67	61	93	43	51	12	80	75	47	572
76 Narbonne	11	100	82	92	17	78	11	56	96	12	35	579
77 Amiens	80	57	63	38	54	80	68	38	54	87	45	584
78 Brive-la-Gaillarde	19	96	69	28	21	38	89	90	27	54	72	584
79 Montauban	82	81	20	51	14	72	63	56	95	38	97	587
80 Cherbourg	50	76	85	76	81	6	99	33	25	36	74	591
81 Toulon	83	37	72	82	92	65	76	81	15	11	67	598
82 Belfort	90	77	91	83	66	25	92	23	7	87	54	605
83 Saint-Malo	35	87	60	36	16	45	87	69	39	90	76	605
84 Vichy	3	94	97	73	84	26	84	52	2	47	49	608
85 Arles	13	64	66	90	49	66	8	99	91	17	60	610
86 Mulhouse	68	12	83	57	91	85	68	65	60	83	31	635
87 Fréjus	83	90	80	47	55	89	25	68	79	2	100	635
88 Montluçon	3	97	89	93	47	15	34	80	35	58	91	639
89 Béziers	34	79	92	65	37	95	50	95	39	7	84	643
90 Lens	62	56	100	97	45	49	37	39	74	100	63	660
91 Alençon	61	80	61	91	13	47	24	97	70	97	81	661
92 Tarbes	65	35	83	99	52	36	98	46	70	53	99	671
93 Ajaccio	2A	99	17	55	87	29	83	89	96	26	93	674
94 Boulogne-sur-Mer	62	69	99	98	77	50	7	43	78	74	86	681
95 Bastia	2B	89	31	94	73	18	78	94	88	23	98	686
96 Agen	47	61	76	86	50	81	94	85	66	27	65	691
97 Calais	62	53	98	100	26	57	54	59	68	85	94	694
98 Charleville-Mézières	8	68	88	96	38	34	9	84	93	96	89	695
99 Nevers	58	84	49	70	63	42	30	93	94	99	88	712
100 Sète	34	93	87	75	74	70	57	78	96	3	82	715

Index

A

B

C

E

F

H

L

M

N

P

R

S

T

W

SURVIVAL BOOKS

Survival Books was established in 1987 and by the mid-'90s was the leading publisher of books for people planning to live, work, buy property or retire abroad.

From the outset, our philosophy has been to provide the most comprehensive and up-to-date information available. Our titles routinely contain up to twice as much information as rival books and are updated frequently. All our books contain colour photographs and some are printed in two colours or full colour throughout. They also contain original cartoons, illustrations and maps.

Survival Books are written by people with first-hand experience of the countries and the people they describe, and therefore provide invaluable insights that cannot be obtained from official publications or websites, and information that is more reliable and objective than that provided by the majority of unofficial sites.

Survival Books are designed to be easy – and interesting – to read. They contain a comprehensive list of contents and index and extensive appendices, including useful addresses, further reading, useful websites and glossaries to help you obtain additional information as well as metric conversion tables and other useful reference material.

Our primary goal is to provide you with the essential information necessary for a trouble-free life or property purchase and to save you time, trouble and money.

We believe our books are the best – they are certainly the best-selling. But don't take our word for it – read what reviewers and readers have said about Survival Books at the front of this book.

To see our current list of titles, visit our website: **www.survivalbooks.net**

CULTURE WISE SERIES

The Essential Guides to Culture, Customs & Business Etiquette

Our ***Culture Wise*** series of guides is essential reading for anyone who want to understand how a country really 'works'. Whether you're planning to stay for a few days or a lifetime, these guides will help you quickly find you feet and settle into your new surroundings.

Culture Wise guides reduce the anxiety factor in adapting to a foreign culture; explain how to behave in everyday situations in order to avoid cultural and social gaffes; help you get along with your neighbours, make friends and establish lasting business relationships; and enhance your understanding of a country and its people.

People often underestimate the extent of the cultural isolation they can face abroad, particularly in a country with a different language. At first glance, many countries seem an 'easy' option, often with millions of visitors from all corners of the globe and well-established expatriate communities. But, sooner or later, newcomers find that most countries are indeed 'foreign' and many come unstuck as a result.

Culture Wise guides will enable you to quickly adapt to the local way of life and feel at home, and – just as importantly – avoid the worst effects of culture shock.

Culture Wise – the wise way to travel

To see our current list of titles, visit our website: **www.survivalbooks.net**

LIVING AND WORKING SERIES

Our ***Living and Working*** guides are essential reading for anyone planning to spend a period abroad, whether it's an extended holiday or permanent migration, and are packed with priceless information designed to help you avoid costly mistakes and save you both time and money.

Living and Working guides are the most comprehensive and up-to-date source of practical information available about everyday life abroad. They aren't, however, simply a catalogue of dry facts and figures, but are written in a highly readable style - entertaining, practical and occasionally humorous.

Our aim is to provide you with the comprehensive practical information necessary for a trouble free life. You may have visited a country as a tourist, but living and working there is a different matter altogether; adjusting to a different environment and culture and making a home in any foreign country can be a traumatic and stressful experience. You need to adapt to new customs and traditions, discover the local way of doing things (such as finding a home, paying bills and obtaining insurance) and learn all over again how to overcome the everyday obstacles of life.

All these subjects and many, many more are covered in depth in our ***Living and Working*** guides - don't leave home without them!

To see our current list of titles, visit our website: **www.survivalbooks.net**

Buying a Home Series

Buying a home abroad is not only a major financial transaction but also a potentially life-changing experience; it's therefore essential to get it right. Our ***Buying a Home*** guides are required reading for anyone planning to purchase property abroad and are packed with vital information to guide you through the property jungle and help you avoid disasters that can turn a dream home into a nightmare.

The purpose of our ***Buying a Home*** guides is to enable you to choose the most favourable location and the most appropriate property for your requirements, and to reduce your risk of making an expensive mistake by making informed decisions and calculated judgements rather than uneducated and hopeful guesses. Most importantly, they will help you save money and will repay your investment many times over.

Buying a Home guides are the most comprehensive and up-to-date source of information available about buying property abroad – whether you're seeking a detached house or an apartment, a holiday or a permanent home (or an investment property), these books will prove invaluable.

To see our current list of titles, visit our website: **www.survivalbooks.net**

OTHER SURVIVAL BOOKS

A New Life Abroad: The most comprehensive book available for anyone planning to live, work or retire abroad, containing surveys of over 50 countries.

The Best Places to Buy a Home in France/Spain: Unique guides to where to buy property in France and Spain, containing regional profiles and market reports.

Buying, Selling and Letting Property: The best source of information about buying, selling and letting property in the UK.

Earning Money From Your Home: Essential guides to earning income from property in France and Spain, including short- and long-term letting.

Foreigners in France/Spain: Triumphs & Disasters: Real-life experiences of people who have emigrated to France and Spain, recounted in their own words.

Investing in Property Abroad: Essential reading for anyone planning to buy property abroad, containing surveys of over 30 countries.

Making a Living: Comprehensive guides to self-employment and starting a business in France and Spain.

Renovating & Maintaining Your French Home: The ultimate guide to renovating and maintaining your dream home in France.

Retiring in France/Spain: Everything a prospective retiree needs to know about the two most popular international retirement destinations.

Running Gîtes and B&Bs in France: An essential book for anyone planning to invest in a gîte or bed & breakfast business in France.

Rural Living in France: An invaluable book for anyone seeking the 'good life' in France, containing a wealth of practical information about all aspects of country life.

Shooting Caterpillars in Spain: The hilarious and compelling story of two innocents abroad in the depths of Andalusia in the late '80s.

Wild Thyme in Ibiza: A fragrant account of how a three-month visit to the enchanted island of Ibiza in the mid-'60s turned into a 20-year sojourn.

To see our current list of titles, visit our website: **www.survivalbooks.net**